Contents

Contents

Affiliations of the Contributors

Nicholas H. Apostoleris, Frances Hiatt School of Psychology, Clark University, Worcester, MA 01610, USA.

James R. Averill, Department of Psychology, University of Massachusetts, Amherst, MA 01003, USA.

John Demos, Department of History, Yale University, P.O. Box 208324, New Haven, CT 06520-8324, USA.

Bradley Duchaine, Department of Psychology, University of California at Santa Barbara, Santa Barbara, CA 93106, USA.

Alan J. Fridlund, Department of Psychology, University of California at Santa Barbara, Santa Barbara, CA 93106, USA.

G.P. Ginsburg, Department of Psychology, University of Nevada at Reno, Reno, NV 89557, USA.

Rom Harré, Linacre College, Oxford, OX1 3JA, United Kingdom and Department of Psychology, Georgetown University, Washington, DC 20057, USA.

Melanie E. Harrington, Department of Psychology, University of Nevada at Reno, Reno, NV 89557, USA.

Paul Heelas, Department of Anthropology, Lancaster University, Lancaster, LA1 4YG, UK.

Inmaculada Iglesias, Department of Psychology, Georgetown University, Washington, DC 20057, USA.

Mark Knapp, Department of History, Carnegie-Melon University, Pittsburgh, PA 15213, USA.

Janet Landman, Department of Psychology, University of Michigan, 580 Union Drive, Ann Arbor, MI 48109-1346, USA.

James D. Laird, Frances Hiatt School of Psychology, Clark University, Worcester, MA 01610, USA.

Catherine A. Lutz, Department of Anthropology, Alumni Building, CB 3115, University of North Carolina, Chapel Hill, NC 27599-3115, USA.

Keith Oatley, Centre for Applied Cognitive Science, The Ontario Institute for Studies in Education, 252 Bloor Street West, Toronto, Ontario, Canada MSS 1V6.

W. Gerrod Parrott, Department of Psychology, Georgetown University, Washington, DC 20057, USA.

Christopher Ricks, College of Liberal Arts, Boston University, 236 Bay State Road, Boston, MA 02215, USA.

Daniel N. Robinson, Department of Psychology, Georgetown University, Washington, DC 20057, USA.

Peter N. Stearns, Dean of the College of Humanities and Social Sciences, Carnegie-Melon University, Pittsburgh, PA 15213, USA.

Gabrielle Taylor, St Anne's College, Oxford, OX2 6HS, UK.

Kenneth T. Strongman, Department of Psychology, Canterbury University, Private Bag 4800, Christchurch, New Zealand.

Luke Strongman, Department of English, Canterbury University, Private Bag 4800, Christchurch, New Zealand.

Preface

The last decade has seen an amazing transformation and broadening in the ways the emotions are understood and in the methods by which they are studied. Many supposedly secure research findings have been upset and taken-for-granted assumptions brought into question. This volume brings together the most recent developments in the psychology of the emotions in what we hope will prove to be a 'handy package'. While taking account of the complexity of the emerging field we hope it will prove to be accessible at all levels. Used as a class text we believe that this book will enable students to acquaint themselves with the most recent developments in the psychology of the emotions.

W. Gerrod Parrott
Rom Harré

Acknowledgements

Some of the chapters have already been published in various forms, some have been newly commissioned for this volume. Reprinted chapters have been drawn from the following works:

Vignette 2 is reprinted from C.D. Spielberger, I.G. Sarason, Z. Kulcsar and G.L. van Heck (eds) (1991) *Stress and Anxiety*, Washington, DC: Hemisphere, Vol. 14, pp. 3–16.

Chapter 3 is reprinted from Gabrielle Taylor (1985) *Pride, Shame and Guilt* by permission of Oxford University Press.

Chapter 4 is reprinted from Carol Z. Stearns and Peter N. Stearns (eds) (1988) *Emotion and Social Change* by permission of Holmes and Meier, New York. Copyright © Holmes and Meier Publishers, Inc.

Chapter 5 is excerpted from Janet Landman (1993) *Regret: The Persistence of the Possible*. Copyright © 1993 by Janet Landman. Reprinted by permission of Oxford University Press, Inc.

Vignette 3 is reprinted from Christopher Ricks (1974) *Keats and Embarrassment* by permission of Oxford University Press.

Chapter 7 is reprinted from Catherine A. Lutz and Lioa Abu-Lughod (eds) (1990) *Language and the Politics of Emotion* by permission of Cambridge University Press, Cambridge.

Chapter 8 is reprinted from R. Harré (ed.) (1985) *The Social Construction of Emotions* by permission of Blackwell Publishers Ltd, Oxford.

Chapter 9 is reprinted from *The Journal for the Theory of Social Behaviour*, 4 (1974): 147–90, by permission of Blackwell Publishers Ltd and the Executive Management Committee.

Chapter 11 contains material drawn from A.J. Fridlund (1994) *Human Facial Expression: An Evolutionary View* by permission of Academic Press, Inc., San Diego.

Chapter 13 is reprinted in part from Charles Darwin (1872 [1955]) *The Expression of the Emotions in Man and Animals*, New York: Philosophical Library, Chapter 13.

We are grateful to the publishers of these books and journals for permission to use this material.

If you do not wish to be prone to anger,
do not feed the habit;
give it nothing which may tend to its increase.
At first, keep quiet and count the days when
you were not angry: 'I used to be angry
every day, then every other day: next,
every two, then every three days!'
and if you succeed in passing thirty days,
sacrifice to the gods in thanksgiving.
                                        – EPICTETUS

INTRODUCTION

SOME COMPLEXITIES IN THE STUDY OF EMOTIONS

Chapter 1

Overview

W. Gerrod Parrott and Rom Harré

The study of the emotions has a special fascination. Not only are the emotions central features of human life, but they are exemplary of the ways in which contemporary psychology faces an irreducible complexity. Emotions are at once bodily responses and expressions of judgements, at once somatic and cognitive. They seem to have deep evolutionary roots, yet they are, among human phenomena, notably culturally variable in many of their aspects. Even the somatic aspect of emotions is complex. There are emotion displays and there are, in some cultures, emotion feelings, and neither is immune from cultural influence. Some displays seem a general feature of human ethology, being established over great numbers of generations by Darwinian selection, whereas others are acquired as habits, and yet others are trained in much the same way as manual skills are trained. Yet, considered functionally, emotion displays have their proper places in unfolding episodes of interpersonal reaction: they are acts embedded in patterns of acts; their display is subject to rules and conventions; they are embedded in culturally specific moral orders and normative systems that allow for assessments of the correctness or impropriety of emotions. In some cultures emotions do not include private bodily feelings as the somatic bearers of judgements – they are all display – yet others take bodily feelings to be one of the salient aspects of emotion.

In this book we are building on but also extending the point of view presented in *The Social Construction of Emotions* (Harré, 1986). We are taking up two lines of investigation. On the functional side we are looking at emotion displays and feelings that have a role in social control, for example embarrassment, shame and guilt. On the somatic side we are taking up the great insight of Luria (1966), that learning new practices actually reshapes the human brain and nervous system. Taking the two lines of investigation together, we are looking at the way patterns of social control enhance the natural human responses and develop specific cultural action patterns, thereby creating the neural basis on which those very responses and patterns depend. We are attempting to bridge the gap between the approaches of the neuroscientist and the cultural psychologist.

It cannot be said that this book completely builds that bridge, but it makes a start by locating some narrows where a bridge might be built and by laying some foundations upon which a future bridge might be constructed. Part of the process involves learning how emotions function within cultures, so that the scope of cultural influence can be understood. Another part involves learning about the somatic underpinnings of emotions, so that the scope for neural malleability can be understood. To accomplish these goals we have chosen to focus on three principal themes, and we have organized the book into three parts corresponding to each. The first theme is the social function of emotions, in particular their role in social control. The second theme is the extent of cultural variation in emotions. And the third theme is the biological dimension of emotions – their embodiment – and its potential for accommodating emotions' social functions and cultural variability. In short, the chapters in this book set out to demonstrate the usefulness of a social constructionist approach and its compatibility with what is known about the somatic basis of emotions.

Like its predecessor volume, the present book contains both original contributions and reprints of statements contributive to the book's enterprise. In addition to the main chapters, this book adds a number of contributions which we call 'vignettes'. These are short pieces which delve into a specific topic or phenomenon which illustrates the book's themes. These vignettes – some original to this volume, others republished classics – illustrate specific applications of the themes developed more generally in the main chapters.

We begin the book with a pair of vignettes which illustrate the complex interrelations of our principal themes. These initial vignettes suggest the integration of levels of analysis to which students of emotion should aspire. The first vignette presents Aristotle's seminal ideas on emotion, which are succinctly described by Daniel Robinson. Aristotle's writings on emotion clearly support the applicability of both discursive and physiological accounts. Aristotle emphasizes that emotions have definite functions. All serve to induce activity, and can be understood in somatic terms. They also can be understood in cognitive and social terms, because all emotions arise from a judgement. For anger, the judgement is that one has been wronged; for shame, it is that what one has done puts one in danger of falling into disrepute. It is because emotions arise from judgements that they can have moral relevance, for the judgements that constitute anger and shame involve moral evaluation.

Certain emotions, such as shame and anger, also function to facilitate social control. This controlling function not only enforces norms but has a developmental purpose as well. By encouraging people to act in socially appropriate ways, the emotions of social control help to build the habits that constitute a virtuous character. For Aristotle, a person of good character is one whose mental functioning has been shaped by culture to function properly within that culture. His notion of character is defined by a person's perceptions and dispositions, the reactions that come *naturally* to a person. In modern terms, he considers the structure and function of the nervous system to be altered by the process of socialization. Aristotle's view that emotion is intimately involved with the development and display of character thus illustrates, as well as anything written since, our goal of linking the cognitive and cultural aspects of emotion with the somatic.

The second vignette also addresses all three of this book's principal themes. In 'Intellectual Emotions', James Averill considers hope, an emotion that appears to lack the bodily symptoms that are commonly considered typical of such traditional emotional prototypes as anger, fear and love. Averill argues, however, that in other respects hope is quite similar to these prototypes. He reports converging evidence that hope, like anger and love, is commonly believed to alter one's thinking and behaviour, to be experienced as beyond one's control, to serve as a source of energy and sustenance, and to be part of human nature. The theme of embodiment is thus addressed in two ways. First, these similarities bring into question the wisdom of emphasizing the sympathetic nervous system and the limbic system as the principal forms of emotional embodiment, as is done in many psychological theories of emotion. Second, they suggest that, because hope motivates behaviour and sustains the pursuit of goals, other means of embodiment must exist.

Averill then addresses a second theme, cultural variation, by examining the similarities and differences of hope in America with its nearest equivalent in Korea, *himang*. Comparisons of these two emotions suggest subtle but important differences between hope in these two cultures, differences that invite analysis in terms of the cultures' values and social structures. The materialism and individualism of Americans was reflected in their greater propensity to hope for material goods and social relationships, whereas the obligations inherent in Korean Confucianism and collectivism appeared to make hedonistic pursuits and freedom from social obligations relatively more prominent among Korean *himang*. Similarly, when Averill asked his American and Korean respondents to report why they might believe they should not hope for something even though it is desirable in some way, he found differences that seem to reflect American pragmatism and Protestantism and Korean collectivism: Koreans were four times more likely than Americans to forgo hoping for an object that would violate social or personal standards; Americans were six times more likely than Koreans to decline to hope for a goal because of a preference for *working* for the goal; Americans emphasized the objective impossibility of obtaining the object of hope whereas Koreans emphasized the object's interference with other goals should it be obtained. National differences in values and social structure must underlie these differences in the expression of hope.

It is this analysis of the reasons for not hoping for something that touches on our third theme, social control. Averill found that the hopes of socialized individuals were constrained by the morals and values prevailing in their society. Evidence of social control could be found in people's beliefs about what hopes should be avoided as well as in their ideas about the relative importance of various desirable objects. Thus, this vignette on hope encompasses this book's themes of embodiment, cultural variation and social control, and thereby provides an exemplar of this book's approach to emotion.

Following these introductory vignettes we move on to examine the first theme in greater detail. Part I contains a set of chapters and vignettes that investigate the social dimension of emotions, especially their role in social control. In Chapter 2 we explore the nature of embarrassment, which contributes to social control by providing a disincentive for violating the social consensus and a means of repairing that consensus once it is violated. The definition and explanation of embarrassment have proved elusive, however, so some attention is devoted to the semantic subtleties that underlie this category. The term 'embarrassment' has multiple uses in everyday speech, and these bear only a family resemblance to each other. Academic usage of terms borrowed from natural languages may strive for more precision, but only at the cost of neglecting some of the richness of the natural category. Precision is good, but omission can be bad, so there is a tension between theorists' need for clarity and their need not to stray too far from the everyday category they initially set out to explain.

It is just this aspect of the English-language category of embarrassment that accounts for the persistence of three very different types of theories of this emotion: dramaturgical theories, decreased self-esteem theories, and negative social evaluation theories. Some aspects of embarrassment are well accounted for by theories that focus on the inability to perform one's role or maintain one's social identity in a social situation; other aspects seem best accounted for by theories that focus on the loss of one's self-esteem in the situation; and still others seem best explained by theories that link embarrassment to concerns that others present will form unfavourable impressions of oneself. These three types of theories do not merely capture different aspects of everyday embarrassment; they are interrelated in subtle and important ways, as when one's need for a certain self-image prevents one from adopting a social role which would end dramaturgic awkward-ness, or when one's forgetting the name of the person one is introducing is simultaneously disruptive of the social interaction and conducive to unfavourable evaluations of oneself by others. Theorists from all three camps have tried to argue that one or another theory describes conditions that are necessary and sufficient for embarrassment to occur, but none has been fully successful (although the exercises have been very helpful in demonstrating the capabilities and limitations of the various conceptions). Whether this lack of clear success is temporary and will eventually be remedied, or whether it is a result of there actually being no necessary and sufficient conditions defining embarrassment's semantic field, we cannot say. What we do believe is that a full understanding of embarrassment will not be had until the interconnections between these three aspects of embarrassment are accounted for.

In Chapter 2 we explore some of these interconnections. In particular, we consider the case of modesty, which is at once a virtue and a social role, and how its attainment involves the juggling of dramaturgy, self-esteem and social evaluation. Many contemporary theorists distinguish embarrassment from shame on the grounds that reactions to one's appearances to others are quite distinct from one's perceptions of oneself, and this is a useful distinction. Yet, it is nevertheless a social fact, noted by Cooley and Mead decades ago, that one's self-esteem is hardly independent of others' esteem for oneself. This is surely one reason for the inclusion of self-esteem in embarrassment's ordinary-language semantic field: even if these two are conceptually distinguishable, in practice they are often interconnected. As a subsequent vignette will suggest, the blurring of embarrassment and shame is even more pronounced in some cultures than in the British-American culture we have focused on here.

Of all the emotions that are involved in the covert control of people's behaviour, guilt and shame are the most prominent, and these are the subject of the next two chapters. Gabrielle Taylor (Chapter 3) begins her analysis of the concept of guilt with a distinction between being guilty and feeling guilty: a person is guilty if he or she transgresses the edicts of some authority; a person feels guilty only if he or she accepts the authority which has forbidden the acts or thoughts or whatever it is that is proscribed. In accordance with the general line we are taking in this book, feeling guilty is the embodied expression of the complex but habituated judgement that one has broken an injunction and that one accepts the rule of the authority that issued it. The structure of guilt cannot be reduced to some covert utilitarian judgement because, as Taylor points out, the thought that one is guilty, expressed in a pattern of bodily sensations, is best glossed as the expression of the realization that one has broken a taboo, because taboos are often authoritative without reason. Guilt does not necessarily express the thought that one has harmed another, though often an edict may be issued just to prevent harm.

Feelings and displays of guilt, Taylor goes on to argue, concern themselves with the harm done, by commission or omission. They are 'localized', as she puts it. Here is the deep contrast with shame, which has all to do with the kind of person one thinks one is. One who feels guilty over some matter is often obsessed with 'making it up' to the person harmed or inconvenienced. The guilty may deserve punishment, but once they have 'made up' for their act their guilt is relieved. Nothing corresponds with this process with shame; all one can do is slip away.

Responsibility too is differently allotted in the cases of guilt and shame. Since guilt always has to do with a sin of commission or omission, acceptance of responsibility is built into the conditions for the application of the concept. But one can be ashamed of many matters that, though intimately connected with one's very being, are not one's responsibility; for instance, one can be ashamed of one's family or of one's physical appearance. In this way embarrassment has some resemblance to shame but has little likeness to guilt. Taylor emphasizes the crucial role that beliefs about agency play in distinguishing these emotions in certain crucial cases.

In cases of shame, argues Taylor, the view I take of myself is that what I have just done 'fits only too well with what I am'. But no such thought troubles the guilty. Rather, since the act is thought not to reflect my true nature, repair and restoration is the appropriate next step. Taylor uses the transformations of the characters of Macbeth and Lady Macbeth to illustrate how one who fails to make recompense for their act, thus rejecting guilt, can so rejig their sense of their own character (Macbeth is transformed from man-of-honour to man-of-action) that they are troubled neither by guilt nor by shame.

Like shame, guilt expresses a reflexive judgement that one is disfigured by what one has done. But with guilt, reparation not only recompenses for the harm done but restores one's sense of oneself as a proper person. Remorse, argues Taylor, is focused wholly on the deed and not at all on oneself as the agent of the act. Unlike regret, which can be felt for something for which one has no responsibility at all, remorse is only appropriate when it is the act one has oneself carried out that one realizes is wrong. Since remorse may prompt to repair and restoration, 'remorse' says Taylor, 'is the means whereby the guilty can regain his former position'. Recognition of guilt is a necessary first step to salvation, but only if it is accompanied by remorse is the moral revival of the person possible. In this way the guilt, above all an emotion of self-assessment, becomes focused on the act, making it possible to 'make it up' to the injured.

The contrasts between shame and guilt as means of social control are clearly illustrated by examining their use in particular cultural and historical circumstances. John Demos (Chapter 4) examines these emotions in the New England region of America, contrasting two historical periods. The first, encompassing roughly the century prior to the American Revolution, he characterizes as relying more on shame than on guilt to accomplish the work of social control. The second, encompassing the first half of the nineteenth century, he characterizes as relying more on guilt. His analysis of these two periods nicely demonstrates the differences between the two emotions.

According to Demos, shame in colonial New England was based on exposure to public scorn, which was central to Puritan culture. The Puritan religion itself placed great value on self-scrutiny, self-assessment and self-abasement, always within the sight of an ever-watchful Deity. This emphasis seems to have made the Puritans very sensitive to abasement by others. Demos documents a cultural focus on reputation, on derision, and on the opinions of others, which might be said to be hypercognized in Puritan culture. He suggests that the Puritans so emphasized the influence of public relations on others that notions related to self-determination might be said to be hypocognized. Interpersonal conflict in particular reveals this cultural preoccupation with shame. Demos cites court records showing that conflicts often revolved around one person's having been perceived as injuring another person's reputation, and many lawsuits concerned slander and defamation. Feuding was often conducted using the 'narcissistic insult', which combined inflation of self with denigration (shaming) of the other. Demos points out that the modes of punishment famously prevalent in this period – stocks, pillories, badges of infamy and so on – all featured public exposure as their central element. Punishment was not considered successful unless it resulted in a public display of shame, in the form of public confession and self-abasement.

During the next century-and-a-half, Demos argues, New England culture evolved away from this emphasis on shame to place more of an emphasis on guilt. The region's predominant Protestant religion shifted from its previous emphasis on salvation through acceptance of one's inherent sinful nature; it came instead to focus on the sacrifices and sufferings of Christ and of members of the church. Religious non-conformity was no longer punished with public scorn and the threat of abandonment by excommunication; it was instead punished with the threat of guilt, a guilt based on a sense that previous sacrifices and sufferings would have meaning only if they led to the subsequent religious conversion of others, and therefore that one's religious shortcomings would render those sufferings in vain and show a lack of appreciation for – and thereby increase the suffering of – those who had sacrificed on one's behalf. As in the previous period, religious belief moulded the general culture. Childrearing practices came to emphasize self-punishment in isolation rather than the parent's administering punishment in public. Incarceration of criminals came to be understood as isolation enforced by a supportive public so that offenders could be punished by their own consciences rather than as a public exposure to society's scorn. Anger was now likely to be expressed in exaggeration of the opponent's villainy (and hence guilt) rather than in belittlement of the opponent's stature (and hence shame). The Puritan's sense of a person's being controlled by external social forces gave way to the nineteenth-century sense of a person's being controlled by his or her own inner moral sense and character.

Demos's analysis raises the issue of the relative advantages and disadvantages of these two means of social control. Demos argues that although the antislavery movement used both shame and guilt to advance its goal, it relied more heavily on guilt. Partly this preference reflected the times, as Demos suggests, but there is also the matter of the motivations to which these two emotions give rise. Shame, to return to a point made by Gabrielle Taylor, limits the shamed person's motives to make things right. The shamed person in effect must accept a debased self as congruent with the wrongful action, and is motivated not so much to compensate for the action as to withdraw from public scorn. Guilt, again following Taylor's analysis, may be coped with by righting the wrong that has been done, because the wrongful action is construed as incongruent with a self that knows better. Assuming that antislavery activists wanted to persuade people to act to end slavery, they may have emphasized guilt over shame for this reason. Thus, the emotional means of social control may be determined for strategic as well as for cultural reasons.

Just as cultural forces may be seen influencing Americans' propensity towards shame and guilt in earlier times, they may be seen influencing the propensity to feel regret in contemporary America. So argues Janet Landman in Chapter 5. Regret, Landman claims, is an emotion particularly sensitive to the prevailing world-view of the society in which it comes under scrutiny. Currently in the United States, regret is downplayed and even deplored as unhealthy and unproductive. What is 'regret'? To a first approximation it is a 'painful state of feeling sorry, for the transgressions and misfortunes of oneself and others'. It is a kind of commentary upon the past. It is the backward-looking character of regret that endows it with such a high degree of cultural ambiguity. Seen in relation to the planning of future activities, regret for tactical mistakes, errors of judgement and bad behaviour in the past can help to improve action in the future. Paradoxically, regret, in being backward-looking, is future-directed. But it can also be seen as dysfunctional, a concentration on past failures to the exclusion of looking to a better future.

Seen negatively, Landman identifies four major ways in which contemporary American culture, as the bearer of a certain world-view, takes regret to be an emotion to be avoided and, if it occurs, to be rid of. In the case of regret as a feature of individual psychology, the expression of phoney regret is a nasty piece of self-serving dishonesty, whereas genuine regret is not much better in that it may easily decline into a sort of perverse self-punishment. In a telling phrase Landman identifies a cultural obsession she calls 'allergy to the past'. Regret, as a backward-looking emotion of great potency, forces the attention where it should not be directed, to the past, a past which has gone and to which nothing can be done. As such, regret is wasteful of scarce cognitive resources and, at the very least, a distraction. Where no remedial action can be achieved, the mind should not rest. It is pointless to regret what has happened in the past, since decisions should employ considerations from the here and now. In general, in a society which, at least in its superficial and overt expression of what it values, the optimistic attitude is to be encouraged. Regret leads to pessimism, and as such is to be deplored and discouraged.

Yet, Landman argues, this tacit cultural evaluation ignores equally obvious benefits that the indulgence of a measure of regret makes possible.

One can hardly deny the 'presence of the past'. There is a dynamic of regret in which, especially in the framework of an optimistic world-view that focuses upon the future, regret is part of a psychological mechanism which enhances the possibility of rational decision making. Regret serves to forewarn of mistakes to come, by focusing attention on those occasions in the past when things did not go as we should have wanted. In this respect it stimulates high-quality thinking. It mobilizes the energy needed for action for change. It is not to be stuck deep in the muddy waters of the past. In relation to an individual life it can enhance integrity, by bringing into focus the ways one has not lived up to one's own expectations of oneself. Insofar as the action one might take is infused with insights drawn from reflection on what one wishes one had done better, the community is frequently the benefactor.

Landman shows how the role of an emotion in everyday life is related to the world-view which that form of life realizes. Interestingly she has also shown how a certain social pressure, even overt social criticism, condemning the indulgence of some emotion, can itself be criticized within the very same framework of concepts from which the original criticism seemed to take its force.

Part I closes with two vignettes illustrating the themes that have been expounded. In these, Christopher Ricks (Vignette 3) and Inmaculada Iglesias (Vignette 4) both probe the cultural boundaries of embarrassment. It is not until the mid-eighteenth century, Ricks points out, that literature indicates a growing sense of the centrality of embarrassment as an emotion revelatory of character. By the nineteenth century embarrassment has become an important and noteworthy psychological phenomenon among the English. Ricks believes that embarrassment is closely tied to indignation, both emotions displayed in a reddening of the face. But indignation, as he puts it, 'drives out' embarrassment. According to Ricks, Keats, as exemplary of the psychology of the English, was 'honourably alive to embarrassment' and at the same time, and as part of the same psychological structure, 'honourably moved to generous indignation'.

Embarrassment is a particularly English emotion. It is the unembarrassability of the French that incurs English suspicions. Indeed, the French language has difficulty with the seemingly simple and radical distinction between flushing (with indignation) and blushing (with embarrassment) – *rougir* must do duty for both. Embarrassment in the French context is more a matter of the violation of modesty than it is a recognition of social or bodily impropriety. Each culture has had its authors who have explored the falsities of their own forms of embarrassment and brazenness. Dickens examined the special qualities of English hypocrisy, whereas de Laclos explored the unembarrassable *hauteur* of the French.

Iglesias' vignette explores a Spanish variant of embarrassment, *vergüenza ajena*, which refers to vicarious or empathetic embarrassment. Her essay, like Averill's on hope, explores the similarities and differences between the emotions in two cultures. The Spanish and English variants of

embarrassment are similar enough to be recognized as corresponding, but
they differ in several notable respects. For example, in Spanish it appears
much more difficult to distinguish embarrassment from shame than it does
in English. Also, *vergüenza ajena*, much more readily than vicarious embarrassment, seems capable of occurring on behalf of people who themselves are not experiencing embarrassment at all, but *ought* to be.

Iglesias suggests a number of features of Spanish culture that might
underlie these characteristics. There is a greater emphasis in Spanish culture
than in British or American culture on maintaining a proper public image.
It is therefore the case that a Spaniard's public image is a more serious
issue, and that their social blunders are less likely to be treated lightly or
humorously (observations that are suggestively reminiscent of ones made
by Demos about shame-oriented Puritan culture). The roots of this
emphasis may be in Spanish culture's strong emphasis on pride, dignity and
honour. Such cultural characteristics may indeed help account for the form
embarrassment takes in this culture.

The topics of historical and cultural variation arose in all the chapters on
social control, and in Part II we shift the focus to these topics. Understanding cultural variations in emotions is a most helpful way to appreciate the extent to which our own emotions have been shaped by our
culture, and is indispensable for demonstrating what degree of plasticity
exists in human emotional nature. Perhaps the most striking demonstrations of cultural variation are those that occur over time within a single
culture. For example, grief seems so deep and central a feature of our
lives that the fact that it varies so greatly from culture to culture and may
even be absent from some seems scarcely credible. Yet there is no doubt
that in the last two hundred years we have seen a radical transformation
of the emotion and its place in our own culture. There has been a huge
rise and then a dramatic fall in the intensity of grief and at the same time
a shift in the location of grief to and from the centre of our cultural
preoccupations.

All this is made clear by Peter Stearns and Mark Knapp (Chapter 6), as
they trace the several transformations of what they have called our 'grief
culture'. In pre-Victorian times the grief occasioned by death was firmly
constrained, and low-key in a world in which emotion generally was
underplayed by our contemporary standards. The generally religious cast of
thought then tended to interpret excessive grief as a sign of too great an
interest in this world. Furthermore, the family was still, at that time, in
many ways more an economic unit, rather than a sentimental one bound by
emotional ties. Death, too, was a social act and the 'good death', slipping
away in the bosom of the family, mostly achieved.

The Victorian death culture was set in a society in which emotion was
heightened in almost every context. 'Love' became the salient bond that
tied the members of a family into a social unit, love between parents and
love between parents and children. Death disrupted this vital tie. At the

same time the beginnings of the belief in progress, which was so to dominate Victorian thought, cast death as a defeat which medical science would combat with all the force at its command.

Startling to our contemporary sensibility is the drawing up of children into the culture of grief. The expression of grief amid the mortuary rituals was a central feature of the social and emotional training of children, who were liberally supplied with funerary toys. Death bed scenes and the intensified and *long-term* display of grief were a staple part of children's stories. In the adult world not only was a life-long display of grief encouraged but there was a vast elaboration of funerary ritual, including the draping of whole houses in black. Within this ritual framework the emotion of grief had free reign.

According to Stearns and Knapp there were two stages in the transformation of this grief culture into the modern form of the emotion. From the religious point of view heavy grief contradicted the official doctrine of the survival of the soul. Practical people began to object to the wastefulness of funerary rituals and the exploitation of grief by undertakers. At the same time, the growing pragmatic cast of thought, particularly in America, led to an impatience with the indulgence of any backward looking emotion as a waste of time and energy (compare Landman's analysis of regret in Chapter 5). This trend was enhanced by the huge death toll of the First World War, and soon silence fell on the subject of death, and grief declined with it.

The second phase of transformation came with the absorption of the Freudian idea that grief-work should be managed according to the principle that 'detachment was the ultimate good'. Anyone persisting in grieving for a loved one was in danger of being diagnosed as suffering from 'chronic grief syndrome'! Death became detached from any strong emotion, as its locale was moved from home to hospital. Etiquette books advised a low-key response to bereavement and loss. Death was hidden. Grief has become a 'problem to be managed'.

If culture can influence the actual experience of emotions, it can influence talk about emotions even more readily. Two of our chapters address emotion talk. In Chapter 7, Catherine Lutz discusses the associations between emotion and gender that may be unearthed in contemporary American talk about emotion. In analysing interviews with a small sample of American men and women she learned something of the contemporary folk psychology of emotion and gender. Many of her informants reported believing that emotion must be controlled, and underlying this belief appears to be a host of beliefs about ways in which emotions can be undesirable, inappropriate, irrational, or otherwise threatening. Many informants also reported believing that women are more emotional than men. Given the many reasons for controlling emotions it might appear that associating the feminine with the emotional suggests a view of women as being inferior to men, but the situation is more complex than that. Emotion has some positive connotations as well, such as indicating intense interpersonal connection or Romantic freedom from convention, and, furthermore, the female gender role may permit or require emotional expressivity not allowed to men.

Another discovery from Lutz's interviews was that women devoted more of their speech to discussing emotional control than did men. Perhaps women's greater discussion of emotional control was a self-presentational strategy intended to counteract concerns that they are prone to succumb to emotional weakness. Interestingly, the gender differences predicted by the folk psychology were not evident in Lutz's analysis of syntactic elements in the speech of her informants: there were no differences between men and women in their use of syntactic elements hypothesized to indicate personalization and hence emotional expressiveness.

Lutz argues that folk psychology can be seen as influencing academic research, a theme that is addressed by other contributors to this volume as well. With illustrations from research on premenstrual syndrome, facial expressions of emotion, and aggression, Lutz points out ways in which cultural notions about gender and emotion have biased theory and interpretation of data.

In Chapter 8, Paul Heelas surveys the huge variety of forms and styles of emotion talk that has been found by historians and anthropologists at different times and in different places. What is the significance and what is the effect of this variety? Heelas discusses this under five headings; how it affects the *variety* of emotions recognized in different cultural milieux, how it directs attention to different *loci* for emotions, how different accounts of the *genesis* and *dynamics* of emotions appear, how ways of *managing* emotions are laid down and highlighted, and, finally, what is the *function* of emotion talk.

It is easy to show that there is a great variety in the emotions expressed in the lexicon of emotion talk. Importantly this variety leads to hypercognition, that is sharply focused attention on some emotions, and to hypocognition, the virtual ignoring of others. This can be tied to distinctive ways in which emotions are seen by Dionysian societies (where elaboration of emotion is valued) and by Apollonian societies in which the management of emotions is all important in the interests of affective calm.

Emotion talk seems to differ in where emotions are said to be located. For some they are organ specific, though Heelas emphasizes that this is not a matter of where they are felt. A liver emotion may not be felt in the liver! Other patterns of emotion talk locate emotions in behaviour, in action. Yet other patterns locate emotions externally but they are said to be personally affective in that they invade the individual.

The generation and dynamics of emotions are also topics of large concern in emotion talk. Again they are said by many cultures to have their origin outside the person, in the activities of other people, in the whims of the gods, or even in such matters as foods, a view shared by Elizabethan English and contemporary Indians. Other styles of emotion talk place the origin of emotions within the person welling up from some source other than the self. These cultures tend to favour something akin to our psychodynamics in their general psychology.

Talk of emotions is also shot through with advice and instruction of how the emotions ought to be managed, be it for their enhancement in the Dionysian manner or their diminution in the Apollonian style. There is much talk of moral orders, of how people should feel, and of what emotions and at what strength they should display them. Much of this is bound up with variations in the powers that emotions are said to have. Obviously too, different ways of talking about the loci of emotions will also have different management techniques associated with them. To some extent the degree to which a form of emotion talk favours psychodynamic explanations will affect the extent to which cathartic management techniques are favoured. Heelas points out that most human societies employ forms of emotion talk that are markedly less 'psychological' than ours. By that he means that our tendency to use talk that highlights and focuses attention on private feelings and motives is rare.

In discussing the function of emotion talk Heelas argues that its main point is the focusing of attention. But these differences are effective in the very formation of emotions: 'Differences in "representation" are actually differences in construction'. In learning our local form of emotion talk we appear to be learning ways of being angry, sad, happy and so on; but whether we are learning to be angry or sad at all, it is difficult to tell from examining emotion talk alone.

In the vignette that concludes Part II (Vignette 5), Kenneth and Leo Strongman sketch the emotion system of the Maori of New Zealand. They point out that there are considerable practical difficulties in this research field due to the paucity of empirical data, a consequence of the biculturalism of contemporary New Zealand society. It is evident, however, that emotionality is prized in much Maori public behaviour. A lexical study discloses four main categories of Maori emotion words – the largest group being those for anger and aggression. The next most numerous categories are words for experiences of perplexity, words for desire and yearning and those for a sense of being diminished. Maori emotion is a rich field for cultural psychology, a unique configuration yet to be deeply explored.

The bodily or physiological aspects of emotion have traditionally been the focus of emotion theory and research, yet the chapters of this book's first two parts focused on other aspects: the cognitive and linguistic, the social, cultural and historical. These other aspects certainly deserve attention, not only because of their prior neglect but because of their importance to the nature of emotions and to human emotional life. Yet, in correcting prior neglect we must not create a new one. Indeed, bodily states are properly considered an important aspect of emotions; what needs to be changed is our understanding of their conceptual relation to emotions' non-physiological aspects. In this book's third and final part are chapters that explore the biological dimensions of emotion, the relation between emotions and the body. The authors of these chapters question and reinterpret the traditional notions that construe bodily states as the central feature of emotions, for example, that emotions can be defined and differentiated by physiological patterns.

The first of these chapters has already become a classic: it is James Averill's analysis of 'psychophysiological symbolism', first published in 1974 and reprinted here in slightly abridged form (Chapter 9). Averill's thesis is that much of the Western tradition of scholarship on emotion is systematically warped by a tendency to employ metaphors and symbols that construe emotion as physiological and primitive. This tendency, in his opinion, goes far beyond what is warranted by the evidence, and therefore deserves the label 'extrinsic symbolism'.

According to Averill's analysis, the symbolism of physiological primitivism manifests itself in three principal ways. First, emotion is contrasted with volition and thus viewed as impulsive and as passively experienced; in the legal and moral realms this contrast sometimes leads to construing emotional behaviour as involving diminished personal responsibility. Second, emotion is contrasted with reason, which results in downplaying emotion's cognitive aspects and in localizing emotion's functions away from areas associated with mentation – in the body and in lower brain areas such as the limbic system. Third, emotion is contrasted with the highest and most human faculties; it is therefore considered something more brutish that humans share with the animals. All three aspects of primitivism carry negative connotations, because in each case emotion is contrasted with something highly valued in Western culture.

Averill documents the historical origins of these ideas in ancient Greek thought and traces their remarkable persistence in philosophy and in physiological psychology. He succeeds in showing that the leitmotiv of psychophysiological symbolism has sounded consistently through the centuries – not by all thinkers, of course, but by many of the most influential, enough that this extrinsic symbolism has had ample opportunity to permeate thinking about emotion to the point of becoming an unnoticed assumption. Of particular interest is his demonstration of how this symbolism made a transition from philosophy to physiology, so that ideas about emotion expressed by Plato came to shape interpretations of neurophysiology in more recent times, including our own century.

Averill goes on to question these assumptions, arguing that the symbolism is indeed extrinsic. How can emotions be contrasted with the most human faculties when humans display more emotions than any other animal? How can emotions be considered primitive when most human emotions require mentation beyond the cognitive capabilities of other animals? How can physiological activity be defining of emotions when it is not prominent in many emotions and when it is common in many non-emotions? How can emotion be localized in lower brain areas when these areas cannot function meaningfully except as part of a larger, more complex system? How can emotion be devoid of cognition when certain appraisals are implied by each of the various emotions? By breaking away the extrinsic psychophysiological symbolism from the intrinsic psychophysiological data, Averill hopes to clear the way for the reinterpretation of the relation between body and emotion.

The social constructionist approach he proposes, like others in subsequent chapters in this section, assigns important roles to culture and socialization in influencing neurological and physiological structure and function. For example, Averill considers the experience of passivity and illustrates why it does not necessarily imply that emotion is primitive. He proposes that the experience of passivity is a form of dissociation that occurs when performing an act for which that person cannot or will not accept responsibility. On his account passivity is a fairly complex phenomenon, one that involves monitoring of social norms and juggling of cognitive attributions to produce a distinctive conscious experience that has meaning in a culture's moral system. He thus points the way towards a new understanding of the role of neurophysiology in emotion.

The other chapters follow in this direction, arguing for emotions' greater sensitivity to context and culture than is usually appreciated. G.P. Ginsburg and Melanie Harrington (Chapter 10) begin their study of the role of the body in emotion by describing a series of experiments that show that the relationships in mimetic facial emotional displays are highly dependent on context, in particular on the line of situated action in that context. Some widespread assumptions in contemporary emotion psychology are queried, for example that emotion reactions/displays spring into being. In fact they have natural histories. Nor is there a reliable correlation between emotions as felt and displayed and specific physiological goings on. Distinct emotions are not correlated with distinct physiological conditions, neither in the central nor in the autonomic nervous system, nor in the associated neuro-chemistry of transmitters. There are very large individual differences in the data, even though there is obviously a physiological underpinning to the display and experience of emotions.

The same conclusion has to be drawn from research in the relation between specific emotions and bodily action patterns. There is no reliable relation between basic emotions (if this contested idea can be permitted) and their specific modes of display. There is a weaker relationship in the enhancement of the pleasantness and unpleasantness of an emotion by the deliberate manipulation of facial expressions. This includes facial displays, that are neither necessary nor sufficient for there to be a specific emotion either reported or experienced. The same holds true for vocalization and posture. The question of whether adopting a certain posture induces an emotion is a quite different question from whether a posture is reliably recognized as the expression of a specific emotion.

The missing element in traditional psychological studies of emotion is context, both as hierarchical and as linear organization. 'Feed forward' accomplishes the accumulation of a 'line of situated action' including physiological states of the body. Feelings, rather than being part of the emotion, are best treated as part of the context. Feelings are in need of appraisal and interpretation and this involves situational information.

To use the word 'emotion' with respect to action sequences serves to disclaim responsibility and to draw attention to some event to which an emotional action is relevant. Emotion 'work' performs a variety of functions. There are, therefore, no necessary physiological corollaries of specific kinds of emotion work. Yet all levels of bodily functioning are candidates for involvement in emotional episodes. Natural history and context are also key features and these require attention to the temporal dimension – the line of situated action.

In Chapter 11, Alan Fridlund and Bradley Duchaine offer a critique of what they call the 'two-factor Emotions View' of facial expressions. The two-factor approach, which has dominated research on facial expressions for the past 25 years, developed from the psychophysiological assumptions described by Averill and Ginsburg. The two-factor approach characterizes emotion as springing from primitive, biological sources which automatically and reflexively generate corresponding facial expressions. Facial expressions of emotion are thus considered to express a person's emotions accurately; in Fridlund and Duchaine's terminology, they are 'authentic,' and like Rousseau's 'noble savage' would naturally signal a person's true, innermost feelings without duplicity or subterfuge if uncorrupted by the influence of culture. But civilization includes rules about which facial expressions are and are not acceptable in various social situations, so with socialization comes a corruption of the face's natural veracity. Civilization superimposes 'display rules' on the natural biological linkage between emotion and facial expression, with the result that, during social interaction – when the display rules are operative – faces cannot be considered a pure index of emotion but rather must be understood as the product of two factors, one innately linked to subcortical structures producing emotion, the other developmentally linked to the culture in which one has been socialized.

Fridlund and Duchaine attempt to undermine the two-factor Emotion View, in particular its assertion that it is possible to distinguish authentic expressions of emotion from social expressions. They address two problems inherent in this assertion. First, they argue against its assumption that people essentially return to their asocial, authentic selves whenever they are not participating in social interaction. Sociality can be present in different ways, and it is difficult to rule out its presence simply on the physical presence or absence of interactants. Even when social interaction is not explicitly present, it may be implicitly present. Humans imagine themselves in interactions with others even when alone, and Fridlund and Duchaine review research suggesting that the presence (real or imagined) of an interactant is at least as important in determining the intensity of facial expressions of emotion as is the presence of a private emotional state. To demonstrate how wide ranging is the human propensity to project sociality into situations, they present new data on the tendency to make faces at inanimate objects. The extreme form of their argument is that it is *never* possible to exclude the possibility of implicit or imaginal interactants. Fridlund and Duchaine admit that their position may be non-disconfirmable, but they want to argue that it is nevertheless scientifically useful. The major implication of this position is that the distinction between an authentic, non-social self and a social self is untenable. It must be replaced with the view that the self is by its nature inherently social.

Second, Fridlund and Duchaine argue that there are conceptual and empirical difficulties with the notion that display rules led to the modification of facial expressions in a social setting. The central problem is the assumption that there can be two situations – one social, one not – that lead to identical emotional states so that the same inner feelings exist in both. It is difficult to satisfy this assumption, and it is arguable that it cannot be met. Social and non-social contexts may well give rise to different meanings and goals and thus lead to the development of different emotional states or to different social motives. Observed differences in facial displays might reflect these differences and not the operation of display rules on otherwise identical facial displays.

In place of the two-factor Emotion View, Fridlund and Duchaine propose an alternative, the 'Behavioral Ecology View'. Rather than analyse the complex subtleties of facial expression as blends of a small number of basic emotions, they postulate the existence of a large number of displays – hundreds or thousands – which are specific to the context, identities and relationships present in the situation. Importantly, these displays are not thought of as linked to particular internal states; rather, they suggest intentions, and are not fixed in meaning but free to have different meanings in different contexts. They are best viewed not as signs of an actual intention to behave but rather as an attempt to manipulate the behaviour of others by suggesting that certain types of behaviour are forthcoming. Facial expressions of emotion, on this account, arise in social situations, as products of a social self.

Just as the arguments of Fridlund and Duchaine may be interpreted as providing a social and cultural basis for facial expressions, so too can those of James Laird and Nicholas Apostoleris (Chapter 12) be interpreted as suggesting avenues by which culture can modify the subjective experience of emotion. Their approach contrasts with what is perhaps the dominant approach to emotional feelings at the present: that feelings somehow arise as the product of activity in certain brain structures, structures that are phylogenetically old. The data and arguments of Laird and Apostoleris do not disprove that some feelings are so generated, but they do suggest another avenue by which feelings of emotion can be produced, one that is highly dependent on interpretations that are easily altered by culture.

According to Laird and Apostoleris, feelings are a type of perception of oneself: feelings are to the self as depth and size are to the visual world, a sort of direct registering of a complex of information. In the case of vision the information consists of texture gradients, relative motion, and the like,

which the perceptual system processes to yield the conscious experience of
'big' or 'close'. In the case of feelings, the information consists of actions,
whether observable by others (such as facial expressions, posture, tone of
voice, or gaze) or not (internal actions as autonomic arousal). Laird and
Apostoleris interpret the results of many studies of emotional experience as
demonstrating that self-perception of such actions contributes not only to
feelings but also to such feelings as confidence, hunger, attraction and
liking.

On this account, it is the perception of automatic patterns of behaviour
that leads to the experience of feeling. Some of these automatic patterns
may be biologically given and universal across human societies, but innate
behaviours are not the only source of automatic patterns of behaviour.
Well-practised behaviours and thoughts can become habitual, and nothing
is second to culture for immersing people in patterns of thought, interpretation and behaviour which become 'second nature'. Just as Fridlund and
Duchaine argue for the importance of social context for determining the
meaning of facial signals, so too do Laird and Apostoleris, along with
Averill, suggest that emotional feelings can be shaped by culture. Feelings,
on their account, are 'our perception of how we are behaving in relation to
the context in which we behave'.

Emotional feelings are not mere epiphenomena, Laird and Apostoleris
argue; they provide important information that is used to guide action, and
nothing illustrates this function as well as does their role in self-control.
Feelings inform our reflective selves about our current automatic tendencies. Only if we are aware of these tendencies can we exercise control over
them. Therefore, if we are to have more control over our emotions we must
become more aware of their existence.

Darwin's classical study of blushing, which rounds off his wonderful
book on the emotions of humans and animals, is excerpted here to help
round off ours (Chapter 13). It does admirably illustrate the thesis of this
book. Although the bodily phenomena of the display or feeling of an
emotion has a physiological origin, the point and source of the emotional
display is some sort of judgement.

Darwin begins his study by pointing out that although blushing is a
matter of the distension of capillary blood vessels, it cannot be caused to
happen by physical means. It is thus unlike laughing and tickling. The
tendency to blush is inherited, and varies from family to family in its
intensity and frequency. This is consonant with the fact that blind people
blush, even as very young children. Generally the blush is displayed by very
young children. Women, at least in Darwin's day, blushed more readily
than men. One may blush for shame, for guilt and for modesty. In each
case there are other gestures that go along with the blush, particularly
gestures of concealment. There is also some confusion of mind, and for this
Darwin gives a simple physiological explanation, in that the blood supply
to the brain is affected by the shunting of blood to the expanded capillaries
on the surface of the body.

The blush is restricted in the body surface on which it appears. Though the whole body may tingle, says Darwin, the visible reddening is generally confined to the face and neck. In some special cases whole body blushing has been reported. Why the face? It has to do with where the mind is focused at the time. All human races blush whatever the colour of their skin, and for the same reasons.

People blush because 'attention has been directed [above all] to personal appearance, and not to moral conduct. [This] has been the fundamental element in the acquirement of the habit of blushing.' It is the face that is seen by others, so it is on the face that the blush appears. Darwin conjectures that in the case of aboriginals who go naked the whole body could be attended to and so could be the blushing surface. Even in those cases where the blush seems to be occasioned by some moral fault, it is regard for the opinions of others rather than the sense of wrong-doing itself that brings about the blush, that is a 'moral cause' as Darwin puts it.

Keith Oatley's vignette also addresses the communicative function of emotions (Vignette 6). On his view, emotions signal the possibility that a goal or plan has become more or less likely to be achieved. Emotions direct attention to this possibility, and they also organize our resources in a manner appropriate to this possibility. Oatley considers there to be a small number of basic emotions that have a biological basis and are a basic part of human nature. These basic emotions can be transformed in a multitude of ways by culture, however, because their experience is coloured by their meaning, and it is culture that supplies the meanings. Aristotle's claim that emotions are necessarily linked to intentional judgements is consistent with Oatley's position that goal-relevant events trigger emotions; yet Oatley argues that this linkage can on occasion be absent, as when moods occur in free-floating form. He presents data on the frequency with which a person's emotion is recognized by another. For one emotion, anger, recognition occurred most of the time, which is consistent with the idea that anger functions to readjust social relationships. The other emotions he studied – happiness, anxiety, sadness, shame and guilt – were recognized as existing by others less than half of the time. These emotions, Oatley suggests, sometimes function through social communication but more often function solely as signals to the self.

In a final vignette that comments on the above themes, K.T. Strongman uses a lively literary description of an incident in which a person is deeply disgusted. Touching something foul has a centrality to the bringing on of disgust, but, like all emotions, disgust is not just a physiological reaction to decaying matter. The moment of touching is embedded within a complex cognitive frame of beliefs and deep-rooted conventions. Disgusting matter is most often stuff that has been expelled from a living body. Touching it brings it once more into proximity, but 'too close for comfort'. In the story Strongman cites, the heroine's disgust leads to vomiting, a kind of symbolic second expulsion of the blood and brains she has inadvertently handled.

In this book we have brought together a very wide range of studies, employing many different techniques. Some have used the methods of analytical philosophy, others of descriptive linguistics, others of historical and cultural comparisons of public practices, others examination of neurophysiological processes in the brain and nervous system. There is a remarkable consensus on the point of view sketched by Luria, that human psychology is a complex pattern of cultural practices, discursive conventions, and physiological processes. None has priority since each interacts with and shapes the others. Nowhere is this picture more true and more fruitful for understanding than in the study of the psychology of the emotions.

References

Harré, R. (1986) *The Social Construction of Emotions.* Oxford: Basil Blackwell.
Luria, A.R. (1966) *Human Brain and Psychological Processes.* New York: Harper and Row.

Vignette 1

Aristotle on the Emotions

Daniel N. Robinson

'The emotions are all those feelings that so change men as to affect their judgements, and that are also attended by pain or pleasure'

(*Rhetoric*, 1378^{a}21–2).[1]

Here, then, is Aristotle's pithiest reflection on the nature of the emotions, a subject that already had received sustained philosophical attention within Plato's *Academy*. From the early to the later dialogues, the Socratic view of the emotions – and particularly that of love – underwent significant changes. Thus, in the *Phaedrus* emotion, once a wild steed to be controlled by rationality, is now the source of creativity, bringing into being what reason alone could never fathom. Aristotle would later characterize such productions as but a species of rhetoric as he himself set about to understand the emotions within his more general theory of human character.

In developing his psychological theory, Aristotle postulates three primary psychological factors in the soul: passions, faculties and states (*Nicomachean Ethics*, 1105^{b}20). Having defended a general teleological theory to account for the regularities of nature, he is committed to the view that all of these, surely including the emotions, are not only natural but for a purpose. Each is to be understood and evaluated according to the extent to which the *telos* is realized or attained. If there is a general function served by the emotions it is that of inducing activity or giving it a certain impulsive character. Different words are used to describe such an influence: *pathos* for emotion in general; *orexis* for a kind of appetite or desire or passion; *ptoēsis* for a dreadful fear, etc.

The moving principles in animals arise from two sources, thought and appetite, rendered in *On the Soul* as *nous* and *orexis* respectively (432^{b}15–433^{a}21). Just how the moving principles are to be understood depends on the sort of account one seeks. One might settle either for a discursive account or one that is scientific. An action prompted by anger, for example, would be explained differently by a scientist and by a dialectician: 'The latter would define anger as the appetite (*orexis*) for returning pain for pain . . . while the former would define it as a boiling of the blood' (*On the Soul*, 403^{a}30–403^{b}1).

The example of anger is useful for it introduces a feature of Aristotle's theory of emotion that connects it directly to his *cognitive* psychology. If there is a strong impulse 'for returning pain for pain', then the emotion must arise from a judgement, and the action impelled by the emotion must bear a coherent relationship to the judgement itself. Were it otherwise, there would be only the feeling. And, as an entirely natural or biological state – indistinguishable in this respect from digestion or breathing – such an emotion would have no moral relevance whatever. The feelings of anger or fear are natural reactions and as such do not provide grounds for praise or blame. It is clear that virtues and vices are not emotions, 'because we are neither called good nor bad . . . for the simple capacity of feeling the passions' (*Nicomachean Ethics*, 1106ª8). Although conferring 'a kind of courage' on animals who defend their litters, Aristotle's restriction of the virtues to man is based on just these considerations. Actions arising from feelings *qua* feelings are of a morally different sort from those seeking a principled end. One is judged to be good or bad, virtuous or vicious, according to the more settled states and dispositions one has; dispositions that determine how one *judges* a situation and then acts when one is angry or fearful in that situation. The question of consequence, then, has to do with what one is disposed to be angry or fearful *about*.

People who feel shame, Aristotle says, blush, whereas those who fear death turn pale. These emotions reflect conditions of the body but are also predicated on different cognitions; in the one case, fear of disrepute, in the other fear of physical pain. As fear of disrepute can have a salutary effect on conduct, inclining persons to live according to the expectations of others, it is a passion well suited to youth. Found in a mature person the emotion of shame cannot be thus useful for it indicates a character still inclined towards what is shameful (*Nicomachean Ethics*, 1128ᵇ10–30). Nor is one to be judged harshly for anger if this passion is unjustly provoked. Rather, it is the instigator who is blameworthy as is one who when treated unjustly is *not* angry! Anger, as Aristotle understands it, is a feeling of pain coupled with a desire for avenging a wrong; one is angry over a 'conspicuous slight at the hands of those who have no cause to slight oneself' (*Rhetoric*, 1378ª31–2).

It is notable, then, that Aristotle's theory of emotion incorporates moral, social, developmental and cognitive considerations within a larger naturalistic framework. It is a theory about the place of emotion within the overall development of personality or what Aristotle called *character*. Where early training has not disciplined the emotions the adult personality is likely to be governed by them and be thus inaccessible to rational modes of persuasion. Passion, says Aristotle, 'seems to yield not to argument but to force', meaning that beyond a certain point proper conduct must be coerced. It is in early life that the right dispositions (*hexeis*) towards emotion are established yielding a character that comes to have 'a kinship with virtue' (*Nicomachean Ethics*, 1179ᵇ30).

Note

1 All quoted passages are taken from the two-volume *The Complete Works of Aristotle*, ed. Jonathan Barnes (1984), Princeton: Princeton University Press.

Vignette 2

Intellectual Emotions

James R. Averill

In ordinary language, a distinction is made between cognition (intellect) and emotion. At least this is true in English, and I assume that it is true in other languages as well. Cognition includes 'higher' thought processes; it is the special domain of the human being – the 'rational animal'. The emotions, by contrast, are 'lower'; they are common to both humans and infrahuman animals, and they are closely linked to physiological change (i.e., they are 'gut reactions').

At first it might seem that distinctions made in ordinary language would have little relevance to scientific theory. Often, however, our theories are little more than formalizations of folk beliefs, clothed in the scientific jargon of the times. Let me illustrate by reference to the seventeenth century philosopher, Descartes. As is well known, Descartes (1649/1968) argued that the human body functions like a complex machine. The human mind, in contrast, belongs to a separate realm, the *res cogitans*. This separation of the mind and body was an implicit recognition that 'higher' thought processes (rationality and choice) are not explicable in strictly mechanistic terms.

According to Descartes, the mind not only acts (reasons and chooses), it is also acted upon, that is, is subject to passions. In the broadest sense, passions are impressions imposed on the mind through its interaction with the body. Some passions are mediated by the sense organs and are attributed to specific events either within (interoception) or without (exteroception) the body. However, other passions seem to have no specific sensory origin – these are *passions of the soul* in the strict sense. These passions arise, Descartes speculated, when animal spirits (extra fine particles distilled from the blood in a region around the heart) rise to the brain. In the brain, the animal spirits serve to keep sensory and motor passages open, so that a frightened individual, say, will continue to flee, even though the stimulus that aroused the fear (e.g., a bear in the woods) is no longer in view.

Descartes's physiological speculations seem quaint by today's standards. The logic of this argument, however, is not foreign to contemporary theories of emotion. In one way or another, most theories emphasize physiological arousal as a necessary, if not sufficient, condition for the experience of emotion; most theories also attribute to the emotions a motivating or sustaining function; and, finally, most theories conceive of the emotions as primitive responses common to both animals and humans.

There is a problem with this traditional conception of emotion, however. Some emotions tend to be primarily cognitive or intellectual in nature, with little bodily involvement. Descartes (1649/1968) also recognized this fact. Thus, he distinguished the passions of the soul from 'interior' emotions (*emotions interieures*). The latter are desires 'which are excited in the soul by the soul itself, in which respect they differ from its passions, which always depend on some movement of the spirits' (Descartes, 1649/1968: Article CXLVII). Descartes used the following examples to illustrate what he meant. A bereaved husband may feel genuine sorrow at the loss of his wife, and yet he may feel 'a secret joy in the innermost parts of his heart, the emotion of which possesses so much power that the sadness and the tears which accompany it can do nothing to diminish its force' (Article CXLVII). Similarly, the theater can excite in us a wide variety of passions – sadness, anger, joy, love and hatred, for example. At the same time, we may experience pleasure in having these passions, 'and this pleasure is an intellectual joy which may as easily take its origin from sadness as from any of the other passions' (Article CXLVII).

Descartes did not elaborate on how the intellectual or interior emotions arise, but they are not simply mild versions of the passions. On the contrary, they 'have much more power over us than the passions from which they differ' (Article CXLVIII).

In short, Descartes clearly recognized that his explanation of passions of the soul was inadequate to account for all emotions. But he did not carry that insight very far; nor did he explore its theoretical implications. I wish I could do here what Descartes failed to do, but I am not so presumptuous. My goals are more limited. Specifically, I examine one emotion that many people might consider 'intellectual', namely, hope.[1] There are good practical reasons for studying hope. For example, persons facing severe challenge, from illness to sporting contests, often do better if they maintain hope; and the loss of hope ('hopelessness') is one of the most common symptoms of depressive disorders. My interest in hope is, however, more theoretical than practical. What is it about hope that would lead us to classify it as an emotion? And, more generally, what would our theories of emotion be like if, instead of focusing on such 'bodily' emotions as anger and fear, we focused instead on such intellectual emotions as hope and pride?

In addressing these issues, I will draw upon data from four studies of hope. The first two studies involved the same procedure (a detailed written questionnaire) and the same sample of subjects (150 American university students). The questionnaire was divided into two conceptually distinct parts. In the first part (comprising Study 1), subjects were asked to describe various aspects of hope in general and a recent experience of hope in particular. The second part of the questionnaire (comprising Study 2) examined the similarities and differences between hope and other, more prototypic emotions, such as anger and love. Study 3 explored the model of hope implicit in Western cultures, as revealed in proverbs, maxims, and slang expressions. Study 4 was similar to Study 1, but involved a comparison of hope among American ($n = 100$) and Korean ($n = 100$) students.

Only a small sample of data from these studies can be presented here. A complete description and analysis is published elsewhere (Averill et al., 1990). Specifically, I allude only in passing to the data from Study 1, which deals with the normative aspects of hope as experienced in everyday affairs. My main focus is on the nature of hope as an emotion, as revealed in Studies 2 and 3, and on differences in the experience of hope among Americans and Koreans (Study 4).

Hope as an emotion

At this point, an objection might be raised. A critic might argue that intellectual emotions are not real emotions and hence are of little theoretical relevance. I shall have much to say in response to this objection as we proceed. For the moment, suffice it to note that throughout much of Western history emotions such as hope (cf. Aquinas) and pride (cf. Hume) have been considered fundamental. Even today, when people are asked to rate the representativeness of various emotions, hope falls within the upper third of the distribution, ahead of such states as disgust, contempt and interest (Averill, 1975; Fehr and Russell, 1984). The latter have been taken by some theorists as basic or fundamental emotions (e.g., Izard, 1977).

But on what grounds is hope classified as an emotion? That is the first issue I want to address briefly.

Similarities and differences among hope, anger and love

Almost everyone would agree that anger and love are good examples of emotion. Study 2 posed the following 'thought experiment' for subjects:

> Think for a moment about two commonly recognized emotions, such as anger and love. What do they have in common, such that they are both classified as emotions? Now compare hope with anger and love (not separately, but in terms of their common features).

This thought experiment was the final item in the questionnaire. It was the first time that reference was made to hope in an emotional context.

Subjects were instructed to list 'two ways in which hope is similar to anger and love' and 'two ways in which hope is different from anger and love'.

Similarities   The most frequently mentioned similarity was that all three states – hope, anger and love – are feelings and/or emotions (16.1 per cent of the responses). Table V2.1 presents the remaining similarities in decreasing

Table V2.1 *Ways in which hope is similar to anger and love*

---

1 All affect the way you think and/or behave (e.g., in obsessional, irrational, or unusual ways). (10.5%)[a]

2 All are difficult to control. (6.3%)

3 All motivate behavior, increase persistence, enable one to keep going. (4.9%)

4 All are common or universal experiences. (3.8%)

5 All can be accompanied by pleasant and/or unpleasant experiences. (2.8%)

6 All can be intense experiences. (2.3%)

7 All can have cathartic effect, provide a release of tension, or a sense of satisfaction. (2.3%)

8 All are highly personal experiences; they come from the 'inside'. (2.1%)

9 All are directed toward external things or events. (2.1%)

10 All can be – and often are – expressed outwardly, e.g., in gestures, words, or actions. (2.1%)

11 All are a necessary part of life. (2.1%)

12 All are indescribable, intangible, and/or abstract experiences. (1.7%)

13 All can come or go quickly, are subject to sudden change. (1.7%)

14 All are states of high arousal or energy level. (1.7%)

---

[a] The percentages in parentheses represent the number of responses, out of a total of 287, that fell within a category. At least 5 responses (1.7% of the total) were required to form a category. The largest category of responses (16.1%) was that hope, anger and love are all feelings or emotions. This category is not included in this table, which concerns the grounds for classifying hope as an emotion. Another 37.5% of the responses were too vague or idiosyncratic to categorize.

order of frequency. (Below, I shall have more to say about the classification of hope as an emotion. For now, our concern is with the grounds for such a classification.)

Nearly all the similarities listed in Table V2.1 represent common characteristics of emotions in general. That is, emotions affect the way a person thinks and behaves, they are difficult to control, they motivate behavior, and so forth. If one wished to construct a prototypic emotion, the list of features contained in Table V2.1 would provide a good beginning.

Differences The most frequently mentioned difference (9 per cent of the responses) was that hope is less demonstrable than anger or love. That is, whereas there are characteristic ways of expressing anger or love, hope – although it leads to goal-directed behavior – need not be expressed in any particular way. The two other most frequently mentioned differences were that hope is less tangible, that is, is more like a dream, fantasy, or illusion (5 per cent of the responses); and that the object of hope is relatively unrestricted (also 5 per cent). This latter difference reflects the fact that anger and love are tied to particular events or targets, for example, an unwarranted affront in the case of anger or a certain individual in the case of love. By contrast, a person can hope for almost any future event, the occurrence of which is uncertain.

The preceding differences can be summarized by saying that hope is more 'open-ended' than are anger and love. This does not mean, however, that there are no restrictions on hope, as we shall see shortly.

There is no need to discuss other ways in which hope differs from anger and love, for our main concern here is with the similarities (see Table V2.1). For the most part, the differences reported by subjects fell along the same dimensions as the similarities – only more or less so. For example, although all three states (hope, anger and love) were described as difficult to control (see Item 2 in Table V2.1), hope was judged as more difficult to control by some subjects (2 per cent of the responses) and as less difficult to control by others (4 per cent of the responses).

Metaphors of hope

To determine whether the similarities among hope, anger and love presented in Table V2.1 were idiosyncratic to the subjects involved (i.e., American university students), the nature of hope as reflected in proverbs, maxims, and other metaphorical expressions was examined. Such expressions can be used as a guide to the models of emotion implicit within a culture. (See Kovecses, 1986, 1988, 1990, and Lakoff and Kovecses, 1983, for detailed discussion and analyses of metaphors of emotion.)

A list of 106 basic-level metaphors was compiled from books of maxims and thesauri, and from student-generated slang expressions. Space limitations preclude a complete content analysis of these metaphors. Instead, I shall use selected metaphors to illustrate some of the reasons why hope is classified as an emotion. Also for reasons of space, I focus on the first four similarities listed in Table V2.1. These are among the most important, or at least the most common, grounds for classifying a response as emotional.

Hope affects the way a person thinks and/or behaves

One of the major connotations of emotional concepts is that emotions involve irrational, or at least nonrational, ways of thinking and behaving. This connotation finds metaphorical expression in such sayings as the following:

He was *blinded* by hope.
She was *grasping at straws.*
The houses hope builds are *castles in the air.*
Hope is a *traitor of the mind.*
Hope is what *dreams* are made of.

Even when hope is regarded as reasonable, it may still be judged by criteria other than the norms of rationality. For example, a seriously ill person who hopes for recovery is not generally asked to justify his or her hope on logical grounds. In general, emotional beliefs are judged in terms of appropriateness, not in terms of truth value. Hope is clearly no exception.

Hope is difficult to control

As we saw in our discussion of Descartes, emotions traditionally have been conceptualized as *passions* – something over which we ostensibly have little control. An implication of passivity is implicit in many of the metaphors of hope. For example, the notion that hope is a 'traitor of the mind' implies not only an irrationality, but also a lack of control.

Lack of control finds more direct expression in such metaphors as the following:

She was a *prisoner* of hope.
He was *consumed* by hope.

Hope is also frequently depicted as a physical object or thing, that is, as something a person has rather than as something a person does. Thus, hope can be *lost* or *found*, *given* or *received*, *shattered* or *restored*, and so forth. One implication of these metaphors is that hope is determined by events external to the self.

In short, a person does not deliberately choose to hope (in the prototypical case). Rather, assuming the object is sufficiently important, the person 'cannot help but hope'.

Hope motivates behavior

Emotions are often treated as a kind of force or energy that motivates behavior. According to Lakoff and Kovecses (1983), the principal (abstract) metaphor of anger is the heat of a fluid in a container. When the heat (intensity of the anger) increases, the fluid rises (wells up), increasing the pressure in the container (the person), until the container blows up (the person loses control).

Hope, too, is depicted metaphorically as a kind of pressure that may *fill* a person until he or she *bursts*. Hope may also *spur a person to industry*, and it may *swell one's sails*.

However, as we pursue the energy metaphor, a difference between hope and other emotions quickly becomes apparent. Consider the following expressions:

Hope *gives you strength*.
Hope is a *poor man's bread*.
Hope is the best *medicine*.
Warmed by hope, frozen by dread.
Hope *lifts you up*.
Hope will *carry you through*.

As these metaphors imply, the 'energy' of hope is more like that found in food than like that found in a coiled spring or a hot fluid. Hope does not only exert pressure for action, it also nourishes, sustains and supports an individual in situations where no action is possible.

Hope is a common or universal experience

The universality of hope is the fourth most frequently mentioned similarity listed in Table V2.1, and the last that I discuss in this chapter. It is particularly interesting for two reasons: (a) it finds frequent support in metaphorical expressions, and (b) it is nevertheless potentially very misleading.

There are many variations on the general metaphorical theme *where there is life there is hope*. The following are three examples:

Hope is the *balm and lifeblood* of the soul.
Hope is the *second soul* of the unhappy.
Hope *springs eternal* in the human breast.

If by *hope*, we mean simply a tendency to persuade oneself that what is desired will come to pass (see Descartes's definition cited in Footnote 1), then hope is undoubtedly a universal and even necessary part of life. But such beliefs are probably better labeled *optimism* than hope. Optimism and hope are sometimes treated as though they were nearly identical (cf. Tiger, 1979); however, it is easy to demonstrate their independence. For example, a person may be so pessimistic that nothing is left but hope.

As an emotional syndrome, hope may not be as universal as is commonly assumed. Boucher (1980) asked informants from various countries to name as many emotions as they could. Ample time was allowed to complete the task (up to a week in most cases). 'Hope' (or its near equivalents in the indigenous languages) was mentioned by informants from the United States, Australia, Puerto Rico and Japan. However, informants from Korea, Indonesia, Malaysia and Sri Lanka did not mention hope among the emotions in their cultures. These data suggest that hope may be constituted differently, at least in its emotional aspects, in various cultures. That is the possibility I explore next.

Hope as experienced by Koreans and Americans

In order to explore possible cultural variations in hope, a questionnaire was administered to a group of 100 students (68 male and 32 female) at Sung Kyun Kwan University in Seoul, South Korea, and 100 students (35 male and 65 female) at the University of Massachusetts, Amherst.

The average age of subjects in the Korean sample was 22.1 years (range = 18 to 29); 24 per cent were sophomores, 73 per cent juniors and 3 per cent seniors. The average age of the American sample was 20.9 years (range = 19 to 34); 15 per cent were sophomores, 35 per cent juniors and 49 per cent seniors (1 American subject did not indicate a grade). More than 80 per cent of the subjects in both samples were social science majors (psychology, business, and education, primarily).

Preliminary analyses indicated no confounding due to age, grade level, or sex on any of the variables reported below.

Intellectual emotions
31

Table V2.2 *Mean ratings and rank orders of hope (*himang*) in terms of superordinate categories by American (*n = 100*) and Korean (*n = 100*) subjects*

Category	Americans		Koreans		p^b
	Mean rating[a]	Rank order	Mean rating	Rank order	
A way of coping (e.g., with a handicap)	1.74	1	1.46	4	<.01
A feeling	1.72	2	1.17	8	<.01
An emotion	1.42	3	1.34	6	NS
An attitude	1.31	4	1.24	7	NS
A voluntary process	1.26	5	1.64	1.5	<.01
A personality characteristic	1.18	6.5	1.64	1.5	<.01
A socially acquired motive	1.18	6.5	1.60	3	<.01
A biologically based need	.84	8	.89	9	NS
An intellectual process	.83	9	1.40	5	<.01
An involuntary process	.69	10	.58	10	NS

[a] 0 = *not at all,* 1 = *somewhat,* 2 = *very much.*
[b] Probability levels are based on analyses of variance.

The classification of hope

The first item in the questionnaire asked participants to rate the extent to which hope belongs to each of 10 basic psychological categories (e.g., an emotion, an intellectual process, or an attitude). Ratings were made on 3-point scales (0 = *not at all,* 1 = *somewhat,* 2 = *very much*). The results, presented in Table V2.2, were analyzed by two-way analyses of variance, with culture and sex as independent variables. The significance levels reported in Table V2.2 are for the main effects of culture.

For the most part, Koreans tend to view hope (*himang*) as a permanent part of personality (albeit socially acquired), closely related to the intellect and will. Americans, by contrast, tended to regard hope as a more transitory state – as a way of coping, a feeling, and/or an emotion. These results support Boucher's (1980) finding that Koreans do not spontaneously list hope among the emotions of their culture.

The bulk of the questionnaire asked subjects to describe a representative episode of hope (one that had begun within the past year). Analyses of these data (see Averill et al., 1990), also support the conclusion that although hope among Koreans and Americans is similar in many respects, the Koreans do not attribute to hope the qualities generally associated with emotional states.

In order to explore in greater detail the norms and values that help constitute hope in Korean and American cultures, subjects also were asked to describe three events that might make their lives easier or more enjoyable, but that they believe they *should not* hope for. They also were asked to describe the reason they did not hope for each event. Descriptions of the events hoped for (henceforth referred to as *fantasy objects*) and the

Table V2.3   *Objects that would make life easier or more enjoyable, but for which subjects believed they should not hope*

Fantasy object[a]	Americans		Koreans		p[b]
	%	Rank order	%	Rank order	
Material goods (e.g., money and car)	32	1	16	2	<.01
Interpersonal relationships (e.g., meeting friends, improved family relations, and getting married)	15	2	6	6	<.01[c]
Achievement: short-term (e.g., success in some academic, artistic, or athletic endeavor)	14	3	5	8	<.01
Change in personal characteristics (e.g., health, intelligence, and beauty)	9	4	1	9.5	<.01[c]
Happiness and well-being (e.g., ease, comfort, and tranquility)	8	5	6	6	NS
Leisure activity (e.g., travel and time off from work)	3	6.5	1	9.5	NS
Achievement: long-term (e.g., a new career)	3	6.5	6	6	NS
Freedom from social and personal obligations (e.g., in order to do what one wants)	2	8	15	3	<.01
Hedonistic pursuits (e.g., sensual pleasures – sex, food, etc.)	2	9.5	17	1	<.01
Social status (e.g., fame, honor, and power)	2	9.5	8	4	<.01

[a] Each subject listed up to three objects. Results are presented as percentages of the total number of objects: The number of American responses was 258; the number of Korean responses was 278. (Eleven per cent of the American and 19 per cent of the Korean responses were unclassifiable.)

[b] Probability levels are based on the chi-square statistic, using all responses.

[c] When only the initial response of each subject was used (thus preserving independence of observation, but greatly reducing the number of observations), group differences were not statistically significant ($p > .05$) for these variables. See text for explanation.

reasons for not hoping were analyzed for content in a manner previously described (see the section on the similarities and differences between hope and other emotions).

Fantasy objects

The categorization of the fantasy objects is presented in Table V2.3. Chi-square tests were used to assess the significance of the differences between Americans and Koreans. Two series of tests were performed, one using all the data (up to three responses from each subject) and the other using only the initial response of each subject. The first series violated one of the assumptions of the chi-square test, namely, independence of observations.

The second series met this assumption, but sacrificed two-thirds of the data. Significance (probability) levels for both series are indicated in Table V2.3.

Both Americans and Koreans tended to fantasize about material objects (e.g., money or a new car), although this was significantly more frequent among Americans than Koreans (by a ratio of 2 to 1). Americans also mentioned improved interpersonal relationships and short-term achievement more than twice as often than did Koreans. On the other hand, Koreans much more frequently than Americans fantasized about hedonistic pursuits (e.g., sensual gratification) and freedom from social and personal obligations.

The data presented in Table V2.3 can best be explained by considering what is most problematic in each culture. Consider the two categories of hedonism and interpersonal relationships. The typical American college student has fewer limitations placed on hedonistic pursuits than does the typical Korean student. On the other hand, a Korean student is more likely than his or her American counterpart to be involved in a network of family and social relationships. Such relationships provide a good deal of support and security, but they also entail a commitment to duty over personal satisfaction. Thus, hedonistic pursuits are more problematic for Korean than for American students, whereas the establishment of meaningful relationships with family and friends is more problematic for Americans than Koreans (and hence more likely to be the object of fantasy).

Reasons for not hoping

The reasons subjects did not hope for the realization of their fantasies are presented in Table V2.4. For ease of interpretation, the reasons have been grouped into four broad categories. These categories, identified on the basis of the data obtained in Study 1 (for details, see Averill et al., 1990), reflect four types of social rules or norms, which I call prudential norms, moralistic norms, priority norms and action norms. Below I explain each type of norm and comment briefly on the differences between Korean and American subjects.

Prudential norms   As discussed earlier, one of the main reasons for classifying hope as an emotion is that it sometimes leads people to act in unusual or irrational ways. This does not mean, however, that hope is typically imprudent. On the contrary, one of the most consistent findings to emerge from the analysis of specific episodes (not reported here) was an emphasis on realism. There should be a reasonable chance of obtaining the object of one's hope. When chances of attainment are unrealistically low, hope is generally regarded as inappropriate. (It is, of course, easy to think of exceptions to this generalization, e.g., the hope of a dying person. We must, however, distinguish between objective and subjective probabilities. It is possible that the fatally ill person, to the extent that he or she maintains hope, subjectively raises the chances of survival.)

Table V2.4   *Reasons for not hoping, categorized according to the norms (rules) of hope*

Reasons[a]	Americans %	Rank order	Koreans %	Rank order	p^b
Prudential norms					
Object is impossible or unrealistic.	28	1	12	3	<.01
Object would be impractical or disadvantageous; it is short-sighted; it interferes with other, more pressing obligations.	9	4	21	2	<.01
Moralistic norms					
Object goes against personal and/or social values; is socially unacceptable; violates personal ideals.	10	3	37	1	<.01
Object is damaging to, or goes against desires of family; fails to meet family obligations.	1	9	4	5	<.05[c]
Priority norms					
Object lacks true worth or importance; it is not really wanted; one can do without it.	7	5	4	5	NS
Action norms					
Hope won't make it happen; one must work for the object.	15	2	0	8	<.01
Object will or will not happen naturally; one has no control over it.	4	6.5	0	8	<.01[c]
Can achieve the object through one's own efforts or hard work; one has control over it.	4	6.5	0	8	<.01[c]
Object would lose value if one didn't work for it; object must be achieved through one's own efforts.	2	8	4	5	NS

[a] Each subject listed up to three reasons. Results are presented as a percentage of the total number of reasons given: The number of American reasons was 258; the number of Korean reasons was 278. (Twenty per cent of the American and 18 per cent of the Korean responses were unclassifiable.)

[b] Probability levels are based on the chi-square statistic, using all responses.

[c] When only the initial response of each subject was used (thus preserving independence of observation, but greatly reducing the number of observations), group differences were not statistically significant ($p > .05$) for these variables. See text for explanation.

Both Americans and Koreans mentioned prudential reasons about equally often when describing why they should not hope for a fantasy object. However, there were important differences within this category. By more than 2 to 1, the Americans stated that the objects of their fantasies were impossible or unrealistic (e.g., the chances of occurrence were slight). The Koreans, in contrast, focused more on the disadvantageousness of the object, should it be achieved. For example, to spend money on hedonistic pursuits, while feasible in an 'objective' sense, might be disadvantageous in that it would hinder one's academic career.[2]

Moralistic norms   The object of hope is circumscribed not only by what is prudent, but also by what is personally and socially acceptable. Fantasies are less restricted in this respect. For example, a young man might fantasize about a rich aunt dying and bequeathing him a large sum of money; yet he would not hope for the aunt to die, for such a wish would be immoral.

There was a marked difference between American and Korean students in the extent to which moral norms dictated the appropriateness of their hope. By almost 4 to 1, more Koreans than Americans indicated that they did not hope for their fantasy objects because such objects would be against social or personal values, or because they would be contrary to family obligations.

Priority norms   Classical analyses of hope generally stop with the assertion that the object of hope is a positive but uncertain event. However, the typical object of hope is not only positive, it also touches upon a person's (or a society's) vital interests, goals and values. What we hope for should have priority over what we merely wish or want. Needless to say, we all hope for trivial events at times (e.g., 'I hope it will be sunny tomorrow'), but that is a rather extended and nonemotional use of the term (cf. 'But I fear that it will rain').

Priority norms were evidenced in a variety of ways. For example, a subject might contend that the fantasy object was not of 'true importance' or that he or she 'could do without it', and hence that it was not an appropriate object for hope. Reasons of this sort were mentioned about equally often by American and Korean subjects.

Action norms   People may want or fantasize about events that they would never act upon. However, to hope for something and not act upon it, given the opportunity, would be inconsistent. People who hope must be willing to take appropriate actions to achieve their goals, if action is possible.

Action norms were indirectly reflected in a variety of the reasons offered for not hoping. For example, a person should not let hope substitute for hard work; nor should a person hope for things that either are or are not completely under his or her own control. Reasons of this type were offered almost exclusively by American subjects.

Cultural background

The reasons for the differences between American and Korean conceptions (and, I would argue, experiences) of hope are undoubtedly many and subtle. One very broad factor is the philosophical and religious traditions of the two countries. America has been influenced by the Judeo-Christian tradition, whereas Korea has been influenced primarily by Confucianism and, to a lesser extent, by Buddhism and Taoism. In Christianity, hope has often been highly prized, not only as an emotional state but also as one of the three 'theological virtues' (along with faith and charity). By contrast, hope has not been emphasized in Confucianism. Rather, Confucianism stresses the self-cultivation of human potential (*jen*); this involves striving to become a morally perfect individual (sage) within a well-defined network of social relationships.

There are, of course, other differences between Korean and American societies that might account for the different conceptions of hope. For present purposes, however, the fact of the difference is more important than its precise explanation.

Implications for theories of emotion

I have now covered two broad topics: (a) the criteria for classifying hope as an emotion and (b) cross-cultural variations in the conception of hope. With regard to the first issue, it might seem that I have devoted an inordinate amount of attention to a rather elementary question: Why is hope classified as an emotion? The issue, however, is of greater theoretical interest than might at first appear. Most contemporary theories do not recognize hope and other 'intellectual emotions' as true emotions. I believe this says more about the nature of our theories than about the nature of hope.

For the most part, our theories of emotion have been erected on a very narrow base. Fear, anger, and, to a lesser extent, love and grief have been the primary emotions investigated. Yet, literally hundreds of emotions are recognized in ordinary language (Averill, 1975; Fehr and Russell, 1984; Johnson-Laird and Oatley, 1989). If a broader sample were made of even the more commonly recognized emotions (of which hope is a good example), I suspect our theories would take on a different character than they now have. For one thing, there would be less emphasis on physiological change and expressive reactions as defining characteristics of emotional states. For another thing, the often heated debate about whether emotions are cognitive or noncognitive would lose much of its force. But most importantly, there would be a greater emphasis on the social determinants of emotion.

Elsewhere (e.g., Averill, 1980, 1982, 1984, 1991), I have argued that emotions can only be understood as part of a broader cultural matrix. From the data summarized in this brief paper, it is evident that hope can only be interpreted within a cultural context. But how far can we generalize from hope to other emotions?

I have already described some of the ways that hope is similar to, and different from, emotions such as anger and love. However, from a logical or conceptual point of view, the most instructive comparison is perhaps between hope and fear. A person cannot hope for something unless he or she also fears that the hoped-for event might not happen. Hope and fear are two sides of the same coin, so to speak; hence, considerations that apply to one also apply to the other.

The close conceptual relationship between hope and fear has been overlooked because the notion of fear can be used in two seemingly different senses. In the first sense, 'fear' refers to short-term *occurrent reactions* characterized, for example, by physiological arousal, attempts to flee, and the like. In the second sense, 'fear' refers to long-term (hours, days, weeks) *dispositions* to engage in any of a wide variety of defensive maneuvers. Most psychological theorizing has focused almost exclusively on the first of these two senses, that is, on occurrent fear or fright reactions. It is primarily in the second (dispositional) sense that fear is the correlate of hope and that similar considerations apply to both emotions. The question then becomes, Which conception – fear as an occurrent reaction or fear as a dispositional state – is primary?

There is not space to address this question here. At the risk of seeming a bit dogmatic, let me simply assert what I believe to be the case, namely, that (a) the distinction between short-term occurrent emotional reactions and longer-term emotional dispositions is not as logically coherent as is often drawn; (b) even short-term emotional states can be conceptualized in dispositional terms; and (c) in the case of fear (and other emotions as well), the dispositional sense is the more important from both a practical and theoretical point of view.

The grounds for the preceding assertions have been presented in detail elsewhere (Averill, 1991). I therefore conclude the present discussion by suggesting that intellectual emotions such as hope be given greater consideration than they have received in the recent past.

Notes

Preparation of this chapter was supported, in part, by Grant MH 40131 from the National Institute of Mental Health. Thanks are due to George Catlin and Kyum-Koo Chon for assistance in collecting and analyzing the data reported herein.

1 For the sake of historical accuracy, it should be noted that Descartes (1649/1968) did not include hope among the intellectual emotions, but rather among the passions. 'Hope is a disposition of the soul to persuade itself that what it desires will come to pass: and this is caused by a particular movement of the spirits, i.e., by that of joy and that of desire mingled together' (Descartes, 1649/1968: Article CLXV).

2 Before the results presented in Table V2.4 are discussed further, a possible source of confounding should be mentioned. We have already noted that Koreans and Americans had fantasies about different types of things (see Table V2.3). Differences in fantasy objects might account for the differences in reasons for not hoping. That, however, was not the case. The trend of the data presented in Table V2.4 generally held, regardless of the nature of the fantasy object.

References

Averill, J.R. (1975) 'A semantic atlas of emotional concepts', JSAS: *Catalog of Selected Documents in Psychology*, 5: 330. (Ms. No. 421)

Averill, J.R. (1980) 'A constructivist view of emotion', in R. Plutchik and H. Kellerman (eds), *Theories of Emotion*. New York: Academic Press. pp. 305–40.

Averill, J.R. (1982) *Anger and Aggression: An Essay on Emotion*. New York: Springer-Verlag.

Averill, J.R. (1984) 'The acquisition of emotions during adulthood', in C.Z. Malatesta and C.E. Izard (eds), *Emotion in Adult Development*. Beverly Hills, CA: Sage. pp. 23–43.

Averill, J.R. (1991) 'Emotions as episodic dispositions, cognitive schemas, and transitory social roles: Steps towards an integrated theory of emotion', in D. Ozer, J.M. Healy and A.J. Stewart (eds), *Perspectives in Personality*. London: Jessica Kingsly Publisher. (Vol. 3, pp. 137–65)

Averill, J.R., Catlin, G. and Chon, K.K. (1990) *Rules of Hope*. New York: Springer-Verlag.

Boucher, J.D. (1980) *Emotion and Culture Project: Lexicon and Taxonomy Report*. Unpublished manuscript, East-West Center, Honolulu, HI.

Descartes, R. (1968) 'The passions of the soul', in E.S. Haldane and G.R.T. Ross (trans.), *The Philosophical works of Descartes* (Vol. 1). Cambridge, England: The University Press. (Original published in 1649).

Fehr, B. and Russell, J.A. (1984) 'Concept of emotion viewed from a prototype perspective', *Journal of Experimental Psychology: General*, 133: 464–86.

Izard, C.E. (1977) *Human Emotions*. New York: Plenum Press.

Johnson-Laird, P.N. and Oatley, K. (1989) 'The language of emotions: an analysis of a semantic field', *Cognition and Emotion*, 3: 81–123.

Kovecses, Z. (1986) 'The folk model of romantic love in America', in C. Kretzoi (ed.), *High and Low in American Culture*. Budapest: L. Eotvos University. pp. 125–32.

Kovecses, Z. (1988) *The Language of Love*. Lewisburg, PA: Bucknell University Press.

Kovecses, Z. (1990) *Emotion Concepts*. New York: Springer-Verlag.

Lakoff, G. and Kovecses, Z. (1983) *The Cognitive Model of Anger Inherent in American English* (Berkeley Cognitive Science Report No. 10). Berkeley: University of California.

Tiger, L. (1979) *Optimism: The Biology of Hope*. New York: Simon and Schuster.

PART I

THE SOCIAL DIMENSION OF EMOTIONS

Chapter 2

Embarrassment and the Threat to Character

W. Gerrod Parrott and Rom Harré

The cognitive discursive structure of embarrassment, its displays and its occasions

In our view, embarrassment, as an emotion of social control, is conformable to a generally discursive approach to the understanding of social phenomena, in that we see emotion displays (and feelings in those cultures that recognize them as relevant to emotions) as having both semantic content and illocutionary force as the performance of social acts. At the same time there clearly is a physiological aspect in the genesis of an emotion display. These displays are rarely preceded by overt deliberation. The aetiology of the tendency to display embarrassment will have to be found in a subtle combination of natural expressions and the training into social habits.

What are the functions of embarrassment? Goffman (1967b) has suggested that there are three subtly related acts that are performed in such displays. Underlying all is the expression of the judgement that other people will think that something about us or something we have done is improper in the context. (Of course, one's belief that this is so may be false!) In displaying embarrassment we express a kind of apology for the real or imagined fault. And, as Goffman points out, the display also serves to present an actor as one who is cognizant of the relevant rules and conventions. Only against the background of such knowledge could inadequacies be realized. So, despite the slip, one is to be seen as a committed member of the society – one does not brazen it out! We shall take this account as a starting point, developing our treatment around it. It is not hard to see that this account construes embarrassment as an 'emotion of social control'.

Occasions and sources of embarrassment

We must begin by discussing some of the occasions of embarrassment. They can be matters of the body-in-public, such as incorrect or exaggerated postures, wrong clothes for the occasion, or improper appearances, like prominent ears. They can be matters of social behaviour, such as insensitive conversational inputs, for instance an ill-placed ethnic joke, or an incorrect pronunciation of a foreign word, such as pronouncing the name of the river where West met East in the Second World War, 'Elb' instead of 'Elbe'. They can be matters of intellect, such as getting hold of the wrong end of the stick in a discussion. The particulars under each of these broad headings are legion. Nor are these categories sharply differentiated. They overlap in various complex ways. Blowing one's nose on one's fingers on ordinary social occasions (a practice attributed to Lincoln by his enemies) is not only an improper way of dealing with a biological necessity, but also displays a louche social personality and massive ignorance of the customs of polite society. Yet, the very people who discretely use a tissue for this purpose would be unembarrassed in following Lincoln's example if far out on the ski slopes. Embarrassment displays have a 'range of convenience'.

Embarrassment is not only tied to disturbances that come from a sense of personal inadequacies. It can be suffered vicariously. It can be felt and less often displayed when someone with whom one has a close relationship displays a deficit in performance or manners, in sensibility, in bodily display, in intellectual competence and so on. It can also be suffered when one is singled out even if it is in a self-enhancing way, as the recipient of honour and praise.

There are other emotion displays that seem to belong in the same group, for instance shame, guilt and chagrin. While the two former (discussed in detail in Chapters 3 and 4) are characterized by the fact that they seem to be occasioned by public exposures and private realizations of moral deficits, chagrin is closer to a species of embarrassment in that it occurs when a person fails to achieve something that they [he or she] had publicly committed themselves to accomplish. In the case of chagrin it is not so much the role that is in question as competence in some well-defined task.

Emotions and emotionologies

In opening up a territory for psychological investigation we need to be able to delineate the phenomena that are to be the targets of our study. Since we live our lives 'within' local variants of our mother tongues, all psychological investigations must begin with a survey of the way the relevant vocabulary is currently (or, in historical psychology, once was) used. The results of such preliminary studies have come to be called 'emotionologies'. There is a subtle relation between emotionologies and the results we obtain by studying the actual display of emotions in concrete situations. We shall return to explore that relation in detail.

Complexities in the use of emotion words

Dictionary definitions or paradigms? In domains other than emotion it seems clear enough that many concepts are multivocal, their applications spread over a field of uses which bear only a family resemblance to one another. This fact makes for some problems with the semantics of many common expressions. We believe that emotion words too, are multivocal. In general there are two main ways of expressing the content of a type word, say 'grandmother'. There is a set of necessary and sufficient conditions for the application of the word, conditions which are the source of most dictionary definitions, such as 'grandmother means mother of one's mother or father'. But most people have some sort of 'picture' of a prototypical grandmother. Both ways of expressing the content of kinship terms seem to be used by people. This may be because identifying an instance of a type may be a different cognitive task from classifying various items as instances of a kind. In most domains there is no incompatibility between working with necessary and sufficient conditions and working with prototypes. Exploring the field of use of an expression like 'chagrin', used to describe an emotion within the general ambit of embarrassment, may require attention to both ways of expressing the content of a type term.

Conjunctive and disjunctive definitions Logicians have used the distinction between conjunctive and disjunctive definitions to give some formal expression to Wittgenstein's conception of a field of uses that are ordered by family resemblance. A conjunctive definition, say of 'cat', consists of a list of attributes all of which must be present for a specimen to count as a cat. The list constitutes a set of conditions which are severally necessary and jointly sufficient. A disjunctive definition, say of 'carbon', consists of a list of attributes any subset of which can certify a specimen as an instance of that element. Each disjunct expresses a sufficient condition for the application of the term. Something is properly called 'carbon' if it is either sparkling diamond, slippery graphite or black amorphous soot. Emotion words could be defined conjunctively by citing the necessary and sufficient conditions for their use, yet could also be defined disjunctively depending on the salience of one or the other feature in particular contexts. In some contexts 'anger' may refer to a violent display, and in others to a grim but constrained expression of tension. Furthermore, for ordinary people a concept such as 'anger' might be used by reference to both conjuctive and disjunctive conditions. They may also use conceptions of typical cases, easily identifiable symptoms, memorable instances, extremely intense states, and the like. The various ways of construing the concept would each be useful for a different task.

The relation between technical terms and everyday uses

There would seem to be a limit with respect to how far the concepts of psychological theory can diverge from the way the relevant psychological vocabulary is used in everyday life. Of necessity a theorist's concepts of 'anger', 'embarrassment', 'pride' and so on must be based on those employed by some cultural group through their use of their local vocabulary of emotion words. Without that constraint we will not be confident that the terms a theorist uses will pick out the same phenomena as the lay person's terms. However, the interplay between ordinary and technical language is quite subtle. It is possible that careful studies of emotion displays and the circumstances in which they occur may change both technical and everyday categorizations. Whales are no longer considered fishes even by the users of ordinary language. But how is it that displays of embarrassment and the conditions under which they occur can diverge from what ordinary folk would understand by 'embarrassment'? It is because the words that we use for emotions do not usually figure in displays of emotion. When we hear someone say 'I'm very angry with you' the chances are that this is a ritual rebuke rather than an expression of genuine anger. And so it seems for the uses of the word 'embarrassed'. Those who say things like 'I'm very embarrassed' are usually using the expression as a ritual opening for presenting an apology. It is perfectly possible then for the occasions and displays of embarrassment to be inadequately described by the relevant words from an emotion vocabulary. This means that the everyday meanings of emotion words are surely somewhat open to modification as a result of psychological studies of phenomena first picked out by the use of the ordinary vocabulary. If studies of the phenomena of embarrassment, say, lead to uses of the relevant vocabulary which are highly discrepant with ordinary usage, an account of how the ordinary usage can be mapped onto the technical usage must be supplied and the need for such a mapping justified.

The conceptual space of 'embarrassment': a family resemblance concept

How there can be three theories of embarrassment

Wittgenstein (1953) introduced the family resemblance idea to describe the semantic fields of expressions that have several interconnected but different uses. He warned repeatedly against the fallacy of assuming that there must be a common element in the phenomena which make up the diverse field of use of many important words, if only we could find it. 'Embarrassment' seems to be just such a word. Its uses are best traced out as a field of family resemblances rather than different realizations of some underlying common essence (Parrott and Harré, 1991). We can explain how there can be three major 'theories' of embarrassment by pointing out that there are three regions of the family resemblance field for which the words 'embarrassed', 'embarrassing', 'embarrassment' and so on are used.

One region is described by dramaturgical theories of embarrassment. In one such account Silver et al. (1987) propose that people construe embarrassment as expressing a person's perception that he or she cannot perform coherently in a certain social situation. Performing a role is such an important prerequisite to satisfactory social interaction that people become distressed and uncomfortable when they find themselves unable to do so and become flustered as t. y unsuccessfully try to think of a coherent way to behave. This flustering is independent of whether the situation provoking it will threaten a person's self-esteem or arouse concern about other people's impressions of them. For example when a woman discovers that she is the guest of honour at a surprise party she may be embarrassed even amid the acclaim. In this view, little more must be added to the classic sociological accounts other than a postulate that flustering and distress are the psychological concomitants that express the perception that one is temporarily deprived of a social role.

In a contrasting account, Modigliani (1968) describes a second region of embarrassments's family resemblance field, proposing that it is a perception of loss of self-esteem that is expressed by a display of embarrassment. In this account embarrassment expresses (a) a person's belief that an audience finds his or her performance to be inadequate to the role being projected and (b) that person's resulting loss of self-esteem with respect to some quality relevant to that role. The crucial difference between these two patterns of embarrassment lies at stage two. In Modigliani's analysis, embarrassment will occur if and only if the actor comes to see him- or herself as inadequate in a way relevant to the interaction. In the analysis proposed by Silver et al. (1987), embarrassment has no necessary relation to self-esteem, only to the ability to perform a role.

A third region of usage is described by theories that maintain that displays of embarrassment express 'social anxiety' that stems from the belief that other people have formed an undesirable impression of one. In one such account, Miller and Leary (1992) propose that embarrassment arises from a person's concern that their behaviour will lead other people to form unfavourable impressions or evaluations of them. Like Modigliani's analysis, and unlike that of Silver et al., this 'social evaluation' theory links embarrassment to decreased esteem for the embarrassed person; but whereas Modigliani stressed the importance of the embarrassed person's self-esteem, Miller and Leary stress that person's perception of the audience's decreased esteem for them.

These should not be taken as competing theories of the aetiology of some one, singular phenomenon. Rather they should be taken as highlighting distinctive regions in the loosely structured field of occasions in which judgements and perceptions of one's inadequacy are expressed in fluster, blushing and the like, the familiar syndrome of embarrassment. On one sort of occasion embarrassment expresses one's sense of a loss of self-esteem, but in a large class of cases a sense of inadequacy in performance or loss of role confidence is all that is involved. Again, there may or may not be a feeling of social anxiety, for example as to how one's actions and appearances are being assessed by others.

In one cluster of cases the words from the embarrassment lexicon are used to identify those feelings and displays that express one's intuition that one can no longer sustain one's role in some situation, nor smoothly adopt another. The embarrassment vocabulary is also used in some situations for feelings and displays which express the anxiety or concern one feels when one believes that one has made an unfavourable impression on other people. And the same vocabulary is also used in yet other situations for those feelings and displays that express one's sense that some aspect of oneself must be considered to be more defective than one would like. As in the prototypic three-circle Venn diagram, these three clusters partially overlap one another. On some occasions the embarrassment vocabulary is used when two regions of usage apply, and in some cases of intense embarrassment all three will apply: feelings and displays of embarrassment on these occasions express one's awkwardness, and one's concerns about other people's impressions of oneself, and one's sense of inadequacy in the situation.

Surely one source of the family resemblance joining these regions is that they often co-occur in the most intense and prototypical instances of embarrassment. One of our students has related a moment of extreme embarrassment that nicely illustrates that portion of the Venn diagram where all three circles overlap. It occurred during a laboratory session of her college chemistry class, near the end of a complex four-hour experiment. As she raised her beaker to make the final measurement, she broke the beaker, which splashed hot water on her, which caused her to break a thermometer and upset some powdered chemicals, producing a cloud which spread throughout the room. Her classmates laughed at her, and, not surprisingly, she felt embarrassed. She flushed bright red, she began sweating and trembling and burst into tears.

She reports aspects of all three accounts of embarrassment. The dramaturgic account addresses her awkwardness in contradicting her role as a competent chemist and her flustering as she failed to repair this role or adopt a new one. The spectacular nature of her accident and of the audience's reaction prevent her or the audience from acting as if nothing had happened, or as if such occurrences were consistent with her role. The one available dramaturgic manoeuvre would appear to have been to adopt a new role consistent with the accident, say, that of 'dismayed student'; too disappointed with the loss of her labour to be aware of her classmates' attention and laughter, or perhaps that of the performing clown, or that of a habitually clumsy person – in American slang the 'class klutz' – announcing in effect 'Oops! There I go again.'

That none of these manoeuvres was attempted – or perhaps even contemplated – can be understood by considering the effects of the two other regions of the family resemblance field of the term 'embarrassment'. Our student reported a great deal of worry about the poor impression her actions might make on her fellow students and on her instructor. She also personally felt stupid, incompetent and inferior to her classmates. Her life-long dream was to attend medical school and become a physician, and she worried about her need to get a good grade in chemistry to realize this goal and her suitability for such a career – so real was her decreased self-esteem that she felt too stupid even to continue with her ambitious academic programme. The accident seemed to her to confirm pre-existing doubts about her abilities, and seemed distressingly congruent with previous, albeit less spectacular, examples of the role of the clumsiest student in the class.

These reactions demonstrate the applicability of the social evaluation and decreased self-esteem accounts to this example but they do more: they show how our student's concerns about her abilities and their perception by others may have limited her dramaturgical options. Perhaps she might have spared herself some embarrassment by playing the role of the class klutz or clown but she did not *want* these roles! She didn't want others to think of her this way, both because she wanted and needed their esteem to achieve her goals and because she privately feared she fitted these roles all too well. So rather than play them and avoid embarrassment, she remained roleless and burst into tears. Such are the subtle interrelations between the three approaches to embarrassment, and such may be the basis of their family resemblance.

How are these uses maintained?

The prototype of embarrassment, abstracted by Parrott and Smith (1991) from lay persons' discourse, contains elements of all three 'theories of embarrassment'. Their study looks into the emotionology of embarrassment by studying the conditions under which people use the 'embarrassment' vocabulary. The dramaturgical theory is evident in much of the impression management leading to and following that which people call 'embarrassment', and also in symptoms involving awkwardness, flustering and the lack of a role to present. The social evaluation theory is evident in items germane to the use of 'embarrassment' reflecting concern that one will be perceived badly by others. Many of the features that fit the dramaturgical theory also involve elements of concern and anxiety about other people's impressions. The 'loss of self-esteem' theory is less evident in the antecedents of embarrassment, although some features involve insecurity or wrongdoing; nevertheless, a common symptom of embarrassment was feeling as if one were somehow defective. The means of coping with embarrassment had little to do with self-esteem. Dramaturgic efforts to repair or escape an awkward situation were mentioned, as were the taking of measures to correct a bad impression. There was virtually no mention by respondents of efforts to repair their own self-esteem. This is not surprising, since in Goffman's theory the display of embarrassment itself is at least a first step towards such repair, though it seems to us that for some people and in some situations it may lead to even more loss of self-esteem.

Given this analysis we can now ask how the norms for the 'correct', that is currently recorded uses of these terms are maintained for each region of the field of cases linked by family resemblance. Is it by reference to necessary and sufficient conditions, and if so is it by virtue of a conjunctive or a disjunctive definition of emotion types? Or is it by reference to proto-types? Our discussion above suggests that all three accounts of the semantics of the type terms from the embarrassment vocabulary have a role to play.

What a display of embarrassment means dramaturgically

Good and bad performances

On a dramaturgic account a good performance is not necessarily one in which positive content is projected – friendliness, competence, niceness, professionalism and so on. We judge a performance dramaturgically by *how well* a part is projected. It is important not to equate the bad per-formance of a character with the performance of a bad character; a lovable portrayal of Lady Macbeth or 'J.R.' is a mistake. According to the dramaturgical account, embarrassment results from a bad performance. A botched portrayal can be due to an actor's inadequacies, to someone else's forgetting lines, or to an act of nature, say, a rainstorm during one's annual garden party. In life, as well as in the theatre, villainous, esteem-lowering interactions can be performed quite smoothly, and heroic, esteem-enhancing ones can result in people stumbling into embarrassment. Goffman puts the point nicely when he contrasts flustered embarrassment with composure:

> Compliments, acclaim, and sudden reward may throw the recipient into a state of joyful confusion, while a heated quarrel can be provoked and sustained, although throughout the individual feels composed and in full command of himself. More important, there is a kind of comfort which seems a formal property of the situation and which has to do with the coherence and decisiveness with which the individual assumes a well-integrated role and pursues momentary objectives having nothing to do with the content of the actions themselves. (1967b: 101)

Embarrassment, as recognized by the local dramaturgical emotionology, can be specified as follows: embarrassment is a flustering expressing our perception that our performance has been spoiled, that we have lost our grip on our role, and that we cannot regain our role or adopt a new one.

Emotion's dramaturgical symptoms are therefore flustering, social dis-comfort and unease. Goffman's description of the embarrassed individual emphasizes the dramaturgical origins of these symptoms.

> He cannot volunteer a response to those around him that will allow them to sustain the conversation smoothly. He and his flustered actions block the line of activity the others have been pursuing. He is present with them, but he is not 'in play'. The others may be forced to stop and turn their attention to the impediment; the topic of conversation is neglected, and energies are directed to the task of re-establishing the flustered individual, of studiously ignoring him, or of withdrawing from his presence. (1967b: 100–1)

Because flustering is itself disruptive for most interactions, a flustered individual may try to conceal signs of embarrassment and fellow interactants may display tact ignoring or helping to conceal such signs. But in some situations, as with our chemistry student, concealment or control of flustering fails, and Goffman describes the dramaturgical aspects of the result:

> he collapses into tears or paroxysms of laughter, has a temper tantrum, flies into a blind rage, faints, dashes to the nearest exit, or becomes rigidly immobile as when in panic. . . . In short, he abdicates his role as someone who sustains encounters. . . . On rare occasions all the participants in an encounter may . . . fail to maintain even a semblance of ordinary interaction. The little social system they created in interaction collapses; they draw apart or hurriedly try to assume a new set of rules. (1967b: 103)

As we shall discuss in a later section of this chapter, complications to this account may arise, however, because in some cases being flustered permits one to act out the 'embarrassed role', a role that displays our qualities of character.

The performing of 'character'

The dramaturgical approach sees social interaction as having a central requirement: Participants must have a 'working consensus' about each other's characters. This working consensus specifies which qualities are relevant to the interactions at hand. It specifies the qualities that each actor can be expected to display (and be sanctioned for not displaying) and, therefore, the qualities that each actor is entitled to treat others (and themselves) as having. Whether the actor actually has these qualities is *not* the concern of the analysis (Goffman, 1967a). Goffman's interest is in how a character's qualities are projected, acknowledged, discredited, sequestered when performing other roles, and so on, regardless of whether the qualities are genuine or illusory. People experience the dramaturgical type of embarrassment when the standard 'texts' of role performance desert them and they do not know what to do next.

If we are to use our dramaturgical account to explain embarrassment, we must first take a further step in developing the emotionology of 'embarrassment' by listing the features that seem to characterize the use of the term 'embarrassment' in more detail. To construct this list we will borrow an example from Silver et al. (1987). Imagine a woman at a formal dinner. As the waiter serving her table reaches past her, he clumsily spills borscht over her white gown. She blushes, is patently flustered, dabbing ineffectually at the stain. This example displays many features associated with embarrassment.

First, embarrassment is typically unpleasant, but it is unpleasant in more than one way. Embarrassed persons think that they look foolish, incompetent, improper or 'wrong' in some way, and in the eyes of others. The thought of adverse judgements in these matters can lead to temporary loss of self-esteem, or to 'social anxiety' for fear of being adversely judged, or to mismanagement of the role or story-line that the person is currently sustaining. All three possibilities are reported. And all three implicate that sense of self-worth we call 'character'. Clearly the borscht episode was unpleasant in two ways: getting in a bodily mess is disagreeable, and thus becoming the focus of all eyes in such circumstances is also disagreeable. We can imagine the victim's feeling that her appearance has been spoiled, that others were forming derogatory impressions of her – and that these feelings lowered her own feelings of self-worth in the situation, albeit for reasons having nothing to do with humans' social natures or our rational natures.

Second, embarrassing circumstances often involve surprises. Clearly the woman was not expecting borscht to be spilled on her dress, and this limited her ability to invent a suitable manner of coping on the spur of the moment. Surprise is thus more closely linked to mismanagement of role than to either loss of self-esteem or to social anxiety.

Third, no matter how surprising an embarrassment is, tact and wit can often rescue the situation and diffuse the embarrassment. If our victim were the president of a canned borscht firm and while looking at her dress she announced that at last she could be an advertisement for her product, everyone around her might laugh and neither she nor they would be embarrassed. Why? Because the woman's joke reconciles her stained gown with the character she is performing, and by exhibiting coolness in rescuing that character from apparent contradiction she projects an even surer command of that character's qualities. One is embarrassed when the untoward event can be taken by others as a display of a defective character.

Fourth, embarrassment appears to be necessarily social. People don't become embarrassed alone unless they are imagining a public. Further, people are rather indiscriminate about what public they are embarrassed before. Even if the woman did not respect or like the people at her table, and even if the other onlookers were complete strangers, our borscht-splattered victim might still feel embarrassed.

What do all four semantic conventions pick out? It is the threat to and display of character that seems to be at issue in each case. Losing a grip on role is a threat to 'character', while displaying cool is a display of it. Loss and gain of self-esteem and feelings of social anxiety seem to be natural concomitants of threats to and defences of character, and, as we have seen, can influence one's grip on role, accounting for the gross structure of the field of family resemblances in the use of the embarrassment lexicon that we explored above.

What a display of embarrassment means for one's self-esteem

One important way in which self-esteem can be threatened is when one's bodily appearance seems to be the focus of unfavourable assessment by others, whether how it appears is one's personal responsibility or not. Perhaps unjustly, but certainly quite widely, 'wrong' bodily appearances are likely to embarrass oneself, perhaps because they create an uneasiness in others. Neither the borscht-drenched dress, nor jug ears, nor some highly visible deformity are the responsibility of the bearer of these stigmata, yet, they are, nevertheless, an embarrassment. There is a kind of cruel residual sense, from our darker past, that those who look horrible according to the standards of the day, should hide themselves tactfully away.

One's personal presence to others is mediated by one's visible, audible, tangible, tastable and smellable body. In our culture smell (and taste) are rarely signs of the tangible presence of bodies, perhaps because we are generally nowadays held responsible for our failure to keep ourselves clean. But in many circumstances one can be looked at. The appearance of one's body can never be denied when one is in company. One can hardly achieve presence without the vulnerability that comes from the possibility of one's body itself being unfavourably assessed by that company. Hence the importance of masks, burkas, cloaks and so on in the achievement of bodily presence without the chances of embarrassment.

Embarrassment and bodily matters like personal appearance are linked through the grounding of rules and conventions of bodily propriety in conceptions of personal honour, that is in matters of character. This should provide a general account of the emotions of corporeal self-attention which transcends the enormous variety of kinds of bodily appearances and exposures that are locally taken to be discrediting. Emotions are not just bodily perturbations. Embarrassment is not just blushing and squirming. It is a particular case of the interplay between social conventions, moral judgements and bodily reactions. The analysis will enable us to juxtapose conventions concerning bodily exposure and those concerning character manifestations within the same conceptual framework and to see how they are sometimes psychologically equivalent. The distribution of credit, however, follows crooked paths. We can be embarrassed by public attention to those matters that are creditable to us as well as those that are discreditable. Even when favourable attention is drawn to our bodily appearances, a display of embarrassment, and of its more potent kin, shame, may itself be creditable, and even be prescribed. Why? Once again the issue at issue is character.

There has been both a shift away from, and back towards, a Victorian relation between displays of bodily parts and attributes and embarrassment. The characterological importance of the concealment of the sexual parts has declined remarkably (more particularly in Europe than in the United States), while the significance of the signs of careful bodily cultivation for character attributions has been enormously amplified. An excessively flabby and ill-kept body is an object of embarrassment (and it may be of shame) both to its possessor and to those who might be unfortunate enough to catch a glimpse of it. We have come to tie body and character in an almost Victorian way. Though the content is vastly different, the underlying structure is similar to the self-attentive bodily emotions of the Victorians, the shame and embarrassment that accompanied inadvertent bodily exposures. Bodily appearances serve as public indices of character.

Starting from the blush as an expression common to this cluster of emotions, Darwin seems to be concerned more with embarrassment than shame. In contrast to Aristotle's emphasis on conduct, it is bodily presence and physical appearance that Darwin mostly finds salient in the occasions for blushing. In *The Expression of Emotion in Man and Animals* Darwin remarks that 'it is not the simple act of reflecting on our own appearance, but the thinking of what others think of us, which excites the blush' (1872/ 1955: 325).

These considerations suggest that embarrassment and shame are not neatly distinguishable by reference to discreditable bodily appearances on the one hand, and disgraceful actions on the other. Bodily shame, on this view, will occur when a wrong appearance in the eyes of others is so tied to personal moral standing that it casts doubt on the virtues of the person involved – that is, when the others take exposure to be a sign of defective moral character. So if I become aware of (or merely believe in) their taking up such an attitude to my dereliction, shame must follow, if I am of good character. Of course if I am a brazen hussy or an arrogant son-of-a-bitch, it will not. So my lack of shame is a second-order display of bad character.

A possible explanation of anomalous embarrassment could invoke the virtue of modesty. A display of self-satisfaction in success would breach the modesty convention as much as an improper body display. Public attention to oneself in the moment of success opens up the possibility that one's natural pleasure in one's achievement may appear to the others as immodest self-satisfaction. Hence, in our culture, one's successes are occasions of threat to one's character as a proper modest person just insofar as one is the centre of attention. But there are cultures in which it would be considered improper not to boast about an achievement or triumph over a defeated rival.

Given that self-esteem and one's standing with respect to character are closely tied, there are three socially normative systems of conventions involved on occasions of embarrassment. There is the system of conventions concerning appearance and conduct whose violation will draw the attention of onlookers. Then, to the sufferer that degree of attention is itself a violation of the rules of address, and so, even in the absence of any first-order infraction can become embarrassing. Finally there is the normative principle that good character is demonstrated in the display of embarrassment. This in turn is relative to either or both of the other two norms, since excessive complacency when the cynosure of all eyes is a display of an unacceptable degree of self-confidence.

How a display of embarrassment influences one's worth in the eyes of others

Infractions of social conventions cannot, in general, be ignored. They must be remedied. Goffman suggests that remedies are needed to dispel the threat of an inference to the conclusion that the participants (and sometimes even the onlookers) are not committed to the local conventions either through vice or through ignorance. One shows that one is the right sort of person, the kind of person with whom others might wish to consort, by putting right one's own infractions and tactfully assisting others to do the same with theirs. Silver et al. (1987) suggest that while the mutual work of face-saving proceeds smoothly, embarrassment does not occur. So it is not the mere fact of failing to maintain the conventions that occasions embarrassment. It is, as we have seen, threats to the character one displays and consequences of those threats in loss of self-esteem and the esteem of other people that structure the feelings, displays and judgements that constitute the emotion of embarrassment.

Time is required to get remedial work under way. An infraction may be forced into public notice just because there has not been time to do the remedial work, be it verbal or practical. The 'working consensus' of the above definition must be about the virtues, qualities and characters of the persons involved. Thus what is at issue, because it is what is at risk, is an unfavourable assessment of character. Unless the skirt is pulled down in time or the self-deprecatory remark dropped in fairly soon after the public congratulation, one runs the risk of being taken to be a shameless floozy, a brash oaf and so on, contrary to the working consensus as to the kind of persons we are and consort with. So, in the end, embarrassment has to do not only with what has been done or not done in itself, but also in how what is done or not done about what has been done or not done provides evidence for assessments of character.

The display may, *in itself*, be sufficient remedy for the infraction, supplying evidence in default of explicit face-work to support an attribution of good character and virtue. Ironically enough, even though one becomes embarrassed because the remedy cannot be carried out in time, being embarrassed *can then become* the remedy. In cultures with high embarrassability, self-confidence, the quality of character that protects against too readily succumbing to embarrassment, is an equivocal virtue. While self-confidence is a quality to be generally admired, it must be displayed with caution since it is perilously close to some generally depreciated attributes such as 'not giving a damn', callousness, arrogance, indifference, contempt and so on. Nevertheless the possibility of a life free from embarrassment particularly attracts the easily embarrassed. Ricks notices that the unembarrassed display 'a self-possession for which the ordinarily embarrassed are grateful to the unembarrassable' (1974: 48).

We are indebted to Ricks (1974) for opening up this issue with a brief remark on the complementary role that indignation can play to embarrassment. The idea seems to be roughly this: a display of embarrassment is, so to say, a mark to be entered in the public record, part of what Goffman called 'character'. It is ambiguous, in that, while it serves to display sensitivity, it also contradicts such desirable impressions as that one is cool, sophisticated and experienced. Embarrassment is not only a sign that one has realized that one has given an impression that is not up to some standard or other, but the embarrassment can itself sometimes be discrediting. Second-order discredit of this sort can sometimes be cancelled by cancelling the impression that one lacks *savoir-faire*. One way of doing that is to display indignation, either on one's own or on someone else's behalf.

Nevertheless, as Aristotle noticed, a display of shame, the moral equivalent of embarrassment, may incur second-order credit, since it shows our awareness of what is proper, if that awareness is a mark of a creditable stage on the way to maturity. As Goffman puts it, 'when an individual, receiving a complement, blushes from modesty, he may lose his reputation for poise but confirm a more important one, that of being modest' (1967b: 108). Hence, as Aristotle observed, the young are to be praised for blushing, though a similar blush would be discreditable among the mature. Is this because the blush shows that one knows what one should have done or how one should have appeared, but that one has failed to follow the rules and that one knows this? Or does the blushing of the older person manifest a childish degree of insecurity of social place or a lack of the nonchalance one would expect from a socially experienced person?

There are many face-saving routes out of embarrassment. One route is that in which creditable embarrassment is its own resolution by the implication that one would be embarrassed only if one knew what was the correct course of conduct etc. Another route is that of indignation, to mount an attack on those that one feels oneself to have been unfavourably judged by, a belief that led to the blush in the first place – 'How dare you presume to judge me!' 'Take that superior smile off your face!' Though most of us just slink away from a situation in which we have let ourselves down, self-esteem can be preserved sometimes by a display of embarrassment, sometimes by a display of indignation.

Bodily awkwardness is both an occasion for, and a manifestation of, embarrassment, feeding on itself. Goffman, following Lord Chesterfield, argues that squirming and casting down of the gaze are best seen as part of the repertoire for concealing emotion, hiding the blush. According to Goffman 'the fixed smile, the nervous hollow laugh, the busy hands, the downward glance that conceals the expression of the eyes, have become famous as signs of the attempt to conceal embarrassment' (1967b: 102). In some cultures the whole face may be covered by the hands. And so these acts become as clear a part of the display of embarrassment as the blush itself. Goffman (1967b: 102) quotes Lord Chesterfield who, icily contemptuous of the middle classes[1] to whom embarrassment is endemic as it is to adolescence, speaks of these actions as 'tricks to keep themselves in countenance' and notices that 'every awkward, ill-bred body' has them.

Modesty: when social anxiety, self-esteem and role-performance meet

We tend to associate displays of embarrassment with the virtue of modesty. Many of the expressions from the cluster have two characteristic contexts of use, illustrating the systematic ambiguity of the concept of 'modesty'. There is the context set by the sense of an unwelcome attention being paid by others to some infraction of the local rules of bodily presence and display. But there may also be attention to our reactions to the attention of others to our first-order infractions. We assign the virtue of modesty as follows: a modest young lady would normally pull down her skirt *and* be embarrassed by it riding up, whereas a shameless hussy would let us see her knickers and not give a damn. A modest young man would wrap a towel around him to change on the beach, whereas an insensitive oaf would pull down his shirt tails a fraction. The same duality of context occurs in more abstract matters. A truly modest colleague would keep quiet about their receipt of an honorary degree and would display some measure of embarrassment when others brought it up. An arrogant bitch or self-satisfied lout would both publicly broadcast the news and show nothing but self-satisfaction in the now-reluctant congratulations of their peers. However, academic honours are not exactly like underwear. A modest pride is acceptable, but it is a tricky note to strike. Modesty is itself a role, but a role the playing of which protects one from the excess of attention that could trouble one with mild anxiety.

Embarrassment, modesty, shame, brashness and so on are concepts that necessarily involve an element of display. Their logical grammar excludes their use for hidden feelings and emotions. To be embarrassed is both to blush and to be discombobulated, while to be bold as brass is both to exaggerate your *décolletage* or the brevity and tightness of your shorts and to seem not to give a damn about anyone taking a look. The element of display is crucial, since the importance of these styles of social behaviour in social life lies not so much in the feelings they betray as in the characters they disclose. Since embarrassment is not a private state, its display is not an expression of an inner state, the 'real embarrassment'. It seems that there could not be 'concealed embarrassment' as there can certainly be concealed or suppressed anger. And this fits with Darwin's important observation that the manifestation of embarrassment, the blush, can be neither inhibited nor feigned. As with all emotion words the boundaries of the usage of 'embarrassed' are not as sharp as the above remarks would suggest. While the core concept does seem to be logically a 'display' concept there are cases in which we do seem to have a use for the distinction between feeling embarrassed and displaying embarrassment. For instance a mother might not display her embarrassment at the behaviour of a child that cast a doubtful light on the standards of the family, and yet for strategic reasons manage to keep her blushes in check.

Many commentators have suggested that modesty is an effect of custom and not its cause. Westermark (1901: 33), for instance, says 'the feeling of shame, far from being the cause of man's [sic] covering his body is, on the contrary, a result of this custom'. Helvétius went so far as to suggest that 'modesty is only the invention of a refined voluptuousness' – that is, that the body is covered to draw attention to it. Mantegazza (1932: 75) remarks that 'covering body parts is an (unconscious) way of emphasizing or drawing attention to them'. But while this may be true, it is far from explaining why shame and embarrassment attend accidental display and the social anxiety that attends the risk.

It is also worth reminding ourselves of the enormous diversity of parts of the body the display of which is thought to be shameful or immodest. Here is a short list: for Islamic women it is the face and elbow, though the breasts may be exposed in public when feeding a child; for traditional Chinese it is the bare feet; for traditional Tahiti clothing is irrelevant, only the untattooed body is immodest; in traditional Alaska (indoors of course) only lip plugs are essential for modesty; in Melanesia clothing is indecent; while in Bali for women to cover the bosom is coquettish at best and a mark of prostitution at worst; before the Ataturk reforms Turkish women were required *by law* to cover the back of the hand, while the palm could be displayed, without shame or embarrassment.

The realization that the occasions for the display of the virtues of modesty are culturally specific and historically variable is a very recent idea. Readers may enjoy the opinion of Judge Phillips in the judgment he delivered in the case of the US v. Harman (45 Fed. Rep. 423, 1891) which runs as follows:

> There is in the popular conception and heart such a thing as modesty. It was born in the Garden of Eden. After Adam and Eve ate from the fruit of the Tree of Knowledge they passed from that condition of perfectability which some people nowadays aspire to, and their eyes being opened, they discerned that there was both good and evil. 'and they knew that they were naked, and they sewed figleaves together, and made themselves aprons'. From that day to this, civilised man has carried with him a sense of shame – the feeling that there were some things which the eye – the mind – should not look upon, and where men and women become so depraved by the use, or so insensate from perverted education, that they will not veil their eyes, nor hold their tongues, the government should perform the office for them in protection of the social compact and the body politic.

As recently as 1935 the following event was reported in Associated News dispatches of 16 and 17 June of that year:

SHOCKED YONKERS'[2] START ROUNDUP OF GIRLS IN SHORTS

> Five young women, handed summonses today for appearing on the streets of Yonkers in shorts, will be treated to the sight of themselves as others see them – and in the movies at that.

> The women were ordered into court tomorrow on the complaint of Alderman William Slater who said he had been besieged by the objections of citizens at having their Sunday afternoon veranda-gazing monopolized by young women in bare legs sauntering about the streets.

Shame, we have suggested, is appropriate in cases of serious derelictions, which would, if publicly noticed, lead to assessments of character so unfavourable as to depreciate one's honour permanently. Embarrassment is the emotion proper to the violation of mere convention, a code of manners. It would be absurd to say that someone who failed to wear appropriate clothing at a Georgetown graduation ceremony was dishonoured by his or her dereliction. Reputation for *savoir-faire* would be lost, but hardly moral character. Nevertheless some measure of social anxiety attends the former.

Reminding ourselves of this distinction can help to explain why earlier writers tended to discuss bodily exposure and the consequent disturbances in terms of shame rather than embarrassment. Particularly when women's honour was at stake modesty was linked to chastity. Exposure of the female body was treated as dishonourably provocative, and so a woman was careful to avoid even an accidental exposure of some forbidden part of herself for fear of being mistaken for the kind of slut who deliberately does so. Once the connection between bodily exposure and womanly honour dissolves (or where in some non-Western societies it has never existed) and the conventionality of choice of bits to cover up is recognized, society wide, then only embarrassment can ensue from the violation of some sumptary rule.

Embodiment opens up the possibility of being looked at, in person, so to say. The fact that our appearance and our honour are tied up with one another we have treated so far as a source of threat and hence an occasion for social anxiety. But every shrinking violet also needs to be noticed, to have his or her existence confirmed. Embarrassment is the adolescent emotion *par excellence*. The predicament of adolescence is precisely the ambiguity of visibility. The enlarged and clumsy body seems only too visible – hence the blush, yet identity as a publicly noticeable being can be confirmed only by being seen to have been seen (and in lesser ways heard to have been heard). To capture this dark moment of adolescence one can borrow a phrase from Ricks about the ereutophobe 'who yet longs to be stared at, and who plays with her (his) cheeks on fire' (1974: 27).

Resolving the multiplicity of emotion 'theories'

That social anxiety is part of the complex phenomenon of embarrassment can hardly be denied. But is that what is *expressed* in the display of embarrassment? Again there can be no doubt that on many occasions of embarrassment a person may suffer a loss of self-esteem. But that may derive as much from the displaying of embarrassment (rather than sophisticated cool) as it does from the singling out of the virtuous and the victorious in public gaze. Furthermore, as we have shown in the case of embarrassing praise, it is the singling out whether for a fault or a virtue that defines most occasions of embarrassment. One can hardly lose one's self-esteem when being publicly praised. But one may be at a loss as to how the role of modest hero is to be sustained or what to do when one realizes that one is improperly dressed and so on. Modesty, from the psychological point of view, is not only a virtue but a role (Emerson, 1970). Yet, and this is what makes embarrassment such an interesting emotion, displays on occasions of fault are expressions of complex discursive acts, and are understood as such. That is shown by the generally pejorative view one takes of those who are brazen or untroubled by gross social gaffes. 'Shamelessness' counts as defiance of social convention just as much as a display of embarrassment expresses conformity to it.

Notes

1 It is well to bear in mind (Grant Webster, personal communication) that modesty conventions have always been class related. Embarrassment is stronger in the middle classes because, in terms of character, they have more at risk.
2 Yonkers is a suburb of New York.

References

Darwin, C. (1872/1955) *The Expression of Emotion in Man and Animals*. New York: Philosophical Library.

Emerson, J.P. (1970) 'Behavior in private places: sustaining definitions of reality in gynecological examinations', in H.P. Dreitzel (ed.), *Recent Sociology No. 2: Patterns of Communicative Behavior*. New York: Macmillan. pp. 74–97.

Goffman, E. (1967a) *The Presentation of Self in Everyday Life*. London: The Penguin Press.

Goffman, E. (1967b) *Interaction Ritual*. Harmondsworth: Penguin.

Mantegazza, P. (1932) *Anthropological Studies of the Sexual Relations of Mankind*. New York: Falstaff.

Miller, R.S. and Leary, M.R. (1992) 'Social sources and interactive functions of emotion: The case of embarrassment', in M.S. Clark (ed.), *Review of Personality and Social Psychology: Vol. 14. Emotion and Social Behavior*. Newbury Park, CA: Sage.

Modigliani, A. (1968) 'Embarrassment and embarrassability', *Sociometry*, 31: 313–26.

Parrott, W.G. and Harré, R. (1991) 'Smedslundian suburbs in the city of language: The case of embarrassment'. *Psychological Inquiry*, 2: 358–61.

Parrott, W.G. and Smith, S.F. (1991) 'Embarrassment: Actual v. typical cases, classical v. prototypical representations', *Cognition and Emotion*, 5: 467–88.

Ricks, C. (1974) *Keats and Embarrassment*. Oxford: Clarendon Press.

Silver, M., Sabini, J. and Parrott, W.G. (1987) 'Embarrassment: A dramaturgic account', *Journal for the Theory of Social Behaviour*, 17: 47–61.

Westermark, E. (1901) *The History of Human Marriage*. London: Longman.

Wittgenstein, L. (1953) *Philosophical Investigations*. Oxford: Blackwell.

Chapter 3

Guilt and Remorse

Gabrielle Taylor

Guilt, unlike shame, is a legal concept. A person is guilty if he breaks a law, which may be of human or divine origin. As a consequence of this action he has put himself into a position where he is liable to punishment, or where, given repentance, he may be forgiven. He will be guilty under these circumstances whether the law is good or bad, pronounced by God or the dictator, backed by good reasons or otherwise. Given only that he is under the legislation of the authority in question, violation of the law is sufficient for guilt.

He may of course *be* guilty and not *feel* guilty, for he may think the law in question bad and oppressive, or he may be quite indifferent towards the authority of the law. To feel guilty he must accept not only that he has done something which is forbidden, he must accept also that it is forbidden, and thereby accept the authority of whoever or whatever forbids it. The person who accepts the authority does not merely recognize its power and so thinks it simply prudent to obey its commands; he also accepts its verdicts as correct and binding. What the authority pronounces to be wrong must not be done. So the authority becomes the voice of conscience. An authority whose commands have to be obeyed has the status of a god, and the notion of the authority of conscience is therefore clearest if it is thought that the voice of conscience reflects the edicts of some god. Otherwise the notion of the authority of conscience remains obscure, though there are of course explanations of how the thought of an authority issuing commands has come to play such an important part in people's lives.[1] The often inarticulate and obscure notion of an authority plays a role in guilt which is analogous to that played by the notion of an audience in shame: in accepting what he has done as something forbidden the person feeling guilty thinks of himself as being under some authoritative command. He may of course come to question and reject the authority; he may for instance come to discard the religion with which he has grown up. As emotional responses notoriously do not keep step with rationally arrived at decisions he may still feel guilty when, for example, he does not go to church on Sundays. His feelings of guilt would then, in his own view, be irrational. Just as a person is guilty if he breaks the law whether or not that law is just or justified, so he feels guilty if what he does presents itself as a wrong, whether or not what he is doing can in fact be regarded as a wrong,

and whether or not he himself thinks it wrong when he views the matter
from a more rational point of view. It is for this reason that it is
illuminating to describe the person who feels guilty as thinking of himself
as having violated some taboo, for this carries the requisite implication of
having done something forbidden, without any further indication that what
is forbidden is so for good reason because harmful in some respect. Taboos
exercise great authority which is often strong enough to survive to some
extent and for some time any rational rejection. The categorical imperative
is on some level still accepted. Taboos will naturally carry varying degrees
of weight, and the struggle to free oneself from them may correspondingly
be more or less prolonged. The agent's thought that he has ignored or
acted contrary to some categorical imperative, or that he has violated some
taboo, must be distinguished from the thought that in doing so he has
caused harm to this or that other person. Whether or not he has done so
will depend on the content of the command, which may or may not
concern the person's behaviour towards others. Guilt, being regarded as a
moral emotion, is sometimes thought to be felt essentially about harm done
to others. Rawls, for example, thinks that when feeling guilty we think of
ourselves as having transgressed what he calls 'a principle of right',[2] so that
the wrong I think I have done must be thought of as some harm to
another. Here, he thinks, is the difference between feeling guilt and feeling
shame, for thinking one has harmed another is not necessary for feeling
shame. The distinction sounds plausible enough and fits the cases that
easily come to mind: suppose you have not spoken up when you think you
should. You will feel shame if your thought is that this just shows what a
moral coward you are. But you will feel guilt if you think that because of
your keeping quiet justice has not been done. Rawls' own example (p. 445)
is of a man who cheats and feels both shame and guilt: he will feel guilt
because by wrongly advancing his own interests he has transgressed the
rights of others; and he will feel shame because he has shown himself to be
unworthy of the trust of his associates. In both these cases feelings of guilt
concern themselves with what one has done to others, while feelings of
shame concern themselves with one's own standing. And it seems true that
guilt does not concern itself with the person's own standing in the way
shame does. Nevertheless, the distinction as drawn by Rawls is not quite
right. That in feeling guilt I should think of myself has having harmed
another applies, perhaps, to the most typical cases, though even here it is
not clear that what in my view has been infringed is a principle of right. I
may feel guilty because I did not have the patience to listen to somebody's
tale of misery, and it seems at least far-fetched to regard this case as falling
under some principle of right. On the other hand, it is true that the person
who feels guilty thinks in terms of duties not performed and obligations not
fulfilled. This is a difference between him and the person feeling shame,
who need not think in such terms at all, and is a difference which reference
to the transgression of a principle of right no doubt includes. What makes
this phrase not wholly suitable as a description of what the guilty think of

themselves as having done, is the implied emphasis on persons other than
the agent himself. It implies, firstly, that the agent's thoughts are primarily
on the rights of others rather than on his own duties. Even if every right
implies a duty, and the other way about, it may still be the case that the
agent thinks of the situation primarily in terms of the one rather than
the other. He may look at it from the point of view of how it most
importantly concerns himself, or of how it most importantly concerns the
other. 'Transgression of a principle of right' fits the latter case rather than
the former, but it is the former which applies to the guilty. Nor is it true (as
the description is also taken to imply) that he who feels guilty must always
think of himself as having harmed another. Principles of right are perhaps
too closely linked with the notion of laws governing social behaviour to be
invoked entirely appropriately for the case of feeling guilty. If feeling guilty
is thought of as the response to having broken such a law then it is
naturally thought of as being the response to harm done to others, for to
avoid such harm is what these laws are all about. But feelings of guilt need
not be so restricted in their scope. I may feel guilty, for example, after a
suicide attempt, not because I think that I have caused a lot of trouble to
others, but because I think it is just wrong to take life, including my own.
Or one may take a Kantian view and think of the deed as an offence
against oneself as an autonomous, rational being. Freud cites the case of a
man who states that 'the thought plagues me constantly that the guilt is
mine for my failure to become what I could have been with my abilities'.[3]
Feelings of guilt are often evoked by the thought that one is wasting one's
time or abilities. I may feel guilty because I watch that silly television serial
rather than improve my mind by reading great literature, but it is hard to
see whom under these circumstances I think I harm other than myself.
Even if I think devoting myself to serious reading will turn me into a better
and wiser person to live with, it may not be for this reason that I feel guilty
when I indulge in more frivolous activity. It is not correct, then, that for
feeling guilt the thought that directly or indirectly I am harming another
must be involved. The crucial thought here is just that what I am doing is
forbidden. It is quite natural, of course, that what is so ingrained in us as
being forbidden should concern our behaviour towards others, for it is in
this area that early childhood restrictions are most likely to be found, that
'moral training' has its central place. But it is not the only area and hence
not what delimits the appropriateness of the guilt-response. What is important for guilt is just that some form of action or abstention should
present itself as obligatory to the agent, but the content of the demand is
not restricted. In this respect guilt does not differ from shame. In either
case it is of course possible that his feelings of guilt or feelings of shame
may be judged irrational, but this is not to deny that he feels one or the
other of these emotions.

In the legal context, to be found guilty is to be found liable to punishment.
Guilt and such liability are conceptually connected. Similarly, if a person

feels guilty she thinks she has put herself into a position where punishment is due. In acting contrary to the authority's command she has offended that authority and so will expect retribution. This thought must again be distinguished from the thought that some reparation is expected of her. This latter thought connects with the content of the command, rather than with the fact that she has disobeyed it. Consequently, although a common thought in cases of guilt, it is not a feature in all of them. The offence may be thought too great for any form of reparation to be thought possible. There was nothing for Oedipus to repair when he realized that his crimes were those of parricide and incest.

A person is guilty if he has done something which constitutes breaking the law. His guilt is thus localized: given that he has at one time broken one law it does not follow that he has also broken others, or that he will go on breaking the law. What he is punished, or possibly forgiven for is the breaking of whatever is the law in question. Punishment is for what he has done and not for what he is. Both guilt and punishment concentrate on the deed or the omission. Similarly, feelings of guilt are localized in a way in which feelings of shame are not localized; they concern themselves with the wrong done, not with the kind of person one thinks one is. This difference is brought out quite well by a distinction drawn by some sociologists between 'primary' and 'secondary' deviance.[4] 'Primary deviance' applies to those cases where a person accepts that he has done wrong but does not think of this wrong-doing as affecting his overall standing as a person. What he has done remains, in his own view, alien to what he really is. The secondary deviant, however, now sees himself not just as a man who at some point, for instance, committed a burglary, but rather sees himself as a burglar. What he has done is not alien to himself but on the contrary expresses what he really is. This second view is appropriate to shame, the former to guilt – though of course neither feeling is a necessary consequence of taking the relevant view, for in either case the individual may remain indifferent or become reconciled to the state of affairs.

If feelings of guilt concentrate on the deed or the omission then the thought that some repayment is due is in place here as it is not in the case of shame. If I have done wrong then there is some way in which I can 'make up' for it, if only by suffering punishment. But how can I possibly make up for what I now see I am? There are no steps that suggest themselves here. There is nothing to be done, and it is best to withdraw and not to be seen. This is the typical reaction when feeling shame. Neither punishment nor forgiveness can here perform a function.

If repayment and punishment are appropriate to guilt but not to shame, then it is natural to assume that guilt is related to responsibility in a way in which shame is not. Normally we are held responsible for what we do in a way in which we are not held responsible for what we are. What we do or fail to do can be set against a background which may at least mitigate the guilt by pleas of ignorance, lack of intention or unfortunate circumstances. Excuses of this sort are irrelevant in the case of shame, for the occasion of shame may be something one could not conceivably do anything about, such as having poor parents or growing old. Similarly, one would suppose, feelings of guilt but not feelings of shame are based on the agent's thinking himself responsible for what he has done. It is indeed true to say that when feeling guilty but not when feeling shame I must think myself responsible for the relevant state of affairs, but this is true only given the widest possible reading of 'responsibility'. I may but need not think of myself as having intentionally or negligently done or omitted to do what I feel guilty about; I may but need not think that I could and should have acted otherwise and so am blameworthy in the accepted sense. Normally, perhaps, I do think myself blameworthy in this sense when feeling guilty, but not necessarily so: while driving my car I knock down and kill a child whom I could not have seen or, once seen, have avoided. I have not been negligent but have taken all possible care, and I know that this is the case. But I have done a terrible thing, and my seeing it as such is enough for me to suffer from guilt. It is of course possible that although I know I have not been negligent I do not quite believe it, and so after all think myself negligent and therefore blameworthy. But this is not the only possible explanation. However little I could have helped the accident, nevertheless I brought it about. In this minimal sense of 'responsible' I am responsible for it. Responsibility of this sort was quite sufficient for the self-condemnation of Oedipus: he had violated the taboos of parricide and incest, and ignorance of what he was doing is quite irrelevant to his feelings of guilt. Causal responsibility is the type that is sufficient for guilt, and that much is also necessary. If I feel guilty about my privileged position in society due to circumstances of birth then I see myself as an agent causally involved: it is *my* birth which has brought about the state of affairs which is my privileged position. The case is quite different if I feel shame about the circumstances of my birth: my agency or otherwise is here irrelevant, it is enough that I think of it as in some way deflating my status. This difference between these two emotions is illustrated by the fact that the deed of another (my child, my compatriot) may make me feel shame but not guilt. Guilt itself cannot be vicarious,[5] and feelings of guilt similarly cannot arise from the deeds or omissions of others. The relationship between myself and, for example, my children is enough for their misdeeds or failures to cause me shame, but it is not enough to cause me feelings of guilt. My son's misdeeds may by me be taken to show my own failure as a parent, but I am not causally responsible for these particular deeds. His own agency has broken whatever causal chain there may be between his defective upbringing and his present behaviour. So I cannot feel guilty about his particular behaviour on this occasion, though I may, of course, feel guilty about my own treatment of and attitude towards him which, in my view, may have contributed to making him the sort of person he now is. It is therefore true that, as one would expect, responsibility, like punishment, is essentially linked with guilt and not with shame. It is because of the agent's thought that he is directly instrumental in bringing about some forbidden state of affairs that he thinks of himself as 'owing payment', as being liable to retribution. But this is a thought which is irrelevant to him who feels shame.

It is also because he thinks himself responsible in this sense that we can account for the effect the deed or state of affairs has on him. The thought involved here is not so much: 'I have done this terrible thing *to him*'; but is rather: '*I* have done this terrible thing to him'. Guilt is a burden he has to carry, he cannot disown it, it must leave its mark upon him. Earlier I suggested as appropriate to the person who feels guilty that he regard what he has brought about as somehow alien to himself, as not being part of what he really is. If he feels guilty about his privileged position then he sees this as the stain on, say, an otherwise admirable communist. It mars but does not destroy the whole. If, on the other hand, he feels shame about his privileged position then he thinks of it as threatening his status as a communist altogether. Similarly, if I feel guilt about my wasted life then I think I have failed to make use of the gifts and capacities I possess, I have not developed what I really am but have led a life that is alien to the 'real' me. But if I feel shame about the way I have lived my life then I see it as being just the sort of life a person of my sort would lead; neither is worth very much. When feeling guilty, therefore, the view I take of myself is entirely different from the view I take of myself when feeling shame: in the latter case I see myself as being all of a piece, what I have just done, I now see, fits only too well what I really am. But when feeling guilty I think of myself as having brought about a forbidden state of affairs and thereby in this respect disfigured a self which otherwise remains the same.

It is because the agent at the time of feeling guilt thinks of himself as the person (causally) responsible for the relevant state of affairs that he sees the disfigurement in himself as brought about by himself. So, if at all possible, he should do something about it. He cannot wipe it out, for what is done is done. But by paying in some way he can make up for it. One form the payment may take is that he accepts retribution. It is from this debit and credit point of view that the notion of punishment as restoring the balance makes its point. Whatever one may think of the virtues and defects of the theory that punishment is a means of restoring the balance, of making it possible for the individual to retake his place in society, this notion of punishment or repayment is essential to the guilty person's view of the situation. There are naturally degrees of feeling guilt, and the thought that he owes payment may on many occasions not be particularly persuasive or lasting. He may manage to live with himself quite happily and to regard the disfigurement as minor enough to be ignored. In serious cases, however, it cannot be ignored, and in such circumstances there are roughly three options available to him who suffers from guilt.

- First, he may make repayment as best he can and regard the matter as closed.

- Second, perhaps not thinking the first solution within his reach, he may adjust himself to the alteration in himself by now continuing in a way consistent with it, by making the disfigurement disappear by disfiguring himself still further.
- Finally, he may just continue to suffer the guilt with possibly serious consequences to himself.

The first solution can take different forms. The 'repayment' may consist in just accepting whatever the punishment may be, or it may consist in a more positive attempt on the agent's part to repair the damage his action may have caused to others. Either way, but particularly in the second case, this solution is the most straightforward and the best for all concerned. It is socially acceptable as the person concerned will have made amends, and it is satisfactory for the person himself as he will have rid himself of an unpleasant and possibly destructive state. The other options may lead to total wickedness or madness respectively.

Macbeth affords a clear example of a case fitting the second solution: he sees his first murder, that of Duncan, as leaving a terrible stain upon him. Immediately after the murder he cannot say 'amen'. 'But wherefore could I not way "amen"?' he asks, and adds, '"Amen" stuck in my throat'. Lady Macbeth, at this point intensely practical, warns him:

These deeds must not be thought
After these ways: so, it will make us mad. (II. ii.)

Macbeth eventually takes her advice and remains quite sane. He acclimatizes himself to the alteration within him by behaving in ways which makes the alteration no longer appear as something alien to the person he is, but makes it appear rather as the norm: driven by overriding ambition, going in for murder is just what Macbeth does. In acting as he does he avoids the threat of shame. When we first meet him he is still a man of honour who takes seriously the relevant code which prescribes how a king and guest ought, or at any rate ought not, to be treated:

. . . He's here in double trust:
First, as I am his kinsman and his subject,
Strong both against the deed; then, as his host . . . (I. vii.)

As a man of honour he must see the murder of his king and guest as disgraceful. But once he has done the deed he changes his point of view. Ignoring obligations to king and guest is part of the man who ruthlessly pursues his aim. From this new point of view it is not the murder he sees as degrading; it is rather the giving up of his ambition which would be cowardly and weak. During his initial period of doubt Lady Macbeth treats him as a moral coward and turns the murder of Duncan into a test of courage:

. . . Art thou afeard
To be the same in thine own act and valour
As thou art in desire? Would'st thou have that

Which thou esteem'st the ornament of life,
And live a coward in thine own esteem,
Letting 'I dare not' wait upon 'I would',
Like the poor cat i' th'adage?' (I. vii.)

The ploy works. What Macbeth now sees as the shameful course is the giving up of his ambition; to abstain from murdering Duncan would be weakness and failure. So he now lives by a new code according to which 'honour' consists in ruthlessly pursuing one's aim at whatever cost to those who happen to be in the way. Bradley has a point when he says that the murder of Duncan is done, 'one may almost say, as if it were an appalling duty'.[6] In a perverted way Macbeth is trying to maintain his integrity.

Lady Macbeth herself is an example fitting the last of the three possibilities given: she is unable to follow her own advice and comes to see her part in the murder as a disfigurement of herself she cannot live with. She was wrong when initially she believed a little water would be enough to clean her. She obsessively washes her hands, but no amount of washing will get rid of the blood. So she suffers the fate she herself predicts for those in her position and goes mad. In her madness she tries to dissociate herself from that part of herself that was accomplice to a murder. What one cannot live with one has to get rid of. Lady Macbeth pursues this course consistently enough by finally committing suicide. Dissociation is a feature of unbearable guilt (normally restricted to cases of murder), and is a consequence of the agent's view that the doer of the terrible deed is alien to his real self. In literature it is therefore not uncommon for the murderer to experience himself as being somehow two selves. Jonas, in Dickens's *Martin Chuzzlewit*, for example, has just murdered a blackmailer and is now on his way home. He is terrified of entering his room. He is supposed to have been in his room all the time while in fact he was otherwise engaged. He knows perfectly well, of course, that at the moment he is on his way to London and not in his own room at all. But it seems as if he had left the 'good' self behind while the 'bad' self went about its business. He sees himself 'as it were, a part of the room', and he is afraid not so much *for* himself as *of* himself. Dickens says of him that 'he became in a manner his own ghost and phantom, and was at once the haunting spirit and the haunted man'.[7]

Macbeth, with his perverted integrity, also and consequently perverts the dissociation: he does not try and dissociate himself from the doer of the terrible deed for this is now not what he sees as alien. He dissociates himself rather from the good and honourable. His murder of Banquo, under whom 'his genius is rebuk'd', would then be seen as Macbeth killing what represents the better side of his nature.

The split experienced in such extreme cases of guilt is comprehensible in the light of the two features mentioned earlier: the agent has brought about something which is yet alien to himself. If he can neither restore himself to his unblemished self nor adjust himself to the altered one, then there seems no alternative for him but to see himself as two distinguishable selves. No doubt some compromise is possible, as psychoanalytic theory suggests: he may conceal from himself the kind of disfigurement it is and persuade himself that it is of a nature which, though bad enough is at least bearable to live with. In 'Dostoevsky and Parricide', Freud suggests that Dostoevsky's feelings of guilt arose from his wish to kill his father. 'As often happens with neurotics, Dostoevsky's burden of guilt had taken tangible shape as a burden of debt.' On this view, Dostoevsky sees his guilt as relating to his gambling whereas it in fact relates to his thoughts about his father. It goes without saying that being an obsessive gambler is better at any rate than being a parricide. One need not accept the whole of that theory to agree that it is plausible that some such replacement should sometimes occur. Equally plausible in the light of the need of the guilty to dissociate themselves from the doer of the deed is Auden's theory about the function of the detective story.[8] The detective story, needless to say, is escape literature, and the fantasy it allows the reader to indulge in is that guilt in the shape of the murderer is uncovered in someone other than himself, thereby proving his innocence.

> The magic formula is an innocence which is discovered to contain guilt; then a suspicion of being the guilty one; and finally a real innocence from which the guilty other has been expelled, a cure effected, not by me or my neighbors, but by the miraculous intervention of a genius from outside who removes guilt by giving knowledge of guilt. (The detective story subscribes, in fact, to the Socratic daydream: 'Sin is ignorance'.)

The satisfaction the detective story therefore provides is the illusion of being dissociated from the murderer, and so it is suitable, perhaps addictive, reading for those who suffer from a sense of sin. No such possibility of escape is provided for those who are prey to recurrent feelings of shame. Dissociation from, or repression of, the alien doer of the deed is not here available precisely because the doer of the deed is not seen as alien but on the contrary as bringing out into the open what the agent really is. For the same reason it is impossible for the person who feels shame to do as Macbeth does and alter himself in such a way that the doer of the deed is no longer alien; all he can do in this respect is to revise his picture of himself and try to reconcile himself to that.

If feeling guilty involved no more than the thought that the agent had harmed another then there would be no reason to regard guilt as an emotion of self-assessment. But this is the class of emotions to which it belongs. From this point of view it is quite different from remorse, an emotion with which it is often linked under the heading 'moral emotions'. The important feature of guilt is that the thought of the guilty concentrates on herself as the doer of the deed. Having brought about what is forbidden she has harmed herself. She has put herself into a position where repayment from her is due, but the point of the payment is not, or is only incidentally, that a moral wrong should be righted. This, the righting of a moral wrong, may well be the form the repayment takes, but from the point of view of the guilty person this is only a means towards the end: that she should be rid of the burden, that she should be able again to live with herself. The painfulness of the guilt-feelings is therefore explained as the uneasiness the person concerned feels about herself. That they so often express themselves as a worry about how to put right an injustice done to others is natural but not essential to the case; it is due to the fact that so often what we regard as the wrong done is an action harming others, so that repairing the harm is necessary to restore the balance. That, in the agent's view, reparation is required is due to her conception of herself as disfigured and the consequent need to do something about it. The greater the supposed disfigurement the greater, of course, such a need – and the more unlikely, perhaps, that the agent should think adequate payment is possible. Hence the self-torments the guilty sometimes let themselves in for.

The thought in remorse, by contrast, concentrates on the deed rather than on the agent as he who has done the deed. Remorse, the *OED* tells us, is a feeling of compunction, or deep regret, for a sin or wrong committed. This is acceptable in so far as it brings out one way in which remorse differs from regret: remorse is felt about a sin or moral wrong whereas regret is felt about what is in some way undesirable, but not particularly morally so. But it would be a mistake to conclude that remorse is regret which operates over a narrower, viz., moral, area. The two emotions differ also in other central respects.[9] Regret but not remorse can be felt about an event for which the agent does not take herself to be even just causally responsible. I may regret the passing of the summer; Hamlet regretted that circumstances had forced him into a position where he had to act against his own nature. He could not, seeing the situation in this way, have felt remorse. Remorse is always felt about an event which the agent sees as an action of hers. It is therefore not surprising that the person who feels remorse and the person who feels regret should view differently the relevant past event. If she feels remorse then she wants to undo the action and its consequences which cause the remorse, but when feeling regret she need not think that she would undo the action if she could. She may regret an action (sacking an employee) which overall she still considers necessary and beneficial (as leading to the more productive employment of labour). It is possible also to regret an action but accept it as the thing to do under the same description: she regrets sacking the employee because the girl was so easily crushed, but she had to be sacked, nevertheless, because she was so inefficient. Perhaps regret always implies acceptance of what has been done. It had to be done although there were unfortunate or disagreeable aspects to the deed. Remorse, on the other hand, never implies acceptance. It is impossible to feel remorse and yet believe that overall it was right to act as one did. The aspect of the action which causes remorse, or the description under which the remorseful agent sees her action, is regarded by her as outweighing any possible good that may have come of it. Agamemnon, for example, whatever else he may have felt about having caused his daughter to be sacrificed, could not have felt remorse about his action while continuing to think that her sacrifice was necessary for the Greek fleet to be able to sail, and that this was the overriding good. He could have felt regret, though unless this is qualified (deep, bitter) it would seem a rather inadequate reaction under the circumstances.

These differences between the emotions are reflected in their respective connection with action. No action need follow from regret, or even need be expected to follow. This is not surprising if the agent may think that all things considered she did the right thing, or did what had to be done. But we do expect some sort of action from her who feels remorse, though of course we may expect in vain. She wants to undo what she has done, and although it is evidently impossible to do just that, she would normally be expected to try and do something towards repairing the damage she takes herself to have brought about. If she takes no such steps the claim that she feels remorse would be suspect.

The person feeling remorse is tied to her action as the person feeling regret is not. She must do something about it, or it will continue to worry her. But at the same time there is a sense in which she remains detached as she cannot do when feeling either guilt or shame. Remorse is not an emotion of self-assessment, the concentration of thought is here not on the self, on its disfigurement or lowly standing, but is on her actions and their consequences. It is more outward-looking than either of the other two. Guilt and remorse may be experienced about the same event. Macbeth initially feels remorse as well as guilt, he wishes the deed could be undone: 'Wake Duncan with thy knocking: I wish thou could'st.' This is different from his guilt-reaction; his inability to say 'amen' indicates that he is now marked as an outsider who has broken his relationship with God. As the beliefs involved in the emotions are different, it is equally possible to feel the one but not the other. While Agamemnon could not have felt remorse under the circumstances I have described, he could have felt guilt, for that an action is thought to be necessary under given circumstances does not interfere with the adverse effect which having done the deed may have on the agent. Jonas, while burdened with guilt, feels no remorse at all, for he does not wish to be back in the situation where he was plagued by a blackmailer.

> Still he was not sorry. No. He had hated the man too much, and had been bent, too desperately and too long, on setting himself free. If the thing could have come over again, he would have done it again. . . . There was no more penitence or remorse within him now than there had been while the deed was brewing. (*Martin Chuzzlewit*, Ch. XLVII.)

It is equally possible that a person should experience remorse but not guilt, where the agent does not see herself burdened or stained by her wrongdoing. The wrong done need not present itself to her who feels remorse as forbidden, she need not think of herself as having disobeyed a categoric demand. Not every action a person sees as morally undesirable and would like to undo need be seen by her as leaving a stain.[10]

Remorse, guilt, and shame are usually classed together as 'moral emotions'. But remorse seems to be 'moral' in a sense in which neither of the others is. Shame, I suggested, may suitably be labelled a 'moral emotion' because of its connection with self-respect, but what a particular agent considers necessary to retain his self-respect may itself not be moral at all. It may be morally irrelevant as when, for example, he regards some physical defect as a threat to his self-respect. Or it may itself be morally wrong, as would presumably be some of the expectations which the arrogant or conceited need to see fulfilled if the basis for their self-respect is not to be undermined. In the case of the guilty, the content of what the agent sees as forbidden or obligatory can hardly seem morally irrelevant, at least to him. But it need not be the case that what he sees in these terms is in fact wrong or evil. In particular, neither of these emotions is moral in the sense of being other-regarding, for the agent's chief concern is for himself. Remorse, on the other hand, seems to be moral in just this sense; though perhaps not necessarily, at least standardly the agent is here concerned with the effect of what he does on others. As it concentrates on the action rather than the actor it also seems the healthier emotion, for in turning the agent away from himself he is less threatened by the possibility of self-preoccupation and self-indulgence.

Sometimes remorse is thought to be of value for the additional reason, that it is only through remorse that the guilty can be redeemed, so that remorse is the means whereby the guilty can regain his former position. The Bible emphasizes that repentance is necessary for God's forgiveness, and it may be that analogously in a non-Christian context remorse is necessary for the guilty to be re-established. This is the view held by Scheler. He regards remorse as the emotion of salvation. On his theory guilt and remorse are related to each other as 'promptings of conscience'. Guilt, it seems, is potentially merely destructive: the man who feels guilty recognizes that he has acted against his conscience, and this recognition will not let him rest and will create a tension within himself. Such torments are in themselves sterile. On the other hand, recognition of guilt is a necessary first step towards salvation; if a person ignores his wrongdoing then we have a case of 'hardening of heart' and nothing fruitful can come of that. It is in remorse that the agent takes a positive attitude towards the situation and himself. It constitutes a 'change of heart', or a totally new attitude, and through it the agent can regain his powers and rebuild himself. Scheler therefore does not stress so much that remorse is outgoing and other-regarding, but sees it rather as that which heals the self and enables it to lead a new life.[11] This does not mean, however, that on this view the thoughts involved in remorse must concentrate on the self, that remorse, too, is an emotion of self-assessment. The healing-process of the self may on the contrary be possible only if the agent looks outward at the world, rather than inward at himself.

On Scheler's view remorse is wholly constructive and guilt is merely destructive. He has made this true by definition: whatever is destructive in the person's attitude and behaviour counts as guilt; whatever constructive counts as remorse. Both points are debatable. There are possible cases of remorse where that emotion seems as destructive and possibly self-indulgent as guilt may be. Far from prompting repair work and bringing about a new and hopeful attitude towards the future, it may just torment the sufferer. A person can make the most of remorse by insisting on seeing what he has done under a description which strikes him as unalterable. A dutiful niece may, after the death of her aunt, feel remorse not because she did not give her the time and care that were needed, but because she did not do so for the right reasons. At the time it suited her to live with her aunt and look after her although her affections were not particularly engaged. What she wants to but cannot undo is her behaviour under the description 'suiting my own purposes' and substitute for it 'devoting myself lovingly and unselfishly to my aunt'. So remorse continues to gnaw at her. Nor does it seem to be the case that, conversely, guilt must always be destructive. In the following quotation Melanie Klein puts a different view:

> The irrevocable fact that none of us is ever entirely free from guilt has very valuable aspects because it implies the never fully exhausted wish to make reparation and to create in whatever way we can. All social services benefit by this urge. In extreme cases, feelings of guilt drive people towards sacrificing themselves completely to a cause or to their fellow beings, and may lead to fanaticism . . . ('Our Adult World and its Roots in Infancy', Tavistock Publications, 1959.)

Scheler's view seems too extreme. It is a more plausible suggestion that, rather than being in this respect so sharply contrasted, both guilt and remorse may be either constructive or destructive, depending on the agent and his view of the situation. There is always the possibility of this view being distorted; like shame, or indeed like any emotion, remorse may be wrongly directed and quite irrational. Feeling remorse no doubt has its value, but this does not mean that it must always be constructive.

But while not acceptable as it stands, Scheler's view nevertheless directs attention to the way in which guilt and remorse both differ from and are related to each other. Earlier I distinguished features which are essential to feeling guilt from those which may quite understandably but still mistakenly be taken to be essential. The person feeling guilt believes that she has done something forbidden and that in doing what is forbidden she has disfigured and so harmed herself. This is the identificatory belief. She may or may not also believe that what she did was harmful to either others or herself. The first, essential, type of harm is the direct consequence of the deed being forbidden; the second, non-essential type of harm is contingent on the nature of whatever it may be the agent sees as forbidden. That may be, for instance, violating another's rights, or it may be neglecting her talents. In the latter case, therefore, the person is harmed under two descriptions, that she has done what is wrong, and that she has not developed her talents. In this case doing the latter also happens to constitute the former, but the specific way in which she thinks she has harmed herself is distinguishable from the harm that is the stain of guilt. Secondly and consequentially, it is central to guilt that the agent sees herself in a position where repayment is due, but not that she thinks she must repair and so in some way undo the damage she has caused. This may or may not be the form in which she thinks she might be able to make up for what she has done.

The two features just rejected as being not essential to guilt are so partly because they need not be present in all cases of it. But even where the person feeling guilt believes that she has harmed another and believes that she should now repair this damage, her thoughts are not primarily on this aspect of the situation, they are primarily on herself. In this sense, too, the thought of damage caused and so to be repaired is inessential. In feeling remorse, on the other hand, it is precisely these thoughts which are the agent's identificatory beliefs, i.e., when feeling remorse the agent believes that she has done harm which she ought to try and repair.

This account agrees with Scheler's insofar as remorse is also constructive. It differs from Scheler's in that guilt need not be wholly destructive; it will be constructive on those occasions when the person feeling guilty believes that repairing the damage is the form her repayment should take. But she, unlike the person feeling remorse, will not regard her repair work as an end in itself. She will see it rather as a means towards self-rehabilitation. There are therefore occasions when the person feeling guilt may do or think she ought to do exactly the same as the person feeling remorse, and it may be impossible for anyone, including the person concerned, to tell whether she is prompted by feelings of guilt or by remorse.

Remorse, though being constructive in that it implies the view that repair-work is due, need not therefore be constructive on all relevant occasions. The remorseful niece is a case in point. But what she feels seems to be a mixture of both guilt and remorse. Insofar as she thinks that she has done damage which she ought to do something about, she feels remorse. But as the damage is caused by the (in her view) non-altruistic reasons for action rather than by her actual behaviour her thoughts also concentrate on the disfigurement of herself as a moral agent, and so there are also guilt feelings. That there can be such hybrid cases is explained by the possibility of a partial overlap of the beliefs involved in these two emotions.

Remorse may be constructive and yet not other-regarding: the repair work the agent thinks should be done may be to mend the damage she has caused herself. This seems at least a possibility; wasting one's talents, spoiling one's chances in life through drug-taking or alcohol may well be a matter for remorse. On the other hand, as the identificatory belief is not directly about the self, remorse, unlike guilt and shame is at least a candidate for other-regarding thought and behaviour. It is, perhaps rightly, thought to be in practice standardly other-regarding. If this is correct, then the reason may be that where a person has caused harm to herself of a nature which can prompt remorse rather than regret, then the harm is likely to be sufficiently serious to concentrate her thought on herself to the exclusion of other possible objects. The person would then in such circumstances be more likely to feel guilt rather than remorse. But whether or not this is so, it is clear that here is a basis for regarding remorse as a 'moral' emotion which is totally lacking in shame and guilt.

On Scheler's account remorse presupposes guilt, for the role of remorse is specifically to heal and re-establish the guilty. While it seemed wrong to restrict the operation of remorse in this way (a person may feel remorse about something he has done and feel no guilt), where the two are linked Scheler's emphasis on the constructiveness of remorse may have a significance not yet allowed for. The point concerns forgiveness. The agent who feels guilty believes that through his wrongdoings he has spoilt his relationship with the god disobeyed or the person harmed. The recipient of the wrong (provided he shares this view of the situation) is now in a position where he may either forgive or withhold forgiveness. For him to forgive is for him to recognize the wrong done to him but to re-accept the agent in spite of it, to re-establish the relationship. But if he so re-establishes the relationship without there being a 'change of heart' on the agent's part then it seems it is not genuine forgiveness he offers, but condonation.[12] For in re-accepting the unrepentant agent he would seem to think little of the wrong done and so compromise his own values. If so, then to be genuinely forgiven and thereby to be re-established in the previous relationship the agent must be sincere in wishing the deed undone, he must, it seems, feel remorse. Nor is the need for remorse restricted to this case: it may be that the agent, if he is to live with himself again, will have to forgive himself, and if genuine forgiveness must be preceded by remorse, then remorse is required on all such occasions as well. Kolnai, in his paper on 'Forgiveness', suggests that forgiveness granted to ourselves is a fairly dubious concept, 'if only because a person cannot "wrong" himself, i.e. infringe his own rights' (p. 106). Kolnai, like Rawls, connects guilt with principles of right, and this itself seemed dubious. It is, however, not this point that matters here. If it is true that forgiveness is necessary to restore a spoilt relationship then the agent himself will have to forgive himself, for *qua* doer of the relevant deed he has alienated himself from himself, and this would seem to be the most important relationship of all to restore. So in all (serious) cases of guilt, for the person concerned to re-establish himself, to regard himself again as a whole and so to live at peace with himself, self-forgiveness is necessary. 'You must learn to forgive yourself' seems in such circumstances very sensible advice. And if genuine forgiveness requires remorse, then so will self-forgiveness. On this view of forgiveness it is true that, as Scheler says, remorse has a very specific constructive function.

The view that genuine forgiveness requires remorse is too extreme to be acceptable as it stands. Whether forgiveness of a wrong is genuine or is a case of condonation will depend on the circumstances of individual cases. It seems quite possible for a generous person to forgive a wrong doer who does not show much sign of a change of heart without thereby being indifferent to whatever wrong he may have committed. Whether forgiveness in these circumstances is wise or foolish is of course a different question. But in the case of self-forgiveness such generosity would hardly be in place; it would suspiciously look like being indulgent towards oneself and making matters too easy for oneself. Maybe in the case of self-forgiveness such charity is always a form of condonation, and if so remorse retains something of the importance Scheler ascribes to it. It would remain at least one means of reconciling the agent to himself.[13]

Remorse was initially introduced to provide a contrast to guilt, and to the emotions of self-assessment in general. As a moral emotion it has in common with guilt and shame only the feature that it requires a sense of value on the part of the agent, an awareness, more or less developed, of moral distinctions, of what is right or wrong, honourable or disgraceful. In other respects it differs from them just because it is not an emotion of self-assessment. In feeling remorse a person's thoughts are not primarily upon himself, it is not the agent himself who occupies the centre of the stage. He is not seen by some audience, nor judged by some authority. The person who feels remorse sees himself as a responsible moral agent, and so sees whatever wrong he has done as an action (or omission) of his about the consequences of which he ought, if possible, to do something. Both guilt and shame are more passive by comparison. In neither of these cases need the person concerned see the occasion for the emotion as an action of his. Shame is passive also in that it leaves the agent helpless. In guilt, the thought that by having done what is forbidden he is now in a position where punishment or forgiveness is appropriate gives him initially the passive role of a possible recipient of the actions of another, rather than that of an active agent. And he may not conceive of himself as a possible active agent at all, for he may be resigned to the view that he who violates a taboo just has to accept whatever retribution is due to him. Insofar as the perceived stain on the self gives him a motive for repair work it is only incidental if it is of the same sort as that prompted by remorse.

Notes

1 For example, Freud: 'At the beginning, therefore, what is bad is whatever causes one to be threatened with loss of love. For fear of that loss, one must avoid it . . . A great change takes place only when the authority is internalized through the establishment of a super-ego. The phenomena of conscience then reach a higher stage. Actually, it is not until now that we should speak of conscience or a sense of guilt.' *Civilization and its Discontents* (The Hogarth Press and the Institute of Psycho-Analysis, 1975), pp. 61–2.

2 *A Theory of Justice*, Part 3, Ch. VII, 67, and Ch. VIII, 72. The 'principle of right' refers to his principles of justice: 'When we go against our sense of justice we explain our feelings of guilt by reference to the principles of justice. . . . The complete moral development has now taken place and for the first time we experience feelings of guilt in the strict sense' (p. 474). Rawls is primarily concerned with the mature person's guilt, or guilt in the 'strict' sense; i.e., he has no particular interest in the occurrence of irrational guilt.

3 Sigmund Freud, 'Determinism, Belief in Chance and Superstition – Some Points of View', in *The Psychopathology of Everyday Life*, ed. J. Strachey (Ernst Benn, London, 1966), p. 244.

4 For example, Edwin Lemert, 'Primary and secondary deviation' (1951), in Cressey and Ward, *Delinquency, Crime and Social Process* (Harper and Row, New York, 1969). I am grateful to Jeremy Waldron for drawing my attention to this literature.

5 Cp. Joel Feinberg, *Doing and Deserving* (OUP, 1970), Ch. IX, p. 231.

6 A.C. Bradley, *Shakespeare Tragedy* (Macmillan, 1929), Lecture 9, p. 358.

7 Charles Dickens, *Martin Chuzzlewit*, Ch. XLVII. Richard III takes a similar view of himself when, on the eve of the battle of Bosworth, the ghosts of all those for whose deaths he is responsible appear to him:

What do I fear? Myself? There's none else by.
Richard loves Richard; that is, I am I.
Is there a murderer here? No. Yes. I am. . . .
All several sins . . .
Throng to the bar, crying all guilty! guilty! (V. iii. 182–99.)

8 W.H. Auden, 'The Guilty Vicarage', in *The Dyer's Hand* (Faber and Faber, 1975), p. 158.

9 For a more detailed discussion of some of these points see Amélie Rorty, 'Agent-Regret', *Explaining Emotions*, pp. 489–506. The Hamlet example is hers.

10 Jane Austen's Emma Woodhouse, after the disastrous party on Boxhill, feels humiliated and remorseful, but she feels no guilt. She thinks of herself as being perfect in her behaviour to others, and it is humiliating to be shown that sometimes she is nothing of the sort. But she is also kind and feels sorry to have hurt Miss Bates's feelings. In order to undo the harm she has done she is prepared to undergo the tedium of a morning visit. She does not think of herself as having neglected a duty or left an obligation unfulfilled, but she thinks of herself as having failed to live up to the standards she has set for herself.

11 Max Scheler, 'Reue und Wiedergeburt', in *Vom Ewigen im Menschen, Ges. Werke*, Band V (Bern, 1954). He describes remorse as from the moral point of view 'eine Form der Selbstheilung der Seele', and as from the religious point of view 'der natürlich Akt, den Gott der Seele verlieh, um zu Ihm zurückzukehren.' (p. 33.)

12 For a discussion of condoning versus forgiving see Aurel Kolnai, 'Forgiveness', in *Proceedings of the Aristotelean Society*, 1973–4. Kolnai concedes, somewhat grudgingly, that remorse is not necessarily required for genuine forgiveness.

13 But not, I think, the only means, e.g. in the last chapter of *Crime and Punishment* Dostoevsky hints at a healing process which is differently based: Raskolnikoff, now a prisoner in Siberia, does not feel remorse. 'He did not repent of his deeds', he merely thought he had made mistakes, and in particular that he had been feeble to confess. Yet there is a change in his attitude, the beginning of a healing process: 'They were both worn and ill, but in those white and worn faces already beamed the dawn of a restored future, and full resurrection to a new life.' His fellow-convicts begin to look kindly upon him, for the first time he is accepted. But this renewal is due not to remorse but to love.

Chapter 4

Shame and Guilt in Early New England

John Demos

Fifty years ago Ruth Benedict made this comparison of American life, past and present:

> The early Puritans who settled in the United States tried to base their entire morality on guilt, and all psychiatrists know what trouble contemporary Americans have with their consciences. But shame is an increasingly heavy burden . . . and guilt is less extremely felt than in earlier generations. In the United States this is interpreted as a relaxation of morals, because we do not expect shame to do the heavy work of morality. We do not harness the acute personal chagrin which accompanies shame to our fundamental system of morality.[1]

Benedict was, of course, a distinguished anthropologist, not a historian. And the foregoing statement seems mistaken – as history. But it does contain a pithy piece of phrase-making, which serves to pose a question. What aspects of American character have traditionally been made to 'do the heavy work of morality'?

The question could be asked about any part of our history, early, late, or in between; but the discussion that follows will be limited to a single geographical region and two segments of historical time. It begins by arguing – in opposition to Benedict – that the 'early Puritans' were notably shameprone, and that shame performed the largest part of their moral 'heavy work'. It further suggests how, in the era of the Early Republic, the burden began to shift – away from shame, towards guilt and 'conscience'. Its focus is New England life and culture,[2] its framework is straightforward comparison. The result is argument, not finished exposition; evidence is introduced more to illustrate than to 'prove' a given point. To these disclaimers must be added two more. Little is said here about the process of change. The period 1650–1750 seems to be one sort of moral/psychological world, and the period 1800–1850 another; but the interim remains (for now) largely obscure. Finally, readers may note an avoidance of certain knotty methodological problems. The psychological disposition of large populations – 'national character', in its most familiar phrasing – is itself a *conundrum*, if not a bottomless pit of academic controversy. And it is necessary to invoke a temporary suspension of disbelief on that score as well.

I

Shame and *guilt*: small words for large and complex forms of experience. Most of us can distinguish them, intuitively, in our personal lives; but it is well, nonetheless, to make some effort at formal definition. Fortunately, there is an abundant scientific literature to bring to bear on that task.[3]

Close to the level of visible behavior, the distinction seems to turn on the presence – and salience – of other persons. *Shame* has an 'external' reference; the pain it inflicts comes by way of an 'audience'. To be sure, the audience is sometimes imagined, not real; but the sense of being watched, of being exposed and unfavorably scrutinized, is central either way. A morality based on shame makes much of *appearances*; one does the right thing because one is concerned to preserve a good reputation. *Guilt*, by contrast, is based on a process that is largely 'internalized'. There is a 'code' of values that individuals carry around inside them – and that serves to regulate their actual deeds. A guilt-prone person feels distressed whenever s/he acts contrary to the inner code – regardless of whether or not anyone else is watching.

The distinction has other, 'deeper' aspects as well, some of which are captured in the following comparative statements. (1) Shame occurs when a standard (a goal; a hope; a fantasy) is not reached; in this almost literal sense it involves 'shortcoming'. Guilt occurs when a norm (a rule; a precept; a principle) is violated – or, one might say, when a boundary is crossed; it amounts, therefore, to 'transgression'. (2) In experiential terms, shame means, 'I am weak, inadequate, inferior'; whereas guilt means, 'I do bad things'. The point implied here is that guilt always has moral connotations, while shame may or may not have them – and also that shame is about the whole self, while guilt is more closely tied to specific acts. (3) The pain experienced, in each case, derives from different unconscious sources. In shame one feels that one is on the receiving end of an attitude of scorn, of contempt; and behind this lies a dread of abandonment. In guilt one seems to be the object, rather, of hatred; and the punishment one fears, at the deepest intrapsychic level, is some form of mutilation. (In psychoanalytic terms, the developmental line leads back to what is called 'castration anxiety'.) These three propositions, in turn, underlie one more; namely, that shame and guilt may both be operant at once, yet usually one of them is in some sense preferred to the other. In practice, shame may cover (or mask, or defend against) guilt – and vice versa.

II

With these theoretical props roughly in place, attention turns to the first part of our comparison – early New England, and, above all, 'Puritanism'. This patch of the historical landscape has, of course, been endlessly picked over by scholars; yet some features remain more or less neglected. Consider the legal system – especially, the punishment system. Here indeed is something wonderfully quaint and curious – and, by most scholarly accounts, inessential, even trivial.[4] It deserves to be taken quite seriously.

Fines were the most common sanction imposed on wrongdoers in early New England. Fines were also, evidently, considered least painful; whenever a choice was offered – pay so much cash, or accept another form of punishment – New Englanders elected to pay. And what were the other punishments? Sitting in the stocks; standing on a pillory; wearing a so-called 'badge of infamy' (in the manner of Hawthorne's scarlet letter) or a simple 'paper' describing the offense in question; branding (in effect, a way of making the 'badge' permanent); being dragged through the streets, tied to a 'cart's tail'; standing in the gallows with a rope tied around one's neck: these were the favorites, with occasional added refinements as circumstances might warrant. What they all had in common was the element of invidious public exposure. And often, in individual cases, the 'public' part was given explicit emphasis. Thus the time and place of punishment would be specified as follows: 'upon some public meeting day', 'on a public training day', 'in the open market place', 'in the open street', 'in the public congregation', 'in some open place in the meeting house'. The purpose of such directions was clear enough: 'that he may be seen of the people', 'so as they may be visibly seen', 'to the open view of spectators', and so on. There was one more kind of punishment – at least as common as the others, and somewhat different in its effects – namely, whipping. The difference, of course, was the physical pain. But scattered evidence from the case files suggests that the pain was not *only* physical. It was an assumed and important part of all whippings that they were public; indeed the term 'public correction' often served, in court records, as a shorthand reference to this procedure.[5]

At least occasionally, shame – that is, the psychological experience itself – was directly mentioned in the records. A man convicted of sexual misconduct was sentenced to be whipped; the woman involved was spared the same punishment, 'considering the weakness of her body', but was ordered to 'be present at the whipping post . . . that she may in some measure bear the shame of her sin'. Another convict boasted, after his punishment, 'that he did not value his whipping the skip of a flea, only for a little shame'. (In one remarkable instance such considerations obtained even with a capital sentence: a murderer 'desired to have been beheaded [rather than hanged], giving this reason, that it was less painful and less shameful'.)[6]

Church congregations, no less than the courts, sought to discipline errant members by way of shaming. 'Admonition' was the means most often employed. 'Temperance Baldwin . . . was called forth in the open congregation . . . and solemnly admonished of her great sin, which was spread before her in diverse particulars': thus one instance among many. Sinners like Temperance Baldwin were urged to 'confess' – or, as it was put in another way, to 'take shame unto her face'. Typically, the result was a long recital of wickedness, given in a tone of abject self-abasement. (For example: 'With all submissive respect, prostrating himself at the feet of your clemency, . . . your poor petitioner . . . humbly desires to acknowledge the justice of God, who . . . hath made his sin obvious to his shame . . .', etc.)[7] If the tone seemed insufficiently abject – if shame was not willingly and visibly expressed – confession was considered meaningless, and the original offense stood compounded. And if admonition failed of results altogether, a church might decide to invoke its most terrible sanction of all, outright excommunication. The gravity of this procedure was underscored in the language used as the minister pronounced sentence:

> For these and many more foul and sinful transgressions, I do here in the name of the whole church . . . pronounce you to be a leprous and unclean person, and I do cast you out and cut you off from the enjoyment of all those blessed privileges and ordinances which God hath entrusted his church withal. . . . And so, as an unclean beast and unfit for the society of God's people, I do from this time forward pronounce you an excommunicated person from God and His people.[8]

If the Puritans were indeed shame-prone, and if the inward experience of shame is rooted in a fearful expectation of abandonment, then surely these words were calculated for maximum effect.

In fact, however, the record of the law and of ecclesiastical discipline does not by itself evince the *experience* of shame in the population at large. It shows that the leaders -- those who made the laws and ran the churches – credited shame with great power, and perhaps it reflects their own psychological tendency. But it is obviously dangerous, when analyzing penal systems, to assume a symmetry of intended and actual effects. How well a given form of punishment 'works' in the offender, or whether indeed it works at all – this is another sort of question.

Unfortunately, we cannot look inside the experience of actual offenders subjected to one or another punishment three centuries ago. We must look, instead, for different – but congruent – evidence. Consider, then, the extraordinary prominence in early New England court records of lawsuits for slander and defamation. In sheer quantitative terms this category of cases makes one of the very largest. And it shows us (as the punishment system does not) many individual persons choosing to act in a particular way. Furthermore, it shows us (at least occasionally) some of the feeling that prompted such action. Here is an illustrative example:

> William Edwards hath entered an action of defamation against Benjamin Price and his wife, his wife saying that the wife of William Edwards was a base, lying woman, and that she would prove her a liar in many particulars.

That is the summary notice on the Court docket; then the depositional evidence begins, with a statement from Edwards himself:

> William Edwards, plaintiff, declares it is a deep wound that is laid upon his wife in that which is expressed against her by Goody Price, for *her life lieth at stake* in this defamation in that it is laid against her that she is a base, lying woman, and that she will prove her a liar in many particulars. Which I also take to be a great

defamation to me and my posterity, in that hereafter it may be spoken, 'here go the brats of a base liar. . . .' I declare that the defamation is such as I would not have made out against my wife for a hundred pounds.[9]

The plaintiff in this case estimated the damage to his wife's reputation as equivalent in monetary terms to more than £100, and other New Englanders made similar calculations. A Rhode Island man, who considered himself 'most ignominiously slandered' by an accusation of theft, pleaded in court as follows: 'Seeing that a man's good name is worth more than wealth, I cannot but charge him [the defendant] with one hundred pounds damage, though it be not a sufficient recompense.' A Massachusetts man challenged a slanderer to fight, saying 'I had rather thou should cut my flesh than give me such words.' A Connecticut town, in establishing its own code of local justice, set the penalty for assault at ten shillings, and that for slander at five pounds – a tenfold difference. And the poet Anne Bradstreet offered this comparison: 'We read in Scriptures of three sorts of arrows: the arrow of an enemy, the arrow of pestilence, and the arrow of a slanderer's tongue. The two first kill the body, the last the good name; the two former leave a man when he is once dead, but the last mangles him in his grave.'[10]

Lawsuits for slander often resulted from larger episodes of personal conflict, and conflict itself bears consideration here. The sources of conflict, the manner, the tone, the results: there is much to be learned from cross-cultural comparison of the ways people *fight*. In early New England the characteristic tone was (what might be called) 'narcissistic insult'. It is heard again and again, whenever the parties to conflict are directly quoted. Here is a modest sampling taken from a variety of depositional records.

He said . . . that Swan was a weak man, and he could drive a dozen such as he before him through the town.[11]

She said that she would make him bare as a bird's tail.[12]

He said he did not care a fart for the Court.[13]

He said, 'We met old Mr. Bradstreet; and my brother . . . crouched and conjured to him, but I knew him well enough, and for my part I never stoved my hat to him, nor reverenced him more than I would an Indian.'[14]

He answered that he would not suffer such an affront from a man – no, not from King Charles himself if he was here, but would trample him under his foot.[15]

He said, . . . 'I shall make a fool of you before I have done with you.'[16]

He put one hand in the waistband of his breeches and said . . . he would deal with him with one hand.[17]

She said . . . that the teacher [i.e., minister] was fitter to be a lady's chambermaid than to be in the pulpit.[18]

He said . . . 'You are too high, you must be brought down.'[19]

She said . . . 'we'll kill them, and flea them, and carry them home in the cart.'[20]

He said that he had as leave to hear a dog bark as to hear Mr. Cobbet preach.[21]

He said . . . that they were but a company of fools for meddling and making themselves ridiculous amongst men.[22]

He said he would humble him, for he had always been a pimping knave to him.[23]

He challenged us [to get] off our horses to try our manhood, and said that he would take me by the eyelids and make my heels strike fire against the element.[24]

He said that his dog's tail would make as good a [church-] member as she.[25]

High versus low, strong versus weak; reverencing versus humbling, trampling versus crouching; smart men versus fools, good men versus knaves, Englishmen versus Indians; kings versus chambermaids, preachers versus dogs; deeds that command respect versus farts and fleas and bare birds' tails. The issues are 'narcissistic' ones[26] in that they involve the management of self and, more especially, of self-*esteem*. When these folk faced off in situations of conflict (with its attendant excitements and dangers), they instinctively sought to inflate themselves, and to denigrate their opponents. Or – to make the same point in other words – efforts of shaming, and of defense against shame, virtually *defined* conflict for many of them.

The causes of conflict are no less revealing than the tonal qualities; and often, in early New England, the cause was some form of 'narcissistic injury'. One man began to fight after declaring that 'his spirit could not bear to be made such a fool of'. Another sued his neighbor in order to 'vindicate my blasted reputation. . . . The world might think that I did cast off the care of my own credit, if I did suffer such reproaches to be laid on me.' And still another – an eminent New England clergyman – lamented man's 'vengeful' nature thus: 'Nothing is more natural . . . than to say so and do so: "I'll be even with him; I'll give him as good as he brings." They think it a disgrace for them to put up [with] an affront, or pass by an injury, without revenge or satisfaction, notwithstanding the Lord chargeth them to forgive those that have done them wrong.'[27]

This last comment leads into the subject of religion; and religion, no less than the law, furnishes important material for the present discussion. Indeed 'Puritan' belief may be viewed as a kind of screen on which the believers could (and did) project a vivid cluster of fantasies, anxieties, and other forms of psychological preoccupation. Consider: A 'good' man is characterized, above all, by 'humility', 'meekness', and the 'forbearance' of pride. (Thus Anne Bradstreet wrote, in praise of her 'honored father': 'High thoughts he gave no harbor in his heart; nor honours puffed him up when he had part.')[28] To become good – or rather to obtain some prospect of 'saving grace' – is to recognize one's profound spiritual weakness. (Recall the subjective experience of shame, as defined earlier: 'I am weak, inadequate, inferior'.) Self-importance is the sin of sins, self-abasement the way to improvement. ('And so the Lord did help me', wrote Thomas Shepard in his *Autobiography*, 'to loathe myself in some measure, and to say often, "Why should I seek the glory and good of myself . . . which self ruins me and blinds me."')[29]

Shepard's autobiography and other personal documents from the period

reflect at every point the importance of self-scrutiny in New England
religious experience. 'Watchfulness' was perhaps the single most common,
and resonant, term for this attitude. Puritans were endlessly watching
themselves, and God, of course, was watching them too. Nothing should be
– or ultimately *could* be – concealed, not even one's innermost preoccupations. In fact, the ability to see everything was a key attribute of the
Deity. Thus, one clergyman referred repeatedly in his private correspon-
dence to 'the eye of God's providence'. A second lamented the tendency of
'foolish creatures . . . to think themselves safe if they can but hide their sins
from the knowledge of men, not considering that the eye of God is upon
them in all their ways'. A third told his congregation that 'it is no matter
whether our neighbours do see our virtuous carriage or no; *God's angels*,
they see it'. And a fourth described the Judgment Day as final, humiliating
exposure: 'We shall every one of us stand naked before Christ's Judgment
Seat . . . [and] all, even the most secret, sins shall be laid open before the
whole world.' (A local court, meanwhile, might admonish an offender 'that
she hath to do with an all-seeing God, who can write her sin in her
forehead' – i.e., for other *people* to see as well.) Seeing and being seen,
watching and hiding: thus a vital nexus of Puritan thought and feeling. Not
surprisingly, Increase Mather believed that 'the eye is the most excellent
member of the body . . . for which way so ever the eye goeth the heart
walks after it'.[30]

Another recurrent element of Puritan religious discourse was the imagery
of height. Shepard repeatedly described himself as 'low sunk in my spirit'.
John Winthrop reported how prayer 'brought me lower in mine own eyes'.
The Reverend Michael Wigglesworth wrote in his diary: 'Lord, I lie down
in my shame, worthy to be rejected'. And the Reverend William Adams,
writing in *his* diary, gave an interesting account of a mishap experienced
while travelling from his home to explore an 'invitation' (in the ministry)
elsewhere: 'As we were coming, . . . my horse stumbled and I had a fall,
though I received no hurt; which causeth me to reflect upon myself whether
I had not been something *lifted up*, that there were so many come to attend
on me; and to adore the wisdom and grace of God in that he can and doth
effectively *bring down high thoughts*.'[31]

Height, of course, is something to be measured; and shame, as noted
earlier, has much to do with subjective measurement. ('I come short of, I
stand below', one or another standard.) The Puritans were much inclined to
measure things, and above all to measure themselves. (To 'watch' the self
was also to measure it.) The pattern could be explored at length in their
various individual writings, and it runs through their collective preoccupations as well. Consider 'declension' – that quintessential category of Puritan
experience. And consider, too, some further points in the psychological
interpretation of shame. According to psychoanalytic theory, shame occurs
in relation to that part of personality structure termed the 'ego ideal'.
Simply described, the ego ideal is a composite of the goals a person has for
him/herself – of all that s/he would most like to be. From a developmental

standpoint, it originates in the very early years, when a child identifies with – and, in a sense, takes into himself – the image he has of his parents. This image has both positive and negative elements. The negative side is the terrifyingly powerful and malevolent 'castrating parent'; this forms the basis of the punishing 'superego'. The ego ideal, by contrast, represents the admired parent – the parent one yearns to emulate – and, in experiences of shame, it becomes the internal point of reference against which one's failings are measured.[32]

These constructs can be pointed directly toward the Puritans, for whom 'declension' meant, first and last, a sense of failure to carry on with the high standards of the founding generation. Cotton Mather's essay *Things for a Distressed People to Think Upon* offers a characteristic statement: 'New England once abounded with Heroes worthy to have their lives written, as copies for future ages. . . . But . . . there seems to be a shameful *shrink*, in all sorts of men among us from the greatness and goodness which adorned our ancestors: We grow little every way; little in our civil matters, little in our military matters, little in our ecclesiastical matters: we dwindle away to nothing.' Recent scholarship has done much to unravel the intellectual history of all this;[33] but perhaps we can better grasp the *emotional* energies involved if we appreciate the pervasive orientation of the Puritans to shame. The failure to 'measure up' to the standards of the founding fathers of New England would be experienced with special intensity by people whose psychic life was structured, in substantial part, around an anxious concern with another – very personal and internalized – father.

Just as 'declension' has served to organize our understanding of Puritan history, so John Winthrop's 'Lecture on Christian charity' is widely taken as an epitome of Puritan ideals. Listen to its most famous passage:

> We must consider that we shall be as a city upon a hill; the eyes of all people are upon us. So that if we shall deal falsely with our God in this work, . . . and so cause Him to withdraw his present help from us, we shall be made a story and a byword throughout the world. We shall open the mouths of enemies to speak evil of the ways of God and all professors for God's sake. We shall shame the faces of many of God's worthy servants, and cause their prayers to be turned into curses upon us, till we are consumed out of the good land whither we are going.[34]

Here, in one densely compacted mass, are virtually all the elements discussed so far: a high hill; staring eyes, open mouths, red faces; curses, false dealing, scornful stories; shame and the threat of abandonment.

Governor Winthrop's private writings reflect on the risks and difficulties involved in embracing the cause of religious reform. And the terms of such reflection recall his famous 'lecture'. 'Methought I heard all men telling me I was a fool, to set so light by honor, credit, wealth, jollity, etc.', he wrote; yet God assured him that he was 'in a right course'. Moreover, God 'and all experience tells me . . . that those which do walk openly in this way shall be despised, pointed at, hated of the world, made a byword, reviled, slandered, rebuked, made a gazing stock, called Puritans, nice fools, hypocrites, hair-brained fellows, rash, indiscreet, vainglorious, and all that nought is.' The city on the hill and the gazing stock are opposite faces of the same psychological coin.[35]

Indeed, Puritans maintained an expectation of *attack* as part of their cultural repertoire. For this, of course, their experience furnished considerable ground; but their psychology contributed as well. The aforementioned Winthrop passages convey a positive reveling in the details of derision. And the same overstated tone appears elsewhere: for example, in the preface of Cotton Mather's important work *Bonifacius, or Essays to Do Good.* These essays, Mather predicted, 'shall be derided, with all the art and wit that [the Devil] can inspire. . . . Exquisite profaneness and buffoonery shall try their skill to laugh people out of them. The men who abound in them shall be exposed on the stage; libels, lampoons, and satires, the most poignant that ever were invented, shall be darted at them; and pamphlets full of lying stories be scattered with a design to make them ridiculous.'[36]

One can summarize all this, and hint at its broader significance, by attempting a sketch of the New England Puritan as a character type. He displayed, as perhaps his most striking personal trait, an extreme sensitivity to the opinions and attitudes of others. Time and again one feels, in the records he has left us, his propensity to search for cues to behavior outside rather than within the self. Has he achieved an important goal, gained some new position or mark of honor? – he will describe in detail the admiration of his friends and neighbors. Has he been disappointed in one or another personal quest? – he will present the view of supposedly neutral parties that he should by all rights have succeeded. Has he been criticized or slighted by other members of his community? – he will immediately call them to account. Does such criticism have some reasonable foundation in fact? – he will jump to his own defense, and will probably try to shift the blame elsewhere. Is he uncertain as to his particular worth and character? – he will ponder how others have defined him.

There is in all this a concern for reputation, an instinct for face saving, a deep dread of appearing deficient in any way, that reaches right to the center of personality. The New England Puritan – considered once again as a social type – was not a weak person; he could act effectively when the occasion required. But often he was reluctant to claim the motives of action as his own. He preferred to picture himself as responding to external influences, especially when his conduct might be open to reproach. He was, in short, not fully self-determining, and he was unable or unwilling to cultivate that existential awareness which modern man has prized so highly. His world was characterized less by stark confrontation with self and more by intense face-to-face contacts with a variety of significant others.

III

The argument so far has scarcely touched on childhood experience – which must, in any culture, reflect and reinforce the prevalent pattern of moral 'heavy work'. Puritan childhood has, in fact, been widely canvassed in recent historical writing, and there is little need to go over the same ground here. Suffice it to say that 'shaming' does seem to have been key to child-rearing practices in New England – and that psychological development, beginning from infancy, laid strong foundations for such practice.[37]

However: child-rearing can serve as an entry-point for the second part of the story. Picture a living room (in a home we would now describe as 'middle-class') where husband, wife, and several children are grouped together, yet are occupied with various individual pursuits. Suddenly, one of the children – a boy named Wallace – spies the family cat despoiling a favorite plaything. Infuriated, he dashes the unfortunate creature into a pot of boiling water. Shrieks of horror come from his siblings – followed by a tension-filled silence. Then father speaks in a measured tone: 'Wallace, go to your room'. Without a murmur, the boy complies. And, hour after hour, day after day, Wallace remains sequestered upstairs, emerging only to go to school. His meals are taken to him, and his other needs remembered; but he has no regular contact with family-members. Finally, after two full weeks of this, he comes solemnly downstairs. He declares to his father his sorrow over his violent misconduct and his determination to prevent any reoccurrence. (He has just withstood – that is, without yielding to anger – some extreme 'provocations' at the hands of schoolmates.) Forgiveness is asked, and received.

This little vignette was, in fact, the centerpiece of a much-read and broadly representative novel by a New England author of the mid-nineteenth century.[37] It may appear, at first glance, to be a tale of 'excommunication' – and thus a domestic replica of 'Puritan' morality from two centuries before. But a second look suggests otherwise. For one thing, the quiet command of the father to 'go to your room' is no equivalent to the minister's sentence of excommunication, as quoted above. For another, the attitude of *all* parties seems significantly different. Initially, they are 'horrified', to be sure; but this feeling is soon superseded by others – by prayerful concern, by 'grief', and above all by deep personal sympathy. Wallace, it seems, is engaged upstairs with some vitally important work with himself; his family cannot help, but they can (and do) *hope*. They are not scorning or censorious; on the contrary, they are openly supportive. Wallace is isolated so that he can more effectively *punish himself*. The penalty for wrongdoing must, in short, be exacted internally (i.e., without reference to an 'audience'). And – in terms of the present discussion – it is a penalty rooted in guilt rather than shame.

Viewed thus, Wallace's lonely struggle was paradigmatic of trends and tendencies in the society at large. His room became, for the space of those critical days, a virtual penitentiary. And surely it is no coincidence that the same era, roughly the first half of the nineteenth century, witnessed the founding of *actual* penitentiaries in New England, and all across the land. Indeed the entire system of judicially imposed punishment now became transformed. Gone were the old forms of 'public correction' and their various accoutrements (the stocks, the pillory, the whipping post, the branding irons, the badges of infamy). In their place arose the prisons which are with us still – though 'penitentiary' does seem the more accurate term for the first, germinal phase. The process of change was, of course, immensely variegated and complex, and one cannot reduce it all to a set of psychological vectors. But surely there were psychological *correlates*. A motive to isolate offenders was central to projects of prison building. And the idea behind such isolation was explicitly – even smugly – psychological. Thus one advocate of the 'Pennsylvania system' of prison organization (which featured a regimen of solitary confinement) could write as follows: 'Each individual [convict] will necessarily be made the instrument of his own punishment; his conscience will be the avenger of society.' And a colleague would point up the inner-life details: '[Each convict] will· be compelled to reflect on the error of his ways [and] to listen to the reproaches of his conscience.'[39]

Penitentiaries, as several scholars have shown us, were infused with the whole spirit of nineteenth-century moral reform. And reform's other branches – peculiarly associated with New England, as they were – deserve our notice too. Consider, for a moment, the temperance movement, that long and ultimately successful effort to curtail the consumption of alcoholic beverages. The literature of temperance was, of course, voluminous: printed sermons and lectures, tracts and pamphlets, personal memoirs and autobiographies. Reduced to their thematic essentials, they told a single story: Hero takes to drink and experiences various forms of personal degradation (loss of job, loss of property, loss of social standing). Hero's family (faithful wife, innocent children, doting parents) are deeply hurt (impoverished, exploited, physically abused, or left 'broken-hearted') in direct consequence. Hero belatedly sees the harm he is causing to those whom he loves most, becomes 'conscience-stricken', and vows to change.[40] Again, it is the relationship between the sin, the sinner, and the others that bears our special consideration. Under the old moral regime, sin might bring shame to the family members (insofar as they shared in the disgrace of the sinner), but it did not injure them otherwise. Moreover, outside the family sin evoked disapproval, disgust, scorn. It was, indeed, to avoid such unpleasant 'external' consequences that one behaved morally, in the first place. The new regime rearranged these elements to a very different end. The inducements away from sin were cast in terms of hurt given *to* others (not inflicted *by* others). And this was precisely the stuff and substance of *guilt*.

The most famous branch of nineteenth-century reform, and the one that left the biggest impression on American history, was, of course, antislavery. The moral and psychological dynamic of antislavery seems considerably more complex than is the case, for example, with temperance, and there is space here only to sample some particulars. One part of the complexity involves the artifacts of language itself; for abolitionists chose to employ the language of *both* shame and guilt. Thus, for instance, William Lloyd

Garrison's antislavery newspaper *The Liberator* includes articles entitled on the one hand, 'O! SHAME SHAME! SHAME!' and, on the other, 'WE ARE ALL GUILTY ... '. And it does appear that antislavery leaders sought to move their compatriots to action by any and every psychological means possible. Still, one feels that the largest share of their energies was devoted to arousing feelings of guilt. They defined slave holding, first and last, as a *sin*, as a pattern of behavior which crossed an absolutely fundamental moral boundary. And they drew that boundary – spotlighted it, and dug it deep – again and again and again. Moreover, the sin of slaveholding was for them expressed in the wrong it did, the *hurt* it *gave*, to other human beings. A favorite abolitionist tactic was to pile up accounts of specific sufferings inflicted on individual slaves; and the most famous, most efficacious, single document in all this literature – Harriet Beecher Stowe's novel *Uncle Tom's Cabin* – is an unrelenting portrayal of slave suffering. The idea was to 'rend the conscience' (as one commentator put it) of 'decent folk' everywhere.

There is another aspect of abolitionist rhetoric that may deserve mention here. Recall, for a start, the prevalent style of conflict in the colonial period (the first part of our comparison). The main thrust, we noted, was by way of narcissistic insult: a tone of disdain, an effort, in short, to belittle one's opponents as much as possible. This seemed consistent with the clinical definition of shame, centered as it is on the dread of becoming an object of scorn, of contempt, of ridicule. Guilt, according to those same definitional categories, involves the sense of being *hated* (something quite different). And hatred – far more than scorn – indeed describes the abolitionists' attitude toward their adversaries. Certainly, they did not belittle those adversaries; on the contrary, their attitude tended toward magnification. Slavery was, in their eyes and words, an 'infernal monster' which 'legalized on an enormous scale, licentiousness, fraud, cruelty, and murder'. Individual slaveholders were 'manstealers', 'tyrants', 'oppressors', and so on. The list could be made very long, but the point is immediately clear. The enemy was in all ways outsize; and the response expressed a fierceness, a hatred, of corresponding dimensions.

And now, one more time, the 'screen' of Protestant religion. Immediately we can see how much the imagery has changed with the passage of two centuries. This is, of course, a well-known story; it bears mention here only to flag some psychological meanings. For example: In the early period the emphasis had fallen on the Lord's all-encompassing sovereignty – and, in explicit contrast, on man's inherent weakness; to be 'saved' was to acknowledge this gap and at the same time to bridge it. Now (that is, in the nineteenth century) the spotlight moved to Christ's sacrifice and suffering; to 'convert' was to accept his sacrifice, even (in a sense) to redeem it. Moreover, resistance to conversion now carried the implication of spurning Christ's sacrifice – and thus of 'hurting' him further. There is an echo here of the reform literature (mentioned previously), in which the wages of sin are exacted from the sinner's family and closest friends. Indeed revival preachers would sometimes present them*selves* as liable to injury by unresponsive congregants. 'I could mention some cases', wrote the famous evangelist Charles G. Finney, 'where ministers have died in consequence of their labors to promote a revival where the church hung back from the work. . . . The state of the people, and of sinners, rests upon their mind, they travail in soul day and night, and they labor in season and out of season, beyond the power of the human constitution to bear, until they wear out and die.'[41] Prayerful wives and children were also at risk; to remain unconverted was to dash *their* hopes and frustrate their labors as well. In short: *convert*, or you will add to Christ's sufferings; *convert*, or you will kill off the preacher; *convert*, or you will distress and demoralize your loved ones.[42] This particular brand of moral 'heavy work' is easy enough to recognize – in the argot of our own time, a 'guilt trip' all the way.

IV

This chapter concludes, as it began, with a brace of qualifiers. Its 'coverage' seems in some respects impossibly large, in others painfully thin and sketchy. At best it frames a hypothesis, and samples the evidence that might be used to develop a full-fledged scholarly project. It does not explore possible class differences around the main thematic line – nor, for that matter, differences of gender, age, and political orientation. The hypothesis stands as a simple (perhaps *over*simple) piece of comparative history in two parts, and treatment of the second part is especially brief. Were the parts to be developed further, they would have to be shaded more carefully. The change between them was not a matter of movement from *all* shame to *all* guilt, but rather a shift in the overall emotional balance. Every regime of moral heavy work taps both kinds of psychological energy (and maintains nonpsychological sanctions as well). Hence this presentation overstates the case – in order to make it more clearly.

But enough of Historian's Humble Pie. The issues here are important ones; the hypothesis itself supports yet another call to 'further research'. Fortunately, New England historians (of both the 'Puritan' and the 'early national' periods) are discovering troves of hitherto unused materials that should make suitable grist for this particular scholarly mill. Court records (especially for the seventeenth and early eighteenth centuries), personal documents (especially for the nineteenth), a huge host of evidence from and about local experience: here, if anywhere, is the basis for reconstructing past emotional life. With all deliberate speed – and with *neither* shame nor guilt – historians must rise to the task.

Notes

1 Ruth Benedict, *The Chrysanthemum and the Sword* (Boston, 1946), pp. 223–4.
2 'New England Culture' is rather loosely construed here. For the first ('Puritan') period

the boundaries are conventional enough; for the second they expand to include the hinterland (New York, the Upper Midwest) peopled largely by New Englanders.

3 The following studies have proved especially helpful on the psychology of shame and guilt: Gerhart Piers and Milton B. Singer, *Shame and Guilt* (Springfield, Ill., 1953); Helen Merrell Lynd, *On Shame and the Search for Identity* (New York, 1958); Helen B. Lewis, *Shame and Guilt in Neurosis* (New York, 1971); Erik Erikson, *Childhood and Society* (New York, 1950), Ch. 7; Heinz Kohut, 'Thoughts on Narcissism and Narcissistic Rage', *The Psychoanalytic Study of the Child 27* (1972): 360–400.

4 Puritan punishments are examined at length in Edwin Powers, *Crime and Punishment in Early Massachusetts, 1620–1692* (Boston, 1966). However, this study is of a purely descriptive nature; its author makes little effort to set his material in the context of Puritan society -- or of Puritan psychology.

5 The details of Puritan punishment can be examined in any set of early New England court records. See, for example, *Records and Files of the Quarterly Courts of Essex County, Massachusetts*, 8 vols. (Salem, Mass., 1911–21). This collection will be cited hereafter as *Essex Court Records*.

6 Charles J. Hoadly, ed., *Records of the Colony and Plantation of New Haven*, 2 vols. (Hartford, Conn., 1867–68), 2: 136; *Essex Court Records*, VIII, 303; J.K. Hosmer, ed., *Winthrop's Journal*, 2 vols. (Boston, 1908), 1: 283.

7 Massachusetts Historical Society, *Proceedings*, 2nd series, VI, 481, *Essex Court Records*, IV, 38.

8 This was the sentence pronounced on Mrs. Anne Hibbins of Boston in February 1641, as noted in Robert Keayne's 'Notes on John Cotton's Sermons' (manuscript document, Massachusetts Historical Society, Boston) and published in John Demos, *Remarkable Providences: The American Culture, 1600–1760* (New York, 1972), pp. 238–9.

9 *Records of the Town of Easthampton, Long Island, Suffolk County, N.Y.*, 5 vols. (Sag Harbor, N.Y., 1887–1904, 1: 33–4.

10 *Records of the Court of Trials of the Town of Warwick, Rhode Island, 1659–1674* (Providence, 1922), 15; *Essex Court Records*, I, 31; *Records of the Town of Easthampton*, 1: 104–5; Anne Bradstreet, 'Meditations, Divine and Moral', in *The Works of Anne Bradstreet*, ed. Jeannine Hensley (Cambridge, Mass., 1967), p. 278.

11 *Essex County Records*, II, 277.

12 Testimony of Thomas Bennett, at the examination of Mercy Disborough (Fairfield, Conn., 1692), MS document, the Willys Papers, Connecticut State Library, Hartford, W-33.

13 *Records of the Suffolk County Court, 1671–1680*, in Colonial Society of Massachusetts, *Publications*, 30: 891.

14 *Essex Court Records*, IV, 105.

15 Ibid.

16 Ibid., II, 353.

17 Ibid., II, 241.

18 Ibid., I, 275.

19 Ibid., V, 310.

20 Ibid., IV, 162.

21 Ibid., I, 59.

22 Ibid., IV, 343.

23 Ibid., VIII, 272.

24 Ibid., VI, 257.

25 Manuscript deposition by Samuel Reynolds, in Files Papers of the Quarterly Courts of Middlesex County, Massachusetts (Middlesex County Courthouse, East Cambridge, Mass.), folder 42.

26 The term is used advisedly, and with some intentional reference to the psychodynamic pattern associated (by clinical theorists) with narcissism. This is not the place to open such a large subject – what psychoanalysts now understand as the 'psychology of the self' – but it does seem to *fit* the Puritans in interesting ways. That fit is explored at some length in John Putnam Demos, *Entertaining Satan: Witchcraft and the Culture of Early New England* (New

York, 1982). Chs 4, 6. (The preeminent theorist of 'self-psychology' is the late Heinz Kohut. See especially his *The Psychology of the Self* (New York, 1971) and *The Restoration of the Self* (New York, 1977).)

27 *Essex Court Records*, VI, 329; ibid., V, 63; Increase Mather, *Solemn Advice to Young Men* (Boston, 1695), p. 23.

28 *The Works of Anne Bradstreet*, p. 202.

29 *The Autobiography of Thomas Shepard*, ed. Nehemiah Davis (Boston, 1832), p. 26.

30 *The Letters of John Davenport*, ed. Isabel M. Calder (New Haven, Conn., 1937), p. 66 and passim; Mather, *Solemn Advice*, pp. 36–7; Commonplace Book of Joseph Green, as printed in Demos, *Remarkable Providences*, p. 356; Hoadly, *Records of the Colony of New Haven*, 2: 268; Mather, *Solemn Advice*, pp. 9, 14.

31 *The Autobiography of Thomas Shepard*, p. 38; John Winthrop, 'Experiencia', in *The Winthrop Papers*, 1: 201; *The Diary of Michael Wigglesworth, 1653–1657*, ed. Edmund Morgan (New York, 1946), p. 20; William Adams, 'His Book', in Massachusetts Historical Society, *Collections*, 4th series, 1: 19.

32 See, for the formulation of all this, Piers and Singer, *Shame and Guilt*.

33 I refer here to the work of Perry Miller and his colleagues.

34 John Winthrop, 'A Model of Christian Charity', as printed in George M. Waller, ed., *Puritanism in Early America*, 2nd edn (Lexington, Mass., 1973), p. 5.

35 Winthrop, 'Experiencia', in *The Winthrop Papers*, 1: 196.

36 Quoted in Kenneth Silverman, *The Life and Times of Cotton Mather* (New York, 1984), p. 226.

37 See John Demos, *A Little Commonwealth: Family Life in Plymouth Colony* (New York, 1970), Ch. 9.

38 Catharine Maria Sedgwick, *Home* (Boston, 1854).

39 Quoted in David Rothman, *The Discovery of the Asylum: Social Order and Disorder in the New Republic* (Boston, 1971), p. 85.

40 A good example of this plot line can be found in the immensely popular story by T.S. Arthur, *Ten Nights in a Bar-Room*, first published in 1854, and recently reprinted, Donald A. Koch, ed. (Cambridge, Mass., 1964).

41 Charles G. Finney, *Lectures on Revivals of Religion* (repr., Cambridge, Mass., 1960), pp. 226–7. A sermon by Cotton Mather, more than a century earlier, stands in direct contrast. The minister, Mather declared to his congregation, 'is above the reach of hurt from your malignity. . . . Do, go on still in your trespasses. You will wound yourselves, and none but yourselves, wretches. Silly children, the minister of God is above all your silly attempts. You can't hurt *him!*'

42 On the matter of shame and guilt in nineteenth-century revivalism, I wish to acknowledge a profound debt to the work of E. Anthony Rotundo. In particular, I am grateful for permission to consult Dr. Rotundo's two (as yet) unpublished essays, 'The Conflict Between Active and Passive in Charles G. Finney's Revival Imagery', and 'Charles G. Finney's Upstate Revivals: Some Emotional Themes and Social Implications'.

Chapter 5

Social Control of 'Negative' Emotions: The Case of Regret

Janet Landman

Western culture generally treats emotion with wary distrust, especially when contrasting emotion with reason in the usual black-and-white way. Therefore, it should not be surprising to find that there are elaborate emotion norms that are passed on from generation to generation, and from the ruling classes to the ruled. A good part of the socialization of children and other societal subordinates involves transmitting civilization's command to regulate the expression, and to some extent, the experience of emotion. The usual generic methods of socialization, which also undoubtedly serve as methods of socialization of emotion, include differential reinforcement, imitation of and identification with models, communication of expectancies, and direct instruction ('Big boys don't cry', etc.) (Saarni, 1993).

The emotion rules differ significantly depending on one's assigned place in the social order. Many cultures, for instance, hold characteristic assumptions about what emotional experiences and expression are appropriate for males versus females. There is evidence that already by the second month of life American parents are treating their infant girls and boys very differently with respect to their emotional experience (Brody and Hall, 1993). The emotional range of males is often constricted by their socialization; and although females are permitted a greater emotional range, certain emotions – notably, anger – are for them culturally censured (Brody and Hall, 1993). Furthermore, Western culture tends to place females in a classic double-bind, expecting them to be emotional but devaluing them for it.

Nearly all of the psychological research on the social control of emotion has so far focused on gender socialization, and on parents as the wielders of social control. This is fine. It needs to be done. I approve. But another part of me agrees with writer Charles Baxter's response to a related issue: 'Confronted with this mode, I feel like an Old Leftist. I want to say: the Bosses are happy when . . . you think the source of your trouble is your family' (1994: 79). What interests me even more than family-based social control is the social control that seems to come out of nowhere but really comes out of everywhere – and reaches everywhere. What to call this 'power [that] operates in covert ways by producing particular kinds of subjectivity' (Cvetkovich, 1992: 9)? Old Leftist or not, I don't think I want to call it the Bosses. We could call it a Mindset, a Worldview, Ideology, The Prevailing Wisdom, The American Way. Let's call it a worldview.

As I see it, a worldview is a set of fundamental values, beliefs, and sentiments about reality which are often tacit and taken for granted. It works like a giant lens through which we characteristically and implicitly perceive, organize, remember, interpret, and emotionally experience the raw material of life. A worldview is difficult to put your finger on, and therefore difficult to analyze. Yet it is every bit as real and as powerful as parents. It is not acquired through magic; undoubtedly worldviews develop and are sustained through many of the same methods entailed in other forms of socialization. A common worldview is one thing that makes a culture a culture rather than a set of unconnected individuals. Individuals in the same culture share a worldview; they can't help it – it comes with the territory. Yet worldviews are not monolithic; individuals in the same culture differ in the extent to which they have internalized every detail of a prevailing worldview.[1]

Understanding the ramifications of a worldview in emotional experience can aid in understanding the persistence of and the difficulty of modifying certain patterns of thought and emotion. Forty years ago Allport (1954/1993) outlined a revealing connection between some prejudice and what I have called worldviews. He posited that certain prejudices are learned 'by subsidiation', rather than by direct teaching, modeling, conformity with social norms, and so forth. To the extent that specific prejudices support or are subsidiary to what Allport refers to variously as the individual's 'philosophy of life' (p. 318), 'whole complex value-pattern[s]' (p. 317), 'broad values (scheme[s one] lives by)' (p. 317), and 'dominant frames of value' (p. 317), they will be especially easy to learn and difficult to unlearn. Conversely, to the extent that specific prejudices *contradict* one's dominant philosophy of life, they will be especially difficult to learn and easy to unlearn.

For example, the individual whose worldview centers on the belief in a just world (that people deserve what they get and get what they deserve) will find it easier to acquire specific prejudices – say, dislike of the poor or others to whom the world has not been kind – because these particular prejudices are readily subsidiated to that particular worldview. Prejudices that are developed by subsidiation to one's worldview will be especially resistant to change.

The principle applies as well to the relationship between emotion and worldview. In fact, it may apply even better to emotion than to the more cognitive aspects of prejudice, for 'an emotion is an integrated response which could therefore be said to commit agents to particular values with greater success than could be achieved by the mere rational comprehension of such values' (Armon-Jones, 1986: 81). To the extent that specific emotions are subsidiary to one's worldview, they too may be especially readily learned and especially difficult to modify. Conversely, to the extent that specific emotions fail to fit with one's worldview, they may be particularly difficult to sustain. Worldviews are not merely peripheral opinions, but become central to who we are. It is possible that one's worldview can be so central to who one is that he or she is unable to generate or assimilate emotions that clash with the worldview.

What I want to explore here is the significant role that worldview plays in emotional life. Specifically, I will focus on how the experience of regret is shaped by the worldview within which it is set. Given the paucity of cross-cultural evidence, I will mostly have to stick with the worldview that I know best, the one that prevails in my culture, twentieth-century *fin-de-siècle* America. It is, I will argue, a worldview in which the emotion of regret is rendered all but socially impermissible.

What are we talking about when we talk about regret? The short answer is that regret is a more or less painful state of feeling sorry for mistakes, misfortunes, limitations, losses, or moral transgressions -- prototypically, one's own, but also those of others. A longer answer is that -- depending on which philosopher, psychologist, statistician, or economist is doing the defining -- regret is (among other things) an emotion (Kahneman and Tversky, 1982), not an emotion (Bedford, 1956–57; Hampshire, 1960), a cold calculation of payoffs (Savage, 1951), a tepid judgment (Taylor, 1985), or a hot self-protective defense mechanism (Festinger, 1957). These disagreements are not, I think, merely semantic. They demonstrate Harré's insight that whenever we define an emotion, 'our answers are, as likely as not, liable to reflect the unexamined commonsense assumptions of our local culture' (1986: 4). In this chapter I will examine some of the unexamined commonsense assumptions underpinning my own culture's attitude toward regret.

Depending in part on how it is defined, regret evokes strong feelings pro and con. But mostly con. A swimming partner of mine insists that regret is wrong -- in fact, a sin -- because all things come together for the good to those who believe. In direct contrast, others view regret as a moral emotion, particularly insofar as it entails a sense of responsibility for moral wrongs (Rorty, 1980). In classic decision theory, whenever we have carefully made the best choice possible at the time, regret for a bad outcome is considered an irrational self-indulgence (Dawes, personal communication, 24 July 1991). Some modern economists disagree, arguing that it is eminently rational to include regret in decision making, since it is one of the inescapable consequences of our decisions (Hershey and Baron, 1987). Then, too, regret can be honored for offering people a consoling sense of temporal continuity and integrity -- as the playwright Eugene Ionesco observed about his own regret at growing old: 'The only thing I have left is my regret at being someone else. It is this regret that makes me continue to be myself' (1940–41/1971: 30). So again there are two sides to this story, a side that rejects regret as wrong, irrational and dysfunctional versus a side that prizes regret as essential to rational decision making and to moral and personal integrity.

Regret repels us and fascinates us. I would bet that Ford Motor

Company has been interviewed at least as often about the Edsel, its flop, as about the Mustang, its star. And although we might hesitate out of delicacy to query our own friends and family about their regrets, my burgeoning file of newspaper clippings on the regrets of public figures like Lee Atwater, Paul Newman, Sammy Davis, Jr, Tallulah Bankhead, B.B. King, Woody Allen and William Burroughs attests to the avid public interest in the topic.

What *is* it about regret? In part, regret shares the attraction of the coin toss, the lottery, and the horror genre. Journalists are not above pandering to this endless fascination with randomness and its role in causing intense regret. At seemingly every air crash, for example, reporters flock to the scene, nosing out the story of the passenger who at the very last minute switched onto (or off) the doomed flight. Perhaps reading accident and disaster stories lets us safely work out how it feels to happen to be in the wrong place at the wrong time. Regret, like horror books and films, may remain perennially fascinating because it allows us to play with forbidden terrors, and thereby master them. Which brings us back to the other side of our uneasy relationship with regret – rejection. Our powerful and conflicting feelings suggest that in this time and place regret, like sex in the Victorian era, may be something of a cultural taboo, something best not spoken of in polite company.

The cultural case against regret

If we as a society were asked to compose a portrait of regret, I imagine her (inevitably, I'm afraid, it would be a female) as a stringy-haired, boneless woman sunk in the dead arms of the past. We would paint her half-sitting half-lying in the shadows of a musty room empty of everything but cobwebs and ghosts – forever staring with glazed eyes out a window, forever straining to hear ancient footfalls, which, were they to appear, would be muffled by the drone of her mutterings about what might have been.

Although this is admittedly a straw person, I think that the cultural disapproval of regret implicit in the portrait is very real. It is the easiest thing in the world to say what is bad about regret. After all, regret is usually self-serving, phony, depressing and paralyzing. Isn't it?

Take RSVPs. Aren't we right to doubt the sincerity of some of those 'I-regret-that-I-cannot-attend's? Probably. Yet, nontruthful RSVPs are often not much more than a fairly innocuous mode of social etiquette. Other sorts of phony regret, however, can prove more serious and more insidious.

Let me explain. A number of philosophers of emotion, including Robert Solomon, view remorse and regret as closely related emotions. Therefore, when Solomon criticizes remorse as 'an extremely self-indulgent emotion, more concerned with its esteem in its own eyes than with the victims of its folly' (1976: 351), we can assume that he intends the accusation to apply as well to regret. Likewise, because guilt and regret are first cousins, surely some of the hazards of guilt acidly articulated by Lillian Hellman also apply to regret: 'I am suspicious of [it] in myself and in other people: it is usually a way of not thinking, or of announcing one's own fine sensibilities the better to be rid of them fast' (1976: 42–3). In 1991 Los Angeles Police Chief Daryl Gates gave the appearance of expressing regret the better to deny it when he said after the videotaped beating by his officers of motorist Rodney King: 'We regret what took place. I hope he gets his life straightened out. Perhaps this will be the vehicle to move him down the road to a good life instead of the life he's been involved in for such a long time' ('No comment', 1991: 10).

Some of the suspicion with which we regard regret probably comes from getting a whiff of the kind of self-serving and socially undermining uses detailed by Solomon and Hellman. Regret primarily concerned with bolstering one's esteem in one's own eyes or the eyes of others is simply phony. Phony regret, what E.M. Forster (1924) [1952: 51] refers to in *A Passage to India* as 'the canny substitute', is perhaps the most obviously bad form that it can take.

Even genuine regret, though, could prove self-serving. Some people may express regret for the purpose of eliciting sympathy from others. Alternatively, forever rehashing regret may serve the 'sick' purpose of perpetual self-punishment. Some individuals may have, as Freeman and DeWolf put it, 'been taught – and deeply believe – that if you err, especially if you err seriously, then you should and must suffer forever' (1989: 85). Emily Dickinson's (1983) assessment of remorse – that it is 'the Adequate of Hell' – applies also to excessive forms of regret: continuous, unending regret could fulfill a need for eternal suffering pretty well.

For others, obsessive regret, though painful, may serve the purpose of relieving existential anxiety that proves even more painful. Such persons may 'prefer' constantly replaying their regrets to acknowledging lack of omniscience or omnipotence. One can imagine a parent whose child is killed on her walk home from school by a hit-and-run driver constantly torturing himself with regrets about not having collected his child from school that day. Still, for this parent, experiencing obsessive regret may actually be less distressing than facing his utter helplessness to have saved his child from an essentially random event. Perhaps this is part of what is meant by writer Jonathan Baumbach's phrase 'the dim solace of regret' (1989: 36).

Beyond these possibly universal defects of regret, our disapproval of regret is in my view part of a larger cultural worldview that repudiates *emotion*. Of course, the bias against emotion is at least as old as ancient Greek civilization. In Plato's *Republic* (1952: 353–4) reason is the 'shepherd', and the passionate and desirous elements of the psyche are the 'dogs'. Like Plato, Aristotle (1935: 179) asserted that the irrational principle should be 'amenable and obedient' to the rational principle. Even 2000 years later, the view of emotion emerging from modern psychological research remains (so far) decidedly cognitive – as if embarrassed to concern itself with what is specifically emotional about emotion.

Clearly we are not the only culture whose distrust of emotion provides fertile ground upon which to breed distrust of regret. However, I suspect there are a number of quintessentially American sources for our discomfort. Our dread of regret may come from the same place as our dread of the limits of forward-looking pragmatism, can-do exteriority, and optimism.

Regret and the cultural allergy to the past

Interestingly enough, the word *regret* has refashioned itself over time. Formerly, the word emphasized losing someone or something dear, as in Shelley's 'that fair lady whom I regret'. That sense of *regret* is now all but archaic; we never hear the term used in this way in contemporary colloquial speech. The former meaning of *regret* has been largely taken over by nouns like *nostalgia*[2] and verbs like *miss* and *long for*. Shelley's 'that fair lady whom I *regret*' would today read 'that fine woman whom I *miss*'. Over time, the romantic, bittersweet connotation of *regret* seems to have drifted to a less romanticized, simply bitter emphasis on gaining something unpleasant. The modern sense of *regret* thus hauls a heavier load of pathology – an emotional tone and a stance that desires distance from an unkind past. It seems to me that part of our modern quarrel with regret concerns our quarrel with the past.

'History is bunk', declared Henry Ford. Although the statement has been widely misunderstood (apparently Ford was criticizing the dry-as-dust mode of *teaching* history [Chapman, 1992]), I suspect that many Americans agree with the (misunderstood) sentiment. Former President Bush, for one. When Mr Bush was asked after his 1988 election whether he had any second thoughts about the negative campaigning conducted by his handlers, his reply was a dismissive 'That's history' (Brinkley, 1990). Our dislike of the past is betrayed by other cultural clichés as well: as in 'That was then; this is now' and 'You can't turn back the clock'.

The past we like best is the sentimental past of nostalgia, a cozy place furnished with golden oldies, retro watches and vintage vehicles. Otherwise, we keep our distance. For to reflect on the real, unsentimentalized past is, among other things, to open oneself up to regret. In shunning the past, we shun regret.

The dominant theory of economic choice links arms with our cultural norms here, telling us that if we want to make rational decisions, we have to ignore the past. Standard decision theory commands us to base decisions only on our best guesses of future consequences. From this perspective, it is therefore imperative to ignore 'sunk cost' – which is what you have already paid into an enterprise in the past (Dawes, 1988; DeSousa, 1987). A classic example of the sunk-cost problem is the case of the money-eating car.

Imagine that three years ago you bought a new car that has clocked more time in the shop than on the road. Now it has just been diagnosed as needing a costly ring job. Some people (but not adherents of standard decision theory) engage in this line of thinking: 'I should get rid of this lemon now and not put another cent into it. But I could have gotten rid of it before and didn't. Now I've sunk too much money into this thing to get rid of it, so I'll have the expensive ring job done.'

According to standard decision theory, this kind of thinking – sometimes referred to as 'knee-deep-in-the-Big-Muddy' thinking (Staw, 1976), because of the sense of being hopelessly mired in a swamp – is irrational. It is irrational because it factors in the past. Decision theorist Robyn Dawes explains: 'Rational decisions are based on an assessment of future possibilities and probabilities. The past is relevant only insofar as it provides information about possible and probable futures' (1988: 31). As philosopher Ronald DeSousa explains, because 'the past is held in common between all possible futures, past investment could not possibly be relevant to the present decision' (1987: 221).

Past-bashing is at least as old as the Enlightenment. Ideologically, the Enlightenment was much occupied with attacking blind faith in and blind obedience to the past, as represented by custom, tradition and religious dogma. The past was even mathematically discredited – by probability theory – which challenged, among other things, the 'gambler's fallacy', that nearly irresistible belief that if, say, a fair coin has turned up heads on ten previous tosses, there just has to be a greater than 50 percent chance of its turning up tails on the eleventh toss. As probability theory points out, no matter now long the string of heads, the best guess of the future probability of the coin's turning up tails is still 50 percent, because the future outcome is entirely independent of past outcomes. 'Coins have no memories', quips Dawes (1988: 28).

The economic analysis clearly has merit when it comes to coins, cars – and extravagant space-based weapons programs. It is arguable, however, whether it applies across the board. For decisions whether to leave or remain with a particular job or partner, for instance, it is not so clear that we should always discount personal history. Since Einstein, we can no longer view time as an incidental, inferior adjunct to reality. Time is at the very heart of reality (Dewey, 1960). And the past is at the very heart of the present.

What was formerly a healthy political, social and mathematical critique seems to have calcified into yet another form of dogma. Many of us recite the catechism. History is bunk. And regret is bunk. Rush Limbaugh says so when he attacks critics of Columbus and proponents of affirmative action:

> I don't give a hoot that he [Columbus] gave some Indians a disease that they didn't have immunity against. We can't change that, we're here. (1992: 45).

> Of course, the argument [in favour of affirmative action] is that black Americans are different from all other groups. They didn't choose to come here; their ancestors were brought here in slave ships. I won't deny that, nor will I defend this country's original sin. But there's nothing we can do about it now. It may not be fair, but we can't change the past. (1992: 208).

Apparently this no-regrets attitude is part of what appeals to some of those twenty million people who in 1994 tuned into Limbaugh's show at least once a week (Edsall, 1994). Lillian Hellman identified the integral connection between the American attitudes toward the past and toward regret when she observed: 'We are a people who do not want to keep much of the past in our heads. It is considered unhealthy in America to remember mistakes, neurotic to think about them, psychotic to dwell upon them' (1976: 152).

But wait. What about Santayana's famous warning about those who cannot remember the past condemning themselves to repeat it? Of course, we are not so foolish as to reject wholesale the idea of looking backward. Even standard decision theory accommodates part of Santayana's idea: the theory acknowledges the rationality of taking account of the past – to the extent that it provides information about future consequences (Dawes, 1988: 31). If there is something obviously *pragmatic* to be gained in regretting a mistake, then we may, however reluctantly, give it a go. Otherwise, regret seems a useless failure of American pragmatism. We Americans can't help but agree with Harry Truman when he said: 'Never, never waste a minute on regret. It's a waste of time' (Romaker, 1991). Or with Katherine Mansfield when she wrote: 'Regret is an appalling waste of energy; you can't build on it; it's only good for wallowing in' (*Correct Quotes*, 1990–91).

Regret and unresolvable conflicts of interest

A related reason for the cultural allergy to regret is an ideal of (a myth of) unconflicted rationality. If conflicting values and needs are resolvable by the application of cost-benefit analysis, then regret is simply uncalled for. If the national budget cannot support both Stealth bombers and student loans, then the rational would-be student cheerfully goes off to the hamburger stand or the barracks rather than to college. If one's health insurance provider judges hospitalization to be unnecessarily costly, then the rational patient picks up her pallet and limps quietly home to mend. In contrast, regret sometimes entails an admission that the available choices are inadequate or incommensurable; that taking one road in that yellow wood means abandoning another heartbreakingly lovely road; that the most cogent calculation of costs and benefits fails to touch human wish, need, and desire.

Regret and interiority

The typically American quality of *can-do exteriority* provides another basis for our quarrel with regret. To entertain regrets is putatively to be thinking things over and feeling bad. But the American way is to be up and *doing*. Regret arouses our discomfort with interiority. Perhaps in part because it is so difficult for us to believe that acts of consciousness can also be great acts, we (many of us) scorn 'navel gazing' and speak mockingly of 'wallowing' in regret.

Regret and paralysis

I once noticed on a bookrack in a doughnut shop a book that on its cover urged: 'Set yourself free from the paralysis of analysis' (Price, 1979). Although this particular advice was based on a stance so intensely anti-intellectual that it is easy to dismiss, it carries a germ of truth – excessive regret *can* provoke excessive hesitation (Hogarth, 1986; Janis and Mann, 1977). It may even replace action. As writer Nora Ephron put it in an essay 'Revision and Life', 'you can spend so much time thinking about how to switch things around that the main event has passed you by' (1986: 7). The helpless passivity of some forms of regret appalls can-do, pragmatic-minded Americans. Besides, there seems to be an irresistible assumption that regret is *in principle* incompatible with action – as if to regret is to choose the fate of Lot's wife, turned to a pillar of salt (and thus immobilized) because she looked back.

Regret and helplessness

Existential discomfort with the limits of personal control may also help explain some of our denial of regret. In an effort to retain a (however beleaguered) sense of being masters of our fate, we suppress regret as irrational. Just as we in scientifically savvy late-twentieth-century America reject fate and destiny as explanatory concepts, we emphatically avoid thinking about those misfortunes that seem unforeseeable, unpredictable, or uncontrollable. When events throw in our face the fact of our helplessness before chance – say, a child was at the last minute switched onto that plane that crashed – we squirm out from under the knowledge.

Regret and agency

Perversely enough, the opposite is also true. It is not only when regrettable occurrences lie outside our control, but also when they lie squarely within our control, that regret chafes. Typically, in fact, regret entails an admission of poor judgment or some other type of personal deficiency (what philosopher Amelie Rorty has called 'character regret'). No one enjoys admitting that his or her judgment, let alone character, is poor. Nor do we welcome what Rorty calls 'agent regret', regret for having contributed to a state of affairs that one judges harmful or undesirable (Rorty, 1980). If we're backed into a corner, we'll grab at just about anything, including the agentless passive voice ('All right, mistakes were made') to try to blur in our own minds and those of others our agency for regrettable outcomes.

Regret and failure

Most of us, moreover, find deeply implausible Elizabeth Bishop's (1980) sadly ironic assertion: 'It's evident the art of losing's not too hard to master', which touches one of America's worst fears – the dread of being a loser. We deny regret in part to deny that we are now or have ever been losers. In the reigning economic models of decision, rational human beings function as calculating machines, deciding their preferences based on the calculation of utilities and probabilities. Insofar as regret implies that we have chosen on grounds other than our own best interests, it is viewed as a violation of rationality. Even people whose choices, though made rationally, have turned out badly fit the unforgivingly elastic cultural category of 'losers'. But losers, with their sticky regrets gumming up the works, not only fail to fit the calculating-machine model, they also fail to fit in the marketplace. We know this and we quake.

Regret and pessimism

Finally, in a militantly *optimistic* society founded on deeply progressivist assumptions, regret (along with similarly 'negative' emotions such as guilt, remorse and sadness) seems a destructive lapse of optimism. This claim has recently begun to receive a bit of empirical attention. Markus and Kitayama (1994), have found, for instance, that Americans report experiencing positive self-relevant emotions much more often than negative ones, but the Japanese show no such difference. Wierzbicka (1994) reports that the strong American norm emphasizing positive emotions and deemphasizing negative ones is absent in Polish culture. Posner et al. (1994) find that negative affect is discouraged in US children but not in Chinese (PRC) children. And, again, Sommers observed that, compared with Chinese young adults, Americans 'mainly value the pleasantly felt emotions, those commonly considered as positive, and devalue the negative emotions' (1994: 332). The one study I am aware of that has specifically explored regret across cultures also observed a pattern consistent with my hypothesis. Psychologist Ilaria Grazzani (1994) found that North Americans (Canadians) were far less likely than Italians to report feeling regret in a situation involving a mistake in joint plans involving another person.

A solid body of psychological research conducted within American culture has demonstrated that those who accurately acknowledge personal shortcomings, unpleasant realities, and lack of personal control tend to show a host of unpleasant emotions, particularly depression (e.g., Alloy and Abramson, 1979; Alloy and Abramson, 1982; Lewinsohn et al., 1980). As Markus and Kitayama put it: 'Good copers [in America] are those who maintain positive illusions about themselves' (1994: 121) among other things.

There is also some evidence directly supporting the intuition that *regret* possesses unpleasant emotional concomitants, including depression and general psychological distress (Gudjonsson, 1984; Weisman and Worden, 1976–77; Lecci et al., 1994). Regret *can be* a mood-dampener – at least in the short run.

But for some reason, we find it hard to think of regret as 'merely' depressing. We tend to think of it more like we think of crack cocaine, as ruinous because inexorably done to excess. In *Brothers and Keepers*, John Edgar Wideman expresses well the torment of regret that is excessively intense and excessively preoccupying:

> We got a sniff of the big time and if we didn't take our shot wouldn't be nobody to blame but ourselves. And that's heavy. You might live another day, you might live another hundred years but long as you live you have to carry that idea round in your head. You had your shot but you didn't take it. You punked out. Now how a person spozed to live with something like that grinning in his face every day? You hear old people crying the blues about how they could have been this or done that if they only had the chance. How you gon pass that by? Better to die than have to look at yourself every day and say, Yeah. I blew. Yeah, I let it get away. (1984: 152)

If jeremiads about the shot you did not take and the chance you let get away grin in your face *every day*, to the point that *death* seems preferable, then regret has become excessive and therefore depressive. In this case, what folk singer Tom Paxton said about nostalgia applies equally well to regret: 'It's all right to look back – as long as you don't stare'.

Another way that regret might be done to excess is by attaching too much importance to the regretted matter. But of course, there is no objective way to rank the relative importance of regrets. Someone may consider it highly important to, in Wideman's words, have failed to take his or her shot at the big time; someone else may consider this particular sort of regret rather trivial. Importance depends to a large extent on deeply personal and subjective matters such as one's values and needs, and what one cares about (Frankfurt, 1988; Frijda, 1986; Klinger, 1975). One person's mountain of regret is another person's molehill. Still, we need not drown in a sea of relativism here; certain matters do lend themselves to consensus – for example, that regret over neglecting a friend who then commits suicide *should* receive greater weight than regret over having eaten the all-pork hot dog instead of the tofu dog. Unfortunately, such distinctions tend to slip more easily out of focus than a blanket condemnation of regret. Like the elderly deposed Prince in Lampedusa's (1960) novel *The Leopard*, we tend to consider all regret a 'perilous slope', a treacherous emotion bound to drag us down to the Slough of Despond.

For all these reasons – regret's sometime admission of randomness, of incommensurable conflicts, and of personal deficiency or blame; its failure of future-oriented optimism, pragmatism, exteriority, and action – regret is un-American. Regret deeply insults our American worldview, which in the language of literary genres is essentially comic (as opposed to romantic, ironic, or tragic) in its Horatio-Alger progressivist assumptions and its preference for action as the solution to life's problems.

The underrated benefits of regret

Hellman is right, I think, that in my time and place regret is viewed as at minimum unhealthy, or worse, neurotic (self-destructively painful), and even irrational. The very titles of both of the other books that I am aware of that are substantially devoted to regret convey a clearly disparaging attitude toward their subject: *Woulda/Coulda/Shoulda: Overcoming Regrets, Mistakes, and Missed Opportunities* (Freeman and DeWolf, 1989) and *Overcoming Regret: Lessons from the Roads Not Taken* (Klein and Gotti, 1992). Both titles promise to tell us how to 'overcome' regret – as if it were a mortal enemy or a fatal disease. In an ethos like ours, the wisdom of the regret-averse adage 'No use crying over spilled milk' seems almost beyond question.

Moreover, as I have acknowledged, regret *is* sometimes a force for no good. Forever recycling, replaying and rehashing mistakes, losses and misfortunes *can* be an exercise in lamentation or immobility. Still, these are arguably less grievous sins than the sins of the other extreme – the complete absence of regret characteristic of overly well-defended optimists, fatalists, rationalizers and sociopaths.

But regret need not fall at either extreme. Moreover, regret properly handled serves a number of beneficial purposes. This claim rests, however, on ideas that are distinctly at variance with the American worldview – starting with respect for the continuity of the past, for regret as a temporally extended and dynamic process, and for emotion as a normal, not irrational, foundation of humanity.

Regret and the dynamics of history

Pragmatist that she was, Lady Macbeth mercilessly berated her husband for his guilty meditations following their multiple murders, insisting: 'What's done is done'. There is, of course, literal truth to the idea of past-as-done-deed. There *is* a sense in which the past is unchangeable and irremediable. Franklin Roosevelt did have a crippling case of polio as an adult. The *Challenger* did explode in 1986. I did once buy a used car not knowing that it needed a costly repair. These things cannot be undone. However, there are other senses in which what's done is not done, the past is neither unchangeable nor irremediable – and anything but dead.

Faulkner highlighted this nonliteral side of the truth when he wrote that 'The past isn't dead. It's not even past' (1929/1987). This is something that Freud knew well too. A foundation stone of psychoanalytic thought is the idea that 'in mental life nothing which has once been formed can perish' (Freud, 1930: 16). In this statement Freud was originally referring to psychic and somatic impulses of an erotic or aggressive nature – the Freudian 'instincts'. However, it applies as well to mental life more broadly – thoughts, feelings, wishes, memories, images and so on. Unwanted psychic matters can be muffled by defensive maneuvers or transformed into salutary forms of expression; but in either case the original processes are not eradicated. Not only do defensive maneuvers fail to eliminate negative emotion, they may amplify it. According to Freud, 'the instinct-presentation develops in a more unchecked and luxuriant fashion if it is withdrawn by repression from conscious influence. It ramifies like a fungus, so to speak, in the dark and takes on extreme forms of expression' (1915: 107). It follows that some excessive forms of regret may actually result from attempts to repress it. In the dark, regret too grows like a fungus, taking on extreme forms.

At the very least then, psychoanalysis as a theory of the human condition tells us that the past ramifies in the present. Psychologically, the truth is: that was then, *this* is then. At the same time, as a method of treatment, psychoanalysis demonstrates the human ability to reformulate the meaning of the past to at least some degree. While it is an implacable fact that FDR suffered polio, that the *Challenger* exploded, and that I bought a car that needed an expensive repair, the significance of the facts can be changed. Insofar as new understanding reveals ways of undoing, redoing, or repairing past misfortunes and missteps, regret becomes no more irrevocable or irremediable than the past.

Furthermore, due to the human capacity for development, regret need not be a static experience like staring or wallowing or inertia. Regret soundly practiced will be a dynamic, changing *process*. Following sociologist Fred Davis's (1979) analysis of nostalgia, I conceive of the dynamics of regret as a chain of events, roughly analogous to the processes of sensation, perception, and cognition. There is first of all the immediate, relatively unreflected 'primary' experience: as in that almost sensory pang I felt when my mechanic showed me the black, metal-flaked transmission fluid from my newly purchased used car. Next, there is a second-order or 'reflexive' process of registering the meaning of that experience – as when I consciously acknowledged my regret to myself: 'Yikes. I think I made a big mistake'. If lingered with long enough, third-order or 'analyzed' regret will develop, which entails further psychological processing of the experience – say, questioning whether one ought to reflect further on it, or suppress it, or engage in 'emotion management', problem-solving, or action to undo, re-do, or repair the regretted matter. In the case of my car-buying mistake, this phase entailed thoughts like: 'I am so sorry I bought that car without having a mechanic look it over. Now I'll have the transmission rebuilt, and learn a good lesson from this mistake for the future.' It is particularly at the higher-order levels that the constructive effects of regret are realized.

But in my culture, the 'rules of prognosis' (Averill, 1986: 107) for regret mandate a truncated time course – preferably no more than a few minutes, it seems. These norms, I would argue, produce a couple of unfortunate and related consequences. First, the practice of prematurely bypassing regret and other negative emotions could result in emotional underdevelopment. In addition, this practice whittles down the possibility of realizing the higher-order benefits of regret, which require not only a longer period of lingering with regret but also a more sympathetic view of emotion than typically obtains in this culture.

Regret and the rationality of emotion

Despite strong cultural presumptions to the contrary, emotion in general and regret in particular are not necessarily irrational. Emotions have enormous epistemological, moral and utilitarian value. Not to assert that reason ought to be ruled by emotion, I argue that reason is necessary but not sufficient to responsible human conduct. Reason and emotion typically play interdependent roles in human conduct. Furthermore, they should.

Due to the strength of the prevailing wisdom, it is not necessary to belabor cases in which emotion threatens rationality. Instead, let us consider an example in which the *suppression* of emotion threatens rationality. Consider a thoroughly 'rational man', Rudolph Hoess.[3] As commandant of Auschwitz for three years, Hoess supervised the murders of 2.9 million individuals. Even while awaiting execution for his crimes, Hoess defended these killings as just and rational.

Oh, he had his reservations: he regretted those acts in which he or his subordinates had experienced or displayed emotion as they carried out the 'Final Solution'. By Hoess's lights, all emotion, whether benevolent or malevolent, was to be suppressed. Thus Hoess condemned both those Nazis who had sadistically enjoyed brutalizing their victims, and also those who had been unable to control their 'good nature and kind heart' (cf. Dawes, 1981: 2). Here is Hoess describing his own difficulty in properly 'stifl[ing] all softer emotions'. It seems his task that day was to force into the gas chamber two small children and their mother. But the children were so absorbed in a game they were playing that their mother could not get their attention. Hoess writes:

> The imploring look in the eyes of the mother, who certainly knew what was happening, is something I shall never forget. The people in the gas chamber were becoming restive and I had to act. Everyone was looking at me; I nodded to the junior non-commissioned officer on duty and he picked up the screaming, struggling children in his arms and carried them into the gas chamber accompanied by their mother, who was weeping in the most heart-rending fashion. My pain was so great that I longed to vanish from the scene; yet *I might not show the slightest trace of emotion.* (cf. Dawes, 1981: 1–2; emphasis added)

As Dawes points out, this chilling self-description of a rational man casts doubt on the assumption that, if only reason were to master emotion, rational acts and decisions would follow. One wishes that Hoess had permitted his emotional reaction to the weeping mother and screaming children to change his mind about what he should do. Instead, his decision to dissociate reason and emotion made him inhuman – monstrously inhuman.

Emotion is a potentially noble part of what it is to be human. To aspire to be something we are not – whether disembodied angels, ideally rational agents, or calculating machines – is futile and counterproductive. We are not warranted in demanding as a condition of rationality the suppression of emotion. In fact, we do well to question the judgment of anyone capable of living life unemotionally.

I want to be very clear here. This defense of emotion should not be taken as an anti-intellectual venture in romanticizing emotion. Clearly, the uninhibited exercise of unreflected gut emotion can make for faulty decisions and acts. We've known that at least since Plato. But the suppression of emotion, and its dissociation from reflective thought, can make for equally faulty acts and decisions. Like cognition, emotion is not nefarious but neutral, and potentially a great force for rationality and human decency. The form of reasoned-emotion or felt-thought that we call regret is likewise neutral, with every bit as much constructive as destructive potential.

Within a worldview open to the possibility of dynamic and constructive experiences of emotion and the past, the benefits of regret begin to come clear: they are utilitarian and ethical in nature; they can occur before or after a decision or event; and they can accrue to the individual or society. Forewarning, instruction, correction, and stimulus to action, integrity, and community are some of the benefits of regret I want to consider here in some detail.

Forewarning, instruction, and correction   Before making a decision of any consequence, it need not be morbid or paralyzing to think through exactly how regrettable the available options would be if they went awry (Janis and Mann, 1977). When I was buying that used car, it would have been smart to have vividly imagined ahead of time my possible regret, and to have allowed that anticipated regret to move me to wait to have the car checked out by a mechanic. The writer Ronald Cassill imagined the biblical Noah using anticipatory regret for the collective good as well: 'I'd like to find and join a chorus of people who say this stuff is rain and it's going to keep coming, so let's build an ark' (1970: 71). Anticipatory regret ('I may regret it if I buy this car mechanic-unseen'; 'we may regret it if we don't build an ark') thus has the power to inform both individual and collective decisions.

Recent research directly supports this claim. In a series of five studies, René Richard (1994) found that anticipated regret increased people's safe-sex behaviors independently of their attitudes, social norms, and perceived self-efficacy. When the salience of future emotional responses, including regret, was increased, subjects' safe-sex behaviors increased as well. Furthermore, retrospective regret, although arguably more tormenting than anticipatory regret, can prove just as useful – in a number of ways.

As mentioned earlier, emotion, like ideation, has informational value. It tells us what we care about, or what we should care about (Oatley, 1992). This function of emotion is less obvious than it appears to those who assume that feelings are transparent to ourselves. Actually, the ability to recognize what we are feeling does not spring forth fullblown in the neonate, but undoubtedly develops over the lifetime. Knowing with immediacy what we feel and what we want is an achievement, not an inevitability.

That achievement is all well and good in the case of positive emotion. But those of us who live and breathe in an emphatically optimistic worldview seem prepared to do almost anything to avoid engagement with negative emotion. This reflex is, however, misguided, for negative emotion has a number of potential cognitive benefits.

First, negative emotion has at least as much informational value as positive emotion. By the early 1990s, most scholars studying emotion had come to appreciate the possible evolutionary usefulness of negative emotion in serving a number of important functions, including survival (e.g., Plutchik, 1980). Once again, negative emotion tells us what we care about, or what we should care about. It can make us think twice in order to avoid doing something we will later regret, or should later regret. Imagine someone who finds himself brooding regretfully about a rather trivial mistake: 'When Pat and I were talking, how *could* I have said "Glad to see the President out on the hastings again" when of course I meant "out on the hustings?!"' This individual could discover from the intensity of his regret how very much he cares about making a good impression with Pat. More serious is the example of Hoess, who could have discovered something vitally important had he treated his negative emotion at the door of the gas chamber with due respect. The pain of negative emotion performs the useful function of pointing to our concerns.

Second, negative emotion can improve the quality of thinking. What? you ask. Doesn't negative emotion, even more than positive emotion, *impair* thinking? Isn't depression, for example, notoriously disruptive of clear thinking? It appears that this piece of conventional wisdom may hold for clinical levels of negative emotions but not for subclinical levels. Compared with nondepressed people (nonclinically) depressed individuals actually often show greater accuracy of judgment about themselves and their actual lack of control over outcomes; the shorthand label of 'depressive realism' describes this counterintuitive phenomenon (Alloy and Abramson, 1979, 1982; Lewinsohn et al., 1980). Also, compared with people in positive moods, people in (nonclinically) depressed moods have been found to show more attentive, more careful, more analytic processing of information (Fiedler, 1988; Schwarz, 1990; Schwarz et al., 1991; Sinclair, 1988). For example, depressed subjects have been observed to be influenced only by strong but not by weak persuasive arguments, while elated subjects were equally influenced by strong and weak arguments (Schwarz et al., 1991). It is as yet not known precisely how sadness produces these salutary effects on thought; it may be because it signals that all is not well that it induces more watchful, more accurate and more cogent thinking.

By extension, it may be that other negative emotions – including regret – stimulate high-quality thinking. For instance, anticipatory regret can enhance decision making by putting on the decision brakes long enough to identify and appraise relevant alternative courses of action and their probable consequences. And of course retrospective regrets 'can be useful when they involve task-relevant information feedback (e.g., how or when to effectively adjust purposive action)' (Lecci et al., 1994: 733). Even though I couldn't undo it, I was better off regretting the unfortunate car purchase. 'It is the non-localized hurts that do the damage', writes poet William Stafford (1970). Conversely, it is the localized hurts that stand a chance of being cured. In fact, lingering a bit with my regret over that mistake did push me to clarify exactly what I might have done differently – that is, not only consult *Consumer Reports* (which I had done), but *also* a good mechanic. The regretter has a better chance than the non-regretter to avoid making the same mistake in the future. Like pain, regret provides information, telling us that something is wrong. To blunt the pain of regret is to forgo valuable information.

Negative emotions entail a third class of potential cognitive benefit. Regret, for instance, has the potential to make for a better future through its association with counterfactual thought, or thought about states contrary to fact. Imagining how things might have been different, for example, has the potential to free one from the thrall of the past to entertain a new future. As Johnson and Sherman put it:

> the risk of experiencing powerful negative feelings generated by counterfactual thinking ('If only I hadn't made that thoughtless remark . . . ') may be worthwhile if thinking of how things might have been otherwise generates possible alternatives that can be drawn upon if similar situations should arise again. (1990: 516)

Imagination is a rebel. In its role as an internal negation of the given, regret stimulates counterfactual thoughts capable of forging a substantial bridge between a regretted past and a better future.

Mobilization to action   Theory and empirical evidence support the claim that imagined action can lead to real action. Sherman et al. (1981) asked people to imagine and explain (and either to explicitly state their expectations or not) a specific hypothetical success or failure on an upcoming anagram task. Those who imagined themselves succeeding in the task and explicitly stated that expectation actually ended up outperforming those who imagined themselves failing. Johnson and Sherman (1990) review a number of other studies in which having people imagining themselves doing something that they can control actually helps make it happen – including reducing the relapse rate of alcoholics and improving the performance of athletes. It also appears that, insofar as regret and other emotion provokes people to imagine a better future, it has the potential to create that better future (Landman et al., 1995).

Not only does emotion have epistemological value then; it has motivational value. In fact the words *emotion* and *motivation* share the same root, the Latin *movere*, to move (Gordon, 1990). We tend to think of *negative* emotions as particularly paralyzing, but in principle they have as much motivational potential as positive emotions. Like physical pain, regret, for instance, may not only tell us that something is wrong, but it can also move us to do something about it. As Lecci et al. put it, focusing thought and emotion 'on a past unattained goal may facilitate decision making, planning, and responsiveness to future similar goals, thereby increasing the likelihood of subsequent goal attainment' (1994: 733). Consequently, it is not wise to dismiss regret over past mistakes as futile and paralyzing.

Those working from a clinical perspective have long stressed the importance of acknowledging and integrating negative feelings and experiences – to the end of unfixating those who were fixated, and unparalyzing those who were paralyzed (sometimes literally, as in conversion disorders). Facing my regret over my car-buying mistake did mobilize me to have a mechanic do a thorough check before I bought my second used Corolla (some years later, after the one with the rebuilt transmission eventually died).

It works that way at the *social* level as well. As the story goes, when the rains began, it would have behooved Noah's friends to use their anticipation of an upcoming disaster to move them to join him in building a whole fleet of arks; their failure to anticipate later regret helped bring it about. Clear-eyed scrutiny of the past, and of the status quo, that residuum of the past, can function as a springboard for collective betterment.

The task of establishing the social benefits of regret is complicated by the cultural dissociation of social and individual, public and private, political and personal. In my culture, emotion is commonly viewed as a purely internal state, a purely private, individual matter – something that takes place in the head and the heart of a solitary individual. But in an analysis of the genre of autobiography, J.N. Morris begins to explain exactly how something so private and interior as reflective self-consciousness might impel action to change the world:

> [T]he great progress made during this century and the last toward more equitable social arrangements and institutions has been achieved partly as a result of the accession to consciousness of literally millions of humble persons of a sense of their worth and dignity as individuals. . . . Almost paradoxically, *the high value that men came to put on private experiences, freeing them from impotent, accepting anonymity, encouraged them to combine with others to force the social recognition of their new conceptions of themselves on the public world.* Self-consciousness is, that is to say, a subversive force. (1966: 219; emphasis added)

Morris's insight appears paradoxical in a worldview that strictly dichotomizes the individual and the social, rather than viewing them as interdependent and interembedded. But his is a deep truth about the human condition: that the richer and stronger one's inner life and sense of self, the richer and stronger one's potential engagement with other people and the world more generally. Social and political consciousness often depend on the cultivation of a certain degree of self-consciousness. And when such reflection is united with its associated emotion, the combination – or what I, again, like to call felt-thought – is especially potent as the 'raw material of social change' (Cvetkovich, 1992: 10).

One way that regret and other forms of felt-thought can advance social change is by functioning as experimental action or prologue to open resistance. Political scientist James C. Scott argues that hidden forms of resistance – including emotions – constitute '*most* of the political struggle of subordinate groups' (1990: 202; emphasis added). Certain processes leading to the fall of communism in 1989 in Poland are illustrative. As Scott points out, this revolution emerged after years in which the populace lived a double life, a public one and a private one; behind this revolution 'lay a long prehistory, one comprising songs, popular poetry, jokes, street wisdom, political satire, not to mention a popular memory of the heroes, martyrs, and villains of earlier popular protest' (Scott, 1990: 212). Private practices – including the private experience of regret for the status quo – can serve to sustain disse through periods when open, public protest is severely repressed.

At times, negative emotions point directly to politically or socially sub-versive concerns. Scott articulates the idea vividly:

> For most bondsmen through history, whether untouchables, slaves, serfs, captives, minorities held in contempt, the trick to survival . . . has been to swallow ones bile, choke back one's rage. (1990: 37)

That bile, rage and other negative emotions serve 'as evidence of trans-gressive impulses, . . . as signs of dissatisfaction with oppressive social structures', and 'as the germ of desire for social transformation' (Cvetkovich, 1992: 7). Women's consciousness-raising groups of the 1970s illustrate the point; they often served not only as a forum for crystallizing previously private feelings (of sadness, regret, frustration and anger, for example), but also as an impetus to collective action and social change.

If self-consciousness is subversive and imagination is subversive, regret is a subversive emotion. This may explain why authors (especially those familiar with totalitarian suppression) frequently take as their theme the strategic deployment of denial of the past, denial of 'negative' emotion, and denial of regret as modes of social control. In the world of *Erewhon*, Samuel Butler's (1872) utopian novel, someone whose spouse dies, who comes down with an illness, or who suffers a financial loss is in trouble with the law. In Erewhon, loss, misfortune and mistakes are literally criminal offenses. As a consequence, people refuse to talk or even think about such things. Similarly, Andrei Platonov, whose work of the 1920s to the 1950s was suppressed by his government (the USSR), wrote in *The Foundation Pit* (1975) about a 'fictional' state in which regret is a political crime, and in which the state mandates 'the duty of joy'. Citizens of this state are constantly exhorted to compete to display the most patriotic – defined as the sunniest – moods. To keep at bay regret for the deficiencies of the system, the government purposely keeps workers' bodies and minds so occupied with physical labor and radio propaganda that they have no time for an interior life, with its potential to engender politically subversive states like regret. In their taboos on regret, Butler's and Platonov's fictional societies are not too different from the society – mine – that Hellman described, where, again, it is 'considered unhealthy . . . to remember mistakes, neurotic to think about them, psychotic to dwell upon them'.

Though swallowing negative emotions may sometimes be necessary for survival in oppressive environments, individuals able to sustain their emotional reactions are in a better position to imagine alternative worlds and take action to free themselves from an oppressive status quo. Armon-Jones has written well about the social functions of emotion, arguing that emotions are 'constituted and prescribed in such a way as to sustain and endorse cultural systems of belief and value' (1986: 57) – or to use my word, worldviews. To the extent that regret is a potential vehicle for social change, it is in the interests of the powers that would be threatened by social change to repudiate regret.

So what about all that intuition and research that tells us that facing a negative reality acts not as a stimulant but as a depressant? No doubt it is right, particularly in circumstances in which that negative reality is difficult or impossible to change. In such circumstances 'regretful realism' could prove demoralizing and immobilizing (though it could also prove beneficial in ways I will detail later). It is equally important to recognize, though, that optimistically putting the best face on things can *also* drain motivation to change things that can and should be changed. To blunt the pain of regret is to blunt the will to take action to correct what has gone wrong.

Inducement to integrity   Regret has instructional uses other than those of a pragmatic sort. In the novel *Under the Volcano* (1947), Malcolm Lowry wrote that 'conscience had been given to man to regret [the past] *only* in so far as that might change the future' (emphasis added). I agree that regret can change the future for the better, but I take issue with Lowry's 'only'. The nonutilitarian – indeed, counterutilitarian – nature of certain regrets is here expressed with eloquent irony by Benjamin DeMott:

> If we pause too long in contemplation of a former self, studying some lesson or other, we run the risk of forgetting how to take our present selves for granted. And down that road there's a risk of starting to treat life as a mystery instead of the way smart people treat it – as a set of done and undone errands. (1982: 14)

Selfhood, personal development, or character is one aspect of life better taken as a mystery than as a set of done and undone errands. Despite the popularity of metaphors like 'finding oneself', it is not useful in my view to construe self-development as a process of uncovering one's inner self – as if the self were the secret heart at the center of an artichoke. Personal development is, I think, better understood as a historical, sociocultural and dialectical process in which (to paraphrase Kierkegaard [1967]) one lives forward and understands backward.[4] Or as I once overheard an unknown graduate student say, the self is a verb.

A good part of the mystery of selfhood lies in its lack of inevitability. Selfhood is an achievement, not a given, and we are bound to make mistakes and suffer misfortunes along the way. In Faulkner's *The Sound and the Fury* (1929) the narrator's father goes so far as to declare that a 'man is the sum of his misfortunes'. This is going too far in a morose direction, but it is half true. There is wisdom in recognizing that we are the sum of our mistakes plus our clever decisions, our misfortunes plus our fortunes.

Moreover, there is wisdom in recognizing that we are who we are partly by virtue of who we are *not*. Limitations and missed boats define a human being as much as positive acts do. Philosopher José Ortega y Gasset understood this:

> Everything that we are in a positive sense is by virtue of some limitation. And this being limited, this being crippled, is what is called destiny, life. That which is missing in life, that which oppresses us, forms the fabric of life and maintains us within it. (cited in Lukács, 1968/1985: xxviii)

Even if we never made a mistake and never lost something wonderful, we are inevitably limited. We cannot simultaneously take all the roads in that yellow wood. Or as Anne Morrow Lindbergh wrote, fashioning a different metaphor: 'One cannot collect all the beautiful shells on the beach'. Anyone who refuses to dissociate feeling and thinking will inevitably experience some regret – for a past that was unlovely, for a self that was stillborn or never conceived, for those beautiful shells that had to be left behind on the shore. Regret is, among other things, the possible pressing its hopeful claims upon the actual.

It's no good telling us that because the possible is unreal, it is irrational to open the door to its knocking. That lecture is too literal-minded for the human psyche. We *will* entertain the possible, especially when the actual fails to satisfy our hopes and dreams. Furthermore, it is a *good* thing that the human mind is not limited by what actually exists. If we are even halfway alive, we will care enough about the particularities of experience to bother to imagine alternatives to reality. To do so is what makes us take a dream and turn it into a reality.

Similarly, it's no good telling us that 'smart people' find regret counter-productive. It is a condition of personal integrity to own one's regret, rather than circumvent it. Genuine regret signifies that we have standards of excellence, decency, morality, or ethics we still care about. In addition, remaining in connection with our better values through regret can further the purpose of moving us to behave differently if a similar situation should present itself in the future.

True, regret is not particularly pleasant. But as one of the moral sentiments, it is essential to a full humanity, as philosopher John Rawls wrote: 'the moral feelings are admittedly unpleasant, in some extended sense of unpleasant, but there is no way for us to avoid a liability to them without disfiguring ourselves' (1963: 141). Like other moral sentiments then, regret functions (in Willard Gaylin's [1979: 82] phrase) as 'a guardian of our goodness'.

In earlier sections of this chapter, I spoke to the potential destructiveness of regret that substitutes for action, and the potential constructiveness of regret that mobilizes action. This consideration of the role of regret in personal integrity suggests a need to qualify a culturally based overcelebration of action perhaps conveyed earlier. As moral philosopher Michael Stocker (1987) points out, not *all* judgment worth having is judgment worth applying directly to action. Even more to the point, regret that does not lead to action is not always worthless or harmful. Once someone told Hume that a particular sorrow of his was fruitless; Hume replied, 'Very true, and for that very reason I am sorry' (cited in Parfit, 1984: 169). Hume's answer applies also to those who blindly dismiss regret over unchangeable matters as useless.

Someone who regrets having neglected a distressed friend who then committed suicide is experiencing regret that is fruitless, in the sense that there is no action that can be taken that will bring back the friend. Yet it is not fruitless, in that it connects the regretful individual with values that are part of what makes him or her humane. Some things are ultimately more important than emotional equilibrium. Insofar as one does not -- despite the personal pain it brings -- repudiate the value of being attentive to and patient with those in distress, one is undoubtedly a better person. It is better to have (right) values, even at the cost of the pain of regret, than to be devoid of them. And it is a 'peculiarly utilitarian or pragmatic crassness which asks only where the action is and gets its answer by looking only at the bottom line', writes Stocker (1987: 106). Radical behaviorism and American action-orientation notwithstanding, human beings are more than the sum of their acts. John Stuart Mill wrote: 'It really is of importance, not only what men do, but also what manner of men they are that do it' (1859: 295). The words are over a hundred years old, and in today's America the sentiment seems almost quaint. But the presence versus absence of something so interior as regret can make all the difference in otherwise identical situations -- whether it is spilling red wine on someone's new white couch, or reflecting on a self-destroying friend.

Safeguard of community Finally, regret (and its cousins such as guilt, shame and remorse) has moral benefits for society. At least three great thinkers of the past converged on this insight. In *The Theory of Moral Sentiments*, Adam Smith (1759/1793) described remorse as the safeguard of society. Spinoza (1952) argued that, although moral emotions like regret are not pleasant, such emotions are 'productive of more profit than disadvantage', precisely because of this social function. Because human beings will inevitably sin, 'it is better that they should sin in this way. For if men . . . were ashamed of nothing, . . . *by what bonds could they be united or constrained?*' Insofar as it embodies a sense of community, regret is a trustee of decency for societies as well as individuals.

In *Civilization and its Discontents*, Freud advanced a similar idea: 'the price of progress in civilization is paid in forfeiting happiness through the heightening of the sense of guilt' (Freud, 1930/1961: 123). The argument here is that the moral feeling of guilt – and, by extension, other moral sentiments, including regret – effectively serve to protect community. Better than the strongest police force, guilt and regret and the other moral sentiments protect civilization from disintegration threatened by the aggressive, erotic and other imperialistic drives of its members – albeit at some considerable emotional cost to the individual. The hope is that the emotional cost to the individual is outweighed by the benefits to the group, and that each individual gains by sharing in those benefits.

Summary and conclusions

There is no doubt about it: regret has a bad reputation in my time and place. The principles of social control and of subsidiation (Allport, 1954/ 1993) help explain why. First, when the prevailing wisdom repeats over and over that history is bunk, negative emotions are counterproductive, and regret is insane, it serves the functions of social control. It does so by suppressing the crystallization of discontent and keeping individuals isolated in their separate emotional cells, where they are unlikely to band together to change a regrettable status quo. Second, regret simply does not conform to the American worldview. At first glance it appears to be anything but an optimistic, action-oriented, pragmatic, future-looking affair; therefore, it is difficult to subsidiate to a worldview that at first glance embodies all those things.

Christopher Lasch, however, articulates the fallacy in this brand of resistance to regret: although 'superficially progressive and optimistic, [it] proves on closer analysis to embody the despair of a society that cannot face the future' (1979: 26). Much as it takes an awful lot of work to keep a beach ball submerged in a pool, forever trying to suppress regret drains us of energy for other things. This may be what Shakespeare meant when he had Albany in *King Lear* say: 'Where I could not be honest, I never yet was valiant'. Facing individual and collective regrets, rather than expending valuable energy forcibly suppressing them, stands to enhance integrity, thus strengthening the individual and the society for future action.

Contrary to the conventional wisdom, regret need not necessarily be a futile waste of time, a failure of rationality, or a 'perilous slope' to paralyzing depression. Regret is better viewed as a form of practical reason appropriately informed by emotion. Regret can blaze a path leading onward and upward. Like anything human, it can go wrong. It all depends on what you do with it.

Earlier in this chapter, regret was personified as a paralyzed woman sunk in the dead arms of the past. By now, another picture has, I hope, emerged. In this new portrait regret is a person of will and integrity standing firm on a base of her own personal past and standing hand-in-hand with others – thereby strong enough to resist being sucked into the tempting but deadly Memory Hole. She may meet life with an ironic expectation of ambiguity, ambivalence, limits, mistakes, and good and bad luck; yet she is not emotionally disengaged. She may be a touch romantic, in that she believes in putting up a heroic struggle against personal and social evils; yet she renounces the romantic demand for absolute answers to the human predicament. This figure of regret is someone whose free and active inner life and engagement with the world fortify her to encounter life with courage.

To reclaim the authority of regret is not to recommend a hair-shirt approach to life. It is merely to acknowledge reality: misfortune, loss, limits and mistakes are an inevitable part of life. So is death. Perhaps it all boils down to death – for if we weren't mortal, we could always re-do the unhappy things in some future. In the face of these realities, regret is inevitable, rational and a moral imperative.

Clearly, emotion is socially constituted. Emotion is also socially constituting. The kind of populace that we are depends to a significant extent on the kinds of emotions that we esteem and value. In one of his *New Yorker* stories, humorist Garrison Keillor once referred to the present as '*a regretless time*' in which:

> your own best friend might spill a glass of red wine on your new white sofa and immediately *explain* it – no spontaneous shame and embarrassment, just 'Oh, I've always had poor motor skills,' or 'You distracted me with your comment about Bolivia.' People walked in and stole your shoes, they trashed your lawn and bullied your children and blasted the neighborhood with powerful tape machines at 4.00 A.M. . . . and if you confronted them about these actions they told you about a particularly upsetting life-experience they'd gone through recently, such as condemnation, that caused them to do it. (1983: 36)

But seriously. It is conceivable that each time regret is dismissed as useless or irrational, the capacity for genuine regret – and therefore decent community – may be weakened, until at last it atrophies. A regret-free world, lacking the potential benefits of regret like those I have just discussed, would no doubt prove a barbarous place to live – even for the Bosses.

Notes

Portions of this chapter were excerpted from my book, *Regret: The Persistence of the Possible*. Copyright © 1993 by Janet Landman. Reprinted by permission of Oxford University Press, Inc.

1 Readers who are interested in reading more about the concept of worldview (specifically the romantic, comic, tragic and ironic worldviews) and its relationship with emotion may want to consult Landman (1995).

2 This contrast was highlighted for me by Fred Davis's book *Yearning for Yesterday: A Sociology of Nostalgia*. There he defines nostalgia as 'a positively toned evocation of a lived past in the context of some negative feeling toward present or impending circumstances . . . that subjective state which harbors the . . . belief that THINGS WERE BETTER (MORE BEAUTIFUL) (HEALTHIER) (HAPPIER) (MORE CIVILIZED) (MORE EXCITING) THEN THAN NOW' (1979: 18; capitals in original).

3 Rudolph Hoess (Höss) was the commandant at Auschwitz; he should not be confused

with Rudolf Hess, Deputy Party Leader of the National Socialist Party under Hitler; he died in the late-eighties at Spandau Prison.

4 Kierkegaard (1967) said this: 'It is perfectly true, as philosophers say, that life must be understood backwards. But they forget the other proposition, that it must be lived forwards.'

References

Alloy, L.B. and Abramson, L.Y. (1979) 'Judgment of contingency in depressed and non-depressed students: Sadder but wiser?', *Journal of Experimental Psychology: General*, 108: 441–85.

Alloy, L.B. and Abramson, L.Y. (1982) 'Learned helplessness, depression, and the illusion of control', *Journal of Personality and Social Psychology*, 42: 1114–26.

Allport, G.W. (1954/1993) *The Nature of Prejudice*. New York: Addison-Wesley.

Aristotle (1935) *Nicomachean Ethics*. (P. Wheelwright, ed. and trans.). New York: Odyssey Press.

Armon-Jones, C. (1986) 'The social functions of emotions', in R. Harré (ed.), *The Social Construction of Emotions*. Oxford: Basil Blackwell.

Averill, J.R. (1986) 'Acquisition of emotions in adulthood', in R. Harré (ed.), *The Social Construction of Emotions*. Oxford: Basil Blackwell. pp. 98–118.

Baumbach, J. (1989) 'Amorality on the rampage [Review of *The Hungry Girls*]', *New York Times Book Review*, 5 February: 36.

Baxter, C. (1994) 'Dysfunctional narratives, or "Mistakes were made"', *Ploughshares*, Fall: 67–82.

Bedford, E. (1956–57) 'Emotions', *Proceedings of the Aristotelian Society*. London: Harrison and Sons.

Bishop, E. (1980) *The Complete Poems 1927–1979*. New York: Farra, Straus and Giroux.

Brinkley, A. (1990) 'A savage and demeaning ritual [Review of *Pledging allegiance*]', *New York Times Book Review*, 14 October: 1, 28–9.

Butler, S. (1872) [1927] *Erewhon: or Over the Range*. New York: The Modern Library.

Brody, L.R. and Hall, J.A. (1993) 'Gender and emotion', in M. Lewis and J.M. Haviland (eds), *Handbook of Emotion*. New York: Guilford. pp. 447–60.

Cassill, R.V. (1970) 'Symposium: The writer's situation', in T. Solotaroff (ed.), *New American Review*, Number 9.

Chapman, R.L. (1992) Letters. *New York Times Book Review*, 23 February: 34.

Cvetkovich, Ann (1992) *Mixed Feelings: Feminism, Mass Culture and Victorian Sensationalism*. New Brunswick, NJ: Rutgers University Press.

Davis, F. (1979) *Yearning for Yesterday: A Sociology of Nostalgia*. New York: The Free Press.

Dawes, R.M. (1981) 'Plato vs. Russell: Hoess and the relevance of cognitive psychology', Tech. Report No. 43. Institute for Social Science Research, Eugene, Ore.: The University of Oregon.

Dawes, R.M. (1988) *Rational Choice in an Uncertain World*. San Diego: Harcourt Brace Jovanovich.

DeMott, B. (1982) 'Funny, wise and true [Review of *Dinner at the Homesick Restaurant*]', *New York Times Book Review*, 14 March: 1, 14.

DeSousa, R. (1987) *The Rationality of Emotions*. Cambridge, MA: MIT Press.

Dewey, J. (1960) 'Time and individuality', in R. Bernstein (ed.), *On Experience, Nature, and Freedom*. Indianapolis, Ind.: Bobbs-Merrill. pp. 224–43.

Dickinson, E. (1983) *The Poems of Emily Dickinson* (T.H. Johnson, Ed.). Cambridge, Mass.: Belknap Press of Harvard University Press.

Edsall, T.B. (1994) 'America's sweetheart [Review of three books by Rush Limbaugh]', *New York Review of Books*, 6 October: 6–10.

Ephron, N. (1986) 'Revision and life: Take it from the top – again', *New York Times Book Review*, 2 November: 7.

Faulkner, W. (1929) [1987] *The Sound and the Fury*. New York: Vintage.

Festinger, L. (1957) *A Theory of Cognitive Dissonance*. Evanston, Ill.: Row, Peterson.
Fiedler, K. (1988) 'Emotional mood, cognitive style, and behavior regulation', in K. Fiedler and J. Forgas (eds), *Affect, Cognition, and Social Behavior*. Toronto: Hogrefe International. pp. 100–19.
Forster, E.M. (1924) *A Passage to India*. New York: Harvest.
Frankfurt, H.G. (1988) *The Importance of What We Care About: Philosophical Essays*. New York: Cambridge University Press.
Freeman, A. and DeWolf, R. (1989) *Woulda/Coulda/Shoulda: Overcoming Regrets, Mistakes, and Missed Opportunities*. New York: HarperPerennial.
Freud, S. (1915) 'Repression', in *General Psychological Theory: Papers on Metapsychology*. New York: Collier.
Freud, S. (1930) *Civilization and its Discontents* (J. Strachey, trans.). New York: Norton, 1961.
Frijda, N.H. (1986) *The Emotions*. Cambridge: Cambridge University Press.
Gaylin, W. (1979) 'On feeling guilty', *Atlantic*, January: 78–82.
Gordon, S.L. (1990) 'Social structural effects on emotion', in T.D. Kemper (ed.), *Research Agendas in the Sociology of Emotions*. Albany: State University of New York Press. pp. 145–79.
Grazzani, I. (1994, July) 'Emotions and errors in joint plans: A cross-cultural comparison between Italy and Canada'. Presented at the Conference of the International Society for Research on Emotion, Cambridge, England.
Gudjonsson, G.H. (1984) 'Attribution of blame for criminal acts and its relationship with personality', *Personality and Individual Differences*, 5 (1): 53–8.
Hampshire, S. (1960) *Thought and Action*. New York: Viking.
Harré, R. (ed.) (1986) *The Social Construction of Emotions*. Oxford: Basil Blackwell.
Hellman, L. (1976) *Scoundrel Time*. Boston: Little, Brown.
Hershey, J.C. and Baron, J. (1987) 'Clinical reasoning and cognitive processes', *Medical Decision Making*, 7: 203–11.
Hogarth, R. (1986) *Judgment and Choice* (2nd edn). New York: Wiley.
Ionesco, E. (1940–41/1971) *Present Past, Past Present: A Personal Memoir* (H.R. Lane, trans.). New York: Grove.
Janis, I.L. and Mann, L. (1977) 'Anticipatory regret', in *Decision Making: A Psychological Analysis of Conflict, Choice, and Commitment*. New York: Free Press. pp. 219–42.
Johnson, M.K. and Sherman, S.J. (1990) 'Constructing and reconstructing the past and the future in the present', in E.T. Higgins and R.M. Sorrentino (eds), *Handbook of Motivation and Cognition: Foundations of Social Behavior* (Vol. 2). New York: Guilford. pp. 482–526.
Kahneman, D. and Tversky, A. (1982) 'The simulation heuristic', in D. Kahneman, P. Slovic and A. Tversky (eds), *Judgment under Uncertainty: Heuristics and Biases*. New York: Cambridge University Press.
Keillor, G. (1983) 'The current crisis in remorse', *The New Yorker*, 11 July: 36–7.
Kierkegaard, S. (1967) *The Journals of Soren Kierkegaard: A Selection*. (A. Dru, ed. and trans.). Bloomington, IN: Indiana University Press.
Klein, C. and Gotti, R. (1992) *Overcoming Regret: Lessons from the Roads not Taken*. New York: Bantam.
Klinger, E. (1975) 'The consequences of commitment to and disengagement from incentives', *Psychological Review*, 82: 1–25.
Lampedusa, G. di. (1960) *The Leopard* (A. Colquhoun, trans.). New York: Pantheon.
Landman, J. (1993) *Regret: The Persistence of the Possible*. New York: Oxford University Press.
Landman, J. (1995) 'Through a glass darkly: Worldviews, counterfactual thought, and emotion', in N. Roese and J.M. Olson (eds), *What Might have Been: the Social Psychology of Counterfactual Thinking*. Hillsdale, NJ: Erlbaum. pp. 233–58.
Landman, J., Vandewater, E., Stewart, A.J. and Malley, J. (1995) 'Missed opportunities: Psychological ramifications of counterfactual thought in midlife women', *Journal of Adult Development*, 2: 87–97.
Lasch, C. (1979) *The Culture of Narcissism*. New York: Warner.

Lecci, L., Okun, M.A. and Karoly, P. (1994) 'Life regrets and current goals as predictors of psychological adjustment', *Journal of Personality and Social Psychology*, 66: 731–41.

Lewinsohn, P.M., Mischel, W., Chaplin, W. and Barton, R. (1980) 'Social competence and depression: The role of illusory self-perceptions', *Journal of Abnormal Psychology*, 89: 203–12.

Limbaugh, R. (1992) *The Way Things Ought to Be*. New York: Pocket Books.

Lowry, M. (1947/1971) *Under the Volcano*. New York: New American Library.

Lukács, J. (1968/1985) *Historical Consciousness or The Remembered Past*. New York: Schocken.

Mansfield, K. In *Correct Quotes*. Software. Novato, Calif.: WordStar International, Inc., 1990–91.

Markus, H.R. and Kitayama, S. (1994) 'The cultural construction of self and emotion: Implications for social behavior', in S. Kitayama and H.R. Markus (eds), *Emotion and Culture: Empirical Studies of Mutual Influence*. Washington, DC: American Psychological Association. pp. 89–130.

Mill, J.S. (1859) *On Liberty*. Great Books of the Western World. Vol. 43. Chicago: Encyclopaedia Britannica, 1952. pp. 267–323.

Morris, J.N. (1966) *Versions of the Self*. New York: Basic Books.

No comment (1991) *The Progressive*, May: 10.

Oatley, K. (1992) *Best Laid Schemes: The Psychology of Emotions*. New York: Cambridge University Press.

Parfit, D. (1984) *Reasons and Persons*. New York: Clarendon/Oxford.

Plato (1952) *The Republic*. Great Books of the Western World. R.M. Hutchins, ed. Chicago: Encyclopaedia Britannica.

Platonov, A. (1975) *The Foundation Pit* (M. Ginsburg, trans.). New York: E.P. Dutton.

Plutchik, R. (1980) *Emotion: A Psychoevolutionary Synthesis*. New York: Harper & Row.

Posner, M.I., Rothbart, M.K. and Harman, C. (1994) 'Cognitive science's contributions to culture and emotion', in S. Kitayama and H.R. Markus (eds), *Emotion and Culture: Empirical Studies of Mutual Influence*. Washington, DC: American Psychological Association. pp. 197–216.

Price, E. (1979) *Leave your Self Alone*. Grand Rapids, Mich.: Zondervan.

Rawls, J. (1963) 'The sense of justice', in H. Morris (ed.), *Guilt and Shame*. Basic Problems in Philosophy Series. Belmont, CA: Wadsworth, 1971.

Richard, René (1994) *Regret is What you Get: The Impact of Anticipated Feelings and Emotions on Human Behavior*. Published doctoral dissertation. University of Amsterdam.

Romaker, R.S. (1991) 'U-M memories', *Ann Arbor News*, 2 December: C1.

Rorty, A.O. (ed.) (1980) *Explaining Emotions*. Berkeley: University of California Press.

Saarni, C. (1993) 'Socialization of emotion', in M. Lewis and J.M. Haviland (eds), *Handbook of Emotion*. New York: Guilford. pp. 447–60.

Savage, L.J. (1951) 'The theory of statistical decision', *Journal of the American Statistical Association*, 46: 55–67.

Schwarz, N. (1990) 'Feelings as information: Informational and motivational functions of affective states', in E.T. Higgins and R.M. Sorrentino (eds), *Handbook of Motivation and Cognition: Foundations of Social Behavior*, Vol. 2. New York: Guilford. pp. 527–61.

Schwarz, N., Bless, H. and Bohner, G. (1991) 'Mood and persuasion: Affective states influence the processing of persuasive communications', in M.P. Zanna (ed.), *Advances in Experimental Social Psychology*, Vol. 24. San Diego, Calif.: Academic Press. pp. 161–99.

Sinclair, R.C. (1988) 'Mood, categorization breadth, and performance appraisal: The effects of order of information acquisition and affective state on halo, accuracy, information retrieval, and evaluations', *Organizational Behavior and Human Decision Processes*, 42: 22–46.

Scott, James C. (1990) *Domination and the Arts of Resistance: Hidden Transcripts*. New Haven, Conn.: Yale University Press.

Sherman, S.J., Skov, R.B., Hervitz, E.F. and Stock, C.B. (1981) 'The effects of explaining hypothetical future events: From possibility to probability to actuality and beyond', *Journal of Experimental Social Psychology*, 17: 142–58.

Smith, A. (1759/1793) *The Theory of Moral Sentiments* (Vol. I). Basil: J.J. Tourneisen.
Solomon, R. (1976) *The Passions: The Myth and Nature of Human Emotion.* Notre Dame, Ind.: University of Notre Dame Press.
Sommers, S. (1994) 'Adults evaluating their emotions: A cross-cultural perspective', in C.Z. Malatesta and C.E. Izard (eds), *Emotion in Adult Development.* Beverly Hills, Calif.: Sage. pp. 319–38.
Spinoza, B. (1952) *Ethics,* in R.M. Hutchins (ed.), Great Books of the Western World (Vol. 31). Chicago: Encyclopaedia Britannica.
Stafford, W. (1970) *Allegiances.* New York: Harper & Row.
Staw, B.M. (1976) 'Knee-deep in the big muddy: A study of escalating commitment to a chosen course of action', *Organizational Behavior and Human Performance,* 16: 27–44.
Stocker, M. (1987) 'Moral conflicts: What they are and what they show', *Pacific Philosophical Quarterly,* 68: 104–23.
Taylor, G. (1985) *Pride, Shame and Guilt: Emotions of Self-assessment.* New York: Clarendon, Oxford University Press.
Weisman, A.D. and Worden, J.W. (1976–77) 'The existential plight in cancer: Significance of the first 100 days', *International Journal of Psychiatry in Medicine,* 7 (10): 1–15.
Wideman, J.E. (1984) *Brothers and Keepers.* New York: Holt, Rinehart & Winston.
Wierzbicka, A. (1994) 'Emotion, language, and cultural scripts', in S. Kitayama and H.R. Markus (eds), *Emotion and Culture: Empirical Studies of Mutual Influence.* Washington, DC: American Psychological Association. pp. 133–96.

Vignette 3

Keats and Embarrassment

Christopher Ricks

Let me set down three propositions. First, that embarrassment is very important in life. Second, that one of the things for which we value art is that it helps us to deal with embarrassment, not by abolishing or ignoring it, but by recognizing, refining, and putting it to good human purposes; art, in its unique combination of the private and the public, offers us a unique kind of human relationship freed from the possibility, which is incident to other human relationships, of embarrassment that clogs, paralyses, or coarsens. Third, that Keats as a man and a poet was especially sensitive to, and morally intelligent about, embarrassment; that the particular direction of his insight and human concern here is to insist upon raising the matter of embarrassability (whereas some other writings and people furnish a different kind of principled relief for us, by means of the cool tactful pretence that the possibility of embarrassment does not arise when we are in their company). I should stress that the attempt is not in any way to search out Keats's psyche, but to get closer to a sense of his special goodness as a man and as a poet; to see the shape of his imagination, and the truth of it. I am aware that this constitutes no kind of biography (but then there have recently been three invaluable biographies, by Walter Jackson Bate, Aileen Ward, and Robert Gittings), and that there are many essential kinds of literary criticism not at all attempted here. But without at all lessening the achievement of Keats' poetry there is a good deal in T.S. Eliot's bringing together Keats, Goethe, and Baudelaire as 'men who are important first because they are human prototypes of new experience, and only second because they are poets'.[1]

Embarrassment is subtle and pervasive in its constraints and pressures. We should value it for this, as does Erving Goffman, the best of the social psychologists who have pondered it:

> By showing embarrassment when he can be neither of two people, the individual leaves open the possibility that in the future he may effectively be either. His role in the current interaction may be sacrificed, and even the encounter itself, but he demonstrates that, while he cannot present a sustainable and coherent self on this occasion, he is at least disturbed by the fact and may prove worthy at another time. To this extent, embarrassment is not an irrational impulse breaking through socially prescribed behaviour but part of this orderly behaviour itself. Flusterings are an extreme example of that important class of acts which are usually quite spontaneous and yet no less required and obligatory than ones self-consciously performed.[2]

But we should be anxious about it too, since there is no power which society rightly possesses which society will not abuse. It can clearly be a good or a bad thing that, as Dr Johnson observed, 'No man finds in himself any inclination to attack or oppose him who confesses his superiority by blushing in his presence' (*The Rambler*, No. 159). Propitiation should be neither blankly spurned nor blankly propitiated. From a different viewpoint, the people who pass by on the other side do so because it is somehow embarrassing to get caught up in all that; the unfortunate who collapses in a railway station needs for his Good Samaritan someone undeterred by the small hot pricklings of embarrassment.

The hot flush of embarrassment rises with special frequency and centrality in the nineteenth century. In this it resembles that other hot flush, of indignation. Indignation is a feeling particularly strongly incited and thought about in nineteenth-century literature. This is partly because of what it is proper to feel about the cruelties visited upon children, as contrasted, say, with those visited upon King Lear; he is so much larger than we are that to feel indignation on his behalf would be to feel something too small, to open to condescension; pity and terror are for Lear, whereas for the Fanny of *Mansfield Park*, the David of the opening chapters of *David Copperfield*, and the Jane of the opening of *Jane Eyre*, indignation is the deep true feeling.

Indignation stands interestingly to embarrassment; the one hot flush drives out the other, as fire fire, so that a common way of staving off the embarrassment one would otherwise feel is by inciting oneself to indignation. One does this when mildly wronged (the wrong change, say) and obliged to attract attention in public to get things put right; the smallish indignation gets factitiously stoked because you will not be ridden by embarrassment once you are hotly riding indignation. Goffman brings together the two words, but not explicitly the two impulses: 'The expectations relevant to embarrassment are moral, then, but embarrassment does not arise from the breach of *any* moral expectation, for some infractions give rise to resolute moral indignation and no uneasiness at all.'[3] Likewise it was to be expected that a man like Keats, so honourably alive to embarrassment, should also have been notably moved to generous indignation: 'He was pleased with every thing that occurred in the ordinary mode of life, & a cloud never passed over his face, except of indignation at the wrongs of others. . . . But if any act of wrong or oppression, of fraud or falsehood, was the topic, he rose into sudden & animated indignation.'[4]

The word 'embarrassment' in our modern sense — 'constrained feeling or manner arising from bashfulness or timidity' — found itself called for at the end of the eighteenth century (the *OED* gives 1774, Burke). As for the adjective 'embarrassed' in our sense, apart from dubious instances in 1683 and 1761 (dubious in that they may mostly represent perplexed and confused rather than constrained and bashful), the first instance comes from the writer whom one would have suspected of having need for it: Sterne. 'As much embarrassed as . . . the lady could be herself' (*A

Sentimental Journey, 1768). By the end of the nineteenth century it had become an ordinary handle to take hold of the bundle, as when Henry James entitled a volume of stories *Embarrassments* (1896).[5] The point is not, of course, that nobody previously blushed, but that blushing and embarrassment came to be thought of as crucial to a great many social and moral matters. In 1839 Thomas H. Burgess published his rich and various book on *The Physiology or Mechanism of Blushing; Illustrative of the Influence of Mental Emotion on the Capillary Circulation; With a General View of the Sympathies, and the Organic Relations of those Structures with which they seem to be Connected*.

Podsnap is, after all, a very nineteenth-century figure:

> The question about everything was, would it bring a blush into the cheek of the young person? And the inconvenience of the young person was, that, according to Mr. Podsnap, she seemed always liable to burst into blushes when there was no need at all. There appeared to be no line of demarcation between the young person's excessive innocence, and another person's guiltiest knowledge. (*Our Mutual Friend*, Ch. 11)

Yet Podsnap, though an ass, is no fool. He was right to sense that the complex of feelings about the young person (so important to the nineteenth century) was at one with the complex of feelings about blushes, blushes to which indeed young persons are markedly prone. For like much else in Romanticism, the young person and the blush both embody paradoxes about innocence and guilt, a disconcerting mixed feeling very different from the old clarity of demarcation. Ruskin was no Podsnap, but he too was moved by this, as in the paradox of blood and iron: 'Is it not strange to find this stern and strong metal mingled so delicately in our human life that we cannot even blush without its help? Think of it, my fair and gentle hearers; how terrible the alternative – sometimes you have actually no choice but to be brazen-faced or iron-faced'.[6] Ruskin was moved, moreover, to make the highest claim for a blush's beauty: 'All good colour is gradated. A blush rose (or, better still, a blush itself,) is the type of rightness in arrangement of pure hue.'[7] The sentiment seems to me a very nineteenth-century one. Perhaps a history of cosmetics – and in particular of rouge – would show the changing attitudes to the blush. Dr Burgess in 1839 (p. 124) quotes Bichât's distinction between a true blush, which is unfeignable, and other emotions: 'Anger, joy, &c, may be imitated by frowning, by laughing, *but it is the* ROUGE *by which the actress represents modesty and innocence*; let it be wiped off, and the paleness of fear and terror instantly appears.'

Is embarrassment not only a nineteenth-century sentiment but a narrowly English one? There is indeed something very English about the great importance accorded to embarrassment, and this is part of that deep Englishness of Keats in which he delighted and which is so vital and honourable. But to say this is not to concede that the preoccupation with embarrassment is therefore a parochialism or a quirk or a disability. It has always been part of the Englishman's objection to foreigners that they are

'brazen-faced', unembarrassable, and therefore untrustworthy. Especially
the French. What the Spaniards said of the South American Indians, the
English might say of the French: How can those be trusted, who know not
how to blush? What was in the one case false physiology (research into the
blushing of the dark-skinned races was a nineteenth-century preoccupation)
might in the other be true philology. How can you trust a people whose
very language does its best to conceal the existence of the blush? *Rougir*
does not in itself offer any distinction between a blush and a flush. Robert's
Dictionnaire shows of course that a context, strong enough virtually to be a
story, can establish the distinction: '*Spécialt. Rougir de pudeur Ne rougir de
rien.* V. Impudent. *Des peintures lubriques qui feraint rougir des capitaines
de dragons. Fig.* Éprouver un sentiment de culpabilité, de honte, de
confusion.' As that last list suggests, the French *embarras* does not exist to
effect the work done by the English 'embarrassment'; the French does
indeed exist – 'État de celui qui . . . éprouve une sorte de malaise pour
agir ou parler. V. Confusion, émotion, gaucherie, gêne, honte, malaise,
timidité, trouble' – but *embarras* as embarrassment neither rules those
synonyms nor rules the many senses of *embarras* as the English 'embarrassment' now does. There are similar problems with the translatability of
'self-consciousness'. But the difference between *rougir* and 'blush' is the
most to the point. Nor is this mere chauvinism. For even if we were to
grant that the total equation that would compare one culture or language
with another is too multifarious to be calculable, it could still be true that
the differences between cultures are at some particular points assessable. '–
They order, said I, this matter better in France –.' More specifically, one
could suggest that English life and literature have had the advantages and
disadvantages of embarrassability, and that the French have had the
advantages and disadvantages of unembarrassability. The falsities of
embarrassability, then, are by a natural paradox an especially rich field for
the English writers: Dickens on Podsnap. The falsities of unembarrassability, by the same token, are ripe for the French writer. No novel has ever
been as unremittingly concerned with embarrassment as *Les Liaisons
dangereuses*; no English novel, perhaps, would ever have been able to be
so subtly and inwardly appalled by the ingenious deceptions and self-
deceptions of unembarrassability. Mme de Merteuil ends a letter to
Valmont: 'Adieu, Vicomte; bon soir et bon succès: mais, pour Dieu,
avancez donc. Songez que si vous n'avez pas cette femme, les autres
rougiront de vous avoir eu' (p. XX). It may be that nobody but the French
would speak so to each other, but then nobody but a French writer would
so unerringly and variously capture their propensity to do so. In this as in
so much else, Byron is Keats's mighty opposite; the English have long felt,
not only that the French overestimate Byron, and esteem him for the
wrong things, but also that there is something a bit too French about
Byron himself. How characteristic are those unheated words imported from
French into English which were so endlessly necessary to Byron in
his letters: 'sang froid' and (a word which the Englishman hardly knows

how to pronounce) 'nonchalant'. Keats's true form of a comforting non-chalance, different from Byron's which has its own truth, is achieved when he explicitly disclaims a false comfortable kind: 'I should, in duty, endeavour to write you a Letter with a comfortable nonchalance, but how can I do so when you are in so perplexing a situation, and I not able to help you out of it.'[8] It will be right to return to Byron whose high achievement wonderfully criticizes and is criticized by Keats's; for the moment, one could suggest that in the end Byron was precluded from being as great a writer as his contemporary Stendhal because Byron's language and culture made it perilously easy for him to treat as mere affectation certain matters – or certain styles – of embarrassability and unembarrassability about which Stendhal was obliged to be in deadly earnest.

Notes

1 *The Criterion*, ix (1930), p. 358.

2 'Embarrassment and social organization', *American Journal of Sociology*, lxii (1956), 264–75; *Interaction Ritual* (1967; 1972 edn., p. 111). See also André Modigliani, 'Embarrassment and embarrassability', *Sociometry*, xxxi (1968), and 'Embarrassment, facework, and eye contact: Testing a theory of embarrassment', *Journal of Personality and Social Psychology*, xvii (1971). On embarrassment as a socializing force, see Edward Gross and Gregory P. Stone, 'Embarrassment and the analysis of role requirements', *American Journal of Sociology*, lxx (1964). On the psychology and psychiatry of embarrassment, see Jerome M. Sattler, *A Theoretical, Developmental, and Clinical Investigation of Embarrassment*, Genetic Psychology Monographs, lxxi (1965).

3 *Interaction Ritual*, p. 105.

4 Benjamin Bailey to R.M. Milnes, 7 May 1849; *The Keats Circle*, ed. Hyder Edward Rollins (2nd edn., 1965), ii. 273–4.

5 *The Spectator*, Aug. 1896, said: 'Really these stories are often *Embarrassments* in a sense other than that intended by their author.'

6 *The Two Paths* (1859); *Works*, ed. E.T. Cook and A. Wedderburn, xvi. 384.

7 *The Two Paths*; *Works*, xvi. 424.

8 To George and Georgiana Keats, 12 Nov. 1819; *The Letters of John Keats 1814–1821*, ed. Hyder Edward Rollins (1958), ii. p. 229.

Vignette 4

Vergüenza ajena

Inmaculada Iglesias

'Vergüenza ajena' is a distinctive and remarkable variation of embarrassment (and sometimes of shame too). The purpose of this vignette is to focus on the effect of culture on the cluster of emotions that includes embarrassment and shame. We will comment on the emotion of 'vergüenza ajena' based on two considerations. First, 'vergüenza ajena' is an emotional cultural variation, especially felt by Spaniards but also by most of the Spanish speaking countries. Second, it is an exception that puts into question the most common perspectives on the study of the causes and circumstances of embarrassment.

'Vergüenza ajena' is the Spanish expression for empathic embarrassment or vicarious embarrassment. Since this is a common expression in Spanish and we are going to refer to the understanding of this emotion by the culture of Spanish speaking people, the Spanish form will be used instead of some English equivalents. Whenever we are talking about this emotion in Spain we will use the Spanish term, whenever we are speaking about investigations by other authors we will use the term used by them. In this way we will be certain that the translation will not affect in any way the concepts and the ideas we are referring to. So the reader should try to remember the words 'vergüenza ajena' with the hope that its meaning will become clearer as the discussion develops.

The concept of 'vergüenza', embarrassment and shame

First we will comment on the meaning of 'vergüenza' and then on the second part of this expression 'ajena', which means alien or pertaining to another person. Finally we will focus on the meaning of the joint term 'vergüenza ajena'.

Although it could sound confusing, *vergüenza* is the Spanish word that can mean either embarrassment or shame. To be precise, we should start by pointing out the definition of 'vergüenza' given by the Dictionary of The Real Academia Española (1992): 'Turbación del ánimo, que suele encender el color del rostro, ocasionada por alguna falta cometida, o por alguna acción deshonrosa y humillante, propia o ajena'. This might be translated as mental confusion, mental fluster, accompanied frequently by blushing, caused by a committed offense, or by a dishonorable, disgraceful, shameful or humiliating action, either one's own or someone else's. There are two important points in this definition that should be pointed out. First, the definition of 'vergüenza' includes both embarrassment and shame. Second, the phenomenon of 'vergüenza ajena' is included in the meaning of 'vergüenza' which gives us a sense of the relevance of this phenomenon in Spanish culture. Based on the assumption of the dictionary's intent to gather and promote the popular understanding of words among the speakers of a language, we could accept this definition in general terms as the common understanding of this emotion by Spanish speakers (in general terms, not in the sense of an exhaustive psychological description, which is not the purpose of a dictionary).

The translation into English of the word 'vergüenza' can be done in three senses; First, 'vergüenza' as *confusion* as in 'Don't embarrass him in front of his friends'. Second, 'vergüenza' involves a sense of *decorum*, decency, dignity as in 'You should be ashamed of yourself'. Third, 'vergüenza' as *disgrace* as in 'Lawyers like him are a disgrace to the profession' (*The Oxford Spanish Dictionary*, 1994). Thus to translate all these examples into Spanish we would use the word 'vergüenza', although they refer to different situations and require the use of different words for translation into another language such as English. *Embarrassment*, based on the Oxford English Dictionary, is defined as perplexity, sense of difficulty or hesitation with regard to judgment or action; constrained feeling or manner arising from bashfulness or timidity; confusion of thought or expression. The definition of *shame* reads 'feeling of humiliation excited by consciousness of (esp. one's own) guilt or shortcoming, of having made oneself or being made ridiculous, or of having offended against propriety, modesty or decency. Embarrassment, shame, mortification, humiliation, chagrin designate different kinds or degrees of painful feeling caused by injury to one's pride or self-respect. Embarrassment usually refers to a feeling less painful than that of shame, one associated with less serious situations, often of a social nature' (*Random House Unbridged Dictionary*, 1983) A similar division of this semantic field is made in Spanish with the exception that embarrassment and shame are covered by the same word, 'vergüenza'. However, there is a Spanish word, 'bochorno', that accounts for the meaning of embarrassment only. It is used in the circumstances of social mistakes and improprieties, but does not imply a moral burden and involves blushing. The word 'bochorno' means, among other things, unease or embarrassment caused by something that offends or is a nuisance or embarrasses (Real Academia Española, 1992). Also it means blushing caused by having received an offense or by feeling embarrassed. It seems like embarrassment focuses on the behavioral and mental difficulties caused by ridiculous situations and shame on a more intense feeling based on humiliation and guilt consciousness caused by dishonest or offensive actions. We can express the differences between embarrassment and shame in terms of the severity of the transgression (social inappropriateness in breaking a moral rule) but Spaniards do not make it an extrinsic distinction. They do not verbalize it; but the 'sentiment' and the social functions seem to be the same. However, the Spanish word seems to be a wider one and to cover both English terms. The use of one word, 'vergüenza', for the different English words, 'embarrassment' and 'shame', although the contexts and situations vary, may be made intelligible by looking for the similarities between them. For instance, self-exposure to another through our actions might be a similarity but with either trivial or more serious or severe consequences and repercussions. Thus a Spaniard would translate 'vergüenza' as embarrassment or shame depending on the severity of the consequences. It might be worth mentioning that in the English speaking world shame and embarrassment are considered to be related and the experiencing individual may be unable to distinguish between them.

The concept of 'vergüenza ajena' and its implications for the theory of embarrassment and shame

'Vergüenza ajena' has different translations in English. Empathic embarrassment, vicarious embarrassment and social embarrassment are among the most common. Even though little attention has been paid to this phenomenon, some research has been conducted on this theme in the last three decades in the English speaking world. Gross and Stone (1964) comment that embarrassment is infectious. It may spread out, incapacitating others not previously incapacitated. There is some empirical evidence that the phenomenon exists. Sattler (1966) studied the situations in which embarrassment occurs by requesting adolescents, college students, normal adults and chronic schizophrenics to describe situations they find embarrassing. A total of 39 categories were derived, including social embarrassment when another person does something that reflects on oneself, and a somewhat different case, being embarrassed for another. By vicarious embarrassment is meant the embarrassment an individual experiences for another person. It is noted that vicarious embarrassment does not necessarily indicate the presence of an embarrassed other. The process of sympathy may result in individuals imagining themselves in the place of a non-embarrassed other. This would be the case in which the other is unsocialized, due to age, culture, subculture or mental state (Fink, 1975). Empathic embarrassment has been defined as embarrassment felt with another even though one's own social identity is not threatened (Miller, 1987). Miller reports two studies that demonstrate the existence of this phenomenon and its relationship to both interactive and personality influences. He studied the reactions of observers to actors' embarrassment by manipulating the nature of the prior interaction between actor and observer (past familiarity with other people may increase our reaction to their embarrassment) and the observational set of the observer (empathic embarrassment is minimized by detached objectivity and enhanced by compassionate empathy) as well as studying the relationship between empathic embarrassment and high embarrassability (dispositional embarrassability substantially determines how strong one's empathic embarrassment will be).

Bennett and Dewberry (1988) propose that others' failures can be a source of embarrassment, particularly when one's own behavior provided social comparison information unfavorable to the other. Thus they bring into question the perspectives that emphasize the actor's failure to present a desired image to others as one of the causes of embarrassment. These studies demonstrate the existence of 'vergüenza ajena' even among non-Spaniards, either as embarrassment felt for another even though the other's actions do not reflect upon oneself (Miller, 1987) or as embarrassment felt for another's failures (Bennett and Dewberry, 1988) or as the embarrassment an individual experiences for another person (Fink, 1975). These studies consider only the embarrassment felt for another's actions, but not shame. However 'vergüenza ajena' covers both emotions and we should not forget this. The existence of vicarious or empathic embarrassment and 'vergüenza ajena' has implications for the theory of embarrassment which is put into question. In order to simplify we will categorize the theories of embarrassment into three basic types (Parrott and Smith, 1991). The social anxiety theories of embarrassment present embarrassment as an experience of anxiety and worry. A second theory is based on the idea of decreased self-esteem. A third type is a dramaturgic theory. However, 'vergüenza ajena' is not brought into being by a difficulty to act or interact since no action is required from the observer and no interaction has been made. Neither does it result from a concern about others' opinion of oneself nor is it derived from evaluating some aspects of oneself as deficient. 'Vergüenza ajena' can be experienced even with no display of felt embarrassment required from the actor.

Can we simply treat 'vergüenza ajena' as a minor cultural variation on empathic or vicarious embarrassment? 'Vergüenza ajena' refers to the embarrassment or shame that is felt by observing another person's action whether the actor feels it or not. Including shame is part of the difference, and although no studies about feeling ashamed for another have been found, expressions such as 'I feel pity for him' are heard sometimes. Someone may feel embarrassed or ashamed for someone whom one does not know or is not related to in any specific way. For instance, it is pretty common to listen to people complain about politicians' performances and scandals and also about the 'vergüenza ajena' these cause to them. People say, among other expressions, 'dan vergüenza' (they make you feel embarrassed), 'es vergonzoso' (it is embarrassing), 'es vergonzoso para el país' (it is embarrassing for the country), and 'qué vergüenza' (what a shame). Another example of how 'vergüenza ajena' works might be an incident experienced by an American professor in Spain where he was giving a lecture. At a certain point of the lecture he made a joke, related to the subject, but unfortunately it was a joke about the Spaniards' way of driving. Even though this joke might be funny in the United States (a sort of teasing) it did not work in Spain for reasons obviously related to our theme here: Spaniards cannot laugh about themselves and their pride is so big that they feel insulted easily; furthermore the speaker felt embarrassed himself in this situation and it probably made the audience feel 'vergüenza ajena' since the joke was 'out of context' due to cultural differences and because they would feel embarrassed themselves in that situation. Another important point is that 'vergüenza ajena' may be felt whether an actor feels it or not. Thus you can feel embarrassed by watching someone on the television putting him- or herself in a ridiculous situation although that would be part of his/her work as in the case of being a comedian. These points can make a difference regarding the intensity with which 'vergüenza ajena' is felt. As a native speaker of Spanish it is my opinion that 'vergüenza ajena' would be more intense in shame-like situations rather than embarrassment-like situations; the more evident the relationship or identification with the actor the more intense the 'vergüenza ajena'; the more intensely and obviously the actor feels embarrassed or ashamed, the more intense the 'vergüenza ajena'.

The effect of culture on emotions: the case of 'vergüenza ajena'

The emotion concept, expression, experiences and eliciting events vary according to the culture. In this way we can pay attention to different, relevant aspects or dimensions that distinguish between cultures to illustrate the effect of the culture on the emotions. For the case of embarrassment, shame and 'vergüenza ajena', the construals of the self and the other have important implications.

Theories of the self distinguish between a construal of the self as independent and a construal of the self as interdependent (Markus and Kitayama, 1991). The independent view is exemplified in North American culture as well as in many Western European cultures. The interdependent view is exemplified in Japanese culture as well as in other Asian cultures, African cultures, Latin-American cultures and many southern European cultures. The distinction between the independent and interdependent construals must be considered as a general tendency to a specific culture as a whole and rather than being a discrete distinction; it is a continuum between extremes. The independent view of the self is based on the belief in the wholeness and uniqueness of each person's configuration of internal attributes, and refers to a conception of the self as an autonomous, independent person. Others are important as sources that can verify and affirm the inner core of the self. On the other hand the interdependent view of the self also expresses a set of internal attributes but these are understood as situation specific. Individual autonomy is secondary and attending to and fitting in with others is emphasized. This could find expression in the importance of concepts like 'dignidad', 'orgullo' and 'honor' (dignity, pride and honor) in Spanish culture in which 'the others' play a major role having as exponent the 'vergüenza ajena' experience.

These construals play a major role in regulating various psychological processes such as emotions (Markus and Kitayama, 1991). How do the emotional processes vary according to the nature of the self-system? In this way a distinction is made between ego-focused emotions and other-focused emotions (Lewis, 1992) that is closely related to the distinction between the construals of the self as independent and interdependent. The ego-focused emotions refer primarily to the individual's internal attributes, whereas the other-focused emotions refer primarily to another person. Anger, frustration and pride would be examples of the former type and experiencing and expressing these emotions emphasizes these self-defining attributes and their assertion in public. Sympathy, feelings of interpersonal communion and shame would be of the latter type and experiencing and expressing these emotions emphasizes one's interdependence and cooperative social behavior. Those with independent selves will express and perhaps experience more frequently the ego-focused emotions. On the other hand, those with interdependent selves will express and perhaps experience more frequently the other-focused emotions. Embarrassment, shame and especially 'vergüenza ajena' have their place in the latter self-system. In this direction we find the research that uses the 'simpatía' script as one of the components of a more general pattern of cultural differences (collectivism versus individualism) between Hispanics and non-Hispanics in which interpersonal behaviors are more important than task achievements in the case of the former than in the case of the latter (Triandis et al., 1984)

Embarrassment is expressed bodily and engendered socially. The experience of embarrassment as well as every emotion has some peculiarities among situations, individuals and cultures. It could be said that the embarrassment phenomenon can be found in every culture and with every individual. But it appears in many different ways and with some variations, for different reasons, in different intensities and with different displays and even different internal concomitants. Cross-cultural studies have been conducted to study how the culture affects the perceived degree of embarrassment and the use of remedial strategies (Sueda, 1990), the consequences of embarrassment (Edelmann and Neto, 1989), and the discussion of embarrassing topics in one's second, compared to one's first, language (Bond and Lai, 1985). A cultural variation of embarrassment and shame is the case of 'vergüenza ajena' in Spain and also among the Spanish speaking people.

Is Spain a society with high embarrassability so the Spanish feel empathic embarrassment very strongly? In my opinion the answer should be an affirmative one and indeed raises some other questions: What is the role that 'vergüenza ajena' plays in the Spanish social life? Why does it seem to be so important in Spanish culture? What is its relationship with other relevant concepts in Spanish culture such as honor, dignity and pride and 'simpatía'?

How do we come to experience embarrassment and shame? Buss (1980) presents an approach that emphasizes socialization practices. In the process of socialization of self-control, modesty, manners and privacy, one of the prime means of socialization is through teasing, laughter and ridicule, which cause intense embarrassment. Subsequently, the reaction of the socialized adults to their mistakes in this area of social behavior will be the experience of embarrassment. Shame will appear in an environment of socialization where there is an ethos of conditional love, lofty goals, a strict code of social conventions with many restrictions and complex rules to follow, and punishment for the failure to achieve and to be socially correct based on withdrawal of affection and ridicule is paramount.

Maintaining a socially proper (accepted) behavior and a positive social image is of such a concern for Spaniards that they would feel 'vergüenza' just for seeing someone else in an (supposedly) embarrassing situation. Some cultures may make empathic embarrassment more likely than others. That is the case for Spain. However, in societies with different socialization practices, the experience of embarrassment and shame might be different in terms of intensity, frequency and even display. Modern China is presented as a society where children are not teased, laughed at, or ridiculed and there is an absence of blushing among young Chinese; however, they may show strong shame reactions (Buss, 1980). It is my opinion that Spaniards avoid ridicule and they cannot laugh about themselves and that is why the previously mentioned anecdote of the American professor in Spain came out that way even though it might have been very amusing in the United States. As a supportive observation, we might point out the high number of successful situation comedy series in television in the United States where the different ethnic groups stereotype and laugh about themselves in contrast with their near nonexistence in Spain. Yet lack of sense of humor is not characteristic of Spaniards. Is Spain a society where social mistakes and improprieties and breaking of (moral) rules are the center of scorn? Or is this strong concern (sense of vergüenza) about social presentation a result of deeper psychological characteristics of this society? The roots of this intense and frequent experience of 'vergüenza' might be in the strong feelings of pride, honor and dignity. As far as I know no studies have yet been conducted in this area. In fact it is characteristic of pride that one feels entitled not to be the object of ridicule or laughter. The conjunction of pride-shame-ridiculousness-humiliation refers to 'face work', the maintenance of a proper public presentation (Crespo, 1986).

Honor is considered a national passion in Spain (Bennassar, 1979) and pride is considered the key to the Spanish attitude toward society (Díaz-Plaja, 1967). Their roots are quite deep in this society and their relevance (in the present time) is evidenced through the numerous terms and expressions related to honor and 'honra'. The Dictionary of Real Academia Española (1992) includes 15 derivatives of honor and 13 of 'honra' in comparison with the 6 terms that the *Oxford Spanish Dictionary* (1994) includes for honor. Besides, honor and 'honra' are very close concepts and have most of their meanings in common, as in the sense of glory and good opinion or reputation acquired through virtue or merit that transcends families, people and actions. Also they share the meaning of showing respect or tribute to someone and the meaning of honesty, modesty and virtue of the woman. There are many common and interesting expressions using the terms 'honra' and honor that point out the semantic closeness of the concepts of honor, dignity, pride and 'vergüenza'. An interesting one is through the derivative 'honrilla' as in doing something 'por la honrilla' meaning (according to the Dictionary of The Real Academia Española, 1992) 'vergüenza' with which someone does or does not do something in order not to appear bad. Similarly the last piece of a sharing (usually food) among a group is called 'el de la vergüenza' meaning that taking the last piece is an occasion for embarrassment since it is not considered good manners to be the one that 'finishes' the sharing. In the expression 'Tener a mucha honra' as to be very proud of, we see the close relationship between pride and 'honra' or dignity. There are several more interesting expressions using the terms 'honor' and 'honra' such as 'honras fúnebres' as funeral rites or to refer to feminine virginity as the honor or 'honra de la mujer' or the good name or honor being sullied, to defend the honor of the family, 'tener el honor de recibir a alguien en su casa' as in having the privilege of welcome or receive someone at home, and 'honorarios' as fees. All these examples corroborate the presence, the relevance and the semantic closeness of these concepts in the Spanish culture.

Honor has a long history in Spain. In the thirteenth century, the Castilian Code of the 'Partidas' defined honor as 'the reputation a man has acquired by virtue of his rank, his high deeds, or his valor' (Bennassar, 1979). This presents honor as motivation for personal action as well as that pertaining to social position. Although honor was a sentiment of chivalric or aristocratic origin and wealth augments a family's capacity to conserve and defend its honor, we find affirmations that certain individuals or families are poor but honorable. (Bennassar, 1979). However, the Semitic character of honor has been pointed out as a result of the coexistence of Jews, Moors and Christians in Spain for centuries (Goytisolo, 1969). This Semitic character refers to the revenge of the defamed even at the cost of another person's life, which was often blameless. At the end of the sixteenth century a black skin was not incompatible with the reputation of being an honorable man, yet a Jewish or Moorish origin was an indelible stain that forbade any claim to honor. More and more honor was defined as a code independent of all morality, a code to which social prejudice and pride or even vanity was the only key (Bennassar, 1979). 'Individual or collective pride, pride of a person or a people, ordinarily grows in proportion to material possessions. Spanish pride does not need this support, because it is an interior pride based on a more intimate wealth, that of race or of religion' (Díaz-Plaja, 1967).

The persistence of honor as an outstanding value in Spain does not mean that its nature and effects remained the same over the centuries. Honor has become the hostage of reputation; its social significance has surpassed its individual significance; it has become wholly dependent on public opinion (Bennassar, 1979). 'El que dirán', which means what they will say, has become a noun indicating the importance of the fear of ridicule and its avoidance. Physical appearance has also assumed great importance: 'the Spaniard adorns himself first with the greatest elegance, even when his food leaves much to be desired, for nobody sees the latter' (Díaz-Plaja, 1967). These aspects are firmly rooted and manifest the importance of 'the other' for the maintenance of 'cara' (face) that is the maintenance of a proper social identity.

Honor is a central and outstanding value for Spaniards and so pride as its exponent is a major trait of Spanish national character, easily recognized by foreigners, that externalize among others this relevant value. This conception of pride and honor transcends the individual through its public character and becomes a socialized value based on reputation which is the expression of an exaggerated fear of public opinion (Bennassar, 1979). Thus it is not surprising that 'vergüenza ajena' has a special place in Spanish culture.

References

Bennassar, B. (1979) *The Spanish Character: Attitudes and Mentalities from the Sixteenth to the Nineteenth Century*. California: University of California Press. p. 213.

Bennet, M. and Dewberry, C. (1988) 'Embarrassment at other's failures: A test of the Semin and Manstead Model', *The Journal of Social Psychology*, 129 (4): 557–9.

Bond, M.H. and Lai, T. (1985) 'Embarrassment and code-switching into a second language', *The Journal of Social Psychology*, 126 (2): 179–86.

Buss, A.H. (1980) *Self-consciousness and Social Anxiety*. San Francisco: Freeman.

Crespo, E. (1986) 'A regional variation: Emotions in Spain', in R. Harré (ed.), *The Social Construction of Emotions*. Oxford: Basil Blackwell.

Díaz-Plaja, F. (1967) *The Spaniards and the Seven Deadly Sins*. New York: Charles Scribner's Sons. p. 21, p. 22.

Edelmann, R.J. and Neto, F. (1989) 'Self-reported expression and consequences of embarrassment in Portugal and the U.K.', *International Journal of Psychology*, 24 (3): 351–66.

Fink, E.L. (1975) *An Empirical Analysis of Vicarious Embarrassment: A Study of Social Interaction and Emotion*. Thesis for Ph.D. Madison: University of Wisconsin.

Goytisolo, J. (1969) *España y los españoles*. Barcelona: Editorial Lumen.

Gross, E. and Stone, G.P. (1964) 'Embarrassment and the analysis of role requirements', *The American Journal of Sociology*, LXX (1): 1–15.

Lewis, M. (1992) *Shame: The Exposed Self*. New York: The Free Press.

Markus, H.R. and Kitayama, S. (1991) 'Culture and the self: Implications for cognition, emotion, and motivation', *Psychological Review*, 98 (2): 224–53.

Miller, R.S. (1987) 'Empathic embarrassment: Situational and personal determinants of reactions to the embarrassment of another', *Journal of Personality and Social Psychology*, 53 (6): 1061–9.

Oxford Spanish Dictionary (The) (1994) New York: Oxford University Press.

Parrott, W.G. and Smith, S.F. (1991) 'Embarrassment: Actual vs. typical cases, classical vs. prototypical representations', *Cognition and Emotion*, 5 (5/6): 467–88.

Random House Unabridged Dictionary (1983) 2nd edn. New York: Random House.

Real Academia Española (1992) *Dictionary of the Spanish Language* (Diccionario de la lengua española). Madrid: Espasa-Calpe.

Sattler, J.M. (1966) *A Study of Embarrassment*. Dissertation for Ph.D. Kansas: University of Kansas.

Sueda, K. (1990) *A Cross-cultural Study of Embarrassment: The U.S. Culture and the Japanese Culture*. Dissertation for Ph.D. Fullerton: California State University.

Triandis, H.C., Lisansky, J., Marín, G. and Betancourt, H. (1984) '"Simpatía" as a cultural script of Hispanics', *Journal of Personality and Social Psychology*, 47 (6): 1363–75.

PART II

HISTORICAL AND CULTURAL VARIETY IN EMOTIONS

'By nature, men are nearly alike; by practice, they get to be wide apart.'

Confucius, Analects, 17.2 (James Legge, trans.) (6th c. BC)

Chapter 6

Historical Perspectives on Grief

Peter N. Stearns and Mark Knapp

Grief can be a powerful emotion. Such is its power that many people assume that grief is a basic reaction to loss, visible not only in humans but in various other mammals who display stunned response to loss for various periods of time – like the dogs whose baying or withdrawal at the death of a master helps them qualify as man's best friend. Yet grief is also a variable (Averill and Nunley, 1988). Its intensity differs greatly from one individual to the next, confronted with otherwise similar loss. Its manifestations – possibly even its existence, in any clearly definable form – also vary from one culture to the next. Some cultures react to loss not with grief but with anger, seeking vengeance or combat. Some cultures, like the Tahitian, limit reactions to loss of any sort; grief is not explicitly recognized. The Ifaluk, in contrast, try to minimize grief while taking pride in displays of empathy with others which are supposed to lead to a return to equanimity on the part of the bereaved individual (C. Stearns, 1993). Grief reactions are, in sum, to some extent at least culturally constructed, quite apart from the oscillations of individual personalities around cultural norms.

Cultural construction means, in turn, that grief can be understood in part through comparisons between contemporary Western patterns and those of other societies but also through tracing major shifts in grief culture that have led up to these same contemporary patterns. This historical work has been only incompletely established up to now, despite a great deal of important research on changes in death practices.

Grief has in fact undergone some surprisingly swift transitions over the last century and a half, in response to changes in attachments in the family (or at least in family ideals) and shifts in actual patterns of death. A rich Victorian grief culture differed greatly from more traditional reactions. But this culture was in turn attacked and partly unseated in a modernist outburst that, oddly, has not been much explored. Only by examining two . successive grief cultures, both arguably 'modern' in some of their pre-conditions, can we understand what contemporary grief involves and why it is in some respects fraught with personal and social tension.

The clearest historical transition, unquestionably relevant to current grief patterns, involves an intensification of grief by the early nineteenth century (Lofland, 1985). Traditional reactions to loss, in Western Europe and colonial North America, seem to have been somewhat muted, though individuals might lose control in grief to the extent of requiring medical attention (a common reason to seek doctors' aid, for example, in seventeenth-century England) (MacDonald, 1981). Grief was felt, to be sure; many parental diaries recorded emotions felt on the deaths of young children. Nevertheless, three related constraints operated to restrain elaborate open displays of grief, and possibly grief itself.

First, undue grief could denote undue attachment to worldly ties, rather than appropriate focus on God's majesty (Stannard, 1976). Neither Protestant nor Catholic Christianity encouraged grief. Children were taught to react to death more with fear than with indulgent grief, at least in Calvinism; death of others was an object lesson in how quickly one could be snatched away to face God's judgment (Fiore, 1992). Second, emotional ties within families were usually somewhat muted. Marriages were not formed primarily on the basis of emotional attraction, nor were intense bonds emphasized between parents and children. The overriding economic concerns of families could cushion the shock of death, which however lamentable was vital to keep family size in manageable bounds. Even spousal death could seem somewhat routine. Evidence of husbands' reactions to maternal mortality in the eighteenth-century South, for example, suggests what to modern ears would seem a shocking callousness (Lockridge and Lewis, 1988). Deaths of older parents could be positively welcome, particularly where land was in short supply, because they alone permitted attainment of full economic adulthood, through inheritance. Hence the French peasant who headed out to a day of ploughing right after his father died, noting 'Now I am a man' (Stearns, 1975).

The nature of death itself provided the third cushion against great grief. Many adults died what historians have labeled a 'good death' – passing away in mature years, from a respiratory ailment sufficiently gradual to permit the family to gather around and affairs to be settled (Ariès, 1981; Stannard, 1975). The act of dying appropriately, in the home, without great pain, seems to have allowed many people to adjust to the prospect of loss such that tremendous outpourings of grief were not necessary. Community support in such circumstances also reduced the need to use grief to gain emotional backing – it was simply there, in close-knit communities.

Key elements of this framework began to change by the early nineteenth century, leading to what one sociologist has termed (somewhat oversimply, as we shall see) the advent of modern grief reactions (Lofland, 1985; Rosenblatt, 1983). Interestingly, death itself did not change much yet, and good deaths were still possible. But the community setting for death declined in some instances, though gradually, as one recent study clearly indicates (Wells, 1994); this could generate more need to use grief to elicit backing from friends and relatives. Two cultural shifts prepared the strikingly innovative Victorian culture toward grief. First, love was now emphasized in the middle-class family (Lystra, 1989). Courtship activities became far more intensely emotional than had been the case previously, and while marriage may well have cooled ardour the assumption that grief should greet the death of spouse derived from the love ideals that courtship had nurtured. (Indeed, if guilt at a love gone stale combined with these ideals, grief would be again a logical result on the death of a spouse.) Emotional ties with one's innocent children gained growing emphasis, enhanced not simply by a new kind of family culture but by the fact of declining birth rates that placed greater emotional premium on each individual child (Hoffert, 1987; Dye and Smith, 1986). Even older parents, it has been hypothesized, came into love's growing orbit, as declining dependence on inheritance, in an increasingly commercial economy, left more room for tender sentiments. Second, growing belief in progress, derived from the Enlightenment and furthered by signs of business and scientific advance, made many deaths seem increasingly inappropriate by the nineteenth century. Deaths of children, particularly, were hard to stomach. Popular women's magazines bombarded readers with criticisms of faulty parental practices that led to totally unnecessary children's deaths – if only they had not been overfed, improperly dressed, these things need not happen. Women began to express growing impatience – and fear – with the customary levels of maternal mortality, as they sought doctors' care well before doctors had much to offer (Lockridge and Lewis, 1988). The disjuncture between what ought to be, in a progressive society, and what was led to a growing sense of guilt when death occurred in the family, and with this a growing need for grief to assuage this guilt. Cultural change, in sum, more than any concrete functional shift, lay behind the burgeoning attention to grief in nineteenth-century middle-class culture.

Certainly in the United States, preoccupation with grief reached new heights, as the emotion blossomed and provided even a certain enjoyment in the Victorian family context.

Grief was, in the first place, frequently discussed, a staple not only of story but also of song. Grief was heartrending, as Paul Rosenblatt has demonstrated (Rosenblatt, 1983; Ariès, 1981; Vinovskis, 1976). The depth of grief followed directly, in fact, from the emphasis on great love, for

Victorian convention held that even the temporary absence of a loved one was a real sorrow. As Nathaniel Hawthorne put it in a letter to Sarah Peabody in 1840: 'Where thou art not, there it is a sort of death'. Death itself, correspondingly, would move one to the core. Despite its pain, the essence of grief was a vital part of Victorian emotional life. Children were prepared for it by frequent references, while adults developed various conventions to permit its open expression. In its intensity and its link to love, grief indeed could have a bittersweet quality: immensely sad, but almost a welcome part of a full emotional experience. It could express and enrich the very love Victorian culture sought. As a Protestant minister put it in a family advice manual of 1882: 'It may truly be said that no home ever reaches its highest blessedness and sweetness of love and its richest fullness of joy till sorrow enters its life in some way.'

Efforts to present grief and death to children in a benign though sorrowful context continued through the later nineteenth century. In McGuffy's Fourth Eclectic Reader (1866), 16 of 29 'poetical lessons' dealt with death, including one entitled 'What Is Death?':

> Child, Mother, how still the baby lies.
> I cannot hear his breath;
> I cannot see his laughing eyes;
> They tell me this is death.
> They say that he again will rise,
> More beautiful than now;
> That God will bless him in the skies;
> O mother, tell me how.

In this case, the mother responds with the image of a butterfly emerging from a lifeless chrysalis. In other poems, again in school readers, the dominant theme was the reunion of loved ones after death in heaven.

> Oh, we pray to meet our darling
> For a long, long, sweet embrace.
> Where the little feet are waiting –
> And we meet her face to face.

Tragic death scenes remained commonplace in stories for children, as they were asked to live through the sorrows of illness and passing while being assured that an outpouring of emotion was valid and ultimately healthy. 'Elsie's grief was deep and lasting. She sorrowed as she might have done for the loss of a very dear brother, . . . a half remorseful feeling which reason could not control or entirely relieve; and it was long ere she was quite her own bright, gladsome sunny self again.' Louisa May Alcott wrote of a sister's 'bitter cry of an unsubmissive sorrow', of 'sacred moments, when heart talked to heart in the silence of the night, turning affliction to a blessing, which chastened grief and strengthened love'. Mother's assurances, repeated references to protecting angels, and the increasing theme of familial reunion in heaven all linked the power of grief to hope and love; but grief's power was not evaded. Stories of death were now disengaged from fear and from moral admonitions about life's transiency to become part of the characteristic Victorian emotional style, in which intense emotions served as a desirable part of life and, ultimately, an enhancement of human ties. The starkness of death disappeared under sentimental overlays in these portrayals, but the inescapability, even the benefit, of a period of deep grief was generally confirmed. Funeral toys associated with girls' doll play both reflected and furthered links between childhood and grief by the 1870s.

The same themes pervaded popular parlor songs in the Victorian decades. The 1839 song 'Near the Lake Where Droop'd the Willow' became an immense success in American concerts and inspired several decades of imitation. The song focused on a girl loved in youth, who had died long ago:

> Mingled were our hearts forever, long time ago;
> Can I now forget her? Never. No, lost one, no.
> To her grave these tears are given, ever to flow,
> She's the star I missed from heaven, long time ago.

In contrast to eighteenth-century songs about death, which were set in the artificial pastoral world of shepherds and written in the third person, Victorian grief songs were personal and immediate. Death and its aftermath became a field for emotional exploration. Minstrel shows dealt with the emotions of death, often without much reference to plot or character. Deathbed scenes, the emotional ties between dead and living, and the idea of ultimate reunion in heaven all figured prominently. Literally hundreds of songs about dying girls were published, particularly in the 1860s, when they obviously served as a combination of focus for and distraction from the terrors of the Civil War: 'Wait for me at heaven's gate, Sweet Belle Mahone'; 'Though we may meet no more on earth, Thou shalt be mine above'; 'Angels guard her with your wings. . . . Bid her dream love-dreams of me – Till I come, sleep, Eulalie.' But along with the sentimentalized heaven came real sorrow on earth, with frequent emotion-laden visits to the cemetery: 'I'm kneeling by thy grave, Katy Darling; This world is all a bleak place to me'; 'All night I sat upon her grave, And sorely I did cry'.

> Oh, a huge great grief I'm bearing,
> Though I scarce can heave a sigh,
> And I'll ever be dreaming, Katy Darling,
> Of thy love ev'ry day till I die.

The pervasive themes of grief and pathos formed an important part of Victorian culture, making the sorrow of bereavement seem natural, even desirable, though also to some degree consolable (Stearns, 1994)). Grief could soar as love did. At the risk of trivializing grief (and certainly Christian doctrines concerning the afterlife), Victorian emotional culture embraced this sorrow openly, returning to it with almost endless fascination at least until the final decades of the nineteenth century (Houlbrooke, 1989).

The distinctive Victorian embrace of grief had both public and personal consequences. Rituals after death clearly changed in the nineteenth century to accommodate heightened emotion. Victorian funeral procedures, unlike those before or since, were intended both to remove the fear of death and to allow open expression of grief through ritual. Increasing use of cosmetics on corpses, and ultimately the rise of professional undertakers and embalmers who took over the handling of death from bereaved families, expressed mainly the desire to allay fear and to direct emotions away from decaying flesh to the bittersweet grief at a loved one's loss. The practice of wearing mourning clothing spread. Funerals became more elaborate, cemeteries and tombstones more ornate and evocative. Scholars have legitimately argued over whether the paraphernalia of middle-class Victorian funerals expressed simply growing wealth and status rivalry, or real grief, and the sensible conclusion has been that both were involved (Cannadine, 1981; Houlbrooke, 1989). Families really did need rituals that would allow them to show their grief. Where child death was involved, funeral monuments of unprecedented size combined with haunting epitaphs to convey the sorrow and love that sent the child to heaven. Gravestone euphemisms about death as sleep, or as going home, expressed the grief-induced need to see death as something less than final (Hoffert, 1987).

On the personal side, the Victorians who expressed themselves in letters, diaries, and often in ritual commonly expected, articulated and felt the sharpness that grief was supposed to generate (Rosenblatt, 1983). Nellie Wetherbee recorded in her diary as she left her family to head west, 'I only cried as the steamer sailed away – bitter, bitter tears'. The death of children produced almost overwhelming emotion, as an 1897 diary reported: 'Jacob is dead. Tears blind my eyes as I write . . . now he is at rest, my little darling Jacob. Hope to meet you in heaven. God help me to bear my sorrow.' Here, clearly, not only the pain of grief but also the conscious handling of grief with references to reunion and divine support reflected the currency of the larger Victorian culture. Men as well as women expressed their sorrow. A Civil War soldier leaves his family in 1863, crying for days before the final departure, then musing in his diary both on his great love and on the 'cruelty' of the separation. A minister, coincidentally in the same year, asks Jesus to 'support me under this crushing blow' – his brother's death. Another man, recording in 1845 the death of a brother-in-law, ended his entry: 'Oh! What sorrow burst in upon us at the melancholy news of his death. . . . All is sorrow and weeping.' Even nostalgic recollection brought grief, as when Sarah Huntington recalled a loss of two years earlier: 'Reading these letters revived all the exclusiveness and intenseness of my love for him I once called husband.'

Some facets of grief varied, to be sure. Different personalities responded differently to death. Death could still call up diary entries dwelling on the transience of life and the uncertainties of God's judgment. Some diaries reported that intense grief followed a death for a month or so, then tapered off; others recorded a fresh renewal of grief well over a year after a death or separation. In the main, however, the obligation to record grief and the felt intensity of grief as a direct reaction to love rather than to fears of death reflected real-life experiences of the culture's emotional standards. Deep loss, hopes for reunion in the afterlife, bittersweet recollections of the ongoing love – all were commonplace in the private reportage.

Of course grief intensities also varied with the level of acquaintance and the kind of death. Deaths that were lingering, providing the chance to prepare, sometimes caused less grief than sudden departures; the concept of a 'good death' may have cushioned grief in the former instances. Where sheer pain dominated, as in the unexpected death of a child, the bittersweet theme might be absent entirely. But efforts to see beauty in death, to emphasize the sharing of grief by friends as well as the consolation of a better life in heaven, expressed some of the qualities urged in the more general commentary on this emotion. Christian resignation entered into the formula, along with frequent references to the 'happier world' beyond and the beauty of the dead body (a clearly Victorian theme expressed for example in death kits for children's dolls, complete with caskets and mourning apparel [Uhlenberg, 1985]), but so did hopes for reunion – a child 'spends this Sunday in Heaven with all her departed relatives', wrote a Schenectady Protestant – and a sense of propriety in the love shared, through grief, in the family circle and beyond (Rosenblatt, 1983; Wells, 1994; Stearns, 1994).

Exploration of Victorian grief culture and its results reveals a distinctive amalgam, linked to religious beliefs and family ideals that did not long survive the nineteenth century. To be sure, as the few chroniclers of modern grief have noted, elements of the Victorian formula have endured. The construct as a whole has not, however, as any observer of changes in death practices could readily predict. What has been missing in the pioneering attempts at grief history has been a recognition of a second, more recent turning point. Post-Victorian grief culture did not unravel all the strands that had emerged since the early nineteenth century, but it ripped the larger fabric. Explicit attacks on Victorian grief culture began to take shape early in the twentieth century, with some hints in popular magazine articles even in the 1890s, as new factors determining grief standards gained ground.

One subtle source of attack on Victorian grief really involved a Panglossian extension of Victorianism itself: if death involved quick union with God and only brief separation from loved ones on earth, why bother to grieve at all, and why dread death? 'Why should it not be to all of us the Great Adventure? Why should we not look forward to it with anticipation, not with apprehension?' In this upbeat Christian rendering, joy, not grief, should predominate, and the bittersweet ambivalence of Victorian culture was muscled aside in favor of assertions of perpetual happiness. In 1907 Jane Belfield wrote on death for *Lippincott's Magazine*, stressing the folly of great pain. After all, not only death but also reunion with family is certain, so death need not involve intense feelings at all but rather 'emotions and aspirations hushed'. Another tack, slightly different from Christian optimism, increasingly emphasized the debilities of old age, such that death could and should be calmly greeted if, as was increasingly the case, it had the courtesy to wait until people had passed through normal adulthood. *Outlook* also took up this theme, stressing death as a pleasant release from decrepitude:

> The stains of travel were gone, the signs of age had vanished; once more young, but with a wisdom beyond young, she started with buoyant step and with a rising hope in her heart; for through the soft mist beautiful forms seemed to be moving, and faint and far she heard voices that seemed to come out of her childhood, fresh with the freshness of the morning, and her spirit grew faint for joy at the sound of them.

Clearly, in this picture, neither fear for one's own death nor grief at the passing of an older relative made much sense (Stearns, 1994).

Popularized science at.. cked grief and fear of death from another interesting angle. A steady, surprising series of articles countered the traditional belief that death involved pain. Many modern spirits argued that this belief was one of the sources of Christianity's hold on the masses, who used religion to counter anticipated suffering, but that it was empirically incorrect. This was not, of course, a direct attack on Victorian emotional culture, which had also downplayed the physical side of death in favor of a vaguely religious spirituality, but it had implications concerning grief. Science, so the modernists repeatedly argued, suggested that most deaths were actually rather pleasant. A *New Englander and Yale Review* article launched a seemingly bizarre debate in 1891, attaching the 'popular belief' that 'the moment of death is to be anticipated as one of bodily pain and mental discomfort'. Granting that there is a natural dread of death in anticipation, the article contended that most deaths involved a 'pleasurable sensation'. Death in old age, most notably, resembled going to sleep; it was 'a slumbrous condition, not unlike that at the end of a toilsome day'. Even sudden death or convulsions, however, did not indicate pain. People under anaesthesia, after all, reported 'delightful sensations' and 'beatific visions'. Whatever pain might be involved was largely unfelt, according to the best medical evidence, in a line of argument that continued to receive considerable attention for over two decades.

Other commentary on emotions associated with death flowed from a series of articles on foreign death practices, which could be used to highlight American gains in objectivity. Another popular theme involved critiques of expensive funeral practices and the increase of professional morticians. A *North American Review* article of 1907 distinguished between appropriate recognition of the gravity of death and the exploitative ceremonies that played on grief: 'Nobody goes to see a man born, but the entire community turns out to see him buried'. Funerals had become perverse: 'We could never understand why old women should, as they unquestionably do, love to attend funerals, or how anybody could be induced, except as a matter of duty, to make a business or profession of the handling of corpses.' The only undertaker worth his salt was the progressive practitioner interested in helping a family save money and curtail needless agonizing, though the author granted that traditional grief should

not be assailed too frontally. A *Harper's Weekly* piece echoed these sentiments, with emphasis on minimization and low cost: a cheap funeral should
be entirely adequate 'to satisfy anyone except those who want really
unnecessary display'. *The Survey*, for its part, condemned grasping undertakers: 'Nothing less than ghoulish are some of the stories of the pressure
put upon grief-distracted people to honor their dead at excessive expense.'
Emphasis, of course, rested on economic good sense, but a corollary
implication was that sensible people would not let themselves be so
overcome by emotion as to fall prey to the greedy.

While death itself received more explicit attention than emotional
reactions to it, up-to-date authors did comment on grief as well. As the
Independent noted in 1908, 'Probably nothing is sadder in life than the
thought of all the hours that are spent in grieving over what is past and
irretrievable'. Time wasted was only part of the problem; loss of control
was the other: 'It is only man [of all the species] that allows his sorrow so
to overcome him that he spends hours calling up the pictures of past
happiness which cannot be brought back.' People know this, but their grief
overwhelms their reason, with the result that they nurse sorrow rather than
looking for happy distraction. Here was a direct attack on Victorian
emotionology: grief has no function, its effort to maintain contact with the
departed being foolish at best, unhealthy at worst. Modern 'psycho-
therapeutics' must be invoked to help people escape conventional grief, and
medical attention was necessary to combat any physical causes of
'melancholic feelings'. A bit of grief might be tolerable, but weeks of tears
suggested 'something morbid, either mental or physical'. Women of course
were the worst offenders: 'When a woman cannot rouse herself . . . from
her grief there is need of the care of the physician.' The *Independent*
editorial acknowledged that grief used to seem consoling, when a young
spouse, for example mourned the death of a partner, but went on to say
that a great deal of unscientific nonsense used to be written about pining
away from grief when often the cause was 'the transmission of the bacillus
tuberculosis':

> This may seem a crude and heartless way to look at such a subject, but it is
> eminently practical and above all has the merit of being satisfactorily therapeutic.
> Nothing is more calculated to arouse people from the poignancy of their grief
> than the realization of a necessity to care for their health.

Thus, although grief might always be with us to a degree, Victorian
wallowing had become ridiculous. Modern medicine suggested that mental
and physical – healing often make grief entirely unnecessary. Even religion
might be legitimately used, if all else fails, to pull people out of their
misery. Whatever the remedy, grief 'in excess' must be attacked. As the
editorial concluded, in an orgy of scientism, grief is a 'contradiction in the
universe, an attempt on the part of a drop in the sea to prevent the tidal
progress of the ocean of life of which it is so small a part, yet every atom of
which is meant to serve a wise purpose in all its events.'

The new view of death and grief was both confirmed and enhanced by recommended reactions to the massive slaughter of the First World War. The dominant theme emphasized the need to put grief aside – as a British article put it, 'to efface as far as possible the signs of woe'. Another journal wanted to use the war to effect permanent improvement in the area of emotion, 'evolving greater wisdom and good sense in our mourning usages'. Grief should, in this revealing argument, become embarrassing: 'To strive to be as natural as possible at such a time is surely the healthy attitude'. Self-control, not excessive sorrow, should predominate, and formal mourning practices, which merely encourage grief, must yield accordingly: 'Let us have more sweetness – and light – in our commemorating of our dear ones'.

After a brief postwar flurry, attacking grief as 'fruitless recollection', the long debate over how to end Victorian approaches to grief and death came to a close. Modernism seemed to triumph in mainstream American public opinion, in interesting contrast to the greater travails of interwar Britain (Cannadine, 1981). Middle-class magazines in the United States turned to other topics as the issue of death and its emotional environment faded from view. Yet the attack on Victorian concepts of grief had three ongoing echoes that incorporated the new hostility to the emotion more fully in middle-class emotionology. These echoes showed how new standards of grief, established during the open campaign against Victorianism, now worked deeper into middle-class emotional culture. First, while discussions of death and grief became far less common, the occasional comment reminded the middle-class audience of the accepted emotional rules; second, the agreement reached about seeking to reduce grief translated into dominant therapeutic emphases; and third, advice to parents sought to develop appropriate socialization strategies to remove intense grief from childhood.

To be sure, one result of the new grief standards was a growing silence. Into the later 1950s discussions of death and emotional reactions to it seemed out of bounds, either not worth pen and ink or too risky to evoke. After this period, by the 1960s, observers of American (and European) death cultures began to talk of death as a modern taboo. They exaggerated slightly, as we will see, but the contrast between the 1890–First World War decades, when active discussion was almost an essayist's staple, and the subsequent cessation of comment was, however, genuinely debatable. It may instead have followed from a sense among the popularizing pundits that the relevant issues were closed, that by now everyone knew the new rules. The largest number of articles during the late 1920s and the 1930s – and they too were infrequent – suggested an assurance that modern Americans were rapidly moving toward appropriate enlightenment about death and grief (Cleghorn, 1923). Beatrice Blankenship, writing of many family deaths, noted how rarely death intruded on the routines of modern life. She criticized ritual remnants such as irrational fear of death or disturbing funerals. Death, even a child's death, while it might elicit some grief, should be treated rationally and calmly, even as modern people were

losing the false certainty of an afterlife. More bombastically, Mabel Ulrich
wrote in 1934 of the decline of religious beliefs and their replacement by
scientific curiosity and self-control. Only a few backsliders remained:

> Is it too far fetched a hope that to these when they have forsaken their wavering
> misty image of heaven there may come a consciousness . . . of the amazing
> relevance of life?

> Modern knowledge . . . offers to the intelligent person today a conception of
> living which is a positive answer to old death fears.

The *American Mercury* proudly boasted that in contrast to emotion-sodden
Europe, 'America Conquers Death'. 'Death, which dominates the European's thought, has been put in its proper place on this side of the water.'
In 1940 *Scholastic* acknowledged real grief but urged the possibility of
allowing life to go on equably even after a death in the immediate family.
Distorting grief, the author argued, usually resulted from some 'unpleasant
and mystifying experience' in connection with death during one's childhood
– a characteristic indication that appropriately low levels of grief depended
on up-to-date child training. Even the Second World War produced little
general reconsideration of death and grief: 'Don't wear mourning too long.
It expresses no real respect for the dead, and it is depressing to the person
who wears it and to friends and family who see it.'

The second transmission of the reconsideration of Victorian grief involved the dominant therapeutic approach. By the 1920s, partly as a result
of Freudian influence but partly, as we can now appreciate, because of shifts
in more general middle-class prescriptions that had so dominated popular
commentary in the anti-grief campaign around 1900, most therapists dealing with grief moved toward what has been called a 'modernist' approach.
Freud had valued grief as a means of freeing individuals from ties with the
deceased, but he had made it clear that detachment was the ultimate goal
and had warned against the stunting that could result if grief were not
transcended fairly quickly. Later modernists downplayed grief even further,
viewing it as a form of separation anxiety, an inappropriate or dysfunctional attempt to restore proximity. In most instances, of course, grief
played itself out as mourners gradually abandoned hope that the lost person
would return; but from the therapeutic perspective there was constant
danger that a more durable imbalance might form. The therapeutic goal,
whether outside help was needed or not, was severance of bonds with the
deceased or departed. Therapy or counseling should work toward this
process of withdrawal, and those who retained grief symptoms must be
regarded as maladjusted. By the 1970s even counseling with older widows
encouraged the development of new identities and interests and promoted
the cessation of grief and its ties to the past. 'Grief work' meant work
against grief and an implicit attack on Victorian savoring of this emotional
state. Appropriate terms were developed for excessive grief – two from the
1960s were 'mummification' and 'despair'. 'Chronic grief syndrome' applied
to a situation of clinging dependency, most common among women, when a

parent or spouse died. The idea that grief followed from love was also attacked; psychologists argued that in cases of spousal death, grief developed particularly strongly when a love-hate tension had existed, grief then picking up on a sense of guilt for the hate rather than a nostalgia for the love. Mental health meant breaking bonds and avoiding dependency. Grief, contradicting both goals, became a target for attack (Stroebe, et al., 1992; Brice, 1991).

Related to the therapeutic approach was the emotional context developed by other health professionals for dealing with death (Wouters, 1990). Because of the desire to avoid grief and emotional entanglement, doctors and nurses, particularly between 1920 and the 1950s, sought to avoid attention to imminent death. Nursing handbooks provided short, matter-of-fact paragraphs on how to recognize impending death and how to lay out a corpse. Both doctors and nurses emphasized concealment of probable death from patients lest unacceptable emotions develop (and in order to protect medical personnel from emotions of their own). Again, grief must be bypassed.

The third area in which the new antigrief regime manifested itself from the 1920s onward lay in a more familiar realm – advice to parents on how to socialize children. Here, the general aversion to Victorian grief was compounded by two factors: the rapid decline in child mortality, which made it progressively easier to dissociate childhood from traditional concern with death; and the rising anxiety about children's fears. From D.H. Thom in the mid-1920s onward, discussions of children's fears frequently embraced the subject of death as popularizers tried to help parents deal with irrational worries about such fanciful prospects as being buried alive. The same new breed of experts warned against the common assumption that children developed attention to death only after their initial years, and they also cautioned that conventional Victorian euphemisms, such as the equation between death and sleep, actually might increase childish fear. As Sidonie Gruenberg noted, '"They go to sleep" is one example of a convenient but dangerous evasion which could make a child approach bedtime with alarm.' (Fiore, 1992). This new approach to death in child-rearing advice was facilitated by the withdrawal of death from the family context, not only because of rapidly dropping child mortality rates but also because of removal of sick adults to hospitals, grandparents to separate residences, and the dead themselves to funeral homes. Further, the decline in adult mourning that followed from the attack on Victorian ceremony also made it easier to separate children from active comment on death, as did the distancing of cemeteries.

In the new context children's fears of death provoked complex reactions among the popularizers. On the one hand, general instructions about fear urged frankness, talking things out. On the other hand, adults themselves were being urged to keep death at an emotional distance, which made it difficult to follow the general line where this particular fear was concerned. A clearer conclusion was that traditional Victorian approaches would not work. Children should not be widely exposed to death ceremonies, and they should not be filled with stories of angels and heavenly reunions. *Parents' Magazine* cautioned against 'conjuring up a heaven of angels and harp playing' for 'inevitably the small girl or boy will discover that mother and father are not certain about the after life. Such a discovery augments the fear of death.' One handbook urged parents to emphasize death's humorous side, while carefully avoiding ridicule – a clear effort to desensitize. Other authors suggested carefully evasive phrasing so that the child would receive no images that he could easily apply to himself. Referring to a grandparent's death as 'all through' might thus be a good idea:

> Fear of death arises when a child imagines not mother or grandmother, or the bird, but himself being covered up with dirt. That much the child can imagine; that much is within the child's observable experience. But if the child gets the idea that a dead person is 'all through', the identification of himself with the dead person or animal is more difficult.

Parents apparently obliged, eager to avoid the necessity of dealing with children's griefs or fears. Thus, a 1943 letter to a child described the death of a family member in these words: 'That door which opens and swings only one way, was thrown open for Dr. Tuttle'. It is doubtful that this imagery would make children stay away from doors or grieve heavily. The entire argumentation assumed that the Victorians were wrong in thinking that children would not be severely touched by grief or might be instructed by it. It also assumed that family unity in grief had somehow become irrelevant, for reactions to death were now gauged purely in terms of their (usually harmful) impact on individual psyches. The whole Victorian grief context had disappeared as grief became simply another problem, though a potentially difficult one, in the emotional raising of children. One of the reasons for abandoning mourning and its colors was to help children ignore death to the greatest extent possible. When information had to be conveyed, 'let us give the facts to the child with as little emotion as possible'. For older children, factual, scientific information would help separate death from powerful emotion – here was a child-socialization variant on the medical modernization approach in adult contexts. Some authorities also urged not only dry facts but maximum avoidance. Alan Fromme for example, advising that children be kept away from funerals, wanted to prevent any glimpse of intense adult mourning. Death itself should be acknowledged quickly, lest children suspect dark secrets, but ceremonies as well as emotions might best be removed (Fromme, 1956). One *Parents' Magazine* author acknowledged that the power of grief makes it difficult for parents to maintain rational control but went on to say that this was precisely why the emotion's power must be combated, for it is necessary to 'maintain some equilibrium to carry on'. Children need not be 'bowed down' with grief as are some misguided adults.

A final sign of the new grief culture emerged, though somewhat belatedly, in the etiquette books offered up to a still-eager middle-class audience. Emily

Post, the leading authority in the interwar period, painted an essentially Victorian picture even in 1934, when she repeated the wording of a long section on funerals that she had initially written in 1922. She urged a variety of mourning symbols and ceremonies, including 'hanging the bell' outside a home, and stressed the importance of punctiliousness precisely because emotional reactions to death ran so high. Her main advice was that readers should acknowledge the intensity of grief and respect its varied courses, expressing active sympathy when the afflicted sought company but also respecting their privacy. Grief had no sweetness in this portrayal, but its vigor was viewed as inevitable. Constraint applied only to those dealing with the mourners, who needed to put selfish interests behind them in the interest of providing comfort and calm. 'All over-emotional people . . . should be banned absolutely' from grief situations. Emily Post attacked overelaborate funerals – though allowing that they were appropriate for those who found solace in them – but she noted that while formal mourning was in partial decline, it could actually serve as a protection against real sorrow. Etiquette, in sum, lagged behind other areas of emotional culture when it came to reactions to death, in part because recommendations were less frequently reworded, in part because advisers assumed that polite form and continuity with past practices were intertwined.

But even in this area change did occur, and it confirmed the earlier shifts apparent in popular magazines and childrearing literature. By 1952, when Amy Vanderbilt issued her etiquette book, the major signals were quite different, although, etiquette being etiquette, there were still forms to observe. Business matters now received as much attention as ceremonies, for the first job of the bereaved was to check on wills, bank accounts and medical formalities. Not only funerals but also mourning had become far more simple – Vanderbilt praised the decline of mourning costumes – and these trends were good because they so lightened the emotional mood. Some bereaved individuals could even express happiness, and this was a positive sign. Friends of the bereaved should still express sympathy, of course, but they should be far more careful than before not to encourage grief itself: 'It is better to avoid the words "died", "death" and "killed" in such [condolence] letters. It is quite possible to write the kind of letter that will give a moment of courage and a strong feeling of sympathy without mentioning death or sadness at all.' Most revealing was the advice to the afflicted themselves, who now had an obligation to control themselves. Whereas Emily Post had readily allowed the emotion to overcome all rational or altruistic capacity for a time, not so Amy Vanderbilt and her peers in the 1950s. Grief simply must not be intense: 'We are developing a more positive social attitude toward others, who might find it difficult to function well in the constant company of an outwardly mourning person.' Whatever went on inside should be kept firmly under wraps. Vanderbilt went on to note, in recognition of the more general culture, that wartime had taught people to restrain their grief because it damaged morale and gave comfort to the enemy. With this, the focus of etiquette shifted largely from appropriate sorrow and condolence to emphasis on restraint and an upbeat mood. Substantial grief had lost its validity in this most conventional and change-resistant of popular advice sectors (Vanderbilt, 1952).

The emergence of a grief culture strikingly different from its Victorian predecessor responded to several new factors, coalescing by around 1900. The larger cultural context shifted, which was crucial given the prominence of cultural ingredients in shaping nineteenth-century grief standards. Religious certainty declined; lessened confidence in references to heaven was explicitly mentioned in new grief advice to parents. To be sure, modernist intellectuals, bent on secular scrutiny of Victorian follies, may well have influenced advice writers more than the larger American middle class, but there was some change in mainstream religious security. Attacks on Victorian grief also reflected a larger campaign against emotional intensity more generally. Grief revisionism, indeed, became an early instance of a general trend, as Victorian standards of anger, fear and even love were also revised (Stearns, 1994).

This larger change, and the explicit hostility to intense grief, also followed from new functionalist concerns. The American economy was shifting toward consumerism and became ever more enmeshed in the tight time schedules of an advanced industrial society. Consumerism helped create a new division between pleasant and unpleasant emotions, the former associated with 'happiness' and often with the savoring of material objects or sexual release (Sommers, 1984). Grief, however valued in the nineteenth century, simply could not qualify in this new environment, and became increasingly rated as negative, one of the emotions toward which Americans were distinctively averse and about which they proved exceedingly reticent. Work schedules figured less directly in grief formulations, but the fact was that the intricate coordination required in big business did not easily mesh with the unpredictable demands of mourning. Mourning, in consequence, declined rapidly, and grief standards – as in the case of etiquette – shifted accordingly (Gorer, 1965).

The erosion of some of the cultural bases for Victorian grief combined with the new functional deterrents almost certainly would have produced some innovations in grief standards. A more specific change – also functional, though in a different way – sealed the combination, while also helping to explain why grief was revised earlier (by a decade or two) than other Victorian emotions in the establishment of new standards. Traditional death rates declined dramatically, beginning about 1880. Infant mortality began its dramatic plunge to under 5 per cent (reached by 1920); maternal mortality saw a similar reduction. Major causes of death, correspondingly, began to move from contagious disease to degenerative illness and accident. In this new context, Victorian grief was not only less needed – there were far fewer children and young adults to mourn – but also began to seem counterproductive. The way to approach death was through combat, by marshaling the resources of scientific medicine, not through emotional indulgence. As death itself began to move from home to hospital – a shift well underway in the United States by the 1920s – previous grief practices either did not fit or seemed positively obstructive.

The power of new customs helps explain why the new grief standards increasingly affected emotional behavior. Public treatment of death unquestionably shifted. Elaborate Victorian mourning began to trail off by the 1920s; first the draping of houses, then even distinctive apparel were largely abandoned, along with more than brief periods of seclusion and disruption of normal schedules (Vanderbilt, 1952). Cemetery markings became less elaborate and less emotional, and cemeteries themselves moved further from daily view (Stannard, 1975). Cemetery visits also declined. Emotional cultures inevitably affect public standards, and this unquestionably applied to the new grief. Standards also affect emotional response to others, and here too the new culture found its mark. Tolerance of prolonged grief declined, just as the etiquette books suggested. From the 1920s onward stories and personal accounts dealt with the theme of peer reactions – 'her friends were again feeling a little critical of her, saying to one another that it would be a pity if poor Marian should allow grief to make her "queer"' (Moore, 1925). Lessened tolerance played a role in the declining space employers offered to mourning employees. It also figured in the new familial reactions to the death of a child. As children's deaths became far rarer, while at the same time tolerance of grief markedly declined, marriage partners increasingly reacted to the death of a child by splitting up, rather than uniting through shared emotion. Guilt and blame contributed, to be sure, but so did the disappearance of a culture in which grief could be indulged. Escape now seemed the most obvious recourse. The rise of therapies designed to help people get over grief without burdening others, and as quickly as possible, reflected the impact of the new grief standards; this use of outsiders had not figured prominently during the Victorian heyday (Stroebe et al., 1992).

Grief, in sum, became a problem, to be managed as unobtrusively as possible – just as the new grief culture suggested. Many individuals, less commonly afflicted by the most poignant instances of death in any event, clearly adjusted without undue difficulty. Grief became a less familiar emotional experience. Yet it did not disappear. Either because some form of grief is a basic emotion or more probably because important elements of Victorian grief culture persisted – particularly in the idealized attachments and guilts associated with family life – many individuals continued to feel an intensity of grief quite similar to the levels recorded in the nineteenth century. Here is where researchers who have used historical materials correctly note a real continuity, even though they have too often ignored the dramatically altered context (Rosenblatt, 1983; Lofland, 1985). Some changes in the incidence of death – particularly, the prominence of sudden, unprepared death as a result of accidents or cardiovascular attacks – could also heighten grief by leaving no time to anticipate bereavement.

Even when grief persisted, of course, the new standards often applied.

Just as the standards influenced reactions to the emotions of others, so they affected evaluations of self. In the new regime, grieving individuals often felt there was something wrong with them because their grief 'cures', undertaken for example with therapists, did not occur as rapidly as the general culture urged. 'I feel like I am just at a standstill in my life, really, just kind of stopped there', said one patient actively fighting her deep grief (Brice, 1991). Again, the actual experience of grief did not change as uniformly or tidily as the culture recommended, but it was deeply affected.

The result was a new complexity, as the larger culture refused to release its hold. Individuals who felt grief intensely, but were denied an indulgent culture or prolonged sympathy from others, had to suffer silently. Or they focused their emotions on desperate attempts to prolong medical treatments, one source of the new and immensely expensive reliance on heroic medicine in hopeless cases. Or, though less commonly, they turned to legal recourse. Revealingly, American law began to shift by the 1970s toward increasing acknowledgment of grief as a legitimate factor in wrongful death suits, which meant that some bereaved could express their emotions in attacks on those held responsible for the death of a loved one. Or they sought therapy. Or, finally, they joined one of the numerous support groups that began to spring up in the 1950s. Groups such as Theos and the Compassionate Friends, spreading to most American cities, constituted an extraordinary emotional development: total strangers turned to each other both because of their shared experience of grief and their distances from the larger culture. The unavailability of sympathetic others, often including family and friends, made the new bond vital and, frequently, extremely efficacious (Kubler-Ross, 1971).

It is possible, of course, that a realization of the limitations of contemporary grief culture will lead to yet another important revision. Certainly death experts, like Elisabeth Kubler-Ross, and even larger institutional movements like the hospices, have worked in this direction since the 1960s. A more tolerant turn in therapy, modifying the idea that 'grief work' consists only of fighting the emotion as quickly as possible, coincides as well. To date, however, the modifications have formed a minor theme amid the persistence of the dominant culture and its attendant complexity. Other trends, such as the growing popularity of cremation, point toward continued efforts to routinize grief reactions.

Summary

Grief was not an easy emotion in traditional Western culture, though arrangements that minimized it seem often to have worked well in the seventeenth and eighteenth centuries. Major change occurred around 1800, leading to the distinctive Victorian indulgence of the emotion. A second, even more explicit revision of standards occurred early in our own century, on the basis of a number of factors that made Victorian reactions increasingly seem excessive and unproductive. Yet this change brought new burdens of its own, in part because the emphasis on intense family relationships, one of the key Victorian components, was often maintained. Grief was redefined, but in a way that created a disjuncture between public expression and the reactions of others, on the one hand, and the experience of some individuals on the other. A variety of efforts to cope with this disjuncture forms one of the more interesting facets of recent emotional history. Correspondingly, grasp of the modern history of grief, and its unexpected though understandable complexity, is an essential step in understanding the emotion itself. Grief is not pure response; it is conditioned by its dependence on an evolving cultural context, highly sensitive to functional and larger cultural issues. The emotion has undergone some surprisingly sharp turns over the past 150 years, and current reactions inevitably mirror this historical pathway.

References

Ames, Kenneth L. (1981) 'Ideologies in stone meanings in Victorian gravestones', *Journal of Popular Culture*, 14: 641–56.

Ariès, Phillipe (1981) *The Hour of Our Death*. New York: Vintage.

Averill, James R. and Nunley, E.P. (1988) 'Grief as an emotion and as a disease; A social-constructionist perspective', *Journal of Social Issues*, 44: 79–95.

Brice, Charles W. (1991) 'Paradoxes of maternal mourning', *Psychiatry*, 54: 781–92.

Cannadine, David (1981) 'War and death, grief and mourning in modern Britain', in Joachim Whaley (ed.), *Mirrors of Mortality: Studies in the Social History of Death*. New York: St. Martin's.

Cleghorn, Sarah N. (1923) 'Changing thoughts of death', *Atlantic Monthly*, 131: 808–21.

Dye, Nancy Shrom and Blake Smith, Daniel (1986) 'Mother love and infant death, 1750–1920', *Journal of American History*, 73: 329–53.

Fiore, Daniel (1992) *Children and the Death Experience from the Eighteenth Century to the Present*. Unpublished honors paper, Carnegie Mellon University, Pittsburgh.

Fox, Vivian and Quilt, Marten (1980) *Loving, Parenting, and Dying: The Family Cycle in England and America*. New York: Psychohistory Press.

Fromme, Alan (1956) *The Parents Handbook*. New York: Harper's.

Gorer, Geoffrey (1965) *Grief and Mourning in Contemporary Britain*. New York: Oxford.

Hoffert, Sylvia D. (1987) '"A Very Peculiar Sorrow": Attitudes toward Infant Death in the Urban Northeast, 1800–1860', *American Quarterly*, 39: 601–16.

Houlbrooke, Ralph (ed.) (1989) *Death, Ritual, and Bereavement*. Boston: Routledge.

Kubler-Ross, Elisabeth (ed.) (1971) *Death: The Final Stage of Growth*. New York: Macmillan.

Lockridge, Kenneth A. and Lewis, Jan (1988) 'Sally has been sick: Pregnancy and family limitations among Virginia gentry women, 1780–1830', *Journal of Social History*, 22: 5–19.

Lofland, Lynn (1985) 'The social shaping of emotion: The case of grief', *Symbolic Interaction*, 8: 171–90.

Lopata, H. (1975) 'On widowhood: Griefwork and identity reconstruction', *Journal of Geriatric Psychiatry*, 8: 41–58.

Lystra, Karen (1989) *Searching the Heart: Women, Men and Romantic Love in Nineteenth-Century America*. New York: Oxford University Press.

MacDonald, Michael (1981) *Mystical Bedlam: Madness, Anxiety, and Healing in Seventeenth-Century England*. Cambridge: Cambridge University Press.

Moore, Anne Shannon (1925) 'Golden sorrow', *Good Housekeeping* 80: 176–81.

Rosenblatt, Paul C. (1983) *Bitter, Bitter Tears: Nineteenth-Century Diarists and Twentieth-Century Grief Theories*. Minneapolis: University of Minnesota Press.

Sommers, Shula (1984) 'Adults evaluating their emotions: A cross-cultural perspective', in Carol Zander Malatesta and Carroll E. Izard (eds), *Emotion in Adult Development*. Beverly Hills, Calif: Sage.

Stannard, David E. (ed.) (1975) *Death in America*. Pittsburgh: University of Pittsburgh Press.

Stannard, David E. (1976) *The Puritan Way of Death: A Study in Religion, Culture, and Social Change*. Ann Arbor: University of Michigan Press.

Stearns, Carol Z. (1993) 'Sadness', in Jeanette Haviland and Michael Lewis (eds), *Handbook of Emotion*. New York: Guilford Press. pp. 547–62.

Stearns, Peter N. (1975) *Old Age in European Society*. New York: Holmes and Meier.

Stearns, Peter N. (1994) *American Cool: Constructing a 20th-Century Emotional Style*. New York: New York University Press.

Stroebe, Margaret, Gergen, Mary, Gergen, Kenneth J. and Stroebe, W. (1992) 'Broken hearts in broken bonds', *American Psychologist*, 47: 1205–12.

Uhlenberg, Peter (1985) 'Death in the family', in N.R. Hiner and J.M. Hawes (eds), *Growing Up in America: Children in Historical Perspective*. Urbana: University of Illinois Press.

Vanderbilt, Amy (1952) *Etiquette*. Garden City, NY: Doubleday.

Vinovskis, Maris (1976) 'Angels' heads and weeping willows: Death in early America', *American Antiquarian Society, Proceedings*, 86: 273–302.

Wells, Robert V. (1994) 'Taming the "Kings of Terrors": Ritual and death in Schenectady, New York, 1844–1860', *Journal of Social History*, 27, 717–34.

Wouters, Cas. (1990) 'Changing regimes of power and emotion at the end of life', *Netherlands Journal of Sociology*, 26: 151–5.

Chapter 7

Engendered Emotion: Gender, Power, and the Rhetoric of Emotional Control in American Discourse

Catherine A. Lutz

In Western academic discourse, emotions have begun to move from their culturally assigned place at the center of the dark recesses of inner life and are being depicted as cultural, social and linguistic operators. In the process, we can ask not only about the cultural foundations of things construed as emotional, but about the organizing category of 'emotion' itself. One important aspect of that category is its association with the female, so that qualities that define the emotional also define women. For this reason, any discourse on emotion is also, at least implicitly, a discourse on gender.

As both an analytic and an everyday concept in the West, emotion, like the female, has typically been viewed as something natural rather than cultural, irrational rather than rational, chaotic rather than ordered, subjective rather than universal, physical rather than mental or intellectual, unintended and uncontrollable, and hence often dangerous. This network of associations sets emotion in disadvantaged contrast to more valued personal processes, particularly to cognition or rational thought, and the female in deficient relation to her male other. Another and competing theme in Western cultural renditions of emotion, however, contrasts emotion with cold alienation. Emotion, in this view, is life to its absence's death, is interpersonal connection or relationship to an unemotional estrangement, is a glorified and free nature against a shackling civilization. This latter rendition of emotion echoes some of the fundamental ways the female has also been 'redeemed', or alternatively and more positively, construed (Lutz, 1988).

In this chapter, I will explore how emotion has been given a gender in some sectors of American culture and, in the process, make two related arguments. First, I will demonstrate that local or everyday lay discourse on emotion explicitly and implicitly draws links among women, subordination, rebellion and emotion by examining interview conversations conducted with a small group of American women and men. In particular, I will explore a 'rhetoric of control' that frequently accompanies women's (and, to a lesser extent, men's) talk about emotion, and argue that talk about the control or management of emotion is also a narrative about the double-sided nature – both weak and dangerous – of dominated groups. Talk about emotional control in and by women, in other words, is talk about power and its exercise. Second, I will argue that this and further aspects of local discourse are echoed and reproduced in many areas of social and natural scientific discourse that deal with the 'emotional female'. Finally, I will present a further, more syntactic analysis of the interview conversations that contradicts at least some of the stereotypical beliefs about the relationship between gender and emotion that these informants, as well as social science, have voiced. This analysis looks at the degree to which women and men might differentially use syntactic patterns that distance, disavow, or depersonalize the experience of emotion. The failure to find systematic differences can be taken as tentative evidence that cultural models that paint women as more emotionally expressive or more comfortable with a discussion of their own emotions remain surface models and do not organize discourse at more microscopic or out-of-awareness levels.

Gender, power, and the rhetoric of emotional control

Western discourse on emotions constitutes them as paradoxical entities that are both a sign of weakness and a powerful force. On the one hand, emotion weakens the person who experiences it. It does this both by serving as a sign of a sort of character defect (e.g., 'She couldn't rise above her emotions') and by being a sign of at least temporary intrapsychic dis-organization (e.g., 'She was in a fragile state' or 'She fell apart'). The person who has 'fallen apart', needless to say, is unable to function effectively or forcefully. On the other hand, emotions are literally physical forces that push us into vigorous action. 'She was charged up', we say; 'Waves of emotion shook his body'. Women are constructed in a similar contradictory fashion as both strong and weak (e.g., Jordanova, 1980), and I will present evidence from the interviews mentioned earlier that when American women and men talk about emotion, they draw on that similarity to comment on the nature of gender and power. This feature of the emotional and of the female produces frequent discussion in the interviews of the problem of controlling one's feelings. Such discussion is found in both men's and women's discourse, but much more frequently in the latter. I will show that this talk about control of emotions is evidence of a widely shared cultural view of the danger of both women and their emotionality. It is also talk that may mean different things to both the speaker and the audience when it is uttered by women and by men, and this factor will be used to help account for differences in the rate of use of this rhetoric of control. Although both women and men draw on a culturally available model of emotion as something in need of control, they can be seen as often making some different kinds of sense and claims from it.

The material I turn to first was collected in four extended interviews on emotion with fifteen American working- and middle-class women and men. All white, they ranged in age from the early twenties to the mid-seventies and included a bank teller, factory worker, college teacher, retiree, housing code inspector and stockbroker. Most were parents. The interviews were usually conducted in people's homes, and the interviewers included myself and a number of graduate students, most of them women. Each person was interviewed by the same individual for all four sessions, and although a small number of questions organized each session, every attempt was made to have the interviews approximate 'natural conversation'. Nonetheless, it is clearly important to keep in mind the context of the discourse to be analyzed, as it was produced by a group of people who agreed on letter and phone solicitation 'to talk about emotion' for an audience of relative strangers who were also academics and mostly females.

Many people mentioned at one or several points in the interviews that they believe women to be more emotional than men. One example of the variety of ways this was phrased is the account one woman gave to explain her observation that some people seem inherently to be 'nervous types'. She remembered about her childhood that

> the female teachers had a tendency to really holler at the kids a lot, and when I was in class with the male teacher, it seemed like he just let things pass by and it didn't seem to get his goat as fast, and he didn't shout at the same time the female may have in the same instance. . . . I think emotional people get upset faster. I do. And like with men and women, things that are sort of important or bothering me don't bother my husband. . . . I think that's a difference of male and female.[1]

One theme that frequently arises in the interviews is what can be called the 'rhetoric of control' (Rosaldo, 1977). When people are asked to talk about emotions, one of the most common sets of metaphors used is that in which someone or something controls, handles, copes, deals, disciplines, or manages either or both their emotions or the situation seen as creating the emotion. For example:

> I believe an individual can exercise a great deal of *control* over their emotions by maintaining a more positive outlook, by not dwelling on the negative, by trying to push aside an unpleasant feeling. I'm getting angry and like I said, he's over being angry, more or less dropped it and he expects me to also. Well we don't have the same temper, I just can't *handle* it that way.

And in a more poetic turn, one person mused:

> sadness . . . dipping, dipping into that . . . just the out-of-*controlness* of things.

People typically talk about *controlling* emotions, *handling* emotional situations as well as emotional feelings, and *dealing* with people, situations and emotions.

The notion of control operates very similarly here to the way it does in Western discourses on sexuality (Foucault, 1980). Both emotionality and sexuality are domains whose understanding is dominated by a biomedical model; both are seen as universal, natural impulses; both are talked about as existing in 'healthy' and 'unhealthy' forms; and both have come under the control of a medical or quasi-medical profession (principally psychiatry and psychology). Foucault has argued that popular views of sexuality – as a drive that was repressed during the Victorian era and gradually liberated during the twentieth century – are misleading because they posit a single essence that is manipulated by social convention. Rather, Foucault postulated, multiple sexualities are constantly produced and changed. A popular discourse on the control of emotion runs functionally parallel to a discourse on the control of sexuality; a rhetoric of control requires a psychophysical essence that is manipulated or wrestled with and directs attention away from the socially constructed nature of the idea of emotion (see Abu-Lughod and Lutz, 1990). In addition, the metaphor of control implies something that would otherwise be out of control, something wild and unruly, a threat to order. To speak about controlling emotions is to replicate the view of emotions as natural, dangerous, irrational, and physical.[2]

What is striking is that women talked about the control of emotion more than twice as often as did men as a proportion of the total speech each produced in the interviews.[3] To help account for this difference, we can ask what the rhetoric of control might accomplish for the speaker and what it might say to several audiences (see Brenneis, 1990). At least three things can be seen to be done via the rhetoric of emotional control: It (1) reproduces an important part of the cultural view of emotion (and then implicitly of women as the more emotional gender) as irrational, weak and dangerous; (2) minimally elevates the social status of the person who claims the need or ability to self-control emotions; and (3) opposes the view of the feminine self as dangerous when it is reversed, that is, when the speaker denies the need for or possibility of control of emotion. Each of these suggestions can only briefly be examined.

First, this rhetoric can be seen as a reproduction, primarily on the part of women, of the view of themselves as more emotional, of emotion as dangerous, and hence of themselves as in need of control. It does this first by setting up a boundary – that edge over which emotion that is *un*controlled can spill. A number of people have noted that threats to a dominant social order are sometimes articulated in a concern with diverse kinds of boundaries (whether physical or social) and their integrity (e.g., Martin, 1987; Scheper-Hughes and Lock, 1987). One of the most critical boundaries that is constituted in Western psychological discourse is that between the inside and the outside of persons; individualism as ideology is fundamentally based on the magnification of that particular boundary. When emotion is defined, as it also is in the West, as something inside the individual, it provides an important symbolic vehicle by which the problem of the maintenance of social order can be voiced. A discourse that is concerned with the expression, control, or repression of emotions can be seen as a discourse on the crossing back and forth of that boundary between inside and outside, a discourse we can expect to see in more elaborate forms in periods and places where social relations appear to be imminently overturned.

This rhetoric of emotional control goes further than defining and then defending boundaries, however; it also suggests a set of roles – one strong and defensive and the other weak but invasive – that are hierarchized and linked with gender roles. Rosaldo (1984) notes of hierarchical societies that they seem to evince greater concern than do more egalitarian ones with how society controls the inner emotional self and, we can add, with how one part of a bifurcated and hierarchically layered self controls another. The body politic, in other words, is sometimes replicated in the social relations of the various homunculi that populate the human mind, a kind of 'mental politic'. When cognition outreasons and successfully manages emotion, male–female roles are replicated. When women speak of control, they play the roles of both super- and subordinate, of controller and controlee. They identify their emotions and themselves as undisciplined and discipline both through a discourse on control of feeling. The construction of a feminine self, this material might suggest, includes a process by which women come to control themselves and so obviate the necessity for more coercive outside control.

There is the example of one woman in her late thirties; she talked about the hate she felt for her ex-husband, who began an affair while she was pregnant and left her with the infant, an older child and no paid employment.

> So I think you try hard not to bring it [the feeling] out 'cause you don't want that type of thing at home with the kids, you know. That's very bad, very unhealthy, that's no way to grow up. So I think now, maybe I've just learned to control it and time has changed the feeling of the hate.

The woman here defines herself as someone with a feeling of hate and portrays it as dangerous, primarily in terms of the threat it poses to her own children, a threat she phrases in biomedical terms (i.e., 'unhealthy'). She replicates a view that Shields (1987) found prevalent in a survey of twentieth-century English-language child-rearing manuals; this is the danger that mothers' (and not fathers') emotions are thought to present to children. In addition, this woman's description of her feelings essentializes them as states; as such, they remain passive (see Cancian, 1987 on the feminization of love) rather than active motivators, a point to which we will return.

In other cases, people do not talk about themselves, but rather remind others (usually women) of the need to control themselves. These instances also serve to replicate the view of women as dangerously emotional. Another woman spoke about a female friend who still grieved for a son who had died two years previously: 'You've got to pick up and go on. You've got to try and get those feelings under control.' (The 'you' in this statement is a complex and multivocal sign (Kirkpatrick, 1987), and directs the admonition to control simultaneously to the grieving woman, the female interviewer, the speaker herself, no one in particular, and everyone in a potential audience.

A second pragmatic effect of the rhetoric of emotional control is a claim to have the ability to 'rise above' one's emotions or to approve of those who do. Women, more than men, may speak of control because they are concerned about counteracting the cultural denigration of themselves through an association with emotion. 'I think it's important to control emotions', they say, and implicitly remind a critical audience that they have the cooler stuff it takes to be considered mature and rational. It is important to note that, as academics, I and the graduate students who conducted the interviews may have been perceived as an audience in special need of such reminders. The speakers would have been doing this, however, by dissociating themselves from emotion rather than by questioning the dominant view both of themselves and of emotion.

Although women may have less access to a view of themselves as masterful individuals, a common aspect of the cultural scheme that *is* available paints them as masterfully effective with others on joint tasks, particularly interpersonal or emotional tasks (social science versions of this include Chodorow, 1978; Parsons and Bales, 1955). This subtly alters the meaning of the rhetoric of control; knowledge of what the feelings are that 'need' control and of what control should be like is perceived and described as a social rather than an individual process. For example, one woman says: 'If you're tied in with a family, . . . you have to use it for guidance how you control your emotions.' This is the same woman whose central life problem during the interview period was coping with her husband's ex-wife and family, who lived across the street from her. The regular, friendly contact between husband and ex-wife has left her very unhappy but also unsure about what to do. The ambiguity over who ought to control or regulate what is evident in her description of an argument she had with her husband over the issue.

I was mad. I was mad. And I said, 'I don't care whether you think I should [inaudible word] or stay in this at all, it's too, and cause I'm going to say it.' And I said, 'How dare you tell me how I'm supposed to feel', you know. Bob [her husband] would say, you know, 'You got to live with it' or 'You got to do this' or 'How dare you tell me this, I don't have to put up with anything' or 'I don't have to feel this way because you tell me I have to feel this way'. You know, it was, in that case Robin is his ex-wife, 'and you have to just kind of deal with it', you know, 'all the problems that she presents in your own way'. And it was almost sort of like saying 'You're going to have to like it'. Well I don't. I don't, you know. And for a year and a half he kept saying, you know, 'You're going to have to like it, this is the way it's going to be, you're going to have to do this, you're going to have to have, be, act, this certain way', you know, act everything hunky-dory, and it wasn't, you know, and I was beginning to resent a whole lot of things. I, I, I resented him for telling me I had to feel that way when I, I wasn't real fond of the situation. I didn't like it. When I would tell him that I didn't like it, it was 'It's your problem, you deal with it'. I didn't like that, that made me really angry because I was saying, 'Help me out here, I don't know how to deal with this'.

This woman is frustrated with her husband for failing to join her in a collaborative project of 'dealing with' her feelings of resentment. Here control is given away to or shared with others. This strategy of control is more complex and subtle than the simple self-imposition described in other parts of the transcripts so far; it aims to control both the emotions of the self *and* the attention and assistance of the other. Note also that she speaks of 'resenting' or 'not liking' (relatively mild terms of displeasure) the overall situation but is most incensed ('mad, mad, mad') about her husband's assumption that she ought not to feel a certain way. She asserts the right to 'feel' unhappy about her predicament but is clearly defining that feeling in the standard contemporary sense of a strictly internal and passive event. Nowhere in the interview does she explicitly state or appear to imply that she wants, intends, or ought to act in concert with those feelings. What is being controlled or dealt with, therefore, has already been defined as a relatively innocuous feeling rather than an action tendency.

Finally, the rhetoric of emotional control can also be employed in both idiosyncratic and 'reversed' ways that may intend or have the effect of at least minimally resisting the dominant view of emotionality, and thus of women. A few people, for example, spontaneously spoke about the problem of emotional control, thereby evoking the whole schema we have just been looking at. They went on, however, to define 'control' in a way that entailed relatively minimal constraints on emotional communication. One woman, a twenty-eight-year-old bank teller, said: 'Let me explain control. It's not that you sit there and you take it [some kind of abuse] and, you know, I think controlling them [emotions] is letting them out in the proper time, in the proper place.' Perhaps more radically, some women (as well as one of the gay men with whom I spoke) denied that they had the ability to control some or many of their emotions.[4] One man in his twenties critically described a previous tendency he had to over-intellectualize problems and explained that he worked against that tendency because

> It wasn't that I wanted to cut off my emotions, I just didn't, they would get out of control, and I found that the more I tried to suppress them, the more powerful they would become. It was like this big dam that didn't let a little out at a time, it would just explode all of a sudden, and I'd be totally out of control.

The question remains, however, of the validity of seeing these latter seemingly resistant uses of the rhetoric of emotional control as 'oppositional' forms (Williams, 1977) within that system.[5] This is certainly a dangerous rhetorical strategy, caught as they (we) are within a hegemonic discourse not of our own making. The opposition to self-control will most likely be absorbed into the logic of the existing system and so come to equal not resistance but simple deficiency or lack (of control).[6] A possibly oppositional intent may have collaborative outcomes to the extent that the denial of self-control is taken by most audiences as a deficit and a confirmation of ideas about women's irrationality.

The culturally constructed emotionality of women is rife with contradiction. The emotional female, like the natural world that is the cultural source of both affect and women, is constructed as both pliant (because weak and a resource for use by civilized man) and ultimately tremendously powerful and uncontrollable (Strathern, 1980).[7] Emotionality is the source of women's value, their expertise in lieu of rationality, and yet it is the origin of their unsuitability for broader social tasks and even a potential threat to their children.

There are vivid parallels between this and the cultural meanings surrounding colonialism that Taussig (1984) and Stoler (1985) have described. Looking at early-twentieth-century colonists' views of the local Columbian labor force, Taussig describes their alternation between fear and awe of Indians who were perceived as dangerous and powerful figures, on the one hand, and disgust and denigration of their perceived weakness and lack of civilization, on the other. Taussig describes the process as one in which a 'colonial mirror' 'reflects back onto the colonists the barbarity of their own social relations' (1984: 495). In a (certainly less systematic or universally brutal) way, a 'patriarchal mirror' can be conceptualized as helping to produce the view of women as emotional – as dangerously 'eruptive' and as in the process of weakly 'breaking down'. A 'paradox of will' seems consistently to attend dominating relationships – whether those of gender, race or class – as the subordinate other is ideologically painted as weak (so as to need protection or discipline) and yet periodically as threatening to break the ideological boundary in riot or hysteria. Emotion talk, as evident in these transcripts, shows the same contradictions of control, weakness and strength. Given its definition as nature, at least in the West, emotion discourses may be one of the most likely and powerful devices by which domination proceeds.

The engendering of emotion in science

Demonstrations of the political, moral, and cultural bases of Western science have been made convincingly in a number of natural and social fields (e.g., Asad, 1973; Fausto-Sterling, 1985; Haan et al., 1983; Sampson, 1981). In like fashion, it can be argued that the sciences of emotion have been, in a significant sense, a product of their social context. In particular, the academic literature on emotion can be considered a form of political discourse on gender relations because of the marked associations between the two domains. That literature thus arises out of and reenters a field of power struggles for the definition of true womanhood. As Haraway (1986) has said of American primatology, it can be seen as 'politics by other means', and in the case of emotions, it is most centrally a politics of gender by other means. By examining several examples of studies of emotion, we will see that much research over the years in biology, psychology, sociology, sociolinguistics and other fields has been implicitly based on everyday cultural models linking women and emotionality, and that this research moves from the assumption of these cultural premises to their 'proof'. Most striking about these studies is the number that naturalize the purported gender differences by attributing them to biological or necessary and universal features of the female role in physical and social reproduction. I will briefly examine several areas of research, including the analysis of premenstrual syndrome and mood, sex differences in the recognition of facial expressions of emotion and in aggression, and studies of the affective components and concomitants of motherhood. Feminist critiques of a number of these latter fields have been intensive, and I will draw on them while extending the analysis of the domain of emotion.

Studies of the relationship between mood and hormonal changes have focused on women's (rather than men's) cycles and in the process have discovered the hormonal disease of premenstrual syndrome. This syndrome is characterized by both physical pain and mood disturbances and has been attributed by the biomedical research community to hormonal imbalances in the women who suffer from it. The syndrome has been used to explain a host of emotions ranging from irritability and mood swings to depression, anxiety and panic attacks. A number of feminist critiques (Archer and Lloyd, 1985; Fausto-Sterling, 1985; Gottlieb, 1987; Whatley, 1986) have pointed out the weakness of the evidence for this syndrome. Assessment of women's mood is usually based on retrospective self-report via questionnaires (one popular version being titled the 'Menstrual Distress Questionnaire'), which allow women to draw on cultural knowledge about the relation between gender, emotion and hormones. Conversely, studies that disguise the purposes of the questionnaire show no significant premenstrual mood changes. The putative therapeutic effects of hormone injections are taken as primary evidence of the female hormonal basis for mood changes, but these studies have not been 'double-blind'. As Whatley argues, this biomedical discourse on emotions and gender may 'cause us to ignore the fact that our premenstrual mood changes . . . may also correlate more closely to a monthly cycle of low bank balances than of hormonal fluctuations' (1986: 183). Moreover, the emotional symptoms of premenstrual syndrome can be seen as a discourse on both the good and the deviant woman, on the necessity of her emotional suffering and the abnormality of, especially, her anger or irritability (Gottlieb, 1987), both common symptoms attached to the syndrome. Normative academic and clinical work on premenstrual syndrome focuses on the emotionality of women as both common and yet as a 'symptom' in need of a cure. This research draws on the entrenched cultural view of emotions as sited in females, as natural in essence (like but independent of the 'naturalness' of females), and as irrational or pathological when they occur.

This line of research follows from and reinvigorates the cultural model in which women are more emotional than men because they are more tied to the biological processes that produce emotion. Wombs, menstruation, and hormones 'predict' emotion. A more tacit part of the cultural logic connecting women and emotion may arise from the view of women as biologically inferior both because they menstruate and because they are smaller, weaker and lack a penis. When viewed as a form of physical chaos or 'breakdown', emotion is one other form of biological weakness suffered by women.[8]

A number of people in the interview study just described spontaneously articulated related ideas about the relationship between women, hormones, emotion and pathology. In several cases, they referred to research as the authoritative source of their assertions, although my argument is that the relationship between everyday and scientific ideas about women and emotion is dialectical rather than an idea system imposed hegemonically on a previously blank or very different lay model. According to one woman, a forty-eight-year-old telephone operator, 'women have been known to have different reactions to the same situation at different times of the month. And that's been a study. I've seen where some women can be downright dangerous, they could be potential killers.'

Another field in which some attention has been paid to sex differences is the study of facial expression of emotion. In one sociobiological account, female emotionality is a product of evolution. Babchuk et al. (1985) interpret studies showing that women are better able than men to read facial expressions of emotions in infants. In their view, this is the result of women's long history of being the primary caretakers of infants and the reproductive value of using these facial cues to detect infant distress. This argument is implausible on many grounds, not the least of which are the redundancy in infants of facial expression and other cues to discomfort, and the theoretically at least equal value of facial expression recognition skills for the prehistoric males, who, in many evolutionary accounts, were engaged primarily in defending the female and infant against threatening and dissembling outsiders. In addition, one of the central studies that demonstrates female superiority in decoding facial expressions of emotion (Hall, 1978) has been reanalyzed and shown to account for less than 4 percent of the variance between individuals in facial expression recognition skills (Deaux, 1984, cited in Shields, 1987).

Despite its obvious problems, this account of the evolution of facial expression identification is a story with some power, as it draws on en-trenched cultural narratives about women, motherhood, children and love. Here, the first premise is that women are more attuned to emotion in themselves and others. Unlike the premenstrual syndrome studies, however, female emotionality is celebrated here, with emotions taking on their positive sense of the interpersonally engaged, the unalienated. Women's emotionality becomes a skill and an asset. It is significant that the sociobiological account focuses on the use of that asset to detect distress (rather than, for example, threat). Distress, of course, calls for nurturance, whereas other facial expressions (in either infants or adults) might call for flight or defense, but only the former behavior is normative for women and mothers.

Another line of research, on sex differences in aggression, also draws on cultural views of emotion and women. This happens, first, because aggression, at least in the Western cultural view, is seen as retrospectively predictive of anger (Montagu, 1978). Anger is the one emotion that is exempted in everyday discourse from the expectation that women feel and express more emotion than men. It is in fact every emotion *but* anger that is disapproved in men and, conversely, expected in women (Hochschild, 1983). This gender stereotype has been shown to have been thoroughly learned by American children as early as the preschool period (Birnbaum et al., 1980, cited in Shields, 1987). A recent, widely accepted, and often cited set of studies makes the parallel claim to have demonstrated a relationship between levels of the 'male' hormone testosterone and aggression. Fausto-Sterling (1985) demonstrates the weakness of the evidence for this claim and questions why it has been taken up so enthusiastically by so many.

The echoes of the lay view in the scientific are followed by the echoes of the scientific view in the lay on this point as well. A professional woman in her forties in the interview study commented on the association between aggression and gender: 'So far the research shows that, yes, little boys are inherently more aggressive than little girls. . . . I think it bothers me that there's a sex link with aggression. There are a couple of sex-linked ones that bother me but . . . but I can't do anything about it.'

A number of studies that use the cultural logic of engendered emotion focus less on physiological differences to account for emotional ones than on universal functions and roles. In particular, they draw on the notion of women's reproductive role and the nurturing role and emotions that supposedly naturally accompany it. From ethological bonding theory (Bowlby, 1969) to some schools of feminism (e.g., Ruddick, 1980), focus is placed on the natural or inevitable emotional concomitants of motherhood (rather than fatherhood), including particularly the positive emotions of love, caring, and attachment. Bowlby follows the prevailing cultural emphasis on women's emotional qualities when he focuses on the emotions of women and their children. He wants to explain the intensity of the bond between mother and infant, and roots that explanation in an instinctual need for attachment in the infant and fear of separation. Feelings of love for the child on the part of the mother are naturalized (cf. Scheper-Hughes, 1985), and disastrous consequences are chronicled should the infant fail to receive sufficient quantities of mother love. These two facets of Bowlby's approach provide the carrot and stick of natural instinct and psychological harm to the child as reasons for continued emphasis on the need for emotionality in women.

Ruddick (1980), on the other hand, identifies 'resilient good humor and cheerfulness', 'attentive love' and 'humility' as among the central features of maternal virtue that follow from (rather than precede) the task of parenting and, by frequent correlation, the task of being female. From these perspectives, women are more deeply embedded in relationships with others (with the mother–infant bond as the primary example and the primary cause). This interpersonal engagement with others is what produces emotion, which is here defined as responses to others with whom one is involved. From the perspective of feminism, male individualism is antithetical to the experience of emotion (see also Chodorow, 1978).

The differences between these two perspectives on mothering and emotion are, of course, crucial. Bowlby-style bonding theory naturalizes the connection between women and affect through evolutionary theory and is continuous with earlier theorizing about the elevated moral status of women achieved through their divinely assigned and naturally embedded mothering skills. Feminist theory most often identifies the social division of labor rather than nature as the ultimate source of such emotional differences. Interestingly, however, both kinds of discourse on emotion elevate women (the first to a domestic pedestal, the second to self-esteem and/or the ability to resist patriarchy) by focusing on positive emotions such as love and by using 'emotion' in its positive Romantic sense of connection and disalienation.

Yet another view of the cultural view of women as emotional is found in the Parsonian normative construction of family roles, in which women are the 'expressive expert' and men the 'instrumental expert' (Parsons and Bales, 1955). These competencies are seen as an outcome of the domestic–market spheres in which the genders differentially participate. Compare this notion, however, with the contradictory view of women's emotional impact on the family noted in the interview example and the child-rearing manual themes described earlier. The point may be that women are expected to be experts in noticing and attending to the emotional needs of others (also per Bowlby), not their own, which are rather objects of control or suppression because they, unlike the emotions of other family members, are defined as dangerous.

Hochschild's (1983) important feminist revision of Parsons and Bales's scheme paints emotion less as a skill than as a form of labor. Women are socially assigned a much heavier burden of emotional labor than are men. Hochschild's ideas contribute to a breaking down of the dichotomy of emotion and thought; they can also extend the notion of women's double day of domestic and wage labor as women are required to contribute both emotional and cognitive labor in both paid and unpaid spheres. In this and other feminist analyses, gender and emotion are related through the relations of production. For Hochschild, emotion is a personal resource that women must self-exploit more than men. It nonetheless remains a psychophysical fact, socially manipulated, rather than a discursive practice that constructs women as more emotional than men.

In sum, social science disciplines women and their psyches. It constructs emotion as an individual and intrapsychic phenomenon and evidences the same concern as lay discourse with the emotionality of women – its frequency, its intensity, its virtues as an emblem of female gender identity, but most of all, its danger and implicitly the need for its control.

Personalization

I now return to the question of how these cultural notions about the emotionality of women, articulated in scientific discourse, are related to everyday discourse. The rhetoric of control that we first looked at was shown to reflect, in multiple and complex ways, relations of power between men and women, and to reflect them in ways that can be said, in large measure, to reproduce the 'emotional female'. By looking closely at some more microscopic aspects of the interview talk, however, we can see that gender differences are minimal, a fact that may speak to the gaps and fissures in the construction of a hegemonic discourse.

In two of the series of interviews, people were asked, first, to describe recent experiences with each of several common emotions and, second, to talk about how they feel about their work and family lives. In an analysis of a sample of 286 randomly selected interview statements that include direct reference to emotions, I have focused on the degree to which the statement 'personalizes' the emotion experience – that is, on a variety of ways emotions, even as they are discussed, can be distanced from the self. It might be expected that women would use more personalizing and immediate syntactic forms if they operate following the cultural model in which women are more emotionally expressive and have a more emotional self-identity.

Personalization, or a nondistancing discursive strategy, was indexed by four speech patterns (see Table 7.1), which will now be discussed.

First, the present tense rather than the past or conditional tense (e.g., 'I *get* [or *am*] angry whenever someone talks to me that way' compared with 'I *was* very angry'), is used. Tense obviously does several things to the meaning that audiences can make of a statement about emotion. First, it can move the emotion experience farther away from or closer to the self or another in time. Second, it can either generalize or particularize the experience; the use of the present tense, for example, can often include the implication that the emotion is habitually experienced by the subject. On both of these counts, the stereotype would lead us to expect more use of the present tense by women speakers. In fact, there is no difference between male and female speakers in the interview sample in the use of the present tense. If anything, men as a group make slightly (insignificantly) more use of it.

Second, another element of a personalizing strategy might include the use of syntactic patterns that more directly portray the speaker as the experiencer of the emotion. Statements were coded as portraying the experiencer as the self, as another person (male, female, or gender unspecified), or as leaving the experiencer unspecified (e.g., '*It* was a very strong feeling of hate' or 'And *that* developed a certain amount of hate toward that individual because of the fact that he . . .') or the emotion as an abstract entity with no particular experiencer (e.g., 'Well, hate and frustration usually go hand in hand, I would say' or '"Love" would be, I think, a good catchall

Table 7.1 *Personalization in syntax*

---

1 *Present tense*
  'I *get* [or *am*] angry whenever someone talks to me that way.'
  Others
  'I *was* very angry.'

2 *Experiencer of the emotion discussed*
  Self, as subject of emotion experience
  '*I'm* very anxious about it.'
  Self, as object of emotion experience
  'It's making *me* angry just talking about this.'
  Other person (male, female, or gender unspecified)
  '*My father* was very annoyed with me for going into that field.'
  Unspecified
  '*It* was a very strong feeling of hate.'
  'And *that* developed a certain amount of hate toward that individual because of the fact
    that he . . .'
  None – emotion as an abstract entity
  'Well, hate and frustration usually go hand in hand, I would say.'
  '"Love" would be, I think a good catchall phrase because . . .'

3 *Cause or elicitor of emotion*
  Self
    'They were angry at *me*.'
    '*I* just kind of giggled and made her even angrier.'
  Other person
    'I hate *her* because she was mean enough to tell me that.'
    'I'm deathly afraid of *dentists*.'
  Event
    'The most anxious moment I had . . . was *my first performance with the . . . Choral
      Society*.'
    'I hate *going out* unless I really have to.'
  Object
    He loves *books*.'
  Unspecified
    Lots of little things are frustrating.'
    'I can't talk anymore, I start screaming to begin with, when I'm really angry.'
4 *Negation*
    'I [or she] was*n't* angry.'

---

phrase because . . .'). The category of self was further broken down by whether the self was portrayed as subject or object of the emotion experience (e.g., '*I'm* very anxious about it' compared with 'It's making *me* angry just talking about this'). The belief in women's emotionality might lead to the expectation that women would more often portray the self (particularly the self as subject rather than object) as the experiencer of emotion, whereas men would portray the other as the experiencer or leave the latter ambiguous.

In the interview sample, it is *not* significantly more common for women, in their discussions of emotion, to focus on the experiencing self as the subject versus the object of the emotion, nor is it more common for men to leave the experiencer unspecified or abstract. In addition, neither women nor men are more likely to portray others as opposed to the self as the experiencer of the discussed emotion. Women and men speak more alike than differently in this sample when discussing the experiencer of emotions.

Third, statements about emotion usually contain an implicit or explicit etiology, that is they specify the cause (usually by specifying the object) of the feeling. Personalizing strategies might include identification of either the self or, secondarily, another person as the ultimate cause of the emotion (rather than the use of syntactic patterns that obscure or fail to identify the cause). Statements were coded as portraying the cause as either the self (e.g., 'They were angry at *me*' or '*I* just kind of giggled and made her even angrier'), another person (e.g., 'I hate *her* because she was mean enough to tell me that' or 'I'm deathly afraid of *dentists*'), an event (e.g., 'The most anxious moment I had . . . was *my first performance with the . . . Choral Society*' or 'I hate *going out* unless I really have to'), an object (e.g., 'He loves *books*'), or as leaving the cause unspecified (e.g., *Lots of little things* are frustrating' or 'I can't talk anymore, I start screaming to begin with, when I'm really angry') (cf. Shimanoff, 1983). Given the associations between gender and affect I noted earlier, we might expect that women more than men would see other people as intimately involved in their own emotion experience and themselves as evoking emotion in others, rather than seeing events as triggering emotion in themselves or failing to specify a cause. The latter strategy can be associated with the view of emotion as nonsensical, irrational, or without ascertainable cause. In fact, there are no significant gender differences in the use of personal versus impersonal causal attribution, nor do women use self versus other attributions more than men.

Finally, a number of statements about emotion in the interviews are essentially denials of emotion in the self or the other (e.g., 'I [or she] was*n't* angry'). The stereotype might lead us to expect more negation in general from men and more negation of particular kinds of female-linked emotions (which include most emotions except anger) by men and of male-linked emotions (notably anger) by women. Here again, women's and men's speech are indistinguishable in terms of the proportion of emotion states that are negated as they are discussed.

The absence of extensive differences might be attributed to the special nature of the people interviewed, all of whom agreed beforehand to talk with a stranger about emotion. The results are consistent, however, with a study of gender differences in emotion language used by Shimanoff (1983), who did a similar analysis of the tape-recorded natural conversations of a number of American college students and married couples, and found few differences in male and female conversations that included reference to emotions.[9] The results are also consistent with the trend in studies of psychological and linguistic sex differences in general, which have tended to show far fewer differences than researchers both expected – on the basis of cultural stereotypes about distinctive male and female styles of thinking, behavior, and speech -- and then often found in self-fulfilling fashion. The absence of differences is more significant given the syntactic nature of the evidence examined; Shibamoto (1987) has concluded that gender differences that are not a response to audience expectations about particular gender identities are more likely to be found in syntactic patterns of use because they are typically outside of our awareness and hence of our easy manipulation, unlike semantic patterns such as those having to do with the notion of 'control' we examined earlier.

Conclusion

In all societies, body disorders -- which emotion is considered to be in this society -- become crucial indicators of problems with social control and, as such, are more likely to occur or emerge in a discourse concerning social subordinates. Foucault has made the claim that power creates sexuality and its disciplining; similarly, it can be said to create emotionality. The cultural construction of women's emotion can thus be viewed not as the repression or suppression of emotion in men (as many laypeople, therapists, and other commentators argue) but as the creation of emotion in women. Because emotion is constructed as relatively chaotic, irrational, and antisocial, its existence vindicates authority and legitimates the need for control. By association with the female, it vindicates the distinction between and hierarchy of men and women. And the cultural logic connecting women and emotion corresponds to and shores up the walls between the spheres of private, intimate (and emotional) relations in the (ideologically) female domain of the family and public, formal (and rational) relations in the primarily male domain of the marketplace.

Rubin has remarked of sexuality that 'There are historical periods in which [it] is more sharply contested and more overtly politicized' (1984: 267). Emotionality has the same historical dynamism, with shifting gender relations often appearing to be at the root of both academic and lay struggles over how emotion is to be defined and evaluated.[10] In other words, the contemporary dominant discourse on emotions -- and particularly the view that they are irrational and to be controlled -- helps construct but does not wholly determine women's discourse; there is an attempt to recast the association of women with emotion in an alternative feminist voice.

Feminist treatments of the question of emotion (e.g., Hochschild, 1983; Jagger, 1987) have tended to portray emotions not as chaos but as a discourse on problems. Some have contested both the irrationality and the passivity of feelings by arguing that emotions may involve the identification of problems in women's lives and are therefore political. Talk about anger, for example, can be interpreted as an attempt to identify the existence of inappropriate restraint or injustice. Sadness is a discourse on the problem of loss, fear on that of danger. By extension, talk about the control of emotions would be, in this feminist discourse, talk about the suppression of public acknowledgment of problems. The emotional female might then be seen not simply as a mythic construction on the axis of some arbitrary cultural dualism but as an outcome of the fact that women occupy an objectively more problematic position than does the white, upper-class, Northern European, older man who is the cultural exemplar par excellence of cool, emotionless rationality. According to a feminist analysis, whether or not women express their problems (i.e., are emotional) more than men, those women's audiences may hear a message that is an amalgam of the orthodox view and its feminist contestation: 'We (those) women are dangerously close to erupting into emotionality/pointing to a problem/ moving toward a social critique.'

Notes

An earlier version of this chapter was presented on the panel 'Emotion and Discourse' at the annual meeting of the American Anthropological Association, Chicago, 18–22 November 1987. The draft has benefited greatly from the comments of Lila Abu-Lughod and Steven Feld. The research on which this chapter is based has been conducted with grants from the State University of New York Foundation and the National Institute of Mental Health and with the help of many people. Kathryn Beach, Robin Brown, Paula Bienenfeld and Walter Komorowski assisted in interviewing and transcription, and the expert analytic work of Angela Carroll and Marion Pratt helped give the chapter its form.

1 The actual process by which these models of gender and emotion are acquired is a fascinating but unexplored question. We might expect that it includes, in part, the child's reasoning from the culturally assigned authority and control of the male teacher to a lack of emotion, the latter perhaps already having been learned to require 'strength' and 'control' to master – in other words, to generalize from the dominant position of males to a presumed lack of emotion (a process that might also have occurred in her teachers' views of themselves).

2 The method used in looking at the transcripts draws on recent developments in the 'cognitive' study of cultural meaning. These focus on the analysis of extended and relatively natural conversations for the cultural knowledge or cultural models (Holland and Quinn, 1987) evident, if not always explicitly stated, in them. By looking at such things as syntax, metaphor, or the propositional networks underlying the sensibility of sentence order, it is possible to draw inferences about the kinds of models individuals are using or, perhaps more aptly, to draw inferences about the kinds of inferences listeners can make about what the speaker has left unsaid but likely wants understood.

3 There are 180 instances in those parts of the women's transcripts analyzed so far, and 85 instances in the men's, with each set of transcripts being of approximately equal length.

4 I have found Woolard's (1985) analysis of the nature of hegemonic and oppositional forms of language use very productive in formulating what I have to say here.

5 Martin (1987) has examined the American discourses on reproduction and women's bodies and has rigorously uncovered the contradiction between a view of uterine contractions during childbirth as involuntary and a view of the woman as in fact in control of the labor process. The women she interviewed about their birth experiences spoke very similarly to the women described in this chapter about their sense of control over the physical process and over their cries of pain and pleasure during labor and birth. She notes a class difference, however, with middle-class women speaking with more approval of control than working-class women. We might then expect men also to express more concern with and approval of control of

emotion, which is not the case here. This is certainly a problem worthy of more study, particularly a delineation of what kinds of control of which domains appear to emerge from what kinds of experience within hierarchical systems.

6 Acknowledgment of one's emotionality may mean very different things to female and male audiences. Women may announce to each other shared identity and solidarity, while asserting difference, submission, or defiance when making similar statements to men.

7 Abu-Lughod's (1986) study of the Awlad 'Ali represents the most detailed and eloquent example of how, in another cultural system, the particular *kinds* of emotions allocated to and voiced by women articulate with other aspects of their ideological and social structural positions.

8 This group of studies obviously follows in the tradition of centuries of expert explanations of hysteria. Although there have been many versions of the explanation (such as one nineteenth-century account that diagnosed its origins as an empty womb and a childhood where the restraint of emotion was not taught [Smith-Rosenberg, 1972]), they have been organized around the connection between female physiology and mood.

9 Shimanoff (1983) found that male and female speakers did not differ in the number of affect words they used, in the tense, valence, or source (similar to the notion of 'elicitor' used here) of statements about emotion. She did find, however, that males made more reference to their own emotions than to those of other people when compared with females.

10 The resurgence of interest in emotion in the late 1970s and 1980s across the social sciences may in part be the result of the feminist movement's revalorization of all things traditionally associated with women (Margaret Trawick, personal communication). Changing gender relations may also be at the root of the reinvigoration of a long-standing Western discourse on the value of emotional expression; the current debate pits expressionists, for whom healthy emotions are vented ones, against those who would dismiss the latter as 'self-indulgent' or 'immature'. This debate no doubt draws in a complex way, in each concrete context in which it occurs, on the gender ideologies and conflicts of the individual participants.

References

Abu-Lughod, Lila (1986) *Veiled Sentiments: Honor and Poetry in a Bedouin Society*. Berkeley: University of California Press.

Abu-Lughod, Lila and Lutz, Catherine A. (1990) 'Introduction: emotion, discourse, and the politics of everyday life', in C.A. Lutz and L. Abu-Lughod (eds), *Language and the Politics of Emotion*. Cambridge: Cambridge University Press.

Archer, John and Lloyd, Barbara (1985) *Sex and Gender*. Cambridge: Cambridge University Press.

Asad, Talal (ed.) (1973) *Anthropology and the Colonial Encounter*. New York: Humanities Press.

Babchuk, Wayne, Hames, Raymond and Thompson, Ross (1985) 'Sex differences in the recognition of infant facial expressions of emotion: The primary caretaker hypothesis', *Ethology and Sociobiology*, 6: 89–101.

Birnbaum, D.A., Nosanchuck, T.A. and Croll, W.L. (1980) 'Children's stereotypes about sex differences in emotionality', *Sex Roles*, 6: 435–43.

Bowlby, John (1969) *Attachment and Loss*, Vol. 1. London: Hogarth Press.

Brenneis, D. (1990) 'Shared and solitary sentiments', in C.A. Lutz and L. Abu-Lughod (eds), *Language and the Politics of Emotion*. Cambridge: Cambridge University Press. Chapter Six.

Cancian, Francesca (1987) *Love in America: Gender and Self-Development*. Cambridge: Cambridge University Press.

Chodorow, Nancy (1978) *The Reproduction of Mothering*. Berkeley: University of California Press.

Deaux, K. (1984) 'From individual differences to social categories: Analysis of a decade's research on gender', *American Psychologist*, 39: 105–16.

Fausto-Sterling, Anne (1985) *Myths of Gender: Biological Theories of Women and Men.* New York: Basic Books.

Foucault, Michel (1980) *The History of Sexuality,* Vol. 1. New York: Vintage.

Gottlieb, Alma (1987) 'American PMS: A mute voice'. Paper presented at the annual meetings of the American Anthropological Association, Chicago.

Haan, Norma, Bellah, Robert, Rabinow, Paul and Sullivan, William (1983) *Social Science as Moral Inquiry.* New York: Columbia University Press.

Hall, J. (1978) 'Gender effects in decoding nonverbal cues', *Psychological Bulletin,* 85: 845–75.

Haraway, Donna (1986) 'Primatology is politics by other means', in Ruth Bleier (ed.), *Feminist Approaches to Science.* New York: Pergamon Press. pp. 77–118.

Hochschild, Arlie (1983) *The Managed Heart: Commercialization of Human Feeling.* Berkeley: University of California Press.

Holland, Dorothy and Quinn, Naomi (eds) (1987) *Cultural Modes in Language and Thought.* Cambridge: Cambridge University Press.

Jagger, Alison (1987) 'Love and knowledge: Emotion as an epistemic resource for feminists', Ms. in possession of author. Department of Philosophy, University of Cincinnati.

Jordanova, L.J. (1980) 'Natural facts: A historical perspective on science and sexuality', in Carol MacCormack and Marilyn Strathern (eds), *Nature, Culture, and Gender.* Cambridge: Cambridge University Press. pp. 42–69.

Kirkpatrick, John (1987) 'Representing the self as 'You' in American discourse'. Paper presented at the annual meetings of the American Anthropological Association, Chicago.

Lutz, Catherine (1988) *Unnatural Emotions: Everyday Sentiments on a Micronesian Atoll and Their Challenge to Western Theory.* Chicago: University of Chicago Press.

Maher, Vanessa (1984) 'Possession and dispossession: Maternity and mortality in Morocco', in H. Medick and D. Sabean (eds), *Interest and Emotion.* Cambridge: Cambridge University Press. pp. 103–28.

Martin, Emily (1987) 'The ideology of reproduction: The reproduction of ideology'. Paper presented to the Upstate New York Feminist Scholars' Network, September.

Montagu, Ashley (ed.) (1987) *The Learning of Non-Aggression.* Oxford: Oxford University Press.

Parsons, Talcott and Bales, Robert (1955) *Family, Socialization, and Interaction Process.* Glencoe, IL: Free Press.

Rosaldo, Michelle Z. (1984) 'Toward an anthropology of self and feeling', in R. Shweder and R. Le Vine (eds), *Culture Theory: Essays on Mind, Self, and Emotion.* Cambridge: Cambridge University Press. pp. 137–57.

Rosaldo, Renato (1977) 'The rhetoric of control: Ilongots viewed as natural bandits and wild Indians', in B. Babcock (ed.), *The Reversible World: Symbolic Inversion in Art and Society.* Ithaca, NY: Cornell University Press. pp. 240–57.

Rubin, Gayle (1984) 'Thinking sex; Notes for a radical theory of the politics of sexuality', in Carol S. Vance (ed.), *Pleasure and Danger: Exploring Female Sexuality.* Boston: Routledge and Kegan Paul.

Ruddick, Sara (1980) 'Maternal thinking', *Feminist Studies,* 6: 70–96.

Sampson, E.E. (1981) 'Cognitive psychology as ideology', *American Psychologist,* 36: 730–43.

Scheper-Hughes, Nancy (1985) 'Culture, scarcity, and maternal thinking', *Ethos,* 13: 291–317.

Scheper-Hughes, Nancy and Lock, Margaret (1987) 'The mindful body: A prolegomenon to future work in medical anthropology', *Medical Anthropology Quarterly,* 1: 6–41.

Shibamoto, Janet (1987) 'The womanly woman: Manipulation of stereotypical and nonstereotypical features of Japanese female speech', in S. Philips, S. Steele and C. Tanz (eds), *Language, Gender, and Sex in Comparative Perspective.* Cambridge: Cambridge University Press. pp. 26–49.

Shields, Stephanie A. (1987) 'Women, men and the dilemma of emotion', in P. Shaver and C. Hendrick (eds), *Sex and Gender.* Newbury Park, CA: Sage Publications. pp. 229–50.

Shimanoff, Susan (1983) 'The role of gender in linguistic references to emotive states', *Communication Quarterly,* 30: 174–9.

Smith-Rosenberg, Carroll (1972) 'The hysterical woman: Roles and role conflict in 19th-century America', *Social Research*, 39: 652–78.

Stoler, Anne (1985) 'Perceptions of protest: Defining the dangerous in colonial Sumatra', *American Ethnologist*, 12: 642–58.

Strathern, Marilyn (1980) 'No nature, no culture: The Hagen case', in Carol MacCormack and Marilyn Strathern (eds), *Nature, Culture, and Gender*. Cambridge: Cambridge University Press. pp. 174–222.

Taussig, Michael (1984) 'Culture of terror – Space of Death: Roger Casement's Putumayo report and the explanation of torture', *Comparative Studies in Society and History*, 26: 467–97.

Whatley, Marianne (1986) 'Taking feminist science to the classroom: Where do we go from here?', in Ruth Bleier (ed.), *Feminist Approaches to Science*. New York: Pergamon Press. pp. 181–90.

Williams, Raymond (1977) *Marxism and Literature*. Oxford: Oxford University Press.

Woolard, Kathryn (1985) 'Language variation and cultural hegemony: toward an integration of sociolinguistic and social theory', *American Ethnologist*, 12: 738–48.

Chapter 8

Emotion Talk across Cultures

Paul Heelas

Emotional life has sparkʟ the human imagination. Members of different societies talk about their emotions in a wide variety of ways, many of which strike us as distinctly imaginative. The Javanese of Ponorogo, for example, employ liver talk: 'it is the liver (*ati*) that appears in idiomatic expressions indicating emotion'; and 'the role of the liver is not altogether just a metaphor' (Weiss, 1983: 72).

In this chapter I shall take the reader on a 'Cooks tour' of societies whose members talk about emotions in an 'exotic' fashion. As we shall see, there are very considerable differences in the number of emotions clearly identified; what emotions mean; how they are classified and evaluated; how the nature of emotions is considered with regard to locus, aetiology and dynamics; the kind of environmental occurrences which are held to generate particular emotions; the powers ascribed to emotions; and management techniques. I hope I am justified in assuming that the relative inaccessibility of much of the ethnography means that many readers will not be aware of the extent to which emotion talk can diverge from our own. But what exactly has this to do with the social construction of emotions? Why do I plunge the reader into an assortment of ethnographic 'curiosities'?

By way of introduction, I shall indicate why I regard emotion talk to be of very considerable constructivist importance. I want to give some idea of the significance of the strange varieties of emotion talk to be encountered. For reasons which will become more apparent later, I shall indicate why emotion talk – clearly a product of the human imagination – does not have imaginary consequences. It in fact has great bearing on the nature of emotional life.

To argue this first means arguing against those who hold that emotions are endogenous. For, if emotions are part of our biological inheritance, emotion talk is adventitious. Just as the stars are impervious to cross-cultural differences in how they are conceptualized, so too are the emotions – at least, in their core properties. I must thus side with Geertz (1980), the constructivist, against Leach, who has written that Geertz's approach is 'complete rubbish' because it ignores 'genetic' factors (Leach, 1981: 32). This is not difficult to do. Perhaps the majority of those psychologists who have found evidence supporting the endogenous approach have also found it necessary to introduce exogenous determinants. Thus Leventhal, distinguishing between 'emotional elements' and 'emotional experiences', argues that biologically generated elements have to be 'enriched' by meanings ('conceptualizations of affect') before becoming emotional experiences (Leventhal, 1980: 192). Incorporating constructivist theorizing, Leventhal accords ample scope for the sociocultural to make impact. Meanings bound up with emotion talk can get to work.[1]

Granted this, what of the importance of emotion talk within the general context of sociocultural determinants? A number of theorists have argued for constructivism without mentioning emotion talk, let alone treating it as important. Mandler writes of 'languages of emotion' in this fashion: 'The label that something is good or the cognate facial expression of acceptance or approval influences the quality of the emotional experience' (1980: 231). Mandler would certainly not want to discount emotion talk, but its *particular* importance is clearly diminished in that moral judgements as a whole can apparently function in generative fashion.

The particular importance I want to attach to emotion talk is seen by what happens when it is ignored. According to Kemper, 'A very large class of human emotions results from real, anticipated, recollected, or imagined outcomes of power and status relations' (1984: 371). More specifically, consider his explanation of how status loss generates anger:

> When we believe the other is the agent of our status loss, whether by insult, intentional infliction of pain, ignoring us when we have a right to be attended to, or depriving us of goods, services, money, or approval that we have earned or deserve according to our understanding . . . the immediate emotional outcome . . . is *anger*. (Kemper, 1978: 128)

Emotion talk, enabling participants to understand the emotional significance of status loss, does not enter the picture. This is unfortunate. It is true that we have acquired a strong tendency to respond to insults and the like in terms of anger, but by no means do we always do so: my status is affected by a public insult and I feel shame; my status is affected when I do not get what I deserve and I feel inadequate; I am deprived of the attention of my wife and feel jealous. Events of the kind mentioned by Kemper, in other words, need not mean that we respond with *anger*. How we respond depends on how we use our knowledge of our emotional life, interpreting an episode as shaming, for example, because it accords with our understanding the episode as being bound up with what we take shame to mean. In short, the fact that we attribute emotion-specific meanings to those more general sociocultural varieties discussed by Kemper explains why the 'immediate emotional outcome' is not always anger.

I do not want to conclude that the meanings provided by emotion talk are the only ones which constructivists should attend to. One consideration is that emotion talk does not exist in isolation from other domains of knowledge. The meaning of 'anger', for example, is obviously bound up with how we have learnt to use this word in connection with the moral domain (cf. Kemper's 'insults'). The term enables us to know (and so have) the emotion in connection with particular moral events precisely because its meaning is not purely psychological. That emotion talk is often bound up with the moral domain is also clearly seen in Peters' observation: 'emotions, such as pride, ambition, guilt and remorse, imply a certain view of our-selves. They are probably not felt in cultures in which little importance is attached to individual effort and responsibility' (1974: 402).

Other reasons for not limiting emotionally significant meanings to emo-tion talk are provided by all those psychologists who do not limit themselves to this domain (cf. Mandler, 1980; and Lazarus et al., who include 'all transactions that the person judges as having implications for her or his *well-being*' (1980: 195)). One final consideration, to do with the fact that the constructivist cannot simply attend to emotion talk when exploring the management of emotions, concerns what social learning theorists such as Bandura (1965) call 'attentional shift'. Do we not often try to manage distressful emotions by thinking of something other than our emotional states?

Having said this, the fact remains that meanings are necessary for the construction of emotions and that particular meanings (of some kind) are necessary for the construction of particular emotions. In the absence of such particular meanings, we are left with those differentiations in experi-ence which occur at the level of what Leventhal calls emotional 'elements'. And it is difficult not to conclude that these particular meanings have more to do with emotion talk than with anything else. Indeed, it might be possible to argue that meanings can constitute different emotions only if they involve emotion terms which provide knowledge of differences. This certainly is what is implied by Lazarus when he writes that 'each emotion quality and intensity – anxiety, guilt, jealousy, love, joy or whatever – is generated and guided by its own particular cognitive theme' (1980: 192). And is not the importance of emotion terms suggested by experimental research (e.g. Schachter and Singer, 1962) apparently showing that emo-tions are states of physiological arousal defined by the actor as emotionally induced? If, indeed, such research shows that differences in knowledge (this situation means 'anger', this 'euphoria') are crucial in determining which emotions are experienced, then emotion talk, providing the linguistic distinctions, lies at the heart of the matter. To an extent, these distinctions *are* the differences in experience.

It is considerations such as these which explain why Lewis and Saarni, for example, place emotion talk at the very heart of the constructivist enterprise. For them, 'emotional experience . . . requires that organisms possess a language of emotion' (Lewis and Saarni, 1985: 8). Other theorists who have emphasized the importance of emotion talk include Malatesta and Haviland ('the emotion words of a culture exert a powerful influence on the actual experience of emotion': 1985: 110); Levy (who introduces 'the idea of emotion as involving information about the relations of a person to his socially constituted world': 1984: 222); Gordon ('Arousal is socially interpreted in terms of sentiment vocabularies, which are sets of meaningful categories that connect sensations, gestures, and social relationships': 1981: 577) and Lutz ('Emotions are culturally constructed concepts which point to clusters of situations typically calling for some kind of action': 1981: 84).

I hope that the ethnographic material now to be presented is not merely of curiosity value. It concerns how people understand their emotional lives. Being those culturally provided forms of knowledge which are most explicitly focused on emotions, they are perhaps the first thing the constructivist should attend to. They involve the attribution of the kind of meaning which is of paramount significance to those interested in exploring how emotions are constructed in the everyday life of other cultures. We might even learn how other cultures so manage things as to diminish, even do away with, distressful emotions such as 'jealousy' or even 'anger'.

Finally, a word about the survey. A number of cultures, we shall see, do not make distinctions of the 'mental–physical', 'body–mind' and 'emotion–cognition' variety. Ethnographers studying societies which do not employ the category 'emotion' clearly have not found it easy to identify what counts as emotion talk. It is difficult to elicit satisfactory replies to the question, 'Does "x" term refer to an emotion?' if respondents' replies could be referring, for example, to what we consider to be bodily states of affairs (such as physiological arousal). There are in fact many interpretative and linguistic problems to do with establishing what counts as emotion talk – and, for that matter, to do with establishing the nature of forms of emotion talk. Although some of these are mentioned in passing, I side-step more thorny problems. I rely on the insights of the ethnographers concerned.

Varieties

Perhaps the most obvious and arresting way in which emotion talk varies from culture to culture concerns the number of emotions which are clearly identified. Hallpike reports 'a general absence of terms to describe inner states' in connection with the Ommura of Papua (1979: 394). Marsella (1976) also writes of cultures which do not label inner mood states. Then there are those cultures which appear to have an extremely limited lexicon. According to Howell, ethnographer of a small aboriginal group in central Malaysia, Chewong emotional vocabulary is limited to: *chan* (glossed as 'angry') *hentugn* ('fearful', 'frightened'), *punmen* ('like something'), *meseq* ('jealous'), *lidva* ('ashamed', 'shy'), *hanrodn* ('proud'), *imeh* ('want') and *lon* ('want very much') (Howell, 1981: 134). In contrast, neighbouring Malays use some 230 words referring to emotion states (Boucher, 1979: 170; cf. Boucher and Brandt, 1981). Going further afield, Chinese (Taiwanese) work with some 750 words (Boucher, 1979). The Taiwanese, it appears, have a richer lexicon than we in the West: Davitz, using *Roget's Thesaurus* to note 'every word that seemed at all likely to be used as the label of an emotional state' (1969: 10), arrives at some 400 English terms.

Although there are grave difficulties in establishing what counts as a member of the emotional lexicon of any culture, it certainly appears that numbers vary.[2] So do meanings of emotion terms. As will become apparent, classificatory differences, differences in how emotions are associated with circumstances, differences in the powers ascribed to emotions and so on all function to ensure that supposedly 'basic' emotions, such as 'anger', show little cross-cultural constancy in meaning. To introduce the subject, I simply draw attention to how emotion terms which are broadly similar to our own nevertheless differ in what they mean. Although such terms involve distinctions which allow translation in terms of our emotion concepts, they also derive their meaning by including states of affairs which do not suit our concepts; which do not suit our understanding of what counts as being afraid, being angry and the like. Consider, for example, La Barre's portrayal of 'guilt' in classical Greek culture:

> Greek guilt was not an agonizing consciousness of sin and not necessarily earned by conscious moral choice after a wrangle with conscience, but rather a quasi-material contamination as the result of sometimes innocently blind acts as in the case of Oedipus. (La Barre, 1972: 448)

Little to do with wilful action, Greek 'guilt' diverges from how we understand the roughly corresponding emotion in our culture. Other illustrations are provided by Davitz's comparison of how emotional experiences are described by Ugandans speaking Luganda, Ugandans speaking English, and Americans. It is true that Davitz found that the first two groups of subjects described 'happiness', 'sadness' and 'anger' in much the same fashion (1969: 178–9). However, comparison of the two Ugandan groups with American subjects show clear differences. Concerning 'happiness', the 'Ugandan adolescent's stress on freedom from pain and worry . . . reflects an important contrast with . . . the American adolescent' (Davitz, 1969: 185). Concerning 'anger',

> in the Ugandan sample, both moving away from others and crying were reported more often than aggression. Moreover, impulses to extreme aggression (e.g., killing, severe mutilation), general discomfort, and various subcategories of inadequacy were far more frequent in the Ugandan sample. Among the United States Ss, impulses to moderate aggression (striking out, hurting, a sense of hyperactivation, and aggressive behaviour) were emphasized. (Davitz, 1969: 183)

Lutz (1985) argues that children learn the meaning of emotion words by attending to the sum of the contexts in which the words are used. Greek 'guilt' and Ugandan 'anger' indicate how variegated contexts can be. The way emotions are talked about shows that the context for 'guilt' includes 'blind acts', while the context for 'anger' includes 'crying'. It is particularly striking that Ugandan 'anger' does not mean what it does for us when it is recalled that half the sample speak 'English'.

Countless examples could be given of emotion terms which are used in connection with states of affairs and activities which diverge from what we take translated 'equivalents' to be about. Malatesta and Haviland write: 'To judge from semantic differential studies, the phenomenology of what we have come to regard as basic, fundamental human emotions can vary in shades of experience, in accord with particular patterns of socialization, for example, by culture and gender' (1985: 98). Studies surveyed show differences of meaning within American society and between two not radically dissimilar language users, American and Norwegian. Thinking now of cross-cultural differences in how the emotions are classified, the implications are considerable. If, indeed, members of those societies employing classifications broadly similar to our own (in that it is relatively easy to effect translation) are working with somewhat different meanings, even these classifications show cross-cultural divergence. If 'English'-speaking Ugandans do not distinguish between 'sadness' and 'anger' as we do (crying being an important feature of our distinction but not for Ugandans), what differences in classification can we expect to find embedded in more alien languages?

The answer is that classifications, and so meanings, vary very considerably. Obvious illustrations are provided by emotion terms which in effect conflate what we keep distinct. Leff, for example, reports that 'in a number of African languages a single word stands for both being angry and being sad' (1973: 301). And, he continues, 'these two emotions are not clearly distinguished linguistically'. Leff also points out that 'Chinese' employ one word 'to stand for worry, tension and anxiety' (Leff, 1977: 322). Another illustration of how the indigenous terms of alien languages can subsume distinctions made in English is provided by Boucher. In his study, 'anger, rage and furious were all translated into the single term *marah* by bilingual Malays' (Boucher, 1979: 171). A yet more striking example is provided by Rosaldo (1980). Examining the key emotion term of the Ilongot, a small group living in the remote reaches of northern Luzon, she points out that the expression is used in a wide range of contexts, including those which she considers to involve 'anger' and 'envy' (1980: 44–7).[3]

Not operating with our distinctions, subsuming what we think of as distinct emotions in alien categories, in general working with meanings which show little (if any) cross-cultural constancy, the evidence suggests that no one classificatory system is the same as another.[4] To emphasize how cultures differ in how emotions are classified, I now present evidence that which emotions are 'hypercognized' and which 'hypocognized' varies with setting. In accordance with Levy's usage, the first of these terms refers to processes whereby emotions come to be well known, the second to processes whereby understanding is 'force[d] . . . into some private mode' (1984: 227). For present purposes, what matters is that hypercognized emotions are those which are culturally identified, hypocognized as being those which receive much less conceptual attention.

It appears that classifications always accord pride of place to particular emotions. 'Love' and 'guilt' for us; 'pressure' for the Rastafarian; 'fear' and 'shyness' for the Chewong (Howell, 1981: 141) and the neighbouring Semai (Robarchek, 1977, 1979); 'passion' or *liget* for the Ilongot (Rosaldo, 1980);

'fear' and 'shame' for the Tahitian (Levy, 1973); *lek* for the Balinese (Geertz, 1973); *sungkan* for the Javanese (Geertz, 1959); *whaka-momore* for the Maori (Gudgeon, 1906); 'gentleness' and 'mildness' for the Utku Eskimo (Briggs, 1970) – all are hypercognized or focal emotions.

It is hardly worth pointing out that herein lies evidence for cross-cultural differences in classification. What is worth dwelling on, however, is the extent to which these core emotion terms are culturally specific. Additional evidence can thus be provided for the claim made earlier to the effect that classificatory systems differ in that there is little (if any) constancy in what emotion terms mean.

Culturally valued focal emotions draw together and otherwise bear on many domains of experience. They are highly ramified. Since what they draw on, bind together, are particular details of particular cultures, it is easy to see why these terms should be so culturally specific.[5] I illustrate with two examples, the first being a term described by Geertz as 'something peculiarly Javanese'. She writes,

> Roughly speaking, *sungkan* refers to a feeling of respectful politeness before a superior or an unfamiliar equal, an attitude of constraint, a repression of one's own impulses and desires, so as not to disturb the emotional equanimity of one who may be spiritually higher. (Geertz, 1959: 233)

The second example is a yet more distinctive term. According to Rosaldo,

> *Liget* is associated most readily with a variety of words suggesting chaos, separation, and confusion, words that point to the disruptive qualities of 'anger' uncontrolled by 'knowledge' – 'anger' that derives from someone else's fury or success. Red ornaments, signifying the *liget* of a killer, can irritate the unaccomplished members of his audience; boasts testify, as they give rise, to *liget* among 'equals'; red in the sky at sunset is a form of *liget* that can make people ill. (1980: 47)

It is already apparent that *liget* includes more than is bound up with what we take 'anger' to mean. But this is not all: *liget* is also associated with what is good in life, and not as a distressful or dangerous emotion:

> Opposed to the chaotic energy of a distracted heart is *liget* that is given form or focus, an 'energy' shaped by 'knowledge', and directed to some end. 'I am full of *liget* when I hunt', a man says, 'because I do not fear the forest'; 'I am moved by *liget* at the thought of eating game'. Unlike wild 'anger', such 'energy' is creative, and whereas unfocused *liget* breeds distraction, *liget* that is concentrated toward a desirable object transcends the challenge and irritation at its roots. Concentrated *liget* is what makes babies, stirs one on to work, determines killers, gives people strength and courage, narrows vision on a victim or a task. (Rosaldo, 1980: 49)

Having introduced hypercognized emotion talk, it remains to say a few words about emotions that are hypocognized. Variations in this regard also reflect differences in classification. Thus, if what we think of as distinct emotions are subsumed by more general categories, they obviously cannot be conceptualized as such by members of the cultures under consideration. Thinking back to Leff's point (that a single word stands for both 'anger' and 'sadness' in a number of African languages), both terms must be missing from the lexicon. A related way in which hypocognition is bound up with more general categories occurs when categories allow for only partial recognition of those emotions which ethnographers report them as subsuming. Ilongot emotion talk serves to make the point: 'Ilongots describe this state [of 'envy'] as *ngelem*, and with a sort of pungent pleasure indicate that the *liget* that underlies it, although disturbing, may also be desirable' (Rosaldo, 1980: 47). Ilongot can talk of 'envy', but not in a fashion which clearly differentiates it from *liget*.

When emotion terms are hypocognized in this fashion, they clearly vary in accord with cross-cultural differences in core emotions. Hypocognition can also occur when classificatory systems do not emphasize emotions which conflict with what is culturally valued. The point can be made by referring to Tahitian emotion talk: not suiting Tahitian values, 'sadness' and 'guilt' receive little conceptual attention (Levy, 1984: 219).

Finally, mention should be made of a form of hypocognition which does not appear to be as cross-culturally variable as those bound up with different classificatory systems. I am thinking of 'depression'. Marsella's review of the literature leads him to the conclusion that the term 'is not well represented among the lexicon of non-Western people' (Marsella, 1980: 242; see also Leff, 1977: 323; Levy, 1984: 230). Why a term with which we are so familiar should be hypocognized in this fashion is something of a mystery.

I have indicated that hypercognized emotions tend to be culturally valued whereas hypocognized states do not tend to be thought of so highly. This leads to another way in which classifications vary cross-culturally – variations to do with the moral significance of emotion talk. A useful approach is to contrast societies which adopt a 'Dionysian' assessment of the emotions with those which favour the 'Apollonian' strategy. Drawing on Nietzsche, this is how Benedict formulates the contrast:

> The desire of the Dionysian, in personal experience or in ritual, is to press through it towards a certain psychological state, to achieve excess. The closest analogy to the emotion he seeks is drunkenness, and he values the illuminations of frenzy. With Blake, he believes 'the path of excess leads to the palace of wisdom'. The Apollonian distrusts all this, and has often little idea of the nature of such experiences. He finds means to outlaw them from his conscious life. He 'knows but one law, measure in the Hellenic sense'. He keeps the middle of the road, stays within the known map, does not meddle with disruptive psychological states. In Nietzsche's fine phrase, even in the exaltation of the dance he 'remains what he is, and retains his civic name'. (1935: 78–9)

Members of Apollonian societies regard the majority of emotions as dangerous threats to themselves and to their institutions. Typically, emotions to do with anything other than those which enhance the power of the established order are accorded negative moral value. The Chewong, for example, encourage 'fear' and 'shyness' but regard all other emotions as dangerous. 'Wanting', 'liking' and so forth are treated as morally reprehensible; they are considered to incur the wrath of supernatural beings (Howell, 1981: 141). The Ommura are another case to hand: 'Generally speaking, what we would describe as "inner states" etc. tend to be treated in most contexts as dangerous, unpredictable, and "asocial" and to be closely associated with sorcery activities' (Hallpike, 1979: 394, reporting a personal communication from Mayer). In contrast, members of Dionysian societies regard the majority of emotions as vital to both themselves and the social order. The Tauade of Papua thus treat 'pride', 'self-assertion', 'envy', 'rage' and so on as 'the normal basis for all behaviour' (Hallpike, 1979: 80–1; 234). These are 'the very stuff out of which social processes are generated (p. 77). 'Fear', 'shyness' and the like, it seems, are little valued.[6]

However, the Apollonian–Dionysian distinction, though useful, does not provide an adequate basis for capturing the intricate ways in which moral assessments of the emotions vary from culture to culture. This will become apparent when we come to discuss how emotion talk includes reference to the powers and management of emotional life. First, however, it is necessary to turn to the matter of how emotions can be described. Talk of powers and management has to wait until this has been done because it often makes use of ways of describing the emotions which ring strange to our ears.

Cursory examination of our own talk of emotions shows that they can be described in various ways. Moving from talk which concentrates on internal states to talk which takes an externalized form, 'vehicles' employed include direct reference to emotions as inner experiences ('I feel angry'; 'I hide my fear'); use of bodily parts including organs ('I vented my spleen'); use of physiological phenomena ('I tingled with fear'); use of behavioural manifestations ('her smile said it all'); appeal to contexts, including social activities ('You can imagine how I felt when I saw the Alps'; 'That cocktail party!'); and use of extremely diverse metaphors and other figures of speech ('Love is like a red, red rose').[7]

It is not surprising that we use various vehicles for talking about the emotions. Psychologically speaking, emotions as inner states are indeed located within the body, associated with physiological arousal and ways of behaving, associated with various contexts, and often experienced as coming from without. But what bearing does this have on cross-cultural differences in how the emotions are described? Rather than members of any other cultures doing what we do – namely, using various vehicles to talk about emotions essentially understood as inner experiences – the evidence suggests that differences in the vehicle employed are (more) literally bound up with different ideas of the nature of emotions: their loci (where they are seated), their generation, their powers and so on.

First, then, how have the possibilities raised by the different ways of describing the emotions been put to use in talk of loci? Regarding emotions as inner experiences, experiences which cannot be reduced to or seen as physiological arousal, intellectual activity or behavioural display, we favour a mentalistic locus. A great many other cultures 'somatize' the emotions.

Emotions are talked of as 'bodily' occurrences, whether in terms of 'organs' such as the liver, which are rarely (if ever) experienced, or in terms of bodily parts such as the stomach and the back of the neck, which can be felt.

Before giving illustrations, I should explain why I have just placed several words in quotation marks. This is to remind the reader that 'somatization' should not be taken to mean that emotions are identified with what we take to be bodily, as opposed to mental, states. As indicated in the introduction to this chapter, many cultures do not make this distinction. Read's point for the Gahuku-Gama of New Guinea almost certainly stands for a great range of societies:

> The biological, physiological and psychic aspects of [man's] nature cannot be clearly separated. They exist in the closest inter-dependence, being, as it were, fused together to form the human personality. To an extent to which it is perhaps difficult for us to appreciate or understand, the various parts of the body . . . are essential constituents of the human personality. (Read, 1967: 206)

'Organs' are, so to speak, 'psychologized'. Organ talk does not mean that emotions are understood to belong to 'organs' as we understand the term.

This said, however, ethnographers have often found it necessary to report a close association between emotions and organs. It is hard to dispute that members of the cultures concerned treat the nature of the emotions in a more organic fashion than we would dream of doing. After all, organ talk provides a way of differentiating between emotions. Thus, Howell writes of the Chewong, 'Whenever they do express verbally emotional and mental states and changes, this is done through the medium of the liver. Thus they may say, "my liver is good" (I am feeling fine) or "my liver was tiny" (I was very ashamed)' (Howell, 1981: 139). The Elema, discussed by Williams, also concentrate on the liver. Emotion talk is somewhat more sophisticated, however, in that members of this society do not simply refer the states of the liver as a whole:

> The Elema have a simple physical psychology by which they allocate all emotion [and] desire . . . to the liver, *iki*. (n. Thus the terms *iki vere*, desire; *iki heaha*, bad temper; *iki bereke*, good temper; *iki haroe*, compassion; . . . .) Of the two sides of this organ the right (*mai-keva*) is the seat of kindliness, sociability; the left (*mai-keva* of the angry passions, strong talk, unsociability. (Williams, 1940: 90–1)

Other illustrations of somatization are provided by Onians ('For Homer the heart and lungs were the emotional centre of the body': 1973: 84); Read (in Gahuku-Gama thought, 'the seat of the emotions is located in the stomach': 1967: 214); Johnson (Israelites conceived man in such a way that 'the various members and secretions of the body, such as the bones, the heart, the bowels, and the kidneys, as well as the flesh and the blood, can all be thought of as revealing psychic properties': 1964: 87); Levy (Tahitians treat the intestines as 'the seat of the emotions': 1973: 515); Smith (for Maori, *ngakau* (associated with the intestines) 'could "feel well", "laugh", "be satisfied" or "sweet"; it could "feel pain", "be weak" or "dark"'; 1981:

152–3); Rosaldo (the Ilongot saying, 'If "anger" and "intent" on action, our hearts may "tense" and "knot" themselves, displaying "hardened" strength and purpose': 1980: 39); and Leff (the Yoruba talk of 'depression' as 'the heart is weak', 'anxiety' as 'the heart is not at rest': 1977: 322).[8]

When organs (and the like) provide the loci, emotions must somehow be thought of as organic in nature. Another option, adopted by a number of societies, is to talk about the emotions as taking place in behaviour. Occurring here, attention is directed to emotions being a form of public action. So let us move from the inner world of organs to explore this more 'Austinian' world of public acts.

I first give an example of how emotions can be seen as bound up with public activities of bodily parts. Discussing how ancient Israelites thought of emotions in terms of a variety of such activities, Johnson includes material on the eye:

> the behaviour of the eye is found to be related to a wide range of physical activity, i.e. pride or humility, favour or disfavour, desire and hope, or disappointment; and in view of the ease with which the eye may be affected by distress of any kind it is not surprising that it should be capable of pity. (Johnson, 1964: 48)

That the eye 'should be capable of pity' suggests that it was not simply regarded as a way of expressing and identifying inner emotions. Emotions were thought of as occurring on the surface.[9] Moving further into the external domain, emotions can be talked about in ways which suggest that they are considered to be as much bound up with social activities as they are with what we think of as inner states. A good illustration is provided by Onians (1973). Homeric Greeks identified 'joy' with going to battle to the extent that the same word ($\chi\acute{\alpha}\rho\mu\eta$) is used for both the emotion and the activity. Joy is 'the spirit of battle' (Onians, 1973: 21). More generally on the Homeric Greeks, Simon and Weiner write that 'What we consider as *inner* mental states or functions are preferentially represented in terms of their concrete, observable, behavioral aspects' (1966: 306). As they continue to make the point,

> Homer is generally much more interested in portraying details about how a character appears, while engaged in a particular mental process, than in the details of the process itself. Thus, the poet does not elaborate the indecision of Penelope but rather Penelope as indecisive – tossing and turning. and unable to sleep. (Simon and Weiner, 1966: 306)

If talk is entirely about behaviour, then it is perhaps best not to regard it as emotional in meaning. The examples I have given count as emotion talk because, although behavioural loci are emphasized, inner experiences are not entirely left out of the picture. Instances of 'emotion' talk which are so bound up with activities, which are so institutionally and morally laden as to lead one to suspect that the talk might not be about the emotions at all, are provided by the Chewong and by the Japanese notion *amae*. I have discussed the problem of deciding whether the Chewong talk about emotions or simply about behaviour elsewhere (see Heelas, 1983a, 1984); *amae* is discussed by Leff (1977: 336) in an interesting albeit brief fashion.[10]

Having begun this discussion of the various kinds of loci accorded the emotions with internalized representations, I close with some examples of the most externalized varieties of talk, namely, those forms which, so to speak, take the emotions away from the 'experiencing' individual and locate them in external agencies. Least radically, this can be effected by talking about inner experiences in terms of figures of speech. Discussing the role of 'visibilia' during the European Middle Ages, Lewis gives a good example of how externalized idioms were employed to communicate emotions: 'If you are hesitating between an angry retort and a soft answer, you can express your state of mind by inventing a person called Ira with a torch and letting her contend with another person called Patientia' (Lewis, 1958: 45). More radically, emotions can be talked about as though they are largely bound up with external states of affairs. Their loci are dissociated from human subjects – or so it is claimed by Hallpike. He reports 'a great deal of evidence . . . that mental states and feelings are often regarded by primitive peoples as external to the person, and as entities whose existence is independent of their being thought or felt' (Hallpike, 1979: 402)

Evidence for the externalization of loci is provided by a number of cultures, including Homeric Greece (Simon and Weiner write of 'strong emotions' as 'outside agencies': 1966: 307). Lienhardt's account of the Dinka (south Sudan) provides one of the best illustrations. Having 'no conception which at all closely corresponds to our popular modern conception of mind' (1961: 149), Dinka talk about emotions as though they were occurring in others. Consider, for example, the role played by the fetish Mathiang Gok:

> This fetish, according to Dinka accounts, works analogously to what, for Europeans, would be the prompting of a guilty conscience. The European emphasis here is upon an integrally interior subject of activity, the conscience. For the Dinka, Mathiang Gok is a presence acting upon the self from without, and employed by someone to do so. The image (as we have called it) of the experience of guilty indebtedness (to take the usual situation in which Mathiang Gok is thought to operate) is extrapolated from the experiencing self. It comes (as memories often do) unwilled by the debtor, and is interpreted as a Power directed by the creditor. (Lienhardt, 1961: 150)

Or consider how 'envy' is conceptualized in terms of beliefs about witchcraft:

> it is possible to interpret them [witchcraft beliefs] as imaging, in another person, states of a person's own conscience. An envious man, for example, not recognizing the envy in himself, transfers to another his experience of it, and sees its image in him, 'the witch'. (Lienhardt, 1961: 151)

Dinka imagination has worked on a possibility provided by the natural phenomenology of emotions, namely, that emotions are felt as happening to us.[11] Coming from outside the 'self', emotional experiences lend themselves in being understood as taking place elsewhere. Lienhardt uses a derivative of the late Latin term *passio* ('The fact or condition of being acted upon or affected by external agency; subject to external force': *OED*) to make the point that 'If the word "passions", *passiones*, were still normally current as the opposite of "actions", it would be possible to say that the Dinka Powers were the images of human *passiones* seen as the active *source* of those *passiones*' (Lienhardt, 1961: 151; my emphasis).

It will be noted that externalization is not quite so comprehensive as is suggested by Hallpike. The Dinka, employed by Hallpike to make his point, do not entirely ignore the natural phenomenological fact that people experience emotions as happening to themselves. Thus, although 'the experience of guilty indebtedness' is accorded a predominantly external locus, it is also acknowledged that it 'comes' to the debtor. Other cultures retain the idea that emotions happen outside the 'self', while giving more explicit acknowledgement that it is people who experience them. This is effected by talking of emotions as external agencies which invade or possess people. The Pintupi Aborigines of the Western Australian Desert sometimes appear to think in this fashion: *kurrunpa* ('fear') is 'having a "wet spirit"' (Myers, 1979: 349).

I close this introduction of loci by reminding the reader that our own emotion talk is derived from an externalized variety. Discussing names of 'feelings' and 'passions' employed by our ancestors, Barfield writes,

> The nomenclature of the Middle Ages generally views them from without, hinting always at their results or their moral significance – 'envy', 'greedy', 'happy' (i.e. 'lucky'), 'malice', 'mercy', 'mildheartedness', 'peace', 'pity', 'remorse', 'repentance', 'rue', 'sin' . . . Even the old word 'sad' had not long lost its original sense of 'sated', 'heavy' (which it still retains in 'sad bread'), and 'fear' continued for a long time to mean, not the emotion, but a 'sudden and unexpected event'. Hardly before the beginning of the seventeenth century do we find expressed that sympathetic or 'introspective' attitude to the feelings which is conveyed by such labels as 'aversion', 'dissatisfaction', 'discomposure', . . . while 'depression' and 'emotion' – further lenient names for human weaknesses – were used till then of material objects. (Barfield, 1954: 169)

I now turn to different ways of talking about the generation and dynamics of emotions. The most widely employed option for us in the West is to consider emotions (inner states) to be generated by external events. Combination of internal locus and external aetiology is probably the option most frequently adopted by other cultures. A number of these cultures also share our emphasis on 'natural' causation. Read reports that the Gahuku-Gama consider 'anger' and 'enmity' to be the consequence of adultery within the clan (1967: 205); Hallpike writes that 'For the Tauade, behaviour is the product of particular situations, and of the emotions generated thereby' (1977: 233); and in his discussion of Norse culture Wax states, 'Trouble and sorrow are seen not as the result of unseemly or offensive conduct toward Beings and Power, but as the logical outcome of an individuals foolish and naïve conduct' (1969: 122).

Emphasis on 'natural' causation is likely to go together with a

'Bandurian' understanding of the dynamics of emotional life. Seen as generated by external events, emotions can be talked about in something akin to the fashion favoured by social learning theorists such as Bandura. Pintupi Aborigines, for example, regard their emotions as being very much bound up with social activities. The (social learning) nature of their indigenous understanding of dynamics is seen in Myers's account:

> How their cultural understanding of 'happiness' works is clear in the following example. Informants frequently told me that Yayayi was 'not a happy place' (*pukulpa wiya ngarrin*); there were fights all the time because there were 'no *corroborees*' (a pidgin term for any ceremonies or organized singing). There should be, they said, '*corroborees* all the time'. On a day of numerous fights and arguments, several men suggested that a 'sing' be organized in order to stop the fighting, to make everyone 'happy'. (Myers, 1979: 353)

While 'naturalistic' understanding of causation is widespread (see for example Hallpike, 1979: 407), it is by no means always emphasized. Members of most societies believe in gods. Most deities are taken to have emotions. 'Supernatural' causation is thus possible. A deity gets angry at a human transgression and threatens punishment: the outcome is 'fear'. Christians would find nothing strange about this extremely widespread way in which deities generate emotions. What is more alien, except perhaps for devout fundamentalists, are those societies whose gods are believed to generate emotions which we would ascribe to 'objective' causes. Smith provides a good illustration: 'The Maori did not consider the emotion of fear to be caused by what we would see as a fear-causing event such as a forthcoming battle, but rather believed it to be inflicted upon a man by a hostile *atua* angered by some violation of a *tapu* rule' (1981: 149). So does Onians. Functioning to 'breathe' emotion into man, gods do more than send distressful states such as *ate*: 'A sudden access of courage or impulse or resolve with its accompanying sense of energy and power as was conceived as the work of a god' (Onians, 1973: 56, 51). Or we can think of Dinka powers (being the 'active source' of '*passiones*') – indeed, of all those societies which place emotions in the hands of their gods.

In these societies, the dynamics of emotions obviously include the workings of gods. This sometimes means that emotions are considered to be outside the control of man. We read in the *Odyssey*, for example: 'We soon made Tenedos, and there, all agog to be home, we sacrificed to the gods. But Zeus had no intention of letting us get home so soon, and for his own cruel purposes he set us all at loggerheads once more.' More frequently, dynamics are thought to include human agency. In Smith's example, the person who violates a *tapu* rule knows the consequences. Emotions are not simply under the control of *atua*. Maori have a role to play in the process. A long and detailed account of a similar form of emotion dynamics is provided by Harris (1978).

External agencies can also include other human beings, operating in 'magical' fashion. Discussing Dinka witchcraft, Lienhardt writes:

If a man hates another, is spiteful towards him, is thought to resent the other's material (not moral) good and envy his possessions, then the Dinka believe that he intends harm towards him, and can cause him to suffer simply by being what he is in relation to his victim – an enemy, but without material weapons or demonstrated hostility. (1951: 317)

Neither should the reader forget that Simon and Weiner include 'strong emotions' among Homeric Greek agencies. That a great variety of things can be called upon to generate the emotions from without is shown by Anderson's analysis of the indigenous psychology of Shakespeare's time:

The elements of all matter (celestial as well as earthly) possess qualities, and the qualities of one substance are capable of acting upon those of another. Man thus lives in close relationship with the world about him. Diet, climate, and the stars may alter his temperament and his spirits. (Anderson, 1934: 46)

In diametric contrast to those cultures where talk is of external causation, there are those which understand causation in terms of something akin to Freud's theory of the id. Emotions well up from within, according to the dynamics of internal organs and the like. The Elema provide a case to hand: Williams writes of 'the man whose liver so to speak secretes the corresponding thoughts, emotions, or desires' (1940: 91; cf. Onians, 1973: 84–5). Generally speaking, however, societies which talk of internal causation do so by combining this with talk of external causation. Such applies to Elizabethan psychological thought: diet and so forth influence 'temperament'; so does, for example, the spleen, as Anderson points out:

The spleen may incline a man to a variety of passions. Its function is to draw to itself and purge the melancholy excrement, normally cold and dry, an excrement which breeds fearful passions, checks passageways, and defiles the whole supply of humours. When it performs this task successfully, man is disposed to mirth. The spleen is thus sometimes said to be the seat of laughter. If the spleen flourishes, the body withers; if the spleen withers, the body flourishes. (1934: 75–6)

Cultures which combine external and internal talk of determinants can often be thought of as possessing indigenous 'psychodynamic' explanations. This is certainly the case for those societies where it is believed that the emotions can be controlled by the ('mental') efforts of participants. Whether because of external or internal ('organic') processes, emotions well up; participants have the responsibility to hold them in check. Thus Anderson writes of Elizabethan 'psychological treatises' which 'accord high praise to the man who is at all times master of himself. They enumerate devices to be used in control of the passions and continually urge to patience' (1934: 174).

Another variant is when (negative) emotions are seen as generated by something other than the 'self' – stored inside, but then regulated by ritualistic activities. Such societies include the Kalabari and the Tallensi (Horton, 1961: 110–16) and the Utku (Briggs, 1970). Utku Eskimos are especially interesting in that their emotion talk makes reference to those psychodynamic processes which we know of as repression and catharsis (see Heelas, 1983b: 394).

Emotions, we have seen, can be regarded as being generated by 'objective' states of affairs, by gods, 'magically' by other people or stars and the like, and by internal organs. They can also be seen as influenced by activities of the 'self'. Dynamics vary accordingly: workings of the gods, of organs, of social activities, of the 'self' – all can be brought to play, and, I should add, all can be combined in various ways. More generally, I have pointed out that some societies favour 'sociodynamics', others 'psychodynamics' and yet others 'id-dynamics'.

Discussion of dynamics has introduced us to differences in how participants of various cultures talk about the management of their emotions. First, though, there is one other important consideration to be raised in connection with aetiology: namely, that there are considerable cross-cultural differences in *what* is held to generate particular emotions.

Chagnon's study of the South American Yanomamö provides a by no means exceptional illustration. Husbands treat their wives, as we would see it, in an abominable fashion – they beat them, hold glowing sticks against them, even kill then. Yet women 'measure their husband's concern in terms of the frequency of minor beatings they sustain', and Chagnon overheard a woman commenting 'that the other's husband must really care for her since he has beaten her on the head so frequently' (1968: 83). What for us would elicit anger here elicits something akin to 'endearment'. Another example is provided by the Semai and Chewong. In both these cultures people who are not given food and the like interpret their state in terms of 'fear', rather than in terms of anger or irritation, as might be expected if our Western understanding is brought to bear.

Ethnographic material provided by Robarchek (1977, 1979) for the Semai, and by Howell (1981, 1984) for the Chewong, shows that members of these two societies have learnt to interpret frustrating situations in terms of emotion words which do not accord with how we would evaluate such situations. The situations are interpreted in terms of 'rules' (*pehunan*, Semai; *punen*, Chewong) which call supernatural agencies into play. These agencies are intent on punishing those who have been frustrated – people who thus have cause to be 'frightened'. The rules in effect mean 'fear'. (See Heelas, 1983a, 1984, for further discussion.)

Moving on to a subject which has already raised its head – indigenous understanding of the *management* of emotions – I should first point out that this is an extremely large and complex subject. This is because indigenous understanding of management can be approached from at least three (interrelated) points of view. One avenue is to concentrate on moral aspects; another is to explore the powers which are ascribed to emotions; the third is to concentrate on indigenous 'theories' to do with loci, generation and dynamics.

Myers points out that 'The determination of when one ought to be angry, when sad, when sorry, when lonely, and how to act, is largely a cultural matter' (1979: 349). A number of theorists have recently drawn attention to the role played by 'display' and 'feeling' rules in this regard

(Ekman, 1982; Hochschild, 1983). Myers explicitly attends to the moral significance of emotion terms themselves. These are what he has in mind when he writes of 'the ideology of the emotions' (Myers, 1979: 365). (Emotion terms are also what Rosaldo has in mind when she writes, 'Psychological idioms that we use in offering accounts of the activities of our peers – or our companions in the field – are at the same time "ideological" or "moral notions"': 1983: 136).

The point is that emotion terms provide information to do with how people should or should not feel (or display their feelings) in particular circumstances. When emotion terms are taken to be associated (in meaning) with particular activities, they provide information as to how participants should feel when they are engaged in the activities. I illustrate by reference to Myers' analysis of how the emotion terms of the Pintupi are bound up with their institutions and morality. Consider his account of 'happiness': 'the central themes of the Pintupi moral order revolve around the ideal of closely cooperating kin, and it is in terms of this understanding that Pintupi attempt to define when and how one should be "happy" (*pukulpa*)' (Myers, 1979: 353). Articulating the values of the kin ideal, the morally laden term *pukulpa* conveys the information that Pintupi should feel happy when acting with kin and should not feel happy when alone. The anthropological literature on kinship terms in a variety of societies suggests that something similar pertains: that kin terms are bound up with 'conventional' emotions; telling people how they ought to feel towards their mother's brother and so on (cf. Needham, 1971: lii–lix).[12]

The implications for indigenous understanding of management are obvious. Often reflecting, perhaps better encapsulating, what society is about, attention to emotion talk enables us to see why participants should feel obliged to manage their emotions as they do. Reflecting cross-cultural differences in moral orders, attention to emotion talk enables us to see why members of different societies select different emotions to emphasize or attempt to do away with. Nor is this all. Emotion talk differs from culture to culture with regard to what people should do if their emotions are to remain in accord with the moral order.

Before exploring this further I want to say a few words about the second way of looking at cross-cultural variations in management. Attention is directed at what has to be handled -- specifically, the powers which are ascribed to emotions. The matter is clearly not divorced from moral considerations. As I have already pointed out, Apollonian societies tend to treat emotions as dangerous threats to the moral order, whereas Dionysian societies tend to treat them as essential for that order. But I want to focus on the subject in order to indicate the extent to which cultures have arrived at different ideas of which emotions are associated with which powers, and in which contexts.

Harris reports that Tahitian 'anger' can kill: 'Mystical agents, including those lying within human persons, were subject to anger and that anger could be manifested in the sickness and death of human adults, their children, and their livestock, or in plague and drought affecting humans in the mass' (1978: 27). More specifically, she reports that

> the rights of persons as members of families and narrow circles of kin, and the rights of domesticated animals as quasi-members, could not be transgressed without mystically endangering the wronged. When such transgressions occurred, the offended one's heart, the locus of the sentiments, became 'hot', or he was 'injured in the heart' (*waßaßwa ngolonyi*), that is, the wronged person or beast became angry and resentful. There followed, as divination would later reveal, suffering of the transgressor. (Harris, 1978: 31–2)

The theme of mystical powers of the emotions of the wronged contrasts nicely with Lienhardt's discussion of Dinka witches: the reader will recall that powers are here those of the wrongdoer. Both of these societies can then be contrasted with the Ilongot. *Liget* (which has an 'anger' aspect) is culturally approved and is exemplified in head-hunting. 'Anger' is one of the factors in motivating Ilongot to go out and 'toss a head': 'Grieving for lost kin, envious of past headhunting, angry at an insult, and bent upon revenge, he and his fellows are concerned, primarily, to realize their *liget*' (Rosaldo, 1980: 55). The positive power of *liget* is seen in the fact that only when it has been 'realized' in this fashion are youths allowed to marry and become adults.

With different views as to the powers of 'anger', the three societies just mentioned employ different management techniques. These are referred to in the following discussion, indicating how different management techniques also go together with different ways of talking about loci, generations and, of course, dynamics.

The third paragraph of the Confucian *Book of Rites* reads:

> The ancient Kings were watchful in regard to the things by which the mind was affected. And so they instituted ceremonies to direct men's aims aright; music to give harmony to their voices; laws to unify their conduct; and punishments to guard against their tendencies to evil. The end to which ceremonies, music, punishments and laws conduct is one; they are the instruments by which the minds of the people are assimilated, and good order in government is made to appear.

Attributing the generation of emotions to ceremonies, these kings operated in a fashion which would win the approval of modern-day social learning theorists and constructivists. Other examples of management strategies involving this kind of understanding of the loci, generation and dynamics of emotion are provided by the Pintupi (their management of 'happiness' has already been introduced) and the Ilongot. Ilongot, it can be noted, are interesting because they combine sociodynamic and psychodynamic understanding of the emotions in a fashion reminiscent of the Western theorist, Berkowitz. Psychodynamic management ('"heavy" feelings were what made men want to kill; in taking heads they could aspire to "cast off" an "anger" that "weighed down on" and oppressed their saddened "hearts"') combines with management couched in terms of sociodynamics. (Adults, exemplifying the social order, teach successful head-hunters *beya*, the 'knowledge' which 'organizes affective life': Rosaldo, 1980: 19, 98.)

Confucians, Pintupi and in some regards Ilongot attach great importance to 'learning models'. A related strategy, found in many societies,
involves working on the emotions in a fashion not dissimilar to that
advocated by cognitive therapists, such as Beck. Buddhists in Thailand and
northern Nepal, with whom I have talked, favour cognitive strategies. And
we can recall what Anderson says of Elizabethan 'psychological treatises'
(cf. Wax, 1969: 123, on Norse management). This strategy, however, is
probably less common than that of taking practical steps to manage
emotions. It is no doubt true that members of all societies are sufficiently
aware of the 'natural' sociodynamics of emotions to do what is necessary
to maintain the emotional order. The variety of management discussed by
Geertz when she writes that, if a quarrel in a Javanese village 'threatens to
erupt into an uncontrollable fight, the opponents forestall it by cutting off
relationships with one another' (1959: 227) is frequently encountered in the
literature.

The reader should not need reminding that, remaining close to our own
cultural understanding, members of many societies think in psychodynamic
fashion. Whether sent by supernatural or natural agencies or coming from
within, certain emotions are thought to well up and cause harm unless
released. Utku, Taita and Ilongot provide illustrations, members of each
society practising what they understand as 'catharsis'. If dangerous emotions remain 'stored', the consequences are grave (Utku, for example, say
that 'a man who *never* lost his temper could kill if he ever did become
angry': Briggs, 1970: 47). Another way in which psychodynamic understanding can be employed is provided by the Gisu (Kenya): Gisu male
initiation rituals involve the idea that fierce 'anger' (*lirima*) is generated
when youths are frustrated (see Heald, 1982).

Then there are those techniques found when externalization is important.
Generated by the gods, the gods must be placated, for example by sacrifice.
As well as pleasing gods, sacrifice can also function to get rid of distressful
human 'emotions'. Dinka sacrificial beasts are 'made the vehicle for the
passiones of men' (Lienhardt, 1961: 293). Sent by *atua*, Maori 'fear' is
exorcised in another fashion:

> Since a man in this position [feeling fear before a battle] was not held to be
> personally responsible for his fear, he could not be held responsible for
> overcoming it. Fear was instead removed by ritual means: one method used was
> to crawl between the legs of a high-born woman or chief, the sexual organs
> (particularly the vagina) having the power to remove supernatural influences.
> (Smith, 1981: 149)

Yet another way of handling the emotions of gods is provided by the
Chewong. For example, they make an effort to avoid subjecting each other
to those frustrations which lead supernatural beings to implement the *punen*
rule (Howell, 1981: 136).

One could go on and on. There is the literature on witchcraft (witches
being external sources of distressful emotions among the Dinka, for

example – see Lienhardt, 1951); there is the literature on those societies
where distressful emotions are thought to derive from food (see e.g. Weiss,
1983: 88); there is the literature on curing rites (see the bibliography
provided by Favazza and Faneem, 1982); there is the literature on classical
Greece (see e.g. Simon and Weiner, 1966, on *ate*); and of course, there is
the literature on Eastern and Western traditions (see e.g. Rawlinson, 1981;
Matthews, 1980). Our own psychotherapeutic techniques can all be found
elsewhere; but, given the variety of ways in which the emotions are
understood, it is not surprising to find techniques which also strike us as
strange.

It is time to draw our 'Cooks tour' to a close. Pulling together a number
of themes, I now want to emphasize something that many of the societies
we have visited have in common: they are less 'psychologically' minded
than we in the West.

Hallpike writes that 'the realm of purely private experience and motives,
as distinct from the evaluation of actual behaviour, is given little attention
in many primitive societies' (1979: 392). This is certainly borne out by the
Pintupi. Myers backs up his claim that 'Pintup use of concepts of the
emotions frequently does not present an introspective view of a person's
feelings' by drawing attention to the fact that he 'found it very difficult to
elicit private or individual interpretations of experience, as in the matter of
a parent's death' (1979: 347). Members of the Western psychological
subculture, intent on exploring their own innermost feelings, would not be
happy in this culture, where, as we have already seen, 'emotions' are
understood as highly social in nature. Neither would we be happy with the
Maori: 'psychology did not interest the Maori very much', writes Johansen;
'conflicts in the mind, unconscious motives, or the like are never mentioned'
(1954: 249). Even members of those societies which emphasize emotions as
inner states would not make good companions in, e.g., encounter groups.
The Ilongot might attach 'commendable' importance to emotions ('without
liget to move our hearts, there would be no human life': Rosaldo, 1980:
47), but the ethnographer presents little evidence that Ilongot are interested
in pondering the subtle inner dynamics of emotional life. And it is not
without significance that it is the Tahitians ('anxious and concerned when
the[ir] inner sense of "enthusiasm" decreases') whom Levy (1984) has in
mind when he presents an externally orientated characterization of emotion
talk: it is used to 'convey and represent information about one's *mode of
relationship* as a total individual to the social and nonsocial environment'
(Levy, 1984: 230; 1973: 271).[13]

The emotion talk of these cultures is clearly not much concerned with
emotions as inner experience. Such experiences are not thought of as
important, as we might put it, *in* themselves. The implications of this, and
of what their emotion talk is concerned with, are addressed in the final
section of this chapter, along with the implications of the fact that some
cultures, such as the Chewong, appear to be even less concerned with
psychological matters.

Significance

First, though, a few words on what is involved in exploring the constitutive significance of emotion talk. Anthropologists, classicists and others provide material on the subject. Psychologists (and philosophers, with their discussion of the 'aboutness' of emotions) find evidence for constructivism, and so provide a way of exploring the significance of emotion talk for emotional life. This, broadly speaking, is the picture. However, the division of labour between ethnographic and theoretical work has meant that not all that much has been done to effect the exploration. In 1979 Boucher wrote that 'systematic studies of the socially learned aspects of emotion in the cross-cultural context are extremely small in number' (Boucher, 1979: 175). The last few years have witnessed a growth of interest in the subject. But I think it is incontestable that we are far from knowing much about how emotions are learnt in 'exotic' societies. And, despite the pioneering work of a number of anthropologists-cum-psychologists, we know even less about the role played by emotion talk.

Perhaps this is not surprising. The subject is fraught with difficulties, it indeed being one thing to claim, on the basis of evidence from experimental psychology, that emotions are socially constructed, and quite another to explore the significance of cross-cultural differences in emotion talk. Consider what is involved in establishing whether or not particular emotions are universal. Can we identify cultures where certain emotions are not conceptualized, and infer from this that the emotions are absent? First, we have to establish that the emotions do not enter into emotion talk. This raises formidable problems to do with identifying emotion talk, for until we know what counts as emotion talk we do not know whether or not certain emotions are being conceptualized. There are also, of course, translation problems to do with the 'logical geography' of terms which might apply to those emotions thought to be absent from emotion talk.

Second, we have to consider the possibility that meanings other than those involved in emotion talk are actually generating those emotions which are not identified in the emotional lexicon. This possibility is raised by those psychologists (such as Lazarus, 1980) who work with broad definitions of what counts as an 'appraisal'. Until we have a clearer idea of the constitutive significance of various domains of meaning (the reader will recall my earlier mention), we cannot rule out the possibility that emotions are generated when not identified as such.

Finally, we have to settle what role to accord to endogenous processes. In this chapter I have been concentrating on differences in representation. But this is not to say that there is no evidence of cross-cultural constancy. Together with evidence for endogenous differentiation and the like, this suggests that culture does not have an entirely free hand in laying down emotions. As I have already argued, the evidence suggests that endogenous processes alone do not generate 'true' emotions. But we still have to take into account the fact that members of cultures which do not provide meanings for particular emotions almost certainly experience, say, 'anger' as a quasi-emotion.[14]

These and other considerations explain why we are far from knowing much about the exact significance, the exact impact, of emotion talk. The following explorations are thus speculative in nature. They are not unrealistically speculative, though. We might not be able to specify the exact significance of emotion talk, but surely we know that it provides the most obvious domain for the constructivist to explore; for it is here that meanings are 'experience-near' (Geertz, 1984: 124), are most directly focused on emotional life.

Emotion talk functions as a kind of spotlight. Depending on culture, it dwells on whatever is taken to be associated with those raw experiences (cf. Leventhal's 'elements') necessary for emotions. Sometimes the beam picks out organs, sometimes witches, sometimes behaviour and social activities, sometimes the gods. How raw experiences are constituted as emotions depends on how they are illuminated. Emotions experienced in the light of organ talk are not the same as emotions experienced in the light of gods (emotions coming from a god will be associated, in *meaning*, with the attributes of that god; emotions coming from an organ will almost certainly be associated, in *meaning*, with different attributes). Emotional elements which have no light thrown on them remain in the dark. And emotions which are focused on become enriched and highlighted in experience.

Anthropological evidence, together with constructivist theorizing, allows us to say that the differences encountered on our tour are not simply metaphorical ways of talking about 'the same thing'. 'Emotional elements' might be universal; 'emotional experiences' are not. As meaningful experiences, emotions differ according to the various meanings which have been introduced in this chapter. Differences in 'representation' are actually differences in construction. Dinka understanding of envy in terms of witches means that envy cannot be the same emotion for them as it is for us. To a degree, then, differences in emotional life can simply be read off from differences in emotion talk. But we can do more than this. We can try and spell out the ways in which emotion talk makes impact.

Attending to ways in which emotional activity might be diminished, consider Leff's claim that 'there is a strong link between the availability of the appropriate words for the various emotions and the ease with which people distinguish between the experiences' (Leff, 1973: 304). More specifically, 'words for denoting emotion whose meaning largely relates to . . . somatic accompaniments cannot be used to distinguish a variety of emotional states with any clarity' (p. 300). Indeed, Leff implies that somatized emotion talk does not function to construct fully fledged emotions, but refers to relatively inchoate bodily states (Leff, 1973: 301; 1977, 324). Levy's account of Tahitian terms to do with 'mild or moderate longing' serves to illustrate. There are, he writes, no unambiguous terms which represent the concepts of sadness, longing, or loneliness. . . . People would name their condition, where I supposed that the context called for 'sadness' or 'depression', as 'feeling troubled' (*pe'ape'a*, the generic term for disturbances, either internal or external); . . . as 'feeling heavy' (*tōiaha*); as 'feeling fatigued' (*haumani*); and a variety of other terms all referring to a generally troubled or subdued state. These are all nonspecific terms, which had no implication of any external relational cause about them, in the sense that 'angry' implies an offense or a frustration. (Levy, 1973: 305)

As Levy elsewhere concludes, 'In dealing with what I took to be "sadness" as, say, "fatigue", the Tahitians were accepting the "feeling" but denying that it was an "emotion"' (Levy, 1984: 220). But there is more to it than this. Hypocognition is not simply facilitated by a somatized mode of attention. There is also the point that 'sadness' can be interpreted in terms of 'the effect of spirits' (Levy, 1984: 223). Attention is thus taken away from what 'really' is 'sadness'-inducing: namely, some loss or another.

There is much more to be said about ways in which cultures so devise things that emotional elements do not get transformed into emotions, or so that particular emotions are not identified and developed. Since it is not my intention now to do anything other than indicate some of the moves which can be made in exploring the constructivist importance of emotion talk, I shall make only one or two more points.[15] One is that absence of linguistic differentiations (as between 'anger' and 'irritation', with regard to Ilongot *liget*) clearly means that particular 'emotions' remain hypocognated. Another is that it could be the case that some cultures do not provide learning models (even of a somatic variety) for certain of what we might want to consider as 'core' emotions. Some might think that it would be a foolhardy person who would try and argue that certain cultures do not provide learning models for, say, 'anger'. Taking my cue from Robarchek (1977, 1979), although perhaps paying more attention to emotion talk than he does, this is what I have tried to argue for the Chewong (Heelas, 1984). Organ (liver) talk is also discussed. (I argue that it directs attention away from emotions as inner experiences by virtue of the fact that it has to do with social behaviour.) And I explore the significance of Chewong 'rules': rules, the reader will recall, which ensure that any 'natural' connection between, say, a frustrating event and 'anger' is overridden by supernaturally implemented 'fear'. Hypocognition gives way to 're-cognition', as perhaps it does with Tahitian 'sadness' when spirits come into play. Attention to supernatural beings, more exactly to the human behaviour which has 'angered' them, comes to the fore.

Chewong, I conclude, are not experts at suppressing their emotions. That they never seem to 'lose control' (Howell, 1981: 135) is because they do not have many strong emotions to get excited about. What, then, of the reverse situation? How can emotion talk function to increase emotional activity? As a rule of thumb, the greater the importance of emotion talk, the greater the importance of emotionality; the greater the number of emotions which are identified, the greater the number of experienced emotions; and the

more an emotion is valued, the more likely it is to be hypercognized and to
be at the forefront of experience. In our own society, some have come
to have richer, more intense, emotional lives by virtue of their belonging to
the psychological subculture. Certain drug rehabilitation units, for example,
might claim to uncover repressed emotions but actually are employing
emotion talk in such a way as to teach people how to be more angry. Every
society, it should go without saying, provides contexts to teach emotions.
Generally informed by the moral domain, rituals very often dramatize and
thereby enrich whichever emotions have, so to speak, been selected for
attention.

Just as emotion talk is of the utmost importance in our psychological
culture, so is it important in many of these rituals (see, for example,
Kapferer, 1979).[16] On more general ways in which emotions are taught by
way of emotion talk, see Geertz (1959), Myers (1979), Lewis (1958), Levy
(1973, 1984) and Gordon (1981). Rather than dwell on this relatively well
discussed topic, I want to end by making the point that there is a
considerable difference between the way in which emotion talk of the
Western psychological subculture generates core emotions and the way in
which a different kind of emotion talk, found in many other societies,
generates emotions of a core or hypercognated variety.

Gordon points out that 'A vocabulary of sentiments is a linguistic
expression of experiences shared by group members, and mirrors their
interests and concerns' (1981: 578). In many of the societies introduced in
this chapter, the 'self' is defined as a social being. This means that the
'interests and concerns' mirrored in emotion talk belong to the social or
moral order. People thus define how and what they should feel in terms of
externalized forms of emotion talk. In other words, since emotion talk
articulates the moral order and defines what people should feel if they are
to be 'themselves' as social beings, it is externalized in terms of that order.

Social locus of identity is reflected in forms of emotion talk which function to bind participants to their true (socially defined) identities. Reflecting
the public domain, emotion talk directs the attention of participants away
from the 'private' and instead concentrates on what it means to be
emotional as that is socially defined. Even when the Pintupi are talking
about the 'private self', their emotion talk takes a sociocentric form. As
Myers writes, 'they seem to present it [private experience] in terms that
reflect more about the cultural system than about the individual' (1979:
348) Whether it is by way of emotion talk as an extension of social
institutions or by way of emotion talk incorporating gods as bound up with
the moral order, or both, the outcome is that emotions of the private self
are little attended to in many cultures. And if they do erupt, as antisocial or
private states of affairs, it is not surprising that they are managed by the
external representatives of true identity.

From a functional point of view, we gain an idea of how emotion talk in
many societies works to bind, 'cathect' in some cases, the emotional lives of
participants to the moral order. Detailed examination of how emotion talk

facilitates this process in different societies will probably show us that cross-cultural differences in emotional experiences can be co-ordinated with differences in both morality and notions of self. This is indicated by comparing what has just been said about some other cultures with how core emotions are generated by the Western psychological subculture. Here, with a highly individualistic morality and self-concept, emotion talk is of course directed within. The locus is internalized. And the outcome of 'psychobabble' is a different kind of emotional life than that found (for example) among the Pintupi. Emotions are not judged as 'right' or 'wrong'; emotions are not experienced (or at least should not be experienced) as bound up with public presentations of the self; and in general, emotional life is differentiated, complex, if not more powerful as a whole. Mirroring individualistic 'interests and concerns', the emotion talk of the psychological subculture almost certainly opens experiences unavailable to those whose emotional lives are bound – by way of emotion talk – to particular social orders. But then, members have to put up with emotions (such as 'anger') which might well be more or less absent in those societies which organize things differently.

To sum up, emotion talk differs from culture to culture. We are still a long way from knowing how to handle all the differences. It seems clear, though, that they can generate quite radical differences in emotional experience; that they can generate differences at the very heart of what it is to have an emotion. It also seems clear that the study of emotion talk provides a fruitful path for exploring the relationship between emotional and social life. It can function to keep the former in alignment with the latter. All this is recognized by Lutz, who has provided what I think is one of the clearest statements on the matter:

> Ethnotheories of emotion describe a fundamental and ubiquitous aspect of psychological functioning. They are used to explain why, when, and how emotion occurs, and they are embedded in more general theories of the person, internal processes, and social life. As they play a central role in the organization of experience and behavior, an examination of the structure of emotion ethnotheories can contribute to both cultural and psychological models of emotion and social action. (Lutz, 1988)

Notes

1 See Heelas (1983b; 1984: 33–9). The evidence strongly suggests that Izard's (1971: 267) claim that 'the subjective experience component of emotion determines Emotion Labeling' be reversed.

2 Concerning numbers, see e.g. Hiatt (1978: 182–7) (Australian Aborigines), Briggs (1970: 375–6) (Utkuhikhalingmiut Eskimo), Needham (1972: 25–8) (Nuer), Weiss (1983) (Ponogoro), Izard (1980) and Averill (1975). See Heelas (1983a; 1983b, 1984) for a discussion of difficulties.

3 More evidence for cross-cultural variations in differentiation is provided by Levy (1973, e.g. p. 322; 1984, e.g. p. 230), Lewis (1967: 70–85), Sorenson (1975, e.g. p. 367) and Marsella (1980, e.g. p. 242).

4 In passing, it can be pointed out that semantic variations, complex differences in

contexts of use, mean that classifications take a polythetic form (see Averill, 1980a: 308; cf. Needham, 1983: 36–65).

5 Culture-specific emotion terms, it can be noted, need not be culturally valued: see, for example, Newman (1964) on 'wild man' behaviour among the Gururumba of New Guinea.

6 Another illustration of how Apollonian and Dionysian societies differ in their attitudes towards particular emotions is provided by the Tallensi and Kalabari of West Africa: the former accord high value to timidity; the latter to aggressive emotionality (see Horton, 1961).

7 Cf. Davitz (1969), Harris (1985) and Frijda (1969). On the particular point of how we employ body talk, see Leff (1973: 301; 1977: 321, 323); on our use of what I have called metaphors, see Hallpike (1979: 393).

8 For more on Somatization see Johansen (1954) (Maori) and Weiss (1983).

9 Cf. Strathern's (1975) 'Why is Shame on the Skin?'

10 Rosaldo (1980, 1983), Myers (1979), Hallpike (1979: 388–409) and Heider (1984) all present interesting material and observations on this topic.

11 See Averill (1980b); cf. Heelas and Lock (1981, e.g. pp. 49–50).

12 The anthropological literature is relatively rich on the topic of 'conventional' emotions (see e.g. Mauss, 1921; Williams, 1932), although emotion talk is generally not dwelt on.

13 Other cultures which to varying degrees are not so concerned with emotions as inner experiences as Westerners include: Chewong (Howell, 1981: 141), Zapotec (Selby, 1974), Hindus (Miller, 1984; Schweder and Bourne, 1984). See also Leff (1977: 344) and Marsella (1976).

14 Ekman and Scherer (1984) present an excellent guide to evidence pertaining to such matters as endogenous elicitation and the kinds of meaning which have to be present. Evidence for cross-cultural constancy has been provided by many: see, for example, Osgood et al. (1975), Ekman (1982) and Levy (1984). Scherer et al.'s (1983) work might prove of great use in this regard. On the issue of establishing what counts as emotion talk, see e.g. Needham (1972; 1981). For general discussion of problems, see Heelas (1983a, 1983b, 1984).

15 Other avenues which could be explored include the ways in which externalization bears on emotional experience: could it be that the significance of 'guilt' is diminished when gods (etc.) are held to be the locus of responsibility? What happens to the experience of 'envy' when it is externalized in Dinka fashion?

16 See also Heald (1982) and Munn (1969), the latter referring to Geertz's (1973) work on 'symbolic models of emotion'. Marsella and White (1982) present a number of articles bearing on the topic.

References

Anderson, R. (1934) *Elizabethan Psychology and Shakespeare's Plays.* University of Iowa Humanistic Studies, vol. III, no. 4.

Averill, J. (1975) 'A semantic atlas of emotional concepts', *JSAS Catalogue of Selected Documents in Psychology*, 5: 330 (MS. no. 421).

Averill, J. (1980a) 'A constructivist view of emotion', in R. Plutchik and H. Kellerman (eds), *Emotion Theory, Research and Experience*. Vol. I: *Theories of Emotion*. London: Academic Press. pp. 305–39.

Averill, J. (1980b) 'On the paucity of positive emotion', in K. Blankstein et al. (eds), *Assessment and Modification of Emotion Behavior*. London: Plenum Press. pp. 7–45.

Bandura, A. (1965) 'Vicarious processes: a case of no trial learning', in L. Berkowitz (ed.), *Advances in Experimental Social Psychology*, vol. 4. London: Academic Press. pp. 167–223.

Barfield, O. (1954) *History in English Words*. London: Faber.

Benedict, R. (1935) *Patterns of Culture*. London: Routledge and Kegan Paul.

Boucher, J. (1979) 'Culture and emotion', in J. Marsella et al. (eds), *Perspectives on Cross-cultural Psychology*. London: Academic Press. pp. 159–78.

Boucher, J. and Brandt, M. (1981) 'Judgement of emotion from American and Malay antecedents', *Journal of Cross Cultural Psychology*, 12 (3): 272–83.

Briggs, J. (1970) *Never in Anger*. London: Harvard University Press.

Chagnon, N. (1968) *Yanomamö: The Fierce People*. New York: Holt, Rinehart and Winston.

Davitz, J. (1969) *The Language of Emotion*. London: Academic Press.

Ekman, P. (ed.) (1982) *Emotion in the Human Face*. Cambridge: Cambridge University Press.

Ekman, P. and Scherer, K. (1984) 'Questions about emotion', in K. Scherer and P. Ekman (eds), *Approaches to Emotion*. Hillsdale, NJ: Lawrence Erlbaum. pp. 1–8.

Favazza, A. and Faheem, A. (1982) *Themes in Cultural Psychiatry*. Kansas City and London: University of Missouri Press.

Frijda, N. (1969) 'Recognition of emotion', in L. Berkowitz (ed.), *Advances in Experimental Social Psychology*, vol. 4. London: Academic Press. pp. 167–223.

Geertz, C. (1973) *The Interpretation of Cultures*. New York: Basic Books.

Geertz, C. (1980) *Negara: The Theatre State in Nineteenth-Century Bali*. Princeton: Princeton University Press.

Geertz, C. (1984) 'From the native's point of view', in R. Schweder and R. Le Vine (eds), *Culture Theory*. Cambridge: Cambridge University Press. pp. 123–36.

Geertz, H. (1959) 'The vocabulary of emotion', *Psychiatry*, 22: 225–37.

Gordon, S. (1981) 'The sociology of sentiments and emotion', in M. Rosenberg and R. Turner (eds), *Social Psychology*. New York: Basic Books. pp. 562–92.

Gudgeon, C. (1906) *Journal of the Polynesian Society*, 15: 163–74.

Hallpike, C. (1977) *Bloodshed and Vengeance in the Papuan Mountains*. Oxford: Clarendon Press.

Hallpike, C. (1979) *The Foundations of Primitive Thought*. Oxford: Clarendon Press.

Harris, G. (1978) *Casting out Anger*. Cambridge: Cambridge University Press.

Harris, P. (1985) 'What children know about the situations that provoke emotion', in M. Lewis and C. Saarni (eds), *The Socialization of Emotions*. London: Plenum Press. pp. 161–86.

Heald, S. (1982) 'The making of men', *Africa*, 52 (1): 15–36.

Heelas, P. (1983a) 'Indigenous representatives of the emotions: the Chewong', *Journal of the Anthropological Society of Oxford*, 14 (1): 87–103.

Heelas, P. (1983b) Anthropological perspectives on violence: universals and particulars. *Zygon*, 18 (4): 375–404.

Heelas, P. (1984) 'Emotions across cultures: objectivity and cultural divergence', in S. Brown (ed.), *Objectivity and Cultural Divergence*. Cambridge: Cambridge University Press. pp. 21–42.

Heelas, P. and Lock, A. (eds) (1981) *Indigenous Psychologies*. London: Academic Press.

Heider, K. (1984) 'Emotion: inner state vs. interaction', Paper delivered to the American Anthropological Association.

Hiatt, L. (1978) 'Classification of the emotions', in L. Hiatt (ed.), *Australian Aboriginal Concepts*. Princeton, NJ: Humanities Press. pp. 182–7.

Hochschild, A. (1983) *The Managed Heart*. Berkeley and London: University of California Press.

Horton, R. (1961) 'Destiny and the unconscious in West Africa', *Africa*, 31 (2): 110–16.

Howell, S. (1981) 'Rules not words', in P. Heelas and A. Lock (eds), *Indigenous Psychologies*. London: Academic Press. pp. 133–44.

Howell, S. (1984) *Society and Cosmos: Chewong of Peninsular Malaysia*. London: Oxford University Press.

Izard, C. (1971) *The Face of Emotion*. New York: Meredith.

Izard, C. (1980) 'Cross-cultural perspectives on emotion and emotion communication', in *Handbook of Cross-Cultural Psychology*. Boston: Allyn and Bacon.

Johansen, J. (1954) *The Maori and his Religion*. Copenhagen: Enjar Munksgaard.

Johnson, A. (1964) *The Vitality of the Individual in the Thought of Ancient Israel*. Cardiff: University of Wales Press.

Kapferer, B. (1979) 'Emotion and feeling in Sinhalese healing rites', *Social Analysis*, 1: 153–76.

Kemper, T. (1978) *A Social Interactional Theory of Emotions*. Chichester: John Wiley.

Kemper, T. (1984) 'Power, status and emotions: a sociological contribution to a psycho-physiological domain', in K. Scherer and P. Ekman (eds), *Approaches to Emotion*. Hillsdale, NJ: Lawrence Erlbaum. pp. 369–83.

La Barre, W. (1972) *The Ghost Dance*. London: George Allen & Unwin.

Lazarus, R. (1980) 'Thoughts on the relations between cognition and emotion', *American Psychologist*, 37: 1019–24.

Lazarus, R. et al. (1980) 'Emotions: a cognitive-phenomenological analysis', in R. Plutchik and H. Kellerman (eds), *Emotion Theory, Research and Experience*. Vol. I: *Theories of Emotion*. London: Academic Press. pp. 189–218.

Leach, E. (1981) 'A poetics of power', *The New Republic*, 4 April.

Leff, J. (1973) 'Culture and the differentiation of emotion states', *British Journal of Psychiatry*, 123: 209–306.

Leff, J. (1977) 'The cross-cultural study of emotions', *Culture, Medicine and Psychiatry*, 1 (4): 317–50.

Leventhal, H. (1980) 'Toward a comprehensive theory of emotion', in L. Berkowitz (ed.), *Advances in Experimental Social Psychology*. London: Academic Press. pp. 149–207.

Levy, R. (1973) *Tahitians*. London: Chicago University Press.

Levy, R. (1984) 'Emotions, knowing, and culture', in R. Schweder and R. LeVine (eds), *Culture Theory. Essays on Mind, Self, and Emotion*. Cambridge: Cambridge University Press. pp. 214–37.

Lewis, C. (1958) *The Allegory of Love*. London: Oxford University Press.

Lewis, C. (1967) *Studies in Words*. Cambridge: Cambridge University Press.

Lewis, M. and Saarni, C. (1985) 'Culture and emotions', in M. Lewis and C. Saarni (eds), *The Socialization of Emotions*. London: Plenum Press. pp. 1–17.

Lienhardt, G. (1951) 'Some notions of witchcraft among the Dinka', *Africa*, 21 (1): 308–18.

Lienhardt, G. (1961) *Divinity and Experience*. Oxford: Clarendon Press.

Lutz, C. (1981) 'Situation-based emotion frames and the cultural construction of emotion', in *Proceedings of the Third Annual Conference of the Cognitive Science Society, Berkeley*. pp. 84–9.

Lutz, C. (1985) 'Cultural patterns and individual differences in the child's emotional meaning system', in M. Lewis and C. Saarni (eds), *The Socialization of Emotion*. New York: Plenum Press. pp. 37–116.

Lutz, C. (1988) 'Goals, events and understanding in Ifaluk emotion theory', in N. Quinn and D. Holland (eds), *Cultural Models in Language and Thought*. Cambridge: Cambridge University Press.

Malatesta, C. and Haviland, J. (1985) 'Signals, symbols and socialization', in M. Lewis and C. Saarni (eds), *The Socialisation of Emotions*. London: Plenum Press. pp. 89–116.

Mandler, G. (1980) 'The generation of emotion: a psychological theory', in R. Plutchik and H. Kellerman (eds), *Emotion Theory, Research and Experience*, Vol. 1: *Theories of Emotion*. London: Academic Press. pp. 219–42.

Marsella, A. (1976) 'Cross-cultural studies of depression: a review of the literature'. Paper presented at the Symposium on Cross-Cultural Aspects of Depression, Tilburg.

Marsella, A. (1980) 'Depressive experience and disorder across cultures', in H. Triandis and J. Draguns (eds), *Handbook of Cross-Cultural Psychopathology*. London: Allyn and Bacon. pp. 237–89.

Marsella, A. and White, G. (eds) (1982) *General Conception of Mental Health and Therapy*. London: Reidel.

Matthews, G. (1980) 'Ritual and the religious feelings', in A. Rorty (ed.), *Explaining Emotion*. London: University of California Press. pp. 339–54.

Mauss, M. (1921) 'Obligatory expression of emotion', *Journal de Psychologie*, 18.

Miller, J. (1984) 'Culture and the development of everyday social explanations', *Journal of Personality and Social Psychology*, 46 (5): 961–78.

Munn, N. (1969) 'The effectiveness of symbols in Murngin rite and myth', in R. Spencer (ed.), *Forms of Symbolic Action*. New York and London: American Ethnological Society. pp. 178–207.

Myers, F. (1979) 'Emotions and the self', *Ethos*, 7 (4): 343–70.

Needham, R. (1971) Introduction, in R. Needham (ed.), *Rethinking Kinship and Marriage*. London: Tavistock Press. pp. xliii–cxvii.

Needham, R. (1972) *Belief, Language, and Experience*. Oxford: Basil Blackwell.

Needham, R. (1981) 'Inner states as universals: sceptical reflections on human nature', in P. Heelas and A. Lock (eds), *Indigenous Psychologies*. London: Academic Press. pp. 65–78.

Needham, R. (1983) *Against the Tranquility of Axioms*. London: University of California Press.

Newman, P. (1964) '"Wild man" behavior in a New Guinea Highlands community', *American Anthropologist*, 1–19.

Onians, R. (1973) *The Origins of European Thought*. New York: Arno.

Osgood, C. et al. (1975) *Cross-Cultural Universals of Affective Meaning*. Chicago and London: University of Illinois Press.

Peters, R. (1974) *Psychology and Ethical Development*. London: George Allen & Unwin.

Rawlinson, A. (1981) 'Yoga psychology', in P. Heelas and A. Lock (eds), *Indigenous Psychologies*. London: Academic Press. pp. 247–64.

Read, K. (1967) 'Morality and the concept of the person among the Gahuku-Gama', in J. Middleton (ed.), *Myth and Cosmos*. New York: Natural History Press. pp. 185–230.

Robarchek, C. (1977) 'Frustration, aggression and the nonviolent Semai', *American Ethnologist*, 4, 762–79.

Robarchek, C. (1979) 'Learning to fear: a case study of emotional conditioning', *American Ethnologist*, 6: 555–67.

Rosaldo, M. (1980) *Knowledge and Passion*. Cambridge: Cambridge University Press.

Rosaldo, M. (1983) 'The shame of headhunters and the autonomy of the self', *Ethos*, 11 (3): 135–51.

Schachter, S. and Singer, J. (1962) 'Cognitive, social, and psychological determinants of emotional state', *Psychological Review*, 69 (5): 379–99.

Scherer, K. et al. (1983) 'Cross-national research on antecedents and components of emotion: a progress report', *Social Science Information*, 22 (3): 355–85.

Selby, H. (1974) *Zapotec Deviance*. Houston and London: University of Texas Press.

Shweder, R. and Bourne, E. (1984) 'Does the concept of the person vary cross-culturally?', in R. Schweder and R. LeVine (eds), *Culture Theory: Essays on Mind, Self, and Emotion*. Cambridge: Cambridge University Press. pp. 158–99.

Simon, B. and Weiner, H. (1966) 'Models of mind and mental illness in ancient Greece. I: The Homeric model of mind', *Journal of the History of the Behavioural Sciences*, 11 (4): 303–14.

Smith, J. (1981) 'Self and experience in Maori culture', in P. Heelas and A. Lock (eds), *Indigenous Psychologies*. London: Academic Press. pp. 145–59.

Sorenson, E. (1975) 'Culture and the expression of emotion', in T.R. Williams (ed.), *Psychological Anthropology*. The Hague: Mouton. pp. 361–72.

Strathern, A. (1975) 'Why is shame on the skin?', *Ethnology*, 14: 347–56.

Wax, R. (1969) *Magic, Fate and History*. Kansas City: Coronado Press.

Weiss, J. (1983) *Folk Psychology of the Javanese of Ponorogo*. Ann Arbor, Mich.: University Microfilms International.

Williams, F. (1932) *Sentiments and Leading Ideas in Native Society* (Anthropological Report no. 12). Port Moresby, Papua New Guinea.

Williams, F. (1940) *Drama of Orokolo*. Oxford: Clarendon Press.

Vignette 5

Maori Emotion

K.T. Strongman and L. Strongman

The New Zealand Maori who comprise approximately one-tenth of the total population of New Zealand, have, since the mid-1980s, enjoyed something of a cultural renaissance in post-imperial New Zealand. While this has led to the legal creation of a bicultural New Zealand nationhood, it has not, except in the broadest sense led to a cohesive Maori and Pakeha (the Maori word for New Zealand white) national identity. To say that one is a New Zealander is now in the mid-1990s to say that one is a member of a society in which New Zealand Maori and Pakeha are in partnership, but nowhere is the precariousness of this partnership better evidenced than in the exchange and fostering of scientific knowledge, particularly social scientific knowledge, about the Maori people. There is simply a paucity of social scientific knowledge about Maori.

One of the central reasons for this is that historically the Maori were a pre-modern race. When Europeans arrived in New Zealand approximately one hundred and fifty years ago they brought with them an imperial modernity, European science, religion, language, technologies and Anglo-Western methods of describing and controlling the world. Over the relatively short period of colonization this often simply displaced the orally based culture of the Maori who had occupied the country – their word for it, 'Aotearoa' – for approximately a millennium before the European. Thus, whatever observations the Maori made of themselves were those of an internationally un-self-conscious tribal culture which had little knowledge of a larger world outside until the coming of the Pakeha. The stories they did tell about themselves were orally transmitted in folklore, or visually related in primitive figurative representations. It was not until the coming of the European in the nineteenth century that these intrinsically Maori narratives were written down, as folklore and myths of creation, and this in the language and form of the colonizing culture which displaced them.

The Maori people are perhaps understandably cautious about giving non-Maori access to their cultural self-knowledge. Cultural boundaries in contemporary bicultural New Zealand are paradoxically carefully guarded by Maori. Generally Maori prefer such engagements only from Maori, almost none of whom is qualified to gather the information necessary for social scientific study – qualified that is in the light of Westernized scientific methods. Should they become so there is the danger that the product will simply be a 'Maori' social science, rather than a general and genuinely bicultural social scientific practice in New Zealand. Here, as elsewhere there is the danger that biculturalism will simply mean a quite banal parallel separatism of two cultures, equivalent dialogues running side-by-side with little exchange between. In post-colonial and post-imperial conditions, there is a world of difference between simply accepting another's culture and attempting to engage in it as an intrinsic part of one's own.

From the outset then, to attempt to come to grips with Maori culture in a social scientific sense is to acknowledge the collision and collusion between two vastly different cultures, it is to acknowledge the problems that lie at the heart of cross-cultural studies: how is it possible to gain access to a culture other than one's own, do justice to the social scientific representation of that culture, preserving both the integrity of Anglo-Western scientific methods and also the authentic representation of the culture which is being studied? There are no simple answers to these perennial questions in cross-cultural social science, and none is particularly to be found in the scientific study of the Maori culture in New Zealand. Often simply to theorize this difficult terrain serves only to build a more sophisticated and scientifically acceptable structure into which is placed a paucity of basic knowledge, which in turn often serves only to abrogate the colonized culture further. Due to the lack of available data about Maori ways of thinking, Maori feelings and emotions, a balance need be set, and concessions made on both sides between Anglo-Western scientific technique and the available sources for the study of Maori emotions. Perhaps these 'concessions' actually in themselves acknowledge a shift away from traditional modernist European scientific techniques to the more language-centred approaches of postmodernism, a recognition that the world is more complexly organized and its ordering of a more fluid and intertextual nature than the practices of a reductive scientific modernism would allow.

Given these largely inhibiting parameters, what then can be said by Pakeha about Maori emotions and in what manner should it be said?

One way of beginning is with observation. For example, consider ritual, an extremely important aspect of Maori affairs. Emotion is built in to many Maori rituals. It ranges from the *wiata* (songs) which express many different emotions depending on the circumstances, to the *haka*, which for example the All-Blacks perform before every rugby encounter. This clearly expresses a war-like, fired up anger and aggression.

Moreover, if a person (whether Maori or Pakeha) speaks formally at a Maori meeting then the speech is meant to be from the heart rather than in a more prepared way from the head. This appears to be aimed at a type of emotional sincerity, more than would be possible were any speech to be more carefully contrived. It seems that in such circumstances emotion is not merely recognized, it is used almost as an indication of integrity.

Within New Zealand culture it is part of the general folk-lore that there is a long tradition of Maori anger and aggression. In recent times, nowhere has this been better portrayed than in the movie *Once Were Warriors*, taken from Maori writer Alan Duff's book of the same name. It is a powerful story of the links between Maori tradition and impoverished city life for the modern Maori.

A central character is Jake the Mus, a man with wife and family who is a natural leader in his community. He leads by force, of both personality and physique. One of the many things portrayed so tellingly in the movie is Jake's occasional lapses into vicious and uncontrolled anger. Rarely has anger been more compellingly characterized than in *Once Were Warriors*, and although there has been some concern among Maori that the book and film exist at all, there has been no quibble at this portrayal.

A further possibility for gaining some insight into Maori emotion is to make an analysis of the words used to convey emotion in a Maori dictionary. Although this may seem to be a curiously old-fashioned approach, in the research climate described earlier, it is one of the few possibilities available. Also, it can be argued that dictionary analyses are a perfectly legitimate part of the broadened concept of scientific method that is characteristic of the discursive approach in general.

The most salient feature of the categories that arise from such an analysis of the Maori language is that by far the largest category contains words to do with anger and aggression. There are nearly three times as many anger and aggression words as appear in the next largest category (perplexed), these representing 17 per cent of the total emotion words in the dictionary. As might be expected, within this category there are great subtleties of meaning and expression which move across a broad range of anger.

At the other end of the scale, there are, from the perspective of the English language, surprisingly few words to do with depression, envy/ jealousy, hate and grief. The smallest category of all is conceit.

Even more interestingly, at least as evidenced by the number of words involved, there appear to be three or four emotional conditions which are important to Maori and which have received very little mention in Western psychology. Second to anger is what might be termed 'being perplexed'. This takes the various forms of being bewildered, confused, unsettled, mistaken, flurried, baffled, incoherent, disconcerted, embarrassed, wandering, unstable, confounded, dumbfounded, uncertain, in turmoil, dazed and giddy. Of course, it is perfectly possible to be perplexed as a non-Maori, but this is not a state which assumes as much importance for members of Pakeha cultures, at least judging from the indirect measures used in the present type of analysis.

Fourth and fifth in the league table of significant emotions are desire and yearning, categories which if combined would be placed second to anger and aggression. Yearning is a very interesting category. It has connotations of great unsettlement and weariness, restlessness, irritation, grieving, fretting, pining and longing for; and has obvious connections with being perplexed.

Another specific emotion category is 'to be diminished'. To our knowledge, this state which is clearly important in the Maori language, has not been previously described in accounts of emotion. It is clearly unpleasant and variously connotes being less, being belittled or despised, being shattered, feeble or debilitated, being powerless or exhausted, being weak, listless and pining away, and being essentially spiritless. A little like the yearning category, all these states are recognizable to a non-Maori experiencer of emotion, but do not assume such categorical significance.

To some extent, the importance of the 'being diminished' category is balanced by the even more important state of 'calmness'. This has all the connotations that might be expected – peaceful, undisturbed, quiet, placid, gentle, still, content, sooL...ng, silent and reserved. But it can also have overtones of being both free from anxiety and prosperous and secure.

This is perhaps sufficient to give an idea of Maori emotion from among the limited sources available. Although it is possible to draw a picture from this type of analysis, it amounts to no more than shadowy images, a set of possibilities. The words available in a language *must* reflect or help to determine the lives of those who express themselves in that language although this is not the place to pursue a consideration of the Whorfian debate. The present approach is a reasonable beginning to the study of emotion from a social constructionist viewpoint and, as mentioned previously, it also fits within the methodologies of postmodern science. At the very least this type of discussion suggests a number of questions it would be pertinent to ask about Maori emotion and hypotheses it would be instructive to test further.

PART III

THE BIOLOGICAL DIMENSIONS OF EMOTION

Chapter 9

An Analysis of Psychophysiological Symbolism and its Influence on Theories of Emotion

James R. Averill

> Now the works of the flesh are plain: fornication, impurity, licentiousness, idolatry, sorcery, enmity, strife, jealousy, anger, dissension, party spirit, envy, drunkenness, carousing, and the like; I warn you, as I warned you before, those who do such things shall not inherit the Kingdom of God.
>
> St Paul, *Epistle to the Galatians* 5: 19–21.

> Of points where physiology and psychology touch, the place of one lies at 'emotion'.
>
> Sir Charles Sherrington, *The Integrative Action of the Nervous System.*

The present article deals with the origins and ramifications of an idea, namely, the notion that emotions are closely linked to physiological change. This idea currently finds expression in many ways. In its most extreme form, emotions are defined as patterns of visceral activity (e.g. Wenger, 1950); less extreme but more common, even among theorists who subscribe to a cognitive orientation, is the assumption that physiological change is an essential component of emotion (e.g. Schachter, 1971). And when physiological change *per se* is not being emphasized, emotions still tend to be viewed as biologically basic, primitive, or instinctive (e.g. Plutchik, 1970). Attitudes and assumptions such as these are reflected in the fact that many of the outstanding theorists of emotion – such as Cannon, Delgado, Gellhorn, MacLean, and Pribram, to name but a few – have had their primary affiliation with physiology and neurology rather than with psychology; and even within departments of psychology, courses dealing with emotion are usually taught by physiological psychologists, as opposed, say, to personality or social psychologists.

In spite of the above physiological emphasis, the topic of emotion has long played an important role in theories of personality and social psychology. Anger, sexual passion, envy, fear and anxiety: singly or in combination, emotions such as these have been taken as the 'drive' without which the individual would collapse, an inert mass of protoplasm, and society would be unnecessary or even impossible. To a disinterested observer, it might seem rather anomalous that psychological processes – the emotions – which are of such interest to personality and social psychology should be conceptualized, researched, and taught largely within a physiological tradition. Why is such an anomaly so taken for granted by psychologists? Ultimately, all psychological phenomena are biologically based and dependent upon physiological processes. Is there something special about emotion in this respect?

It is sometimes the case that psychological processes become linked to physiological structures not on the basis of empirical fact, but rather, on the basis of symbolic relationships which are extrinsic from a scientific point of view. I have termed this process of predication *psychophysiological symbolism* (Averill, 1969). The traditional link between emotion and physiological activity is a special case of psychophysiological symbolism. It stems from communalities in attitudes which are deep-seated in Western intellectual and ethical traditions – attitudes towards things emotional, on the one hand, and things bodily, on the other. To the extent that the association of emotional reactions with physiological change is based on psychophysiological symbolism, it proves a hindrance to an adequate understanding of emotional phenomena. This is especially true when it comes to questions concerning the relationship of emotion to cognition, and with regard to the role of society in shaping emotional behaviour. [. . .]

The role of symbolism in psychophysiological theory

The relationship of symbolism to science

If it is assumed that one function of science is the symbolic representation of reality, then any aspect of a scientific concept or symbol which accurately fulfils this function may be said to be *intrinsic* from a scientific point of view, and any aspect (e.g. culturally imbued surplus meaning) which does not refer to objective fact is scientifically *extrinsic*. This is, admittedly, a difficult distinction to draw, and perhaps an example will help clarify the difference between intrinsic and extrinsic symbolism. A circle is a closed curve, every point of which is equidistant from the centre. This is its logical meaning or, from a mathematical point of view, its intrinsic symbolism (for the points and lines of the geometer are nothing more than symbols for abstract relations). In many cultures, the figure of a circle also has acquired meanings related to cosmological, religious, and even sexual events. Such symbolism is extrinsic to the logical or scientific meaning of 'circle'. [. . .]

The intrinsic or scientific meaning of a physiological concept refers to the actual function of the designated organ or tissue; the extrinsic symbolism refers to some attribute conceived within a non-physiological framework. Since accurate physiological knowledge has been slow to accumulate, and is still in a relatively primitive state, it is not surprising that historically many physiological concepts have been strongly imbued with extrinsic symbolism. For example, an organ or tissue may be assigned significance not on the basis of its actual physiological function, but on the basis of its use as food, involvement in ritual sacrifice, presumed role in sexual activity, and so forth.[1]

The intrinsic and extrinsic symbolism of psychological concepts is more difficult to explicate than that of physiological concepts. At this point it suffices to note that everyday psychological concepts do not just describe the objective characteristics of behaviour; they also place behaviour within an interpretative framework or system of judgment, which often involves moral, aesthetic, legal, and other social considerations. Psychological concepts taken from the vernacular are thus replete with connotations and presuppositions which may be superfluous from a scientific point of view. [. . .]

The psychophysiological symbolism of emotion

Let us turn now to a consideration of the psychophysiological symbolism of emotion, i.e. the association of emotional with physiological processes on the basis of extrinsic symbolic relationships. We will begin with an examination of the concept of emotion in both its intrinsic and extrinsic aspects. [. . .]

The term 'emotion' is derived from the Latin, *e + movere*. It originally meant to migrate or to transfer from one place to another. It also was used to refer to states of agitation or perturbation, both physical (e.g. the weather) and psychological. It is in this latter, somewhat metaphorical usage, that the etymology of 'emotion' has sometimes been offered in support of the thesis that affective states involve high arousal and disturbance. It is important to note, however, that the term 'emotion' has only recently been applied widely and consistently to affective states. For approximately two thousand years, from the time of the Greeks to the middle of the eighteenth century, it was common to speak of emotions as 'passions'. The term 'passion' derives from the Latin, *pati* (to suffer), which in turn is related to the Greek, *pathos*. Also derived from *pati* are such terms as 'passive' and 'patient'. At the root of these concepts is the idea that an individual (or physical object) is undergoing or suffering some change, as opposed to doing or initiating change. Historically, 'passivity' has been the generic term used to express this idea. It may thus be said that emotional concepts imply passivity or, following Aristotle, that emotions belong to the category of passivity (Peters, 1962). (In order to avoid confusion, it must be emphasized that 'passivity' in this sense has nothing to do with lack of energy or vigour, and hence is not to be contrasted with 'activation' as the latter term is often used in theories of emotion.)

In ordinary discourse, the passivity of emotion is expressed in many ways. We are 'gripped', 'seized', and 'torn' by emotion; we act 'uncontrollably', as if 'possessed'. This connotation of passivity has led to a host of legal, moral, and other types of evaluative judgments which are not intrinsic to the concept of emotion. Legally, for example, a person is less culpable for behaviour committed during emotion ('crimes of passion'). Morally, on the other hand, one is admonished to avoid situations likely to induce strong passions. In general, Western ethical and intellectual traditions have placed a high value on rational, deliberate action. Thus, although a person may not be held responsible for emotional reactions (one cannot be responsible for behaviour beyond his control), the emotions more often than not have been considered negatively, being viewed as irrational, involuntary, and animal-like. It is evaluative judgments such as these which form the extrinsic symbolism of emotion. Let us examine them a little more closely, starting with the view that emotions are irrational.

Emotion and rationality   The distinction between passion and reason can be found quite early in Western thought. For example, the Greek philosopher Anaxagoras (born 500 B.C.) identified the divinity with *nous* (mind). *Nous* was conceived of largely as an agent of rationality and was described as *apathes* (without passion). There is a sense, of course, in which the emotions are antithetical to rational behaviour. Rationality involves the weighing of evidence by appeals to general principles and according to standards of inference (standards which may be explicit, e.g. rules of logic, or which may be largely implicit and unformulated, but nevertheless recognizable). Emotional reactions, on the other hand, tend to be unpremeditated, intuitive, and impulsive. To this extent, at least, the antithesis between rationality and emotion presents no problem as far as extrinsic symbolism is concerned. The difficulty arises when the favourable connotations typically associated with rationality accrue to cognitive and intellectual functions in general; and then, by contrast, emotions come to be viewed as being noncognitive, as not requiring a great deal of intellectual competence, and as being dependent upon bodily structures different from those which subserve 'higher' mental processes.

Emotion and voluntary action   Emotions are often viewed as involuntary as well as irrational. Obviously, however, emotional reactions are not involuntary in the same sense that behaviour induced by external coercion is involuntary. The person who is angry *wants* to harm his enemy; the lover *wants* to possess the object of his passion; the fearful person *wants* to flee. In other words, during emotion an individual is 'coerced', if at all, by his own desires. In scholastic philosophy (O'Brien, 1948), this fact led to a distinction between fully voluntary acts (to which the individual gives full assent) and perfectly voluntary acts (which are performed after due deliberation and forethought). According to this distinction, emotions are fully voluntary but not perfectly voluntary. In more modern terminology, one might say that emotions involve strong commitment but little freedom of choice.

What is the extrinsic symbolism which surrounds the notion of emotions as involuntary? If we focus attention on the restricted view that emotions are not perfectly voluntary, then many of the same considerations apply as were discussed above with regard to rationality. That is, to be perfectly voluntary an act must involve rational deliberation regarding means and ends. Of course, most persons do not make such fine distinctions as that between fully and perfectly voluntary acts, and the fact that emotional reactions are in *some* sense involuntary has been sufficient to enmesh them in a whole network of prejudicial attitudes related to such issues as freedom of the will.

Emotion and animality The ideals of rationality and free will, either singly or in combination, have formed the cornerstones of Western intellectual and ethical traditions; indeed, within this tradition, these ideals have been considered the hallmark or very essence of mankind. It is of little wonder, then, that for over 2000 years the emotions have been viewed as somewhat less than human – as 'brutish', 'bestial', 'instinctive', and the like. Stated in more neutral terms, the emotions have long been considered to be a function of that part of the soul or body common to animals and man. As will be demonstrated below, this supposed animality of emotional reactions has played an important role in physiological analyses of emotion.

On the basis of this brief review of the symbolism of emotion, it is to be expected that emotional reactions would become associated with physiological structures which are viewed with some degree of negativity or distaste, which are believed to be distinct from the substratum of rational thought, which are considered outside of voluntary control, and which are thought to be shared by animals and man. Rightfully or wrongfully, this set of characteristics has been applied to the broad class of structures known as the viscera, and even sometimes to the body as a whole (i.e. when a contrast is made not between bodily structures *per se*, but between the corporeal and the spiritual). On the basis of psychophysiological symbolism, then, one would expect to find a close conceptual link between emotion and physiological change, especially visceral activity.

Historical and contemporary examples of the psychophysiological symbolism of emotion

The distinction between extrinsic and intrinsic symbolism is not easy to make conceptually and is even more difficult to recognize in practice. Not surprisingly, therefore, the workings of psychophysiological symbolism can best be seen with the aid of hindsight. This is why it may be useful to look at speculations regarding the relationship between emotion and physiological change from an historical perspective. Though we obviously cannot provide a comprehensive history, we can illustrate the influence of psychophysiological symbolism through selected examples. Hopefully, such examples will make the operation of psychophysiological symbolism in contemporary psychological theory more readily discernible. The first half of the review is devoted to philosophical speculation from Plato to Descartes; in the second half, an examination is made of the views of some leading anatomists and physiologists since the time of Descartes. [. . .]

Examples from philosophy

Plato provides an excellent introduction to psychophysiological symbolism, both because his symbolism is so vivid and because there can be little pretension that during the fourth century B.C. localization of function was based on physiological fact. Since primitive explanations of the universe generally mix psychology with cosmology, the creation myth in Plato's *Timaeus* also illuminates his psychophysiological symbolism. We are told there that the immortal principle of the soul is self-motion; anything which receives its motion through outside forces can cease to move and, *ipso facto*, to live. Self-motion, according to Plato, is also the motion of thought; hence, the immortal soul is the rational soul. In contrast, the mortal soul is passive, 'subject to terrible and irresistible affections'. The psychological meaning of the distinction between the immortal and mortal soul is thus quite clear; it is the distinction between deliberate, self-initiated (rational) behaviour, on the one hand, and affective, externally-initiated (irrational) behaviour, on the other.[2]

Having drawn the distinction between immortal and mortal souls (deliberate and affective behaviour, broadly conceived), Plato went on to localize them within the body. Since the motion of thought is circular, it was natural to place it in a spherical structure such as the head. Plato adduced two additional reasons for this localization: First, the head imitates the spherical shape of the universe (which, it will be recalled, is also besouled with rationality); and second, the head is closest to the heavens and the celestial divinities.

Having located the immortal, rational soul in the head, the placement of the mortal soul – and hence emotion – followed quite naturally. In order not to pollute the rational soul any more than necessary, the mortal, affective soul was placed in the trunk of the body. The neck thus served as

an isthmus or boundary to help separate the rational from the irrational
elements of the soul. The mortal or irrational soul was in turn divided into
superior and inferior parts, located above and below the midriff, respectively. It is with the superior part, high-spirited and contentious, that man
feels anger. This spirited aspect of the mortal soul was localized by Plato in
the chest, with the heart as its principal organ, 'in order that being obedient
to the rule of reason it might join with it in controlling and restraining the
desires when they are no longer willing of their own accord to obey the word
of command issuing from the citadel' (*Timaeus*, 70). The cravings which
must be controlled and constrained have to do with such things as food,
drink, sexual arousal, and even such seemingly cognitive desires as the love
of money (*Republic*, 581a). Plato considered these all to be a function of the
appetitive or inferior part of the mortal soul, located in the abdomen below
the diaphragm 'as far as might be from the council chamber, making as little
noise and disturbance as possible, and permitting the best part to advise
quietly for the good of the whole and the individual' (*Timaeus*, 71).

It is not insignificant that Plato first localized intellectual functions in the
head. The assignment of emotions to the viscera then followed quite
naturally. The emotions, being affections or passions, are not self-moved
and hence belong to the mortal, irrational parts of the soul. They are
located in visceral cavities so that they will contaminate reason as little as
possible.

It might be objected that even in Plato's day physiological knowledge –
not to mention common sense – was sufficient to attach considerable
importance to the head and brain for intellectual functions and to the
viscera for emotional reactions. Thus, Hippocrates, an older contemporary
of Plato, considered the brain to be the seat of intelligence and offered a
variety of empirical reasons for so believing (e.g. the sense organs lead to
the brain; and injury to the brain may result in loss of speech, sight, etc., or
in paralysis and death). However, the evidence adduced by Hippocrates for
the brain as the seat of intelligence was by no means compelling or itself
free from mythological overtones. This is indicated by the fact that
Aristotle assigned intellectual functions to the heart, which he observed to
be in the centre and warmest part of the body and the first organ to show
life in the fetus. The brain, Aristotle believed, could not subserve reason
since it is insensitive to direct stimulation.

We can thus see how Plato's ethical and cosmological beliefs led him to
distinguish emotional from higher mental processes and to associate the
former with bodily (visceral) functions. These are two different aspects of
the extrinsic symbolism of emotion discussed in the previous section. With
regard to the third aspect, namely, the presumed animality of emotional
behaviour, Plato postulated a kind of reverse evolution in which the various
animal species were created out of men who lived according to their
passions rather than to the dictates of reason. [. . .]

Aristotle did not show the Platonic disdain for or distrust of the body,
nor did he view the emotions as generally evil. It is therefore not surprising

that the psychophysiological symbolism of emotion is less stark in Aristotle than in Plato. Moreover, when Aristotle did offer specific physiological explanations for behaviour, he relied more on empirical than cosmological arguments. His empiricism did not necessarily lead to greater accuracy, however, as indicated by his attribution of thought processes to the heart. On the whole, most ancient philosophers tended to follow Plato rather than Aristotle with regard to localization of function. Thus Galen (A.D. 130–200), whose authority in physiological matters remained virtually unchallenged for nearly 1500 years, adopted and embellished Platonic notions with regard to the body-soul relationship: He placed the rational soul in the brain; the spirited, irascible soul in the heart; and the appetitive, concupiscent soul in the liver. The Platonic influence, however, is even more evident in the work of Plotinus (A.D. 204–270). [. . .]

Plotinus linked the emotions (other than mystical experience) to bodily change. Ordinary emotional experience is [. . .] a function of that 'modified corporeal nature' which consists of the association of the body with the passive or sensitive aspects of the soul. Emotional feelings are the result of bodily changes being sensed by the passive soul, and these feelings in turn become the object of knowledge or judgment. With regard to more specific localization of function, Plotinus maintained that the soul itself is unitary (although various aspects may be distinguished) and hence not located in any particular organ. The body, however, is not unitary and different bodily parts do subserve different functions: the brain – reasoning and thought; the heart – spirited impulses of defence; and the liver – bodily appetites. Plotinus was aware that both the liver and the heart have extensive vascular connections, and he believed the emotions to be closely associated with the vital powers of the blood. In this, as well as in his general view of emotional experience as the perception of bodily change, his theory is remarkably similar to the views of James and Lange (especially the latter). But more of that later.

While Plotinus was a Neo-Platonist, St. Thomas Aquinas (1225–1274), was in the tradition of Aristotle. Aquinus' discussion of emotion may be found in the *Prima Secundae* of his *Summa Theologiae*. The organization of this part of the *Summa* is itself of interest with regard to the symbolism of emotion. It consists of 114 Questions regarding human activity and its goals. Questions 1–5 concern the ultimate goal of human life; Questions 6–21 deal with acts leading to this goal which are exclusively human; Questions 22–48 with acts which are common to animals and men. These latter are the *passiones animae*, passions of the soul. In short, for Aquinas as for his predecessors, the emotions are part of man's animal nature.

Aquinas began his analysis by asking whether the soul is actually subject to passion. To answer this, he distinguished three uses of the Latin verb *pati*, from which the noun *passio* is formed.

> First, in a perfectly general sense, it is used whenever any quality is received, even if the recipient loses nothing in the process: for instance, one might say that the air 'suffers' or 'undergoes' illumination. However, this would be better styled

'acquiring' a new quality than 'suffering' something. More strictly, the word *pati* is used when a thing acquires one quality by losing another; and this may happen in two ways. Sometimes the quality lost is one whose presence was inappropriate in the subject: for example, when an animal is healed, it may be said to 'undergo' healing, for it recovers its health by shedding its illness. At other times, the opposite happens: for example, a sick man is called a 'patient' because he contracts some illness by losing his health. It is this last kind of case which is called *passio* in the most correct sense. For the word *pati* is used when a thing is drawn to some agent; and the more a thing is withdrawn from that which properly belongs to it, the more naturally it is said to be drawn to something other than itself. . . . Now *passio*, in each of these three senses, may be found in the soul. For first, the remark *thinking and understanding are in some sense passions* applies to that kind of passion which involves reception pure and simple. Those kinds of passion in which some quality is lost, however, always involve some bodily change; passion strictly so called cannot therefore be experienced by the soul except in the sense that the whole person, the matter-soul composite, undergoes it. But here too we must distinguish: the bodily change may be for the better or for the worse; and it is in the latter case that the term *passion* is used more properly. Thus sorrow is more naturally called a passion than is joy [1a2ae. 22, 1].

There are two things worthy of note in this passage. The first is the statement that the kinds of passion in which some quality is lost, which include emotion, always involve bodily change. No empirical evidence is adduced for this observation; rather, it is based on Aristotelian metaphysics. Second, there is the contention that the term 'passion' is more properly applied to negative (e.g. sorrow) than to positive (e.g. joy) states. Aside from its metaphysical rationale, this observation perhaps reflects the fact that the attribution of emotion involves a certain abnegation of responsibility for the consequences of an act. However, people tend to assume responsibility for acts considered positively by themselves or society. Hence, emotional concepts are less likely to be applied to positive than to negative states (Averill, 1973). (Note that the phrase 'good deeds of passion' sounds very peculiar.)

Having established that the soul is in fact subject to passion, Aquinas then set out to determine whether emotions are a function of the appetitive or of the cognitive faculty of the soul. Among his arguments for placing the emotions in the appetitive faculty, and hence for separating them from cognitive functions, was the following appeal to theology:

Now passion or passivity implies by its very nature some sort of deficiency: a thing is passive in so far as it is in potentiality to being actualized and thus improved. Those creatures therefore that come nearest to God, the first and completely perfect being, have little of potentiality and passivity in them; others, of course, have more. Accordingly one will find less of passivity, and so less of passion and the emotions, in the cognitive faculties, since they are the more primary powers of the soul [1a2ae. 22, 2].

It will be noted that there is a difference in tone in the psychophysiological symbolism of Plotinus as compared to Aquinas (as there is between that of Plato and Aristotle). Nevertheless, some of the major features of psychophysiological symbolism are still quite evident, in the work of the latter. To summarize briefly, Aquinas believed that the emotions are essentially non-cognitive[3] (belonging to the appetitive faculty of the soul), necessarily involve bodily change (since passivity implies potentiality, which in turn implies a material substratum), and are common to both animals and man.

As a final example of psychophysiological symbolism from the philosophical literature, we shall consider briefly Descartes (1596–1650), who [. . .] argued that any event could be both an action and a passion, depending upon how it is viewed: It is an action from the perspective of the agent which causes it, and a passion from the perspective of the subject to which it happens. Thus, an action of the body, by affecting the soul, can be a passion of the soul. Thoughts which are self-initiated and deliberate are actions of the soul; passions are thoughts impressed upon the soul through its interaction with the body. [. . .]

Considering Descartes' explicit rejection of earlier teachings as being without merit, the similarities between his views and those of Plato are striking. Both men characterized reason as a form of self-movement, which is a recognition of the sense of choice in rational, deliberate behaviour; both considered emotions to be externally initiated, which is a recognition of the experience of passivity during emotion. But these psychological insights, however valid in themselves, become intertwined without cosmological, theological, and ethical considerations which were primarily responsible for the localization of function. For Descartes, as for Plato, reason became identified with a separate entity (the soul), which somehow interacts with the body. Plato thought the point of interaction was the head, which conformed to his ideas regarding circular motion. [. . .] Descartes singled out the pineal gland because it conformed to his own conception regarding the nature of thought (as solitary and simple). Having located the rational aspect of man, i.e. the point of interaction between soul and body, the emotions were assigned to structures of a lower nature because of their unfavourable contrast with reason. They became a function of the body-machine, with the soul only passively affected.

With Descartes, we reach the threshold of the modern period. Obviously our sketch thus far has been highly selective. In particular, no consideration has been given to positions which do not illustrate the influence of psychophysiological symbolism. The Stoics, for example, treated the emotions as a form of (false) reason or judgment. This intellectualistic approach was adopted in spite of the fact that the Stoics held emotional behaviour in quite low esteem. Or to take another counter-example, Augustine explicitly argued against (albeit not very consistently) the idea that all passions of the soul have their origins in the body. But if there is validity to the argument that the traditional link between emotion and bodily change is based on extrinsic symbolic factors, then counter-examples such as these should not be difficult to find. Psychophysiological symbolism implies an adventitious and not a necessary connection between psychological and physiological processes and hence unanimity of opinion would not be expected. [. . .]

Examples from physiology

It might be expected that the psychophysiological speculations of philosophers would be highly metaphorical and symbolic. The case should be
different among scholars whose primary concern is bodily function. But
even the most empirical observation must be given an interpretation, and
hence is subject to extrinsic symbolic influences.

As previously noted, Galen – the last great physician of ancient times –
incorporated Platonic notions regarding the soul into his medical system,
thus lending his authority to much of Plato's psychophysiological
symbolism. Galen is also important to the present enquiry for the following reasons: First, he advanced the doctrine that sympathy or mutual
influence among organs is due to the flow of animal spirits through
anastomotic nerves (i.e. interconnecting tubules). Second, he described the
ganglionic nerve chains along the spine, which he considered to be branches
of the vagus. Third, he elaborated within a physiological context on the
distinction between voluntary and involuntary movements. The former
presuppose intention; the latter encompass all activity, including visceral
functions, which do not involve the use of reason. As we shall see, these
three trends eventually became fused in speculation surrounding the role of
the sympathetic nervous system in reflexive and emotional behaviour.

There was little advance in physiological knowledge during the Middle
Ages; we can therefore pick up the course of the above Galenic trends with
Thomas Willis (1621–75), an English contemporary of Descartes and
leading anatomist of his time. Willis recognized the independence of the
vagus nerves and the spinal ganglionic chains, but he attributed the origin
of both (the latter indirectly) to the cerebellum. These nerves form a system
which, according to Willis, is concerned with the regulation of involuntary
movements and which serves as the basis for 'sympathy' among organs.
From a psychological standpoint, Willis' clear distinction between voluntary and involuntary movement was his most important contribution.
Voluntary behaviour is due to animal spirits (cf. Descartes) produced in the
cerebrum. Willis made the cerebellum the centre for involuntary behaviour
primarily on *a priori* grounds, or as he put it, 'from the Analogy and
frequent Ratiocination . . . to which afterwards happened an Anatomical
inspection, which plainly confirmed me in this opinion' (1664, p. 111). The
analogy and ratiocination employed by Willis should be familiar by now.
The cerebellum is like a separate appendage to the brain; this means that
the animal spirits for involuntary movements will mix with and disturb as
little as possible the spirits from the cerebrum. 'If the range or furious
motions of the Passions and Instincts should be carried in the same path in
which the forces of sensible things are carried, their acts might be greatly
confounded by the mutual meeting or gathering together of the animal
Spirits' (1664, p. 109). This is essentially the same rationale used by Plato
in placing the affective soul in the thoracic and abdominal cavities.

Willis' anatomical observations not only 'plainly confirmed' his opinion relegating emotions to cerebellar and hence visceral activity, but they also plainly illustrate the influence of psychophysiological symbolism on the interpretation of empirical data. For example, Willis observed that the nerves leading from the cerebellum innervated the visceral organs and 'did serve the Functions, wont to be performed by the Instinct of Nature or the force of the Passions' (1664, pp. 111–12). This is a *non sequitur*, since it assumes rather than demonstrates, the association of emotion with visceral activity. Willis also observed that the cerebellum does not vary greatly among different animal species as does the cerebrum; therefore, the former must serve functions common to all animals, namely, visceral, affective (involuntary) reactions. The cerebrum, on the other hand, serves intellectual (voluntary) activity, which differs greatly among animals. Implicit here is the assignment of emotions to structures on the basis of their common primitive or animal-like characteristics.

From Willis, two lines of thought could be traced which are of considerable interest to the problem of psychophysiological symbolism. First, Robert Whytt (1714–66) extended the notion of voluntary and involuntary movements, noting that the latter are dependent upon local stimulation. Whytt also discarded the notion of anastomotic nerves and made the central nervous system the mediator of 'sympathy' among organs. These innovations laid the physiological foundation for the reflex arc concept, about which we will have more to say later.

The second line of thought leading from Willis concerns the evolution of ideas regarding the autonomic nervous system (Sheehan, 1936) and its relationship to emotion. In 1727, the French surgeon Pourfour du Petit demonstrated that the spinal ganglionic chains do not arise from the cerebellum. Winslow (1772) accepted this view and gave them the name 'great sympathetic nerves' (*nervi sympathetici majores* or *maximi*) 'because of their frequent communications with almost all the other principle nerves of the body' (p. 126). Thus, the ancient doctrine of sympathy achieved its modern neural justification. Of more substantive importance for later theories of emotion was Winslow's view of the sympathetic ganglia as a series of 'little brains'. This laid the foundation for Bichat (1771–1802) who completely separated the sympathetic from the central nervous system and, in the process, emotion from intellectual activity.

Bichat divided life into two aspects, animal (*la vie animale*) and organic (*la vie organique*), and described neural and muscular structures corresponding to each. [. . .]

[He] included the emotions among organic functions because they are supposedly independent of the will and intellect – by now a familiar theme. [. . .]

As one indication of Bichat's influence, it may be noted that his *la vie organique* became the *milieu interieur* of Claude Bernard, which in turn helped lay the foundation for Walter Cannon's concept of homeostasis. Bernard did not deal extensively with the emotions and what he did have to say on the topic followed closely the analysis of Bichat. Thus, Bernard believed the heart to be the most sensitive organ of the vegetative or organic life, and the brain to be the most sensitive organ of the animal life. [. . .]

The emphasis by Bernard on circulatory changes as the cause of emotional experience is also found in the work of Carl Lange, the Danish physician whose name is often associated with that of William James. Actually, Lange's position was in important respects different from that of James. Whereas the latter (James, 1890) defined emotion as subjective experience dependent upon bodily change, Lange had gone a step further and defined emotion as the bodily event itself. In Lange's (1885) own words:

> We have in every emotion as sure and tangible factors: (1) a cause – a sensory impression which usually is modified by memory or a previous associated image; and (2) an effect – namely, the above mentioned vasomotor changes and consequent changes in bodily and mental functions. And now we have the question: What lies between them? If I start to tremble when I am threatened with a loaded pistol, does a purely mental process arise, fear, which is what causes my trembling, palpitation of the heart, and confusion; or are these bodily phenomena aroused immediately by the frightening cause, *so that the emotion consists exclusively of these functional disturbances of the body*? [p. 64, italics added].

Lange clearly rejects the first alternative, that a mental process intervenes between the perception and bodily change, and in this respect he is like James (cf. also the earlier discussion of Plotinus). Moreover, Lange insinuates, but never states unambiguously, that he would answer the latter question in the affirmative; that is, an emotion consists *exclusively* of bodily change (primarily within the circulatory system), and subsequent subjective experience is only tangential. In an explicit extension of what he believes to be Lange's position, Wenger (1950) has defined emotion as activity of the autonomic nervous system and the organs it innervates – and nothing else. Subjective experience, activity of the striated (voluntary) musculature, etc., may accompany emotion, i.e. be part of an emotional complex, but they are not part of the emotion *per se*. With this statement of the problem we seem to have reached the logical conclusion of a long history of thought: emotions are not just closely associated with visceral activity, they are visceral activity. The best argument against a position is sometimes to carry it to its logical conclusion.

Let us now retrace our steps slightly and examine some 'central' theories of emotion, starting with Walter Cannon. Cannon is important because he provided a functional interpretation of visceral changes during emotion, and because he focused attention on the central rather than peripheral aspects of visceral activity. [. . .]

It might be objected that Cannon was really breaking with tradition by emphasizing the central nervous system in emotion. But the break with tradition was not as great as might at first appear. Cannon suggested that the perception of an emotional stimulus excites the thalamus and related diencephalic structures. If released from cortical control, these discharge downward producing the visceral changes characteristic of emotion. At the same time, they discharge upward, adding the quality of emotional experience to the original perception. This is essentially the view of James, except for the substitution of thalamic for peripheral feedback. Cannon's position is traditional in other respects also. In discussing the thalamus (1929, pp. 245 ff.) he emphasized that the neural organization for the display of emotion is located in a phylogenetically ancient portion of the brain (the diencephalon), thus accounting for the common features of emotion in man and animals. Moreover, he assumed that the viscera are solely under diencephalic control and hence cannot be influenced by a direct act of will – a function of the cortex. This association of emotion with animalistic, involuntary portions of the brain is reminiscent of the arguments of Willis regarding the role of the cerebellum in emotion. [. . .]

Emotion and bodily change – science or symbolism?

The foregoing historical review lends credibility to the assertion that psychophysiological symbolism has had a major influence on speculation regarding emotion and bodily change. By itself, however, it does not establish this assertion. For the latter, a further step is required; namely, it must be demonstrated that the close historical link between emotion and visceral activity is not warranted on logical or empirical grounds, and consequently that the symbolism upon which it is based is extrinsic from a scientific point of view. Such a demonstration, at least in broad outline, is the purpose of the present section.

What we have seen, so far, is that emotional concepts imply passivity, and that this distinction has led to a number of contrasts based on ethical and other philosophical considerations. Thus, in contrast to rational, deliberate behaviour (actions), the emotions (passions) have tended to be associated with man's baser qualities. Specifically, extrinsic symbolism has linked the emotions to the irrational, non-cognitive, primitive, animal-like, and visceral. We will now examine the relevance of these prejudices to three major themes: (a) the biological (evolutionary) foundation of emotion; (b) the physiological correlates of emotion; and (c) the relationship between emotion and cognition. Each of these themes will be examined briefly in order to demonstrate that the traditional link between emotion and bodily change is, in fact, more a matter of (extrinsic) symbolism than of science. To help complete the argument, a fourth issue will be touched upon, namely (d) the social construction of emotional behaviour.

The biological foundation of emotion

After the classic work of Darwin (1873) in the expression of emotion, it has been common to view emotional reactions as products of man's evolutionary past. However, it is important to remember that the comparison of emotion with animal-like characteristics is quite ancient and is more a reflection of philosophical (especially ethical) than biological considerations. It will be recalled, for example, that Plato described animals as degenerate forms besouled by humans who, in previous existence, failed properly to exercise the faculty of reason. In physiological research, such moral attitudes should not play an important role in the interpretation of data. But no scientist can fully prevent the general assumptions of his culture from colouring his work. Thus, Willis assigned emotional functions to the cerebellum, in part because of the relative similarity of this structure in various animal species. This was not an evolutionary argument (in the seventeenth century), but probably reflected an implicit value judgment. Similarly, when theorists like Cannon and MacLean have assigned emotional functions to phylogenetically old structures, cultural prejudices may have slipped by unrecognized under the guise of evolutionary theory. Darwin, by using the emotions to demonstrate continuity between animals and man, provided a seemingly scientific rationale for an age-old tradition; he did not thereby make the tradition any more valid – only less obvious in its moral aspects.[4]

The phrase, 'a seemingly scientific rationale', is used advisedly, for man is the most emotional of animals, both in the quality and quantity of his affective experiences. A few examples will suffice to illustrate this fact. Richardson (1960) estimates that from 1820 to 1945, a period of 126 years, 59,000,000 human beings were killed in wars and other violent acts. While this figure reflects technical capabilities as much as biological predispositions, it is nevertheless clear that aggression is hardly an 'inhuman' characteristic, except perhaps in a moral sense. Or take sexual behaviour. While all lower animals restrict mating to certain periods (estrus), man is the only species with a continuous mating pattern. So prominent is sexuality in man that psychoanalytic theorists have made it the touchstone of human development – normal and pathological. And similarly with fear: no animal has as many as man, not only of concrete, earthly dangers, but also of a whole pantheon of spirits and imaginary evils as well. Violence, sex, and fear, it should be noted, are only a few of the supposedly more 'primitive' passions; they certainly do not exhaust the repertoire of emotions. What about hope, love, jealousy, awe, envy, guilt, pity, pride, grief, and the myriad of other emotions experienced by man? These are observable in animals in only the most rudimentary or extended sense.

This is not to say that emotions have no biological roots, but rather that emotional predispositions are not biologically more primitive than, say, intellectual capacities. Both emotion and intelligence are biological adaptations which have reached their highest degree of complexity in the primates, and especially in humans (Hamburg, 1963; Hebb and Thompson, 1954; Jolly, 1966). In short, the presumed animality of emotional behaviour *vis-à-vis* 'higher' mental processes is more a prejudice than a fact. It is, however, a prejudice which is not easily laid to rest. [. . .]

Physiological correlates of emotion

Now let us consider the tendency to emphasize physiological (especially autonomic) activity during emotion. No one, of course, wishes to deny that emotions have physiological correlates. The question is primarily one of emphasis, especially on the theoretical level. In considering this question, we shall look first at the presumed association between emotion and peripheral physiological activity, and then discuss briefly the localization of emotional processes within the central nervous system.

Emotion and peripheral physiological activity   It would be fatuous to argue that emotional reactions do not involve peripheral physiological change. However, it can be argued that the emotions are not peculiar in this regard. In the first place, not all emotions are characterized by marked physiological arousal and, secondly, physiological arousal is indicative of many non-emotional as well as emotional states. With regard to the first point, it might be noted that most research on emotion has been confined to a very few states, especially anger, fear, and sexual arousal. These are emotions which involve vigorous muscular exertion, at least in their most common manifestations. It is therefore not surprising that they are also accompanied by physiological arousal, as is any form of strenuous exercise. Emotions which do not normally involve strong physiological arousal (e.g. hope, gratitude, contentment, enjoyment, admiration, affection, and envy, to name a few), have been the object of little investigation, and have had only minor impact on psychological theory. It might, of course, be objected that states such as these are not true emotions. In answer to this objection, it can only be pointed out that these states are in fact considered to be emotions by the average layman (cf. Davitz, 1969). To deny them the status of emotions because they do not conform to our pre-conceived notions regarding physiological arousal would only be to prejudge the issue. The role of psychological theory is to describe and explain behaviour, not to legislate what is or is not to be considered an emotion.

But let us look at the matter from a somewhat different perspective. Even if it be granted that not all emotions involve physiological arousal, it still might be argued that physiological reactions are more indicative of emotion than non-emotional processes. Until about the mid-1950s, in fact, physiological responses were used almost exclusively for the assessment of emotional reactions. For example, in their comprehensive review of experimental psychology, Woodworth and Schlossberg (1954) devoted three chapters to emotion; one of these dealt with expressive reactions and the other two with physiological changes, e.g. in skin conductance, heart rate, respiration, etc. Indeed, about the only references to peripheral physiological activity in the entire book were contained in these two chapters. In recent years, this one-sided emphasis has been changing with the recognition that physiological responses can be sensitive indicators of psychological processes other than emotion. Much of the credit for this recognition goes to Lacey and his colleagues (e.g. Lacey, 1967; Lacey and Lacey, in press), who have emphasized the 'transactional' nature of physiological responses. That is, physiological changes cannot be assumed simply to reflect some psychological state like 'emotionality' or 'arousal', but must be interpreted in terms of the transactions of the individual with his environment. [. . .]

Localization of emotional processes within the central nervous system

We have seen how emotions have been localized by various authors in supposedly primitive parts of the brain, e.g. the cerebellum, hypothalamus, or limbic system. But what does it mean to localize emotion in a physiological structure? Is it that some neural structure is a *necessary* condition for emotion to occur? Such a criterion is not sufficient for the localization of function. Thus, to take a rather trivial example, the eye is necessary for vision, but vision is not 'located' in the eye – or in the thalamus, or in the occipital cortex, whose destruction also will produce blindness. Other criteria could be stipulated for the localization of function, but this is not the place to go into such detail; in the final analysis the entire issue simply is not very meaningful (cf. Bullock, 1958; Gregory, 1961).

Consider the following electronic analogy. If a resistor is removed from a radio (ablation) or an extraneous source of current is introduced into the circuit (stimulation), a wide variety of things might occur. Amplification might decrease (though the function of a resistor is not to amplify), static might appear (though static is not 'suppressed' by the resistor), and so forth. What, then, is the function of the resistor? In one – physical – sense, its function is to impede the flow of electricity, but this does not tell us much about its role in the radio. To determine the latter, we must understand how the resistor functions as part of a larger system. The same resistor may, in fact, serve different functions depending upon which circuit of the radio it is switched into. Now let us apply this analogy to the case of emotion and the central nervous system. The brain is a complex system, and the workings of any of its parts can only be understood in relationship to other parts. This introduces a variety of difficulties, not the least of which is the fact that at present we know very little about how the brain operates as a system. What can he said, however, is that most neural structures play a role in a variety of behaviours and it makes about as much sense to segregate such structures into classes on the basis of, say, emotional versus intellectual outputs, as it does to classify parts of a radio on the basis of whether they subserve music or news broadcasts.

It might be argued that the above analysis is a caricature, more descriptive of phrenology than of modern neuropsychology. True, it is oversimplified; no modern investigator is so naive as to believe that psychological functions can be neatly assigned to particular areas of the brain in the manner of the phrenologists. And yet it would be a mistake to overlook the strong appeal that localization of function has had – and still has – on psychological speculation. As Von Holst and Saint-Paul (1960) have emphasized, questions of 'how' and 'why' are too frequently turned into the seemingly more simple problem of 'where'. The recent past has been a period of great neuroanatomical progress, made possible by advances in electronic recording and stimulating devices; unfortunately there is little sign of corresponding progress in the conceptualization of psychophysiological relationships. The macroscopic phrenology of Gall and Spurzheim may be dead, but a kind of microscopic phrenology is alive and well in many a neurophysiological laboratory.

There is an alternative to localization of function in the broad sense described above. This may be illustrated briefly by reference to some of the speculations of Pribram and his colleagues regarding the relationship between limbic structures and psychological activities. To begin with, Pribram (1960) notes that the limbic system has undergone phylogenetic development like the rest of the brain, portions of it actually being quite 'young', i.e. first appearing in primates. Moreover, autonomic functions are not mediated solely by the limbic system; it is not *the* visceral brain. Pribram therefore concludes: 'The limbic system cannot be conceived as the neural substrata of motivation and emotion if these are thought of exclusively in terms of visceral-autonomic activities nor if they are felt to be old, primitive, innately determined processes' (1960, p. 12). Conversely, one might add, if emotions are not conceived as old, primitive, etc., then one of the major reasons for assigning them to the limbic system in the first place is gone. A second point which Pribram notes is that limbic structures have been implicated in memory functions, especially with regard to ordering of sequential acts. That is, the limbic system seems to be involved in intellectual as well as emotional behaviours. Integrating these two points, Pribram argues that: 'Limbic system lesions can be thought to interfere with behaviour because of some defect in the planning mechanism, and not because of disturbed emotion or motivation, nor primarily because of some global defect in memory. Limbic system function is thus conceived to be related primarily to the mechanism of the execution of complex sequences of action' (1960, p. 13).

Pribram (1967, 1971) recently has analysed in considerable detail the possible role of certain limbic structures, viz. the amygdaloid complex and the hippocampus, in both emotional and intellectual behaviours. The details of this analysis need not detain us here, for we are not concerned with the validity of any particular hypothesis regarding the neural substrates of emotional behaviours. What is important about Pribram's analysis for the present discussion is the fact that he does not attribute emotional functions *per se* to the limbic or to any other area of the brain. Rather, physiological structures (e.g. the amygdala and hippocampus) are examined for their relationship to processes (e.g. types of afferent inhibition) which might enter into – *but do not constitute* – emotional and problem-solving behaviour. Like the resistor in the previous radio analogy,

the same structure may serve a variety of functions depending upon the
state of the entire system and the particular 'circuit' into which the structure is switched at the moment.

Emotion and cognition

The term 'cognition' is ambiguous. When contrasted with emotion it often
denotes rational, deliberate, problem-solving activity. We have no quarrel
with the distinction in this sense; phenomenologically, emotions are not
conducive to orderly thinking. But 'rational' thought (however broadly
conceived) is only one aspect of cognitive activity. Psychophysiological
symbolism is fostered when this fact is ignored and emotion is contrasted
with any and all forms of cognition. It is easy to lose sight of the many
aspects of cognition related to emotion since, in philosophy and academic
psychology alike, the rational processes have been the primary focus of
interest.

Let us consider first the appraisal of emotional stimuli. Numerous
authors (e.g. Kenny, 1963) have pointed out that emotional concepts imply
objects; that is, we must be angry *at* something; afraid *of* something; proud
of something; and so forth. Moreover, the connection between an emotion
and its object helps delimit or define the nature of the response. Without
special explanation, for example, a person cannot be angry at the good
deed of another, sorrowful at his own good fortune, jealous of someone
stepping on his toe, or proud of the stars. This connection between
appraised object and emotional response is what Peters (1962) has aptly
called the 'cognitive core' of emotion; it, and not physiological or behaviour response patterns, forms the primary basis for distinction between
commonly recognized emotional states. In other words, cognitive appraisal
is not simply an ancillary precursor of emotion, it is an integral part of
what we mean by 'emotion'.

Turning now to the response or output side of emotion, cognitive processes are apparent here also. A few examples will suffice to illustrate the
point. Working within the Freudian tradition, Schachtel (1959) has distinguished two broad classes of emotion, which he calls activity affect and
embeddedness affect. The former is a directed, active mode of coping, as in
normal attack and avoidance; the latter may involve much non-directed
motor activity, as in a temper tantrum, but largely entails cognitive
attempts at conflict resolution. This distinction of Schachtel's is in some
respects similar to one made by Lazarus (1968) between direct action
tendencies and intrapsychic modes of coping. An even more thorough-going
cognitive approach to emotion is Kelly's (1955) theory of personal constructs. Kelly views each man as an incipient scientist, formulating
constructs (hypotheses) by which he may predict and control his environment. Emotions are defined in terms of such constructs and the cognitive
systems of which they are elements. Sartre (1948) also has presented an
analysis in which cognitive responses, or what he has described as attempts

to 'magically' transform reality, are made the *sine qua non* of emotion. Such a position is extreme, but no more so than the opposite reliance on physiological change as the fundamental aspect of emotional reactions. If nothing else, these examples illustrate that too close an association between emotion and physiological activity can be achieved only by overlooking a contrary and – to some theorists – an equally compelling set of facts.

Finally, let us consider the basic distinction between reason and affect, for it is the tendency to identify cognition with the former that has led to the view of emotion as non-cognitive. Psychologists interested in clinical phenomena and in creativity have long recognized two types of reasoning, variously called rational vs. intuitive, logical vs. prelogical, realistic vs. autistic, secondary process vs. primary process, and so forth. Although the former type generally has been associated with intellectual behaviour and the latter with emotion, this is more a reflection of prejudice than of fact. Problem solving – even that involved in rigorous disciplines such as mathematics (Polyani, 1964; Polya, 1957) – relies heavily on intuitive, prelogical thought, while many emotional behaviours may be quite 'logical', e.g. the delusional system of a paranoid. In short, similar cognitive processes – in the broad sense – may enter into both intelligent, problem-solving behaviour and emotion.

The social construction of emotional behaviour

The preceding arguments indicate that the emotions are not primitive in a biological sense but, rather, that they are complex cognitive processes. But a major question remains. In Part I, it was argued that a primary reason for the negative contrast between emotion and 'higher' mental activities is the experience of passivity. To be 'gripped' and 'overcome' by emotion is a real experience and not a cultural prejudice. What are the origins of this experience if it is not a reflection of biological and physiological mechanisms? To answer this question would take – indeed, has taken (Averill, 1976) – an essay as long as the present one. At this point, only the barest outline of an answer can be given.

There is no doubt that some emotion-like responses have their roots in man's biological heritage. Examples include startle to a loud noise, avoidance of certain natural dangers (e.g. high places), attacking the source of pain, etc. Responses such as these undoubtedly were of functional significance during the evolution of our hominid ancestors. However, most standard emotional reactions transcend any biological imperatives related to self- or species-preservation. They are based instead on human capabilities above the animal level and, in particular, on the ability of man to create symbolic systems of thought and behaviour (i.e. culture).

In order to understand the role of sociocultural factors in determining emotional experience, the following fact must be emphasized: the relationship between man and culture is a dialectical one. Not only is culture a human product, but man is also a cultural product. Through the process of socialization, aspects of culture are internalized to form parts of an individual's own character structure. The source of passivity during emotion is to be found in the character structure of the individual and, ultimately, in the sociocultural system which helps shape that structure.

In contrast to the view that emotions are biologically primitive, the present position is that most standard emotional reactions are social constructions. On this assumption, the experience of passivity may be treated as a kind of illusion. Emotions are not something which just happen to an individual; rather, they are acts which a person performs. In the case of emotion, however, the individual is unwilling or unable to accept responsibility for his actions; the initiation of the response is therefore dissociated from consciousness. In this respect, it is instructive to compare emotional with hysterical reactions. The hysteric may be assailed by inner voices, semi-hallucinated images, and the like, which seem to have a source independent of himself. On a deeper level of analysis, of course, it is evident that such behaviours are the individual's own doing, i.e. that the experience of passivity is a kind of defence mechanism. By restricting awareness of his own self-responsibility, the hysteric may help alleviate personal feelings of anxiety and guilt. In the case of standard emotional reactions a similar process occurs, but here we must look to social norms and customs, as well as intra-psychic processes, for an explanation of the experience of passivity.

The manner in which social norms and customs contribute to the experience of passivity during emotion has been discussed in detail elsewhere (Averill, 1976). The present remarks will therefore be limited to a few examples which illustrate the underlying dynamics. Newman (1964) has described an emotion-like syndrome among the Gururumba, a people of the New Guinea highlands. This syndrome is called by the natives 'being a wild pig'. The individual so affected engages in a variety of aggressive acts, including looting, shooting arrows at bystanders, and the like. Serious harm seldom occurs in these 'attacks', and after the episode has passed the individual is accepted back into society without recrimination. The explanation offered by the Gururumba for this behaviour is that the affected individual has been bitten by a ghost, thus releasing primordial impulses. As Newman points out, however, the behaviour is tolerated only in certain persons – young men with pressing and seemingly unavoidable social obligations. After an episode of 'being a wild pig' such obligations may be reassessed by the group and the social pressures lightened. In short, 'being a wild pig' is a way of realigning obligations within the community while still proscribing any *deliberate* deviation from established norms (see also, Salisbury, 1966a, 1966b).

As cultural outsiders, it is not difficult to see how 'being a wild pig' is a socially constructed behaviour pattern. One might almost consider it a form of community mental health. The Gururumba, however, do not view it that way. As its name implies, they consider the response to be very primitive, like the behaviour of a domesticated pig gone wild.[5] And although the affected individual cannot help what he does, and hence is not responsible for his actions, it is a condition definitely to be avoided.

'Being a wild pig' is not a standard emotional reaction even among the Gururumba; this response might more appropriately be conceptualized as a socially sanctioned form of hysteria. The difference, however, is not critical for the present discussion. By its exaggerated nature, 'being a wild pig' illustrates well certain of the features of standard emotional reactions, especially the functional significance of the experience of passivity. To be 'overcome' with emotion helps mitigate personal responsibility for the consequence of an action. To illustrate this point further, consider the legal treatment of 'crimes of passion' in our own culture. The person who kills in a fit of anger is liable to be found less culpable than one who kills with premeditation. In a sense, society is saying, 'Thou shalt not kill', while at the same time providing an escape hatch. When the provocation is 'adequate' (see Perkins, 1946, for the legal definition of this term), an attack may be allowed and even encouraged. But the attack must be carried out in such a way as not to violate the general proscription against intentionally harming another.[6] [. . .]

These few cursory remarks necessarily oversimplify the social construction of emotional behaviour, which is a very complex issue. However, to extend the argument further would be beyond the scope of the present chapter. The major objective of this essay has been to illustrate the workings of psychophysiological symbolism and only secondarily to examine the nature of emotion.

Concluding observations

The phenomenon of psychophysiological symbolism extends, of course, beyond the problem of emotion. [. . .]

Extrinsic symbolic relationships probably play a role whenever one theorizes about the physiological correlates of psychological phenomena on the basis of inadequate empirical data – and at the present time there is still little other basis. This is not to gainsay recent advances in physiological knowledge, but simply to recognize the complexity of the problems involved. The present article, therefore, is not a polemic against psychophysiological theorizing; rather, it is an argument for an increased sensitivity to potential symbolic influences on the acceptance and interpretation of ostensibly empirical facts.

Notes

Preparation of this paper was supported, in part, by a grant (NEG-00-3-0139) from the National Institute of Education, Department of Health, Education, and Welfare, U.S.A.

1 The interested reader may refer to Onians (1951) and Thass-Theinemann (1968) for analyses of the symbolic significance of certain bodily structures during the early development

of Western civilization. Douglas (1970) discusses body symbolism in a general fashion as it relates to social organization, the examples being drawn primarily from African tribal cultures. Werner (1972) and Berlin, Breedlove and Raven (1973) have reviewed recent anthropological research on ethnobiology. To date, most of this research has dealt with the principles underlying folk taxonomies of plants and animals. Relatively little attention has been paid to prescientific conceptualizations of anatomy and physiology, although this situation appears likely to change in the near future.

2 See the reference section for complete citation of the edition and translation of the works of Plato, Aristotle, and other classical authors quoted in the text.

3 See Arnold (1960) for a cognitive approach to emotion which owes a considerable debt to Aquinas.

4 The fact that the theory of evolution met stiff opposition from traditional theological circles does not contradict this statement. It was acceptable to postulate a commonality between man and animals with regard to certain functions, including emotional reactions, as long as a dualism was maintained between man's animal and human natures. The implications of Darwin's theory, of course, did not stop with the emotions or strictly bodily functions, but encompassed all of human existence.

5 In the preceding historical review of the psychophysiological symbolism of emotion, emphasis was placed on the unfavourable contrast between emotional behaviour and certain values esteemed by Western cultures, e.g. rationality and freedom of the will. Values such as these are, of course, not limited to Western societies; no group could endure for long if in practical matters of survival it favoured the irrational and the whimsical. One might therefore expect emotion-like behaviours to be viewed as primitive in most, if not all, cultures. 'Being a wild pig' is a case in point.

6 Although the examples used here have involved negative (aggressive) responses, the present analysis can be extended *mutatis mutandis* to the case of positive emotions (Averill, 1973).

References

Aquinas, St. Thomas (1967) *Summa Theologiae*. Vol. 19. *The emotions* (1a 2ae. 22–30). E. D'Arcy (transl.). New York: McGraw-Hill.
Aristotle (1941) *The Basic Works of . . .* R. McKeon (ed.) (Oxford Translation). New York: Random House.
Arnold, M.B. (1960) *Emotion and Personality* (2 vols). New York: Columbia University Press.
Averill, J.R. (1969) 'Emotion and visceral activity: a case study in psychophysiological symbolism'. Paper presented at the meetings of the Society for Psychophysiological Research, Monterey, Calif., October.
Averill, J.R. (1973) 'Why are there not more positive emotions?' Paper presented at the meetings of the American Psychological Association, Montreal, August.
Averill, J.R. (1976) 'Emotion and anxiety: Sociocultural, biological and psychological determinants', in M. Zuckerman and C.D. Spielberger (eds), *Emotion and Anxiety: New Concepts, Methods and Applications*.
Berlin, B., Breedlove, D.E. and Raven, P.H. (1973) 'General principles of classification and nomenclature in folk biology', *American Anthropologist*, 75: 214–42.
Bernard, C. (1878) *La science experimentale*. Paris: Libraire J.B. Ballière & Fils.
Bichat, X. (1824) *General Anatomy, Applied to Physiology and the Practice of Medicine*. 2 vols. London: S. Highley.
Bullock, T.H. (1958) 'Evolution of neurophysiological mechanisms', in A. Roe and G.G. Simpson (eds), *Behaviour and Evolution*. New Haven: Yale University Press.
Cannon, W.B. (1929) *Bodily Changes in Pain, Hunger, Fear, and Rage* (2nd edn). New York: D. Appleton.
Darwin, C. (1873) *The Expression of the Emotions in Man and Animals*. London: Murray.
Davitz, J.R. (1969) *The Language of Emotion*. New York: Academic Press.

Descartes, R. (1968) 'The passions of the soul', in E.S. Haldane and G.R.T. Ross (transl.), *The Philosophical Works of Descartes*. Vol. 1. Cambridge: University Press.

Douglas, M. (1970) *Natural Symbols*. New York: Pantheon Books.

Gregory, R.L. (1961) 'The brain as an engineering problem', in W.H. Thorpe and O.L. Zangwill (eds), *Current Problems in Animal Behaviour*. Cambridge: University Press.

Hamburg, D.A. (1963) 'Emotions in the perspective of human evolution', in P.H. Knapp (ed.), *Expressions of Emotion in Man*. New York: International Universities Press.

Hardie, W.F.R. (1964) 'Aristotle's treatment of the relation between the soul and the body', *Philosophical Quarterly*, 14: 53–72.

Hebb, D.O. and Thompson, W.R. (1954) 'The social significance of animal studies', in G. Lindzey (ed.), *Handbook of Social Psychology*. Vol. 1. *Theory and Method*. Cambridge, Mass.: Addison-Wesley.

James, W. (1890) *The Principles of Psychology*. Vol. 2. New York: Henry Holt and Co.

Jolly, A. (1966) 'Lemur social behavior and primate intelligence', *Science*, 153: 501–6.

Kelly, G.A. (1955) *The Psychology of Personal Constructs*. Vol. 1. New York: Norton and Company.

Kenny, A. (1963) *Action, Emotion and Will*. London: Routledge and Kegan Paul.

Kimble, G.A. (1961) *Hilgard and Marquis' Conditioning and Learning*. New York: Appleton-Century-Crofts.

Lacey, J.I. (1967) 'Somatic response patterning and stress: Some revisions of activation theory', in M.H. Appley and R. Trumbull (eds), *Psychological Stress*. New York: Appleton-Century-Crofts.

Lacey, J.I. and Lacey, B.C. (in press) 'On heart rate responses and behavior: A reply to Elliot', *Journal of Personality and Social Psychology*.

Lange, C. (1922) 'The emotions' (orig. publ. 1885). In C.G. Lange and W. James *The Emotions*. Baltimore: Williams and Wilkins.

Lazarus, R.S. (1968) 'Emotions and adaptation: Conceptual and empirical relations', in W. Arnold (ed.), *Nebraska Symposium on Motivation*. Vol. 16. Lincoln, Nebr.: University of Nebraska Press.

Miller, N.E. (1972) 'Experiments on psychosomatic interactions'. Paper presented at the meetings of the Eastern Psychological Association, Boston, April.

Newman, P.L. (1964) '"Wild man" behavior in a New Guinea highlands community', *American Anthropologist*, 66: 1–19.

O'Brien, V.P. (1948) *The Measure of Responsibility in Persons Influenced by Emotion*. Washington, DC: Catholic University of America Press.

Onians, R.B. (1951) *The Origins of European Thought about the Body, the Mind, the Soul, the World, Time, and Fate*. Cambridge: Cambridge University Press.

Papez, J.W. (1937) 'A proposed mechanism of emotions', *Archives of Neurology and Psychiatry*, 38: 735–44.

Perkins, R.M. (1946) 'The law of homicide', *Journal of Criminal Law and Criminology*, 36: 391–454.

Peters, R.S. (1962) 'Emotions and the category of passivity', *Aristotelian Society Proceedings*, 62: 117–34.

Plato (1961) *Collected Dialogues of* . . . Edith Hamilton and H. Cairns (eds). New York: Bollingen Foundation.

Plotinus (1969) *The Enneads*. S. MacKenna (transl.) (4th edn) New York: Pantheon Books.

Plutchik, R. (1962) *The Emotions*. New York: Random House.

Plutchik, R. (1970) 'Emotions, evolution, and adaptive processes', in M.B. Arnold (ed.), *Feelings and Emotions: The Loyola Symposium*. New York: Academic Press.

Polya, G. (1957) *How to Solve it* (2nd edn). Garden City, NY: Doubleday.

Polyani, M. (1964) *Personal Knowledge* (rev. edn), New York: Harper & Row.

Pribram, K.H. (1960) 'A review of theory in physiological psychology', *Annual Review of Psychology*, 11: 1–40.

Pribram, K.H. (1967) 'Emotion: Steps toward a neurophysiological theory', in D.C. Glass (ed.), *Neurophysiology and Emotion*. New York: Rockefeller University Press.

Pribram, K.H. (1971) *Languages of the Brain*. Englewood Cliffs, NJ: Prentice-Hall.

Richardson, L.F. (1960) *Statistics of Deadly Quarrels*. London: Stevens and Sons.

Salisbury, R. (1966a) 'Possession on the New Guinea highlands: Review of literature', *Transcultural Psychiatric Research*, 3: 103–8.

Salisbury, R. (1966b) 'Possession among the Siane (New Guinea)', *Transcultural Psychiatric Research*, 3: 108–16.

Sartre, J.P. (1948) *The Emotions: Outline of a Theory*. New York: Philosophical Library.

Schachtel, E.G. (1959) *Metamorphosis*. New York: Basic Books.

Schachter, S. (1971) *Emotion, Obesity, and Crime*. New York: Academic Press.

Sheehan, D. (1936) 'Discovery of the autonomic nervous system', *A.M.A. Archives of Neurology and Psychiatry*, 35: 1081–1115.

Thass-Thienemann, T. (1968) *Symbolic Behavior*. New York: Washington Square Press.

von Holst, E. and von Saint-Paul (1963) 'On the functional organization of drives', *Animal Behavior*, 11: 1–20.

Wenger, M.A. (1950) 'Emotions as visceral action: An extension of Lange's theory', in M.L. Reymert (ed.), *Feelings and Emotions: The Mooseheart-Chicago Symposium*. New York: McGraw-Hill.

Werner, O. (1972) 'Ethnoscience', *Annual Review of Anthropology*, 1: 271–308.

Willis, T. (1965) 'The anatomy of the brain and nerves' (Tercentenary edn) (orig. publ. 1664). Montreal: McGill University Press.

Winslow, J.B. (1772) *An Anatomical Exposition of the Structure of the Human Body*. Vol. 2. (6th edn). Edinburgh: Alexander Donaldson and Charles Elliot.

Woodworth, R.S. and Schlosberg, H. (1954) 'Experimental psychology' (rev. edn). New York: Holt.

Chapter 10

Bodily States and Context in Situated Lines of Action

G.P. Ginsburg and Melanie E. Harrington

Emotions and their representation in talk, literature and art have been a part of human affairs throughout recorded history. Emotions are said to constitute the richness of experienced life, and ahedonia – flatness of affect and the absence of emotional reactivity – is held to be a pathological state, even a symptom of schizophrenia. The recognized importance of emotion in ordinary life and the problems created by pathological emotion states and reactions have generated an immense body of empirical research. Although the amount of research in recent decades has exploded, the study of emotion has gone on for centuries, partly because of the diagnostic potential of abnormalities in emotional reactions and displays. Yet, there is active and continuing disagreement about the nature of emotions, their linkages to bodily states, and the roles they play in life. It is our purpose in this chapter to consider these matters, and to propose a fundamental reconstrual of emotion and its relationship to bodily states.

Emotion and the body: current status

Some anomalous observations of facial displays

In anticipation of a project on deficits in empathic facial reactivity among psychopaths, we chose the procedures reported by Dimberg (1982) as a simple and apparently reliable means of evoking mimetic facial reactions. Dimberg presented facial display slides taken from Ekman and Friesen (1976) and reported that angry faces evoked relatively higher brow region (corrugator) activity, while happy stimulus faces evoked greater cheek region (zygomatic) activity. The Dimberg findings were well enough accepted in the field so that we ran a small pilot only to check out our equipment. However, we found that pilot subjects were not responding differentially to the positive and negative slides as expected.[1] Therefore, we conducted a formal replication of the Dimberg study, following his procedures very closely.[2] Based on 30 subjects, we found that activity in the brow muscle did increase more in the presence of a frowning stimulus than a smiling one, and more than did the cheek muscle to frowning stimuli. This replicated Dimberg's findings with regard to 'angry' facial stimuli.

However, we also found that activity in the cheek muscle increased as much to a frowning stimulus as to a smiling one, and activity in the brow muscle increased as much to a smiling stimulus as did activity in the cheek muscle. Further, we imposed an incidental 'live' display: for a subset of subjects, the experimenter smiled or frowned while adjusting the subject's electrodes. Subjects' cheek region activity during E's smiles was reliably higher than during baseline and happy slide presentations. Thus, Dimberg's findings of facial mimicry to still, acontextual photographs were only partially replicated.

In addition, to our knowledge there has been no exact replication of the Dimberg (1982) results, although there have been a few partial attempts. But the replications either did not match the original results (e.g., Cacioppo, Bush and Tassinary, 1992) or involved altered procedures (e.g., Voglmaier and Hakerem, 1989). Despite the common citation of the Dimberg (1982) results, our experience has made us very sensitive to the possibility that mimicry is highly contingent on the context. This is consistent with the earlier findings of Stotland and his colleagues (see Stotland, 1978), in which psychophysiological empathic reactivity was found only when subjects were asked to feel the way the target person must be feeling (or otherwise to role-take). It is our view that facial mimesis is contingent on the viewer having taken an empathic or affiliative orientation.

Our pilot studies also indicate that the relationships between reported affect and facial displays are contextually contingent. In setting up procedures for a series of studies of empathic facial reactivity in different types of close personal relationships, we employed an 'emotional contagion' videotape sent to us by Hatfield. The videotape depicts a young man telling, in one instance, the happiest thing that had ever happened to him (a surprise party), and in another instance the saddest thing (the death of his grandfather). We used these two clips and a third – a baby playing in a bathtub and laughing infectiously – to assess the impact of subjects' knowledge that we were interested in emotional reactions and empathy. Half of the subjects were told that we were studying their emotional reactions to the videotape, while the remaining subjects were given neutral instructions that did not make any reference to 'emotion'. After video viewing, we collected subjects' self-reported recall of their emotional states while viewing the clips. We also videotaped the subjects while they were watching the stimulus tapes and coded the occurrence of smiles (with and without eye-crinkling) and frowns. Eye-crinkle smiles (Duchenne smiles) are held by some (Ekman and Friesen, 1982) to characterize 'true happiness' and we wished to assess the capacity of the two happy stimuli to elicit such D-smiles. For the Sad tape, we found as expected that frowns were much more frequently among subjects who knew we were interested in emotion and empathy. For the two Happy tapes, however, the results were more complex. Instructions did not influence smiling of either type. However, the relationship between self-reported 'felt happiness' and Duchenne smiles varied with the context. In the moderately 'happy', narrative situation, subjects made few Duchenne smiles, and *non*-Duchenne smiles were correlated with self-reported happiness. In the more intense 'happy baby' context, subjects more frequently made Duchenne smiles and the postulated relationship occurred: Duchenne smiles correlated with reported happiness and non-Duchenne smiles did not. A factor analysis of the data revealed a similar pattern. It yielded a felt emotion factor which contained self-reports of happiness, D-smiling to the very happy tape (the baby), and *non*-Duchenne smiles to the moderately happy tape (narrative).[3]

In sum, facial displays are contextually contingent, as is the relationship between those displays and reported emotional states. A relationship between type of smile and self-reports of 'happiness' found in one context cannot be presumed to hold for other contexts. Material that reliably elicits frowning brow activity under one orientation of the viewer may not do so under another orientation. Furthermore, it is worth noting here and will be emphasized later that the line of situated action on which the person has embarked is an important feature of the context. This is generally omitted from the construals of emotion which are current in the field today. Typical features of these construals are discussed below.

A critical examination of current construals of emotion

Most psychological research on emotion in the last several decades has presumed, sometimes implicitly, a model in which emotions are construed as internal states which have expressive, subjective and physiological components. The emotion state is construed as springing fully blown into being, as having causal force in that it can instigate and coordinate various responses, and as involving internal states that are each unique to a given emotion. Some models also construe emotions as having unique physiological signatures as well, either autonomically or centrally. Furthermore, most models accept the ordinary language construal of emotion as something that happens to one – as a non-agentive occurrence.

Ekman (1994a), for example, proposes seven characteristics that distinguish emotions from other phenomena. These include automatic appraisal, which refers to rapid, non-thoughtful recognition of the dangers, pleasures, and so on inherent in the stimulus array to which the organism is reacting; commonalities in antecedents, which refers to essential similarities in the variety of circumstances that precipitate specific emotional reactions, such as fear; presence in other primates; rapidity of onset, a corollary of automaticity of appraisal; brief duration, which Ekman and some of his colleagues see as 3–5 seconds; unbidden occurrence; and a distinctive physiology. It is worth examining the major themes of these typical contemporary construals.

The natural history of emotional reactions   Do emotional reactions actually spring fully blown into being? Apparently not. At a microanalytic level, the various muscles involved in an emotional facial display, such as surprise, begin their contractions, reach and hold their apices, and end their contractions at different times. Different facial displays have different natural histories, and this is probably as true within a display type but across occasions as it is between display types. Furthermore, the physiology of muscle contraction entails the recruitment of small motor units first, with larger units recruited a bit later in the progressive activation of the muscle. Muscles of facial expression follow this process, and in the very early stage of emergence of a display, the amplitude of the contraction is low, and the display is typically not yet visible. Electromyographic recordings reveal the presence of such low amplitude, incipient contractions, but they are unrelated to specific affective states – they distinguish only positive from negative (Cacioppo et al., 1986). Thus, the emotional display takes shape over a span of time, even at a most microanalytic level. It does not simply spring into being.

Emotion instances form over time at a more macro level, as well. There appears to be an interval of objective ambiguity that characterizes the transition between the ending of one emotional interchange and the beginning of another (Hsu et al., 1989). During that transition, interaction partners jointly create a coordinated, new but related interchange. The joint creation of rounds of affectively toned activity has been amply demonstrated in mother-infant dyads by Fogel and his colleagues (Messinger et al., in press). There is no question that emotional interchanges – and the emotional reactions of the individual participants – have natural histories of formation, and that there are intervals in their formation when their identity is objectively ambiguous and readily susceptible to alteration. Moreover, we will point out later that the natural histories of emotion instances are interwoven with the situation and the lines of action in which the parties are engaged. For the moment, though, it is sufficient to emphasize the fact that emotion instances do not spring fully blown into existence, but rather have natural histories of emergence at both micro and macro levels of analysis, and that there are time spans in its emergence when the identity of the instance is ambiguous and particularly susceptible to modification.

The reliable physiological distinctiveness of emotions   Are there coherently organized physiological components which differentiate emotions reliably? This is a matter of considerable debate in the literature. We will address it on four grounds – autonomic nervous system patterns, central nervous system structures and processes, central neurochemical patterns, and the important matter of individual differences. We will consider coherently organized motoric patterns, including facial displays, in a subsequent section. Our discussion is not intended as a review of the relevant literatures, but as an extraction of basic themes pertinent to the physiological distinguishability of emotions.

The *autonomic nervous system* (ANS) has long played an important role in the conceptualization and study of emotion, in part because of its presumed importance for 'arousal' (Blascovich and Tomaka, 1996). Some contemporary investigators contend that measures of ANS patterns already can differentiate at least some 'basic emotions' (Levenson, 1992, 1994; Levenson et al., 1990; Ekman, 1994a, although with some qualification), or are likely to be discovered to do so in the near future (Blascovich and Tomaka, 1996). For example, Levenson et al. (1990) found that facial configurations of anger, fear and sadness were associated with higher heart rates than happiness or disgust, when subjects contracted particular facial muscles in accord with experimental instructions. At a somewhat more abstract level, Blascovich and his colleagues (Blascovich and Tomaka, 1996) have found potentially important cardiovascular differences between subjects who appraise a stressful situation as a threat and those who appraise it as a challenge. Specifically, those who see it as a threat show blood pressure increases and moderate heart rate increases along with increased resistance of the peripheral vasculature; in contrast, those who see the situation as a challenge show blood pressure increases, large heart rate increases, and increases in cardiac output (including increased ventricular contraction). This has been replicated in our laboratory (Hartley, 1995; Hartley and Ginsburg, 1995) using a self-presentational task, either allowing or not allowing some degree of control by the subject. The potential importance of this finding lies in a possible link between persistent increases in total peripheral resistance and later coronary heart disease, which in turn would imply a linkage between an affective reaction type and health. Thus, there is evidence which supports claims of autonomic differentiation of emotions, at least to some degree.

On the other hand, a careful examination of the replicability of the findings yields a very different impression (Zajonc and McIntosh, 1992): There is little or no consistency of patterns across laboratories, and relatively little across studies within a single laboratory. As Zajonc and McIntosh note, 'Heart rate is perhaps the best discriminator among emotions . . . But even heart rate is far from discriminating consistently and fully among the emotions.' Stemmler (1989), in a well designed assessment of both convergent and discriminant validity of multiple measures of a variety of emotion states, found little evidence of robust ANS differentiation among emotions.[4] Cacioppo et al. (1993) reviewed a large number of studies containing at least two emotions and at least two ANS response variables, and found very little consistency across studies. In addition, it was noted that there were many examples of specific emotions occurring in the absence of ANS differentiation, implying that specific ANS changes are not *necessary* for a specific emotion to occur.

Therefore, the evidence to date does not support the claim of differential ANS signatures for different emotions. Although advances in our understanding of the complexities of ANS functioning (Cacioppo et al., 1993) and technological advances in our measurements of ANS parameters (Blascovich and Tomaka, 1996) might lead to the discovery of differentiating patterns, we consider it unlikely. The ANS functions primarily in the service of metabolic needs, including phasic demands in support of physical activity. It is unlikely that there will be 'an' ANS pattern for 'an' emotion that is not a function of the line of situated action in which the individual is emotionally engaged. We will return to this point later.

The *central nervous system* (CNS) also has played an important role in emotion research and theorizing. MacLean (1949) built upon prior observations by Papez to hypothesize an emotion circuit in the brain which he named the 'limbic system'. It contained a variety of regions, including the hypothalamus, hippocampus, amygdala and septal nuclei, and incorporated a 'recapitulation' assumption – that ontogeny recapitulated phylogeny. The emotion circuit was construed to involve phylogenetically older and more primitive parts of the brain, and was overlaid by the more recently developed, more advanced neocortex. The recapitulation conception is now recognized as essentially flawed (Fridlund, 1994: 108) – all parts of the brain are equally evolved – but it was compatible with the notion of emotion as atavistic. MacLean's proposal was widely accepted and was buttressed by the striking findings that began to emerge in the 1950s of self-stimulation areas in the septal and hypothalamic regions (see the early report by Olds and Milner, 1954). Indeed, Olds' work was frequently interpreted by others as evidence of 'pleasure centers' in the brain.

The picture today is much more complex. The limbic system concept has proven difficult to define, and some of its classic constituents are now known to be more integrally involved in cognitive processes than emotional processes (LeDoux, 1993, 1995). On the other hand, some regions of the brain clearly are central to emotional instances. The amygdala is one such set of structures (Weiskrantz, 1956; LeDoux, 1995; Rolls, 1992, 1994), although it does not operate in isolation. It has outputs to the lateral and medial hypothalamus, to autonomic nervous system centers in the medulla oblongata, and indirectly to the basal ganglia, hippocampus and orbitofrontal cortex. It thereby has influence on motor, autonomic and limbic systems, and it has backprojections to those very areas of the cortex from which it receives input (Rolls, 1994). In fact, the richness of its afferent and efferent connections seems critical in its emotion role. Amygdala neurons are sensitive to the hedonic qualities of stimuli, and they participate in the acquisition of associations of rewards and punishments with stimuli (and therefore in the acquisition of learned emotional responses; see Rolls, 1992: 158). LeDoux (1995) distinguishes between emotional respondents and emotional operants, the former referring to such involuntary 'emotional' reactions as freezing, fleeing, facial reactions, and autonomic and endocrine reactions. Emotional respondents are presumed to be defense patterns that have been conserved through evolution, and to be susceptible to classical conditioning. Emotional operants are less well understood but are tied to instrumental (operant) conditioning which can occur after emotional operants are expressed. They are likely to involve a variety of brain systems but to work in conjunction with the amygdaloid system. The latter would underlie automatic, evoked aspects of fear and anxiety, while the operant systems would be involved in the cognitive phase of fear and anxiety.

More general CNS models also abound, but they, too, reflect the complexity of contemporary findings, largely by involving multiple structures and by proposing different subsystems for different sets of emotional activities. Gray (1994), for example, proposes a tripartite CNS emotion model which incorporates a behavioral approach system, a behavioral inhibition system, and a fight-or-flight reaction system. All three are sensitive to the reward and punishment potentials of environmental inputs. Zajonc has proposed a very different model. He theorizes that minor variations in brain temperature will affect subjective emotional experience by increasing or decreasing the turnover rates of critical neurotransmitters. In its current form, Zajonc's model (Zajonc et al., 1993) conceives of facial displays as modulating the venous flow of blood from certain regions of the brain, especially the hypothalamus, thereby modulating temperature in those regions. Hypothalamic temperature, the model postulates, is modulated in part by the cooling of arterial blood in the internal carotid as it passes through the venous cavernous sinus, which in turn is cooled by nasal breathing. Facial veins assist in the modulation process because they can change the direction of venous flow, draining either into the external jugular or the cavernous sinus. Changes in the direction of their flow appears to be dependent on temperature. Zajonc and his colleagues infer that breathing patterns and facial muscle action can control venous flow and temperature in veins that drain to the cavernous sinus, which in turn modulates brain temperature, which influences subjective affective state. They see this as a process by which 'physical action can *cause* changes in subjective feeling' (Zajonc et al., 1993: 214). They have produced a variety of intriguing experiments in support of the various aspects of the model.

Another CNS model of emotion with an impressive body of empirical support is that of Davidson (1993, 1994). He distinguishes between emotions that entail approach and those that entail withdrawal, with states of happiness instantiating the former and states of depression as instances of the latter. Over a very large number of studies, Davidson has demonstrated that approach-related positive emotions (happiness, amusement) are associated with relatively enhanced activation of the left prefrontal and anterior temporal cortex regions, withdrawal-related negative emotions (fear, disgust) with relatively enhanced activation of the right anterior region, and negative emotions that entail decrements in approach activities (sadness, depression) with relative damping of the activation in the left anterior region.[5]

The atavistic underpinnings of the conceptualizations also are still apparent, as in the title of a recent chapter by one of the strongest proponents of CNS models of emotion: 'The neurobiology of human emotions: Of animal brains and human feelings' (Panksepp, 1989; also see Panksepp, 1994). There is a continuing construal of emotion as primitive, as evolutionarily older than higher cognitive capacities.

Integrally related to the possibility of unique CNS signatures for various emotions, the *neurochemistry* of the central nervous system, especially the brain, has also received much attention as a causal or constitutive source of emotions. A recent review by Panksepp (1993) summarizes the current state of the field and is an important source for the following comments. The neurochemistry of the CNS as it pertains to emotions involves primarily the wide variety of neurotransmitters, although that should be understood to include inhibitory as well as facilitative functions. However, the neurotransmitters range in effects from those that are system wide to those that are relatively specific; and they range in complexity from relatively simple amino acids to complex hypothalamic and pituitary peptides.

An example of a relatively simple amino acid is glutamate, which has as an end product of its metabolism gamma-aminobutyric acid (GABA). GABA is believed to have inhibitory effects through the CNS, but its effects have proven most interesting and useful in their inhibition of those areas of the brain that appear to be involved in fear reactions. The minor tranquilizers (benzodiazipine antianxiety agents) are believed to work by facilitating the inhibitory effects of GABA on fear circuitry in the brain. It is worth noting that GABA appears to modulate the state of the CNS system generally.

Many of the active neurochemicals seem associated with more specific states of the system, although not uniquely with specific emotions. The catecholamines (epinephrine, norepinephrine, dopamine) have been recognized as playing a role in affective rectivity and affective states for decades, in addition to their more basic central functions. Dopamine, for example, is associated with positive affect: heightened DA levels are related to heightened positive affect. Depression also has been linked to catecholamines, but the linkage is complex; in some species, depression is associated with low catecholamine levels, while in other species the reverse has been found.

Indoleamines, such as serotonin (5-hydroxytryptamine), also have been discussed as related to specific emotions or to more general emotional states. The evidence, however, is conflicting; but 5-HT does seem to lead to some damping of emotional processes, perhaps by an inhibitory effect.

Other relatively specific system state effects can be found for acetylcholine (ACh), which has CNS involvement in arousal and attention (in addition to its peripheral role as a primary neurotransmitter in the parasympathetic nervous system). There is some evidence suggesting it is involved as well in such negative states as rage and separation distress. A related neurotransmitter, adenosine, can suppress behavioral activation and wakeful consciousness; it appears to be a soporific agent.

Some of the greatest interest in recent years has been given to the neuropeptides, such as those produced by the hypothalamus and pituitary. More neuroactive peptides are being discovered and given names which reflect the relative lack of understanding of their full functions (Neuropeptide Y, Substance P), but many have been known and studied for decades. The neuropeptides often are associated with, or modulate, relatively specific states of the system in its interaction with the environment, although a few just-fine tune the intensity or duration of a reaction sequence. The affect-related functions of a few of the hypothalamic and pituitary neuropeptides are well documented, and these are discussed briefly below along with the opioid peptides.

Two of the hypothalamic neuropeptides which are known to modulate affective states or reactions centrally are corticotrophin-releasing factor (CRF) and oxytocin (OXT). Both appear to be produced in the paraventricular nuclei of the hypothalamus, but their routes from that point differ. CRF is part of the adrenal stress response sequence and is carried by the portal vessels from the hypothalamus to the anterior pituitary, where it stimulates the release of adrenocorticotrophic hormone (ACTH). ACTH, in turn, is carried through the blood to the adrenal cortices, where it precipitates the production and release of glucocorticoids which are key agents in the response to stress. OXY, on the other hand, migrates in neural tissues directly to the posterior pituitary, when it has both central and peripheral consequences. Peripherally, it facilitates the release of milk on stimulation of the nipples and somehow also appears involved in the birth process, since it is a uterine contractive agent (that is the source of its name). It also is involved peripherally in sexually related states, for it is produced during the female orgasm (probably via an amygdaloid-hypothalamic linkage), perhaps as part of the uterine contraction process, and facilitates lordosis in females and penile erection in males in certain species. Centrally, however, it appears to facilitate maternal behavior and bonding, provided the circumstances are appropriate (e.g., an object toward which to express maternal behavior). CRF also has central consequences: CRF produced by neurons nearby to those of the paraventricular source mentioned above appears to participate in a central stress response or state which behaviorally includes agitation and separation distress. Again, note that the state of the system is affected, but primarily with regard to its interaction with specific environments.

Two of the several peptides of the anterior pituitary also are worth noting in terms of their relationships to emotional actions. Prolactin is involved in the production of milk; but it also is associated with sustained maternal behavior, and therefore potentially with bonding because of prolonged, positive interaction with the offspring. ACTH, as mentioned, is part of the adrenocortical stress response sequence; but centrally, it is described by Panksepp (1993) as leading to a state of 'anxious disaffection'.

A final class of peptides that may be very important in setting the state of the system with regard to affective reactivity is the opioids. The opioid peptides include β endorphin and the enkaphilins. The former is powerfully addictive, and its central administration both induces positive affective states and reduces negative states. The negative states that are reduced include both physical and psychological pain, separation distress and aggressiveness. The actions of the enkaphilins are much less clear; they act more rapidly and with briefer duration than β endorphin, but also appear to have positive affect linkage.

There are many other identified neuropeptides, but their CNS ties to emotion states and reactions are not clear. These include several important gastric neuropeptides, other hypothalamically produced releasing factors, and a number of well-known anterior pituitary peptides, such as thyroid-stimulating hormone and the gonadotrophic stimulating hormones. If we consider the central nervous system actions of the neurochemicals described above with regard to emotion states, it seems clear that changes in their levels or activity rates can be a condition for enhanced or reduced readinesses, capacities, or susceptibilities to engage the environment in ways we would call emotional, and to persist in such behaviors or react with greater or lesser amplitude. A change in either the general state of the system, as with changes in GABA, or in the states of the more specific subsystems, can enhance or reduce reactions and reaction readinesses to the environment. This strikes us not as a set of causes of emotions, nor as a unique linkage between a neurochemical change and a specific emotion or emotion family, but as a change in the powers and liabilities – the capacities and susceptibilities – of the organism in its interaction with its environment. We will return to this point in our general discussion of environmental affordances.

Most of the physiological patterns discussed so far account for statistically significant but relatively small proportions of variance in emotional state or reaction, primarily because of the very large *individual differences* that characterize the data in this field. For example, in a study of electrocardiographic t-wave amplitudes in astronaut trainees under a variety of stressful conditions, we (Kline et al., in preparation) found that 85 percent to 88 percent of the variance was due to differences between subjects, even though the different conditions had significant effects once the between-subject differences were partialled out. Cacioppo (1994) also reported very large individual differences, although reactivity patterns were stable within individuals across tasks. Kagan (1994), too, has stressed the point that there are important differences between individuals, which are reflected in different patterns of psychophysiological reaction. After reviewing work on human infants and other species, Kagan distinguishes between defensive and nondefensive temperaments and notes a variety of neurophysiological differences: the basal amygdala is more reactive to threatening stimuli (not to all) in defensive cats, the projections from the amygdala to the ventromedial hypothalamus are more excitable in defensive cats, and the reactivity of that linking circuit is independent of the reactivity of the amygdala. He proposes, then, that 'inhibited' children (a temperamental category on which he has done extensive research) may have lower thresholds of responsiveness to unfamiliar events and greater excitability of the projections to the hypothalamus. The result would be both greater vigilance and responsiveness and more dynamic motor reaction in children of one temperament than in those with other temperaments. Therefore, in view of the differences between individuals, it is unreasonable to expect a specific physiological pattern to be tied uniquely to a specific emotional reaction.

This matter is further complicated by the fact that even similar ANS reactions to particular types of stimuli might be due to different underlying mechanisms. The research of Blascovich and his colleagues, and of Hartley and Ginsburg, mentioned earlier, are a case in point. Cacioppo (1994) provides a detailed summation of related findings in his review of stress and its bifurcated effects. Specifically, many people react to stressful events or circumstances with heart rate increases, but those could reflect increased sympathetic activity, decreased parasympathetic activity, or a reciprocation between sympathetic and parasympathetic systems (where increases in one are reciprocated by decreases in the other). All of these are known to occur, and they appear to differ with the type of stress. For example, postural stress entails a reciprocal reaction pattern, while a demanding arithmetic task leads to relatively independent activation of the sympathetic and parasympathetic systems. These in turn can entail very different neuro-endocrine pathways: sympatho-adreno-medullary system, versus hypothalamic-pituitary-adreno-cortical system, with the former leading to increased catecholamine activity and the latter to increased corticosteroid activity. The latter is believed to have deleterious health implications.

Thus, individual differences may exist in underlying mechanisms, even when surface physiology of reactions by different people to a particular type of emotionally evocative event is similar. In addition, the surface physiology patterns of response of different people to emotionally evocative events are themselves very different from each other. At least with respect to peripheral physiology, and perhaps central physiology as well, there are differences in reaction patterns across circumstances within a particular class of emotionally evocative material, and across people who differ in surface reaction patterns, and even across people who differ in underlying mechanism when the surface physiology is similar.

Therefore, it strikes us as unrealistic to expect a unique physiological pattern which is tied reliably and exclusively to a particular emotional state. This seems true even at the level of the CNS. Although activity in certain CNS regions clearly is involved in reactions that we are likely to call emotional, that is very different from concluding that specific patterns of CNS activity are necessary and sufficient for particular emotional reactions, and also uniquely involved in a particular emotion (or emotion family) and not with other reactions. The data do not support such a strong conclusion.

Coherent, organized bodily action patterns   Are there coherently organized patterns of bodily action that reliably indicate and discriminate among emotions? Here, too, the evidence is mixed and complex, and for certain bodily actions, the debates are intense.

Facial actions have received a great deal of investigative attention, by far exceeding the attention given to vocal or postural actions or to movement patterns. Probably the singly most important line of research on facial actions has been the study of facial expressions of putatively basic emotions, as pursued by Ekman and his colleagues (Ekman, 1973) and by Izard (1971) both of whom were influenced by the earlier work of Silvan Tomkins (1962, 1963). Although some of the evidence is confusing and inconsistent, and there are disagreements over methods and interpretations (see Russell, 1994; Fridlund, 1994), certain matters are clear. There is a small set of facial displays that are highly recognizable as reflecting specific 'basic' emotions around the world when subjects are asked to choose from among that small set (see Ekman, 1973, 1994b; also see Izard, 1993; Frijda, in press). Recognition rates do vary somewhat with regions – they are a bit lower in Asia and Africa, and recognition data for some specific displays are less consistent (e.g., contempt), but overall the linkage of facial displays to such emotional states as anger, fear, disgust, happiness or joy, and sadness is clearly reflected in the recognition data.

On the other hand, a careful examination of naturally occurring facial displays reveals inconsistent evidence regarding the occurrence and emotional linkage of the facial displays so strongly supported by the recognition studies. For example, Camras (1994: 347–8) notes that infants do not necessarily or reliably produce the facial displays that particular eliciting circumstances would indicate. Smiles appear during REM sleep; surprise facial displays may occur in the presence of familiar but exciting elicitors but they occur rarely in response to violations of object permanence; fearful facial displays seldom occur upon approach by a stranger; and facial configurations of anger, sadness and discomfort occur over such a wide range of circumstances that they cannot reasonably be taken as expressions of discrete emotional states. Based on these observations as well as others, Camras concludes that there is not an innately concordant relationship between the facial configurations described by discrete emotion theorists and the purported discrete emotions. Fogel and his colleagues (Messinger et al., in press) come to the same conclusion.

Moreover, evidence of the occurrence of discrete, full facial displays of explicit emotions in infants is mixed. Isolated components of those displays occur relatively frequently – but sometimes with elements from other displays.[6] On the other hand, Izard and his colleagues (Izard et al., 1995) coded approximately 20,000 codable facial displays from videotapes of about 100 middle-class infants of ages 2.5 to 9 months and found that roughly one-fifth of the codable displays were 'joy', and that nearly all of those were full-face configurations. However, 'anger' and 'sadness' together made up another 15 percent of the displays, and half of those displays were either partial or blends with components of other displays.[7,8] Messinger et al. (in press) also found, in their longitudinal observations of face-to-face interactions of parents and infants and in their reviews of the literature, that infant facial displays were not well described by the facial configurations examined in the recognition studies. The facial actions often were fleeting; they sometimes contained other elements that indicated a different emotional state, as when a smile contained elements of a grimace; and elements of purportedly emotional facial displays are sometimes parts of non-emotional actions, as when an infant raises its brows to see what is above it. Therefore, it is not clear that a basic set of highly organized facial displays exists in preprogrammed form, and there is some question about the existence of a small set of basic emotions as coherent organized entities. The composition of facial displays of more complex emotional states such as pride and shame is a further complication. That is, it is unclear whether the 'basic emotions' are supposed to serve as building blocks for displays of more complex states.

In sum, it is not clear whether the displays of more complex emotions in children are constructed from the displays of basic emotions; full facial configurations as described by discrete emotion theories and the emotion recognition studies do occur in infants and babies, but their separate components also occur in the absence of the full configuration; displays of one sort may contain elements of another sort; and conditions that should elicit a particular emotional state – and appear to do so, given the general line of activity of the baby – do not necessarily elicit the relevant facial configuration. The linkage between specific emotional states and specific facial displays therefore seems questionable, even in infants and babies too young to be influenced by the display rules of their culture.

Nevertheless, certain facial displays, when formed, often lead to reports of feelings that are consistent with emotions with which the facial displays are typically associated. This occurs even when the facial displays are formed apparently independently of any emotion induction. For example, subjects who contracted those muscles involved in the facial configurations held to be expressions of certain basic emotions (fear, disgust, anger, happiness, surprise, sadness) reported subjective states consistent with the facial configurations (Ekman et al., 1983; Levenson et al., 1990). In these experiments, steps were taken to minimize any emotion cues and to bring about facial configurations only through the anatomically based instructions. However, as noted earlier in the discussion of ANS patterns, these same experiments produced apparent ANS effects which differentiated among basic emotions, but those differences generally proved unreliable across experiments (Zajonc and McIntosh, 1992). The reliability of this strong form of a facial feedback effect remains to be demonstrated.

There is considerable evidence of a weaker form of facial feedback using muscle induction, however. Over a period of years, James Laird has demonstrated that the pleasantness and unpleasantness of subjective experience can be enhanced by manipulation of appropriate facial configurations while performing other tasks. The effects were found while subjects were engaged in activities as varied as viewing cartoons and emotional slides, writing speeches, recalling emotional material, and wearing eyeglasses (see Laird, 1984, for a review and elaboration of this work). Zajonc and his colleagues also have shown apparent facial feedback, basing their experiments on the vascular theory described earlier in which facial configurations are believed to modulate venous flow and thereby brain temperature, which in turn is postulated to influence subjective experience of pleasantness and unpleasantness (Zajonc et al., 1993). The effect sizes of these studies are moderate, reflecting considerable individual differences. Laird (1984; Laird and Bresler, 1992) addressed that fact explicitly and found that facial feedback effects were influenced by differences in self-perception – for example, facial configuration instructions were more effective for people with less facial fat (inferred from total body weight). But here, too, cross-laboratory replication is needed, especially since experimental subjects for whom the instructions or stimulus materials are ineffective are typically removed from the analyses.[9] In addition, although elaborate procedures have been used to minimize 'hypothesis guessing' by subjects, the close association between emotional displays and emotional talk makes it extremely difficult to rule out demand characteristics as a potential alternative explanation for 'facial feedback' results.

One facial display configuration in particular has been associated with both a specific subjective state and a specific EEG pattern, strongly suggesting a CNS underpinning linking both the display and the subjective state. The configuration in ordinary terms is a smile with crinkled eyes. More technically, the configuration has come to be known as a Duchenne (D-) smile (Ekman, 1989). The Duchenne smile is generally associated with positive self-reported emotional states, especially happiness judgments on scales or checklists. It also is associated fairly strongly and discriminatively with higher relative EEG activation of the left anterior temporal cortex and prefrontal cortex, which Davidson has shown to be selectively indicative of positive, approach oriented affective states (Davidson et al., 1990). Davidson and Ekman interpret the Duchenne smile as being associated with true happiness and thus as a physiological marker of a specific emotional state. However, others interpret the data differently, and some data are inconsistent in particular details with those reported by Davidson et al. (1990).

For example, Fogel and his colleagues (Messinger et al., in press) consider the contraction of *orbicularis oculi* (the muscle surrounding the eye and contracted in the eye crinkle of the Duchenne smile, especially the lateral part of the muscle) to be a constituent of enhancement of an affective state, whether a positive state (pleasure, happiness) or a negative one (anger). Their interpretation, though, is based primarily on infant facial displays during mother–infant interaction episodes, and there may be developmental changes in the configurational role of the *orbicularis oculi*. A hint of such differences can be found by comparing the EEG pattern reported by Davidson et al. (1990) for adults during Duchenne smiles with the pattern reported by Fox and Davidson (1988) for infants during comparable smiles but in a different circumstance (return of the mother after brief absence). In the latter case, Duchenne smiles were associated with elevated activation of the left frontal cortex but not the right frontal (which remained at baseline level); but for adults (Davidson et al., 1990),

Duchenne smiles were associated with elevated activation of both the left and the right frontal hemispheres. The unique association of D-smiles and left frontal activation in the adult data came from the return of left frontal activation to baseline levels in the presence of non-Duchenne smiles while the right frontal level remained elevated, which was a different basis for 'uniqueness' from that of the infants.

Fridlund (1994) gives extensive attention to the Duchenne smile, and particularly to the *orbicularis oculi* contraction, which he describes as a grimace. Similarly to Fogel and his colleagues, Fridlund expresses serious reservations about the necessary and unique linkage between the smile-with-eye-crinkle and states of 'true happiness'. The pilot data that we described earlier also revealed some complexity in the relationship between Duchenne smiles and self-reported happiness, since the claimed relationship occurred in the presence of one affectively positive videotape but not the other. With the latter tape, it was *non*-Duchenne smiles that were associated with reports of positive affect. We interpreted the difference in patterns to be due to intensity differences in the tapes, but the tapes could also be construed to differ in type of positive content. It could be that the tape of the baby laughing in her bath evokes spontaneous, unthoughtful amusement and affection through an emotional contagion mechanism (see Hatfield et al., 1992), while the tape of a young man describing a surprise party as the nicest thing that ever happened to him elicits a more reflective, somewhat skeptical, but empathically positive reaction. Either interpretation, however, introduces a contingent quality to the association between smile-with-eye-crinkle and positive affect.

Finally, the design of experiments may preclude the desired inferences regarding the association between the Duchenne smile and emotional state. Typically, as in the Davidson et al. (1990) study cited earlier, a psychological state is induced (by instruction or by stimulus-based evocation), and physiological and video measures are then taken. Thus, the conditional probability of a Duchenne configuration given the occurrence of a true state of enjoyment can be estimated. The logic of the design is $\wp[\phi_D|\psi_{Hap}]$ – that is, the likelihood of a Duchenne configuration given the occurrence of true happiness. But this does not give the probability of a true state of enjoyment given the occurrence of a Duchenne configuration ($\wp[\psi_{Hap}|\phi_D]$). Therefore, it remains unclear whether the Duchenne smile configuration – i.e., the mouth smile and the crinkled eyes – is a unique index, component of producer of 'true enjoyment', because the data indicate only that in the presence of 'true enjoyment', the D-smile is likely to occur. The data do not specify whether in the presence of a Duchenne configuration, 'true enjoyment' and only 'true enjoyment' will occur.[10]

The above reservations notwithstanding, the relatively tight linkage between facial displays and emotional experience claimed by Ekman and his colleagues, especially for the D-smile (Davidson et al., 1990; Ekman et al., 1990), has an interesting implication. As Ekman et al. (1990) note, emotions are experienced as 'happening to' a person, but the person can generate some aspects of emotional experience by willfully making a facial expression. This view is compatible with that of Laird (1984), and also with a variety of sociological writings (e.g., see Hochschild, 1979) to which we will refer later in the chapter. But a corollary implication is that facial displays, being somewhat under volitional control, are not necessarily expressions of an internal emotional state, and certainly not necessarily caused by an antecedent internal emotional state. However, this is still a matter of very active debate in the literature, particularly with regard to whether facial and other bodily displays are readouts of internal emotional reactions (see Buck, 1984, 1995, for a readout view, and Fridlund, 1994, *contra*). Fridlund, for example, considers facial displays to be essentially communicative in function, serving as incipient indicators of actions that might be performed if the situation doesn't change. He argues that having a display mechanism tightly locked to a biologically reflexive action could potentially ruin the organism's likelihood of success in reproductive competition, since the reactions often occur in circumstances that pose great risk to the life or well-being of the organism. Other writers adhere to a view of facial displays as expressions of emotional states (and as components of those states), but explicitly acknowledge (Izard, in press) that observable expression is not a necessary component of emotion.

In sum, facial displays are an important part of many emotional episodes, but the linear relationship of facial displays to emotional states is not established – that is, the antecedent, componential or constitutive, and consequent linkages are unclear. Neither the necessity nor the sufficiency of facial displays as aspects of emotional episodes or emotional experience is clearly established. That is, a facial display is neither necessary nor sufficient for an emotion to be said to exist. The linkage between a facial display and an emotional state appears to be contingent on a variety of contextual factors, including situations and perhaps intensities of affect. There also are limitations of logical inference imposed by common research design and analysis strategies which make ambiguous the uniqueness of the tie between a facial configuration and an emotional state. Furthermore, the volitional nature of facial displays implies that to the extent that a facial display is tightly linked to an emotional state, a skilled 'displayer' could induce that state by willfully making the facial display. Finally, the most persuasive data linking specific facial configurations to specific emotions come from recognition studies, which in turn are susceptible to a number of methodological and logical problems. It seems most judicious to conclude this section by acknowledging the importance of facial displays as aspects of those episodes that we would call emotional, either as observers or as experiencers, but to withhold judgment on the nature of the relationships.

The relationship of *other bodily actions* to emotions also has been investigated, particularly vocalizations. The picture for vocalizations is similar to that for faces, in that there is demonstrably high recognizability – observers can classify streams of vocalizations within a fixed set of emotion labels with a high degree of inter-observer agreement. Furthermore, it does appear that humans are capable of distinguishing a highly differentiated array of emotional states on the basis of vocal production alone (Pittam and Scherer, 1993), and by implication capable of producing vocal signals differentially tied to a wide range of emotional states. These complementary capabilities would be compatible with the more general principle of joint evolution of signal and vigilance – perceptual sensitivity to a type of signal and ability to produce the signal evolve jointly (Fridlund, 1991, 1994). However, the specific linkages between the production of vocal signals of emotion and the comprehension of those vocal signals remain to be established, especially with regard to the roles of biological and cultural factors (Pittam and Scherer, 1993: 195), but also with regard to the action context within which the vocal signals are embedded and are displayed. The same uncertainty about linear relations as noted above for facial displays exists here: antecedent, constitutive, and consequent relationships between signal and state remain to be established.

The relationship between emotional states and movement, posture and gestures also has received some attention, although the restrictive constraints of laboratory studies have limited the types of postural and movement sequences that could be observed. Argyle (1975) reviewed studies of postural components of emotion expressions, and Laird and Bresler (1992) reported that postures as well as facial configurations could affect subsequently reported affective feelings. Bloch and her co-workers (Bloch et al., 1987; Santibanez-H. and Bloch, 1986) found evidence of 'emotion effector patterns' that included specific postural and respiratory patterns and which were helpful to actors in making dramatic presentations of particular emotions. Bull (1951) also described in considerable detail the postural patterns that she found to be critical in the performance and experience of a variety of emotional states. We will discuss her work in detail later, but it is relevant here to note that she found specific postural conflicts and hesitations to be essential features of the feeling aspect of evoked emotional sequences. That is consistent with the work of Hochschild (1983) with airline hostesses, who were able to induce positive emotional states in themselves as they interacted with passengers, regardless of their own initial states, by acting in positively expressive fashion – by performing facial displays and positive patterns of movement and postures.

Nevertheless, in developmental (Lewis, 1993) as well as adult literature, there is a relative dearth of systematic research on the relationships between emotions and movements and postures. It is reasonable to say that there is modest evidence of recognizability, but it is potentially confounded by cultural and regional differences. On the other hand, as we will emphasize later, it does appear that bodily preparation for action and the patterns of action that are performed during a situated emotional episode are indeed very important.

Summary of current status   In sum, it appears that there is little evidence of physiological patterns which *reliably* differentiate emotions. This is particularly the case for autonomic patterns, although there is some indication of within-person stability of autonomic patterns specific to broad categories of emotional reactions. There also is serious question about the existence of 'basic' emotions, although the issue remains actively disputed in the contemporary literature. There is, however, strong evidence for a high degree of recognizability of a simple set of facial displays, although methodological questions have been raised regarding the assessment of agreement. There is an intriguing linkage between one facial display – a smile with crinkled eyes – and EEG patterns previously associated with self reports of pleasant states. However, the crinkled eyes may reflect a higher amplitude of affect, which would reduce the linkage to one of amplitude rather than categorical quality. Recognizability of broad affective categories also has been established for certain vocal patterns. Finally, there is considerable evidence that facial displays, certain postures and other actions can alter reports of feeling states, and may be used by the individual to induce such states. This is compatible with writings about emotion in the sociological literature, and both sociologists and psychologists have speculated that by taking certain postures, facial displays, or other actions, people can induce emotional states in themselves. This is held to be a socialized skill. Nevertheless, as our review should have made clear, the theoretical and empirical states of affairs regarding emotion are confusing, albeit intriguing. Particularly absent from the predominant psychological research on emotion is context (although increasing attention is likely – see Izard, in press). We will turn to this topic now, and point out how it has to be taken into account even when considering physiological states of persons.

Context and its accumulation

Structure of context

The context of any event or process has two structural features. One is hierarchical organization, and the other is linear or sequential organization. Hierarchical organization refers to the embeddedness of events in larger events or processes, and the embedding of smaller processes and events as constituents of a given event. At the level of actions, one can construe an action as a component of a larger act, the accomplishment of which is facilitated by the successful completion of the component actions. For example, a kiss helps to accomplish a greeting, or caustic and denigrating comments help to accomplish an argument.[11]

The linear or sequential aspect of context reflects the notion that what already has occurred in a stream of activity constitutes a set of conditions under which subsequent actions occur. Put more formally, actions at prior times in the course of an act constitute the context for current actions in that act. This includes emotional aspects of prior actions; emotional reactions at earlier points can be the context for actions at the current point. It is compatible with Clark's (1985) characterization of conversation as the progressive accumulation of common ground.

These two structural characteristics of context – the hierarchical and the linear – are applicable across all levels of analysis. The multilevel, cumulative character of context draws attention to the fact that when a person embarks on some particular act, preparatory actions have already occurred, including physiological preparation, and they constitute part of the context of that act. People can bring about specific emotions by engaging in certain actions (Hochschild, 1979; Davidson et al., 1990: Laird, 1984); those actions serve as context for subsequent actions and also jointly with those subsequent actions are constituents of the emotion. Thus, actions not only occur in a context in part given by prior events and processes, but also constitute part of the context for subsequent events. Their influence feeds forward.

The feedforward mechanism

A feedforward mechanism is a basic operating feature of all living systems, including persons and their settings of action. Current actions are in part a function of the state of the system, such state being a cumulative context, and those current actions become incorporated as part of the context for subsequent actions. Humoral, autonomic, somatic, perceptual, cognitive and motor systems are all included in the operation of this principle; they are all involved in the progressively accumulating situated line of action. This has interesting implications for the relationship between physiological processes and emotional states. For example, the physiological status of the body at a point in time is a cumulative function of prior activity, and also serves as part of the context for current reactions. This is illustrated by a study conducted in our laboratory.

We modified the Zillman (1983) excitation-transfer paradigm[12] by giving male participants various levels of exercise and various periods of rest after the exercise, and then showing them a frankly erotic film. We recorded their heart rates continuously over the course of the film, and found what appears to be a carryover context effect – a feedforward effect. Specifically, those participants who entered the film setting while their heart rates were still considerably elevated by the prior exercise did not show the usual return to their baseline heart rates, as did the other groups whose heart rates had not been as elevated by exercise upon entering the film setting. Instead, the heart rates of the participants in the heavy exercise conditions asymptoted during the film at about 100 beats per minute, well above their baselines of about 74 bpm. Moreover, their heart rates remained in that elevated region (falling only to the high 90s) for the full 12-minute length of the film. Our interpretation of this finding, which awaits our replication, is that the high heart rate groups had their heart rates 'captured' by the affordances of the situation – the erotically arousing nature of the film. That is, the residual arousal from the exercise should be seen as part of the

context of the present situation; if the residual arousal is compatible with
the arousal implicitly called for by the new situation, the person will be
more likely to become fully and readily engaged in the new situation. This
same process may also play a role in emotional contagion (Hatfield et al.,
1992).

Feelings and felt experience as context in emotional episodes

Most discussions of emotion include feelings and felt experience as integral
aspects of the phenomenon. A careful examination of the matter, however,
suggests that they actually are part of the context. We will consider the
issue briefly, starting with a distinction between felt experience and talk
about felt experience.

Talk about felt experience   The measurement of feelings through self-
report scaling procedures is a form of talk about felt experience and should
be distinguished from the putative reference phenomenon – that is, the
experience to which the talk refers and which we seem to experience
directly, which we seem to 'have'. Talk about experience confounds the
issue of the nature of emotion and its bodily states by presuming that
emotion constructs used in talk are primitive or basic categories of the
material world, so that reference to them in talk is denotative reference to
coherent material entities. But as Russell (1991) and others have pointed
out, although emotion talk uses terms that are essential in ordinary
language and everyday interactions, those terms are not necessarily appropriate for technical discourse and for the scientific study of the phenomena
to which ordinary language emotion terms are believed to refer. Therefore,
talk about one's emotional experience should not be taken as referring
denotatively to extant entities. On the other hand, emotion talk unquestionably is important, but as an aspect of social interaction and as part of
the context for subsequent action.

Felt experience   Apart from talk about it, felt experience also stands in
unclear relationship to emotion phenomena. At the least, felt experience
necessitates some form of reflection by the experiencer on what is going on.
LeDoux (1995), in his succinct review of the role of the amygdala in fear
and other emotions, emphasized the importance of distinguishing between
conditioned fear and the experience or feeling of fear. The phenomena are
not the same.
   Other authors have made similar points, either explicitly or implicitly.
Rolls (1994) for example, in his chapter on emotion and consciousness
from a neuroscience perspective, treats feelings as entailing reflective
appraisal and as requiring language-like processing abilities. Cacioppo,
Berntson and Klein (1992) implicitly assume reflective appraisal on the part
of a 'feeling' person. They argue that somatovisceral reafferentation is
inherently ambiguous in that a given pattern can be part of any of several

reactions to any of many different circumstances. Moreover, a particular type of event can engender different somatovisceral patterns, depending on circumstances, activity and state of the organism at the time, and so on. Therefore, somatovisceral reafferentation is a basis for 'somatovisceral illusions', analogous to visual illusions with ambiguous figures. The implications of this argument are that people reflect on somatovisceral feedback as a step in their experience of feelings, and that that feedback is inherently ambiguous. Disambiguation presumably requires situational information.

In a monograph published 45 years ago, Bull (1951) proposed that the feeling which we take to characterize a given emotional state occurs only during a pause in the sequence from the 'motor attitude' to the instrumental action. The pause can be due to a conflict between competing motor attitudes, or to an imposed delay, or even to the absence of any clear instrumental act. Bull emphasized that these familiar affective states – the feelings – are spinoffs of patterns of bodily response, and in her work she identified response patterns (brief action sequences) which correspond to disgust, fear, anger, depression, triumph and joy. Feelings are frequent concomitants of such situated sequences but not central components, since a situated action sequence could in principle run off without the pause necessary for feeling. But on the occasions when a pause and feeling do occur, the feeling certainly is part of the context of the subsequent actions.

Intensity Feelings also vary considerably in their intensity, and this is often used as an index of the intensity of the emotion. Moreover, emotions that differ in the intensity of feeling may have different behavioral and physiological features, even if the emotions are of the same category (Izard, in press). However, it should be noted that not all intense activities are emotional, even if the intensity is experienced. Intense concentration, as in learning, or in trying to solve a puzzle, would not ordinarily be considered an emotional state, either by the experiencer or an observer. Nor would intense physical effort, as in weight lifting, be considered an emotional state. Finally, even weakly felt affective experiences may be called emotional, both by the experiencer and by an observer.

There are several troubling implications of this overview of emotions, feelings and context. Feelings do not seem to be a central part of emotions, but rather are frequent concomitants. Also, emotions do not appear to be internal states that are internally coherent and are evoked and expressed, sometimes dramatically. And emotions are not necessarily intense experiences, nor are intense experiences necessarily emotions. Thus, there does not appear to be a set of bodily states which are uniquely and reliably tied to specific emotional states and only to them. The bodily instantiations of what we refer to as emotions appear to be variable and unreliable, although there is evidence of bodily structures and processes that are relevant and even necessary for the conduct of some emotional episodes. But if specific bodily states are not uniquely, necessarily and sufficiently tied to particular emotions, and if emotions are not necessarily intense experiences, why is emotion so important a concept in human affairs? Perhaps, as Averill (1974, and Chapter 9 of this volume) has suggested, we should look at the social and personal functions served by emotion talk and emotion display.

Functions of emotion talk: the use of emotion terms

Our intention in this section is to consider emotion as a term, as a concept – that is, to consider its *use* in speech and text. Since this topic is considered in detail in other chapters in this volume, we will just set out some bald statements, with little attempt to defend them. Our purpose is to set a framework for our concluding comments about the relationships of bodily states to 'emotion'.

The use of emotion terms in speech and text is as a claim that an action or series of actions is of a sort not fully under control of the actor. The actor is less than fully responsible for his actions or their consequences, and his action is not instrumental – that is, he is not acting that way to achieve some end. Specifically, any situated behavior or action is a candidate for a claim of emotion to the extent that

1 it can be construed to imply a reduced responsibility on the part of the actor;
2 the actor is not under such identifiably exogenous influences as drugs, injury or physical disease; and
3 the actor is responding to some finite event, whether external or internal (otherwise the action would be an expression of the actor's permanent temperament).

The claim of less than full responsibility can be made by the actor about his own past, present or future action, or by the actor's interaction partner, or by an outside observer (such as a psychologist). The functions served by the claim will differ across these claimants. Furthermore, the claim can be made directly, through such descriptive statements as, 'Joe is happy' or 'Mary is angry', or it can be made indirectly by actions or talk which imply an emotional state (behaving angrily or sadly or joyously). The consequences of direct claims may differ from those of indirect claims, and it would be interesting to work out the differences, much as discourse investigators are doing for direct and indirect speech acts.

A socially and culturally competent person usually can choose or decide to be emotional. That is, a person generally is capable of performing those movements and expressions, and of thinking those thoughts, that *constitute* a particular emotion. The person actually will be *in* a particular emotional state, as we all are capable of doing at a funeral, or in a bedroom, or as a theater audience. We are guided in these accomplishments by the situated emotion norms and rules of emotion work (cf. Hochschild, 1979). Once an action is accepted as emotional, it has a variety of functions, as has been suggested by Harré (1986). These include interpersonal force, as in the emotional contagion process (Hatfield et al., 1992), and sincerity implications. However, it should be noted that 'acceptance' of an action as emotional does not itself require reflective appraisal. Acceptance may be built into the perspective of the interaction partner, such as a mother playing with her baby or a culturally competent audience at a theater production.

According to this view, any behavior or action which implies a reduced responsibility on the part of the actor and is construable as a reaction to some finite event but at the same time is not performed while the actor is reacting to some exogenous influence, is a candidate for a claim of emotion. Therefore, there is not *necessarily* anything common to all emotions, or even to all instances of a particular emotion, although prototypical instances of a particular emotion may well have a common and unique set of features (features common to all prototypical instances of an emotion, and only to that emotion) that allows ready identification of the emotion. Furthermore, the common and unique set of features may have been biologically selected; but none of this requires that *all* instances of a particular emotion will have that set of features, nor that that set is a *necessary* set for an instance of that emotion. Contraction of *zygomaticus major* is not *necessary* for a claim of happiness to be legitimate, nor does every form of anger *require* contraction of the *corrugator* muscles. Similarly, some of the common and unique features may be virtually or literally reflexive in the context of certain classes of events, as when an infant averts its head in the presence of a rapidly looming object, or cries when a nipple is withdrawn before it has finished nursing; but once again, the legitimate making of an emotion claim is *not* dependent on a reflexive or prewired or highly overlearned, automatic response, whether behavioral or physiological. Automaticity is not a ground for the claim.

Emotion and its relationships with bodily states

Implications

Our review of the current status of the relationships between 'emotion' and bodily states and processes has a number of implications for research and theory, positive as well as negative. On the negative side, there appear to be no clear internal or display markers of emotions. There also may not be any biological features or processes that are necessary for the occurrence of emotions in general or of specific emotions in particular. Evidence is very strong for the importance of the amygdala in reactions of animals that we readily would label 'fear', but that might not be different categorically from saying that the heart is necessary for happiness. The issue is one of necessity and sufficiency taken jointly. There do not appear to be any organized structures of part and processes, including neurological, which uniquely and necessarily specify the common identity of multiple instances of an emotion. This raises very serious doubts about the existence of prewired emotion programs in the central nervous system.

On the positive side, it is clear to us that all levels of body functioning are prime candidates for involvement in emotional episodes. Furthermore, we would expect variations in involvement of bodily parts and processes as a function of intensity level – the physiology of instances of weak anger is very likely to be significantly different from the physiology of instances of intense anger. In addition, emotional episodes are likely to vary in form and content across settings, roles and cultures. All of these are legitimate topics for study. Moreover, emotional episodes have natural histories in which emotional qualities emerge and dissipate across time. The natural histories of paradigm instances of emotional episodes can be studied profitably, and at multiple levels.

The matter of natural history deserves serious investigative attention, which has generally been lacking in the emotion field. For example, facial, vocal and postural displays of emotions can help to mark or indicate the identity of the act that is under way. They can serve as early indicators of the situated line of action in which the person is engaged, or which could eventuate if a particular course of action continues to develop. Therefore, they can play an important regulatory role in social interaction, and can be a nonverbal topic of interactional negotiation.

The matter of context is closely related to that of the natural history, or unfolding, of the emotional episode. To the extent that early actions in a developing act entail preparations that include a high degree of physiological and somatic arousal, those early actions and their constituent processes serve as context which will influence the person's sensitivity to the environment and its affordances, and constrain the range of likely directions the interaction will take.

There is a remaining matter to which we only alluded in our review, but which has important implications for research and theory in emotion. In the last decade, research from a dynamic systems perspective has emerged in developmental psychology (Camras, 1994; Fogel, 1993; Fogel and Thelen, 1987; Messinger et al., in press), social psychology (Vallacher and Nowak, 1994), and sociology (Harvey and Reed, 1994), that persuasively indicates that executive functions of the sort typically sought in and imputed to the brain are not necessary for the complex functioning of a system. Instead, local coordination emerges by virtue of the capacities and constraints of the interdependent constituents of the system. This is not to say that the central nervous system is not necessary for the occurrence of emotional reactions, but rather that it is but one of the constituents of the person-environment dynamic system, the behavior of which is forming over extended durations of time. From this perspective, it is essential that the study of emotion include the observation of the emergence and dissipation of emotional episodes and their contexts, and preferably at multiple levels of analysis. The temporal dimension of emotional episodes – what we have called the situated line of action – must be part of the research.

ow
'emotion' is construed. In the course of our review we pointed out the
contextual contingency of displays in emotional episodes and noted that the
component features of emotional episodes vary with the situational affordances for action. This applies to autonomic and skeletal components,
neuroendocrine components, and perhaps CNS components. The case
seems not to be one of an emotion occurring which then causes various
displays, thoughts, feelings, behaviors and physiological reactions. Instead,
the displays, behaviors and physiological reactions, when they co-occur,
constitute the satisfactory conditions for our imputation of a specific
emotion label. The claim that an act was emotional, and the acceptance of
that claim as legitimate, have important social utility.

This point of view places emphasis on the examination of emotional
episodes, preferably in natural contexts of occurrence. For example,
instances of happiness could be facilitated by setting up happy interactions,
videotaping them and having the participants review the tapes later to pick
out happy segments. Assuming psychophysiological recordings had been
taken, happy segments could be compared against other segments and the
progressive development of each instance of happiness could be charted
physiologically and behaviorally.[13] We might even find incipient physiological changes that presage the identified instances of happiness – changes
which went unnoticed by the participant. For example, we would expect
incipient contractions in the *zygomaticus major* region to increase in
frequency and spectral power before each identified segment of happiness,
indicating a progressively increasing readiness for the person to *be* happy.
Furthermore, the initial components of an emotional reaction, even if they
are reflexive, probably are readily modulated – i.e., amplified or suppressed
– by the person *or* by the flow of interaction in which the person is
immersed. For example, a person can amplify and display an incipient
smile; or the initial sacral reflexes producing tumescence of erogenous tissue
can be amplified by the passionate behavior of the interaction partner.

As a final point, the modulation of an emerging emotional act does not
require self-conscious control by the person. In fact, this probably would
interfere with the emotional quality of the act. Instead, the person need
merely *embark* on the act; from that point on, two factors will come into
play in the modulation. One is the person's own chunked skills at *being*
angry or sad or happy or proud, and the other is the environment,
especially the social environment. If you embark on an episode of anger,
your partner often will act so as to facilitate or to damp the further
development of that episode.

So, we see emotions as biosocial phenomena that have a time course of
emergence and disappearance. Both social and biological study are
essential, and so is microanalysis of the development and dissipation of
emotional instances. One quality that strikes us as special about 'emotions'

(as opposed to everything else that we do and experience in life) is the social function that emotion serves. But the situated bodily changes and kinds of actions that often serve as the conditions for making and accepting emotion claims are themselves interesting and important phenomena. They can be studied as emergent phenomena, and at the same time as part of the progressively accumulating context from which situated lines of action unfold.

Notes

1 Several subjects yawned repeatedly, and a few appeared to fall asleep. A few others giggled.

2 We used a video display rather than a slide projector, but the retinal angle subtended was similar, and the faces, projection times and average inter-slide interval were the same.

3 The pilot studies described here have been reported in detail. See Harrington and Ginsburg (1994) and Harrington et al. (1993).

4 Ekman (1994a) notes Stemmler's findings but criticizes his procedures.

5 Relative enhancement of activation refers to a *reduction* in the spectral power of the alpha range of frequencies in the electroencephalogram of one hemisphere, relative to the spectral power of the other hemisphere, with that relationship between the two compared with the relationship obtained during baseline measures.

6 Camras described instances of this at a Nags Head workshop on facial displays and emotion in 1993.

7 Izard et al. (1995) found that nearly half of all codable facial configurations were displays of 'interest', and that almost all of those were full-face configurations. However, 'interest' strikes us more as an attentional orientation than an 'emotion' in common parlance.

8 In Izard's discrete coding system (MAX) no upper face blends of 'joy' are allowed because the upper face features of 'joy' are ambiguous when they occur without the lower face components (e.g., raised cheeks and narrowed eyes could be a squint rather than part of a joyful expression). This reasonable coding decision, though, makes unknown the number of joyful displays that were only partial – i.e., the number that contained some but not all of the 'joy' components. Thus, the finding that almost all joy displays were full-face configurations is partly artifactually inflated.

9 Laird noted, in a Social Psychology seminar presentation at the Department of Experimental Psychology, University of Oxford, 1 November 1993, that a fairly large proportion of subjects have to be discarded because they see through the disguise or subterfuge. This is not an uncommon procedure in social psychological research; a subject who does not find a video clip of a dog playing with flowers amusing, indexed by the absence of a smile, will not allow for a test of the hypothesis that 'happiness' is associated with a unique and differentiating set of ANS changes. However, the consequence of such subject exclusions is to bias the sample in a manner equivalent to self-selection, thereby posing a serious threat to external validity (and perhaps to internal validity, if the exclusions are differentially related to experimental conditions).

10 It should be noted that this comment pertains only to the kinds of inference that can be drawn from the usual designs. It does not bear upon issues raised by others and cited above regarding the multiple roles of the crinkled eyes, as in grimacing or as augmenters of a variety of affective states. Nor does it bear upon the very serious problem of identification of a 'true' affective state, such as 'true enjoyment', independently of the facial configuration hypothesized to be a marker or component of such a state.

11 Since an event can be part of more than one hierarchy, it would be more accurate to refer to this organizational feature as heterarchical.

12 Zillman (1983) and his colleagues had demonstrated in several experiments that people

would react more emotionally to emotionally evocative events or circumstances if they were still physiologically aroused from some prior activity, which itself was irrelevant to the current, evocative event. Exercise was often used as the arousing manipulation. A critical and replicated finding was that the prior arousal – the exercise – must end several minutes before the newly evocative event in order to have the enhancing effect. This finding was typically interpreted in terms of misattribution: The residually aroused subject is unaware of the source of the residual arousal, given the lapse of time, and therefore attributes it to the new, evocative circumstance and reacts more strongly. The design of most of the excitation transfer experiments, however, confounded time since arousal and residual level of arousal; we ran our study to disentangle those two factors.

13 This is very similar to the procedure used by Gottman and his colleagues (see Gottman, 1993, for a summary) in their research on distressed couples, but they have not conducted microanalyses over the temporal span that we are suggesting. Their objectives are different, and their findings have proven very interesting within the frame of those objectives.

References

Argyle, M. (1975) *Bodily Communication*. New York: International Universities Press.

Averill, J.R. (1974) 'An analysis of psychophysiological symbolism and its influence on theories of emotion', *Journal for Theory of Social Behaviour*, 4 (22): 147–90.

Blascovich, J. and Tomaka, J. (1996) 'The biopsychosocial model of arousal regulation', in M.P. Zanna (ed.), *Advances in Experimental Social Psychology*, 28: 1–51. San Diego, CA: Academic Press.

Bloch, S., Orthous, P. and Santibanez-H., G. (1987) 'Effector patterns of basic emotions: A psychophysiological method for training actors', *Journal of Social and Biological Structures*, 10: 1–19.

Buck, R. (1984) *The Communication of Emotion*. New York: Guilford Press.

Buck, R. (1995) 'Social and emotional functions in facial expression and communication: The readout hypothesis', *Biological Psychology*, 38 (2/3): 95–116.

Bull, N. (1951) 'The attitude theory of emotion', *Nervous and Mental Disease Monographs*, No. 81.

Cacioppo, J.T. (1994) 'Social neuroscience: Autonomic, neuroendocrine, and immune responses to stress', *Psychophysiology*, 31 (2): 113–28.

Cacioppo, J.T., Berntson, G.G. and Klein, D.J. (1992) 'What is an emotion? The role of somatovisceral afference, with special emphasis on somatovisceral "illusions"', in M.S. Clark (ed.), *Emotion* (V. 14). London: Sage Publications.

Cacioppo, J.T., Bush, L.K. and Tassinary, L.G. (1992) 'Microexpressive facial actions as a function of affective stimuli: Replication and extension', *Personality and Social Psychology Bulletin*, 18, 515–26.

Cacioppo, J.T., Klein, D.J., Berntson, G.C. and Hatfield, E. (1993) 'The psychophysiology of emotions', in M. Lewis and J.M. Haviland (eds), *Handbook of Emotions*. New York: Guilford Press.

Cacioppo, J.T., Petty, R.E., Losch, M.E. and Kim, H.S. (1986) 'Electromyographic activity over facial muscle regions can differentiate the valence and intensity of affective reactions', *Journal of Personality and Social Psychology*, 50 (2): 260–8.

Camras, L.A. (1994) 'Two aspects of emotional development: Expression and elicitation', in P. Ekman and R.J. Davidson (eds), *The Nature of Emotion: Fundamental Questions*. New York: Oxford University Press.

Clark, H.H. (1985) 'Language and language users', in G. Lindzey and E. Aronson (eds), *Handbook of Social Psychology, Vol. II* (3rd edn). New York: Random House.

Davidson, R.J. (1993) 'The neuropsychology of emotion and affective style', in M. Lewis and J.M. Haviland (eds), *Handbook of Emotions*. New York: Guilford Press.

Davidson, R.J. (1994) 'Complexities in the search for emotion-specific physiology', in P.

256 *The Emotions*

Ekman and R.J. Davidson (eds), *The Nature of Emotion: Fundamental Questions*. New York: Oxford University Press.

Davidson, R.J., Ekman, P., Saron, C.D., Senulis, J.A. and Friesen, W.V. (1990) 'Approach-withdrawal and cerebral asymmetry: Emotional expression and brain physiology I', *Journal of Personality and Social Psychology*, 58 (2): 330–41.

Dimberg, U. (1982) 'Facial reactions to facial expressions', *Psychophysiology*, 19: 643–7.

Ekman, P. (1973) 'Cross-cultural studies of facial expression', in P. Ekman (ed.), *Darwin and Facial Expressions*. New York: Academic Press.

Ekman, P. (1989) 'The argument and evidence about universals in facial expressions of emotion', in H. Wagner and A. Manstead (eds), *Handbook of Social Psychology*. New York: Wiley.

Ekman, P.E. (1994a) 'All emotions are basic', in P. Ekman and R.J. Davidson (eds), *The Nature of Emotion: Fundamental Questions*. New York: Oxford University Press.

Ekman, P. (1994b) 'Strong evidence for universals in facial expressions: A reply to Russell's mistaken critique', *Psychological Bulletin*, 115 (2): 268–87.

Ekman, P. and Friesen, W.V. (1976) *Pictures of Facial Affect*. Palo Alto: Consulting Psychologists Press.

Ekman, P. and Friesen, W.V. (1982) 'Felt, false and miserable smiles', *Journal of Nonverbal Behavior*, 6: 238–52.

Ekman, P., Davidson, R.J. and Friesen, W.V. (1990) 'The Duchenne smile: Emotional expression and brain physiology II', *Journal of Personality and Social Psychology*, 58 (2): 342–53.

Ekman, P., Levenson, R.W. and Friesen, W.V. (1983) 'Autonomic nervous system activity distinguishes among emotions', *Science*, 221: 1208–10.

Fogel, A. (1993) *Developing Through Relationships: Origins of Communication, Self and Culture*. Chicago: University of Chicago Press.

Fogel, A. and Thelen, E. (1987) 'The development of early expressive and communicative action', *Developmental Psychology*, 23: 747–61.

Fox, N.A. and Davidson, R.J. (1988) 'Patterns of brain electrical activity during facial signs of emotion in 10-month-old infants', *Developmental Psychology*, 24: 230–6.

Fridlund, A.J. (1991) 'Evolution and facial action in reflex, social motive, and paralanguage', *Biological Psychology*, 32: 3–100.

Fridlund, A.J. (1994) *Human Facial Expression: An Evolutionary View*. San Diego: Academic Press.

Frijda, N. (in press) 'Facial expression and modes of action readiness', in J.A. Russell (ed.), *New Directions in the Study of Facial Expression*. New York: Cambridge University Press.

Gottman, J.M. (1993) 'Studying emotion in social interaction', in M. Lewis and J.M. Haviland (eds), *Handbook of Emotions*. New York: Guilford Press.

Gray, J.A. (1994) 'Three fundamental emotion systems', in P. Ekman and R.J. Davidson (eds), *The Nature of Emotion: Fundamental Questions*. New York: Oxford University Press.

Harré, R. (1986) 'An outline of the social constructionist viewpoint', in R. Harré (ed.), *The Social Construction of Emotions*. Oxford: Basil Blackwell.

Harrington, M.E. and Ginsburg, G.P. (1994) 'Failure to replicate Dimberg's "Facial Reactions to Facial Expressions" in potentially expressive subjects [Abstract]'. *Proceedings of the Annual Meeting of the Society for Psychophysiological Research*.

Harrington, M.E., Ginsburg, G.P. and Bissett, R.T. (1993, April). *Instructions to Subjects Influence Facial Displays of Emotion*. Presented at the Annual Convention of the Western Psychological Association, Phoenix, AZ.

Hartley, T. (1995) *A Situated Action Approach to Stress and Cardiovascular Reactivity*. Unpublished doctoral dissertation, Department of Psychology, University of Nevada, Reno.

Hartley, T. and Ginsburg, G.P. (1995) 'Self presentation and cardiovascular reactivity [Abstract]'. *Proceedings of the Society of Behavioral Medicine Annual Scientific Sessions*.

Harvey, D.L. and Reed, M.H. (1994) 'The evolution of dissipative social systems', *Journal of Social and Evolutionary Systems*, 17: 371–411.

Hatfield, E., Cacioppo, J.T. and Rapson, R.L. (1992) 'Primitive emotional contagion', in M.S. Clark (ed.), *Emotion* (V. 14). London: Sage Publications.

Hochschild, A.R. (1979) 'Emotion work, feeling rules and social structure', *American Journal of Sociology*, 85: 551–75.

Hochschild, A.R. (1983) *The Managed Heart: Commercialization of Human Feeling*. Berkeley: University of California Press.

Hsu, G., Stuart, J., Chiasson, C. and Ginsburg, G.P. (1989) 'Emotional interactions as dyadic developmental achievements'. Poster presented at the joint meeting of Western Psychological Association and Rocky Mountain Psychological Association, Reno, NV.

Izard, C.E. (1971) *The Face of Emotion*. New York: Appleton.

Izard, C.E. (1993) 'Organizational and motivational functions of discrete emotions', in M. Lewis and J.M. Haviland (eds), *Handbook of Emotions*. New York: Guilford Press.

Izard, C.E. (in press) 'Perspectives on the development and significance of emotional expressions', in J.A. Russell (ed.), *New Directions in the Study of Facial Expression*. New York: Cambridge University Press.

Izard, C.E., Fanauzzo, C.A., Castle, J.M., Haynes, O.M., Rayias, M.F. and Putnam, P.H. (1995) 'The ontogeny and significance of infants' facial expressions in the first 9 months of life', *Developmental Psychology*, 31 (6): 997–1013.

Kagan, J. (1994) 'On the nature of emotion', in N.A. Fox (ed.), 'The development of emotion regulation: Biological and behavioral consequences'. *Monographs of the Society for Research in Child Development*, 59 (2–3, Serial No. 240): 7–24.

Kline, K.P., Ginsburg, G.P. and Johnson, J. (in preparation) *Evaluation of Beat-to-Beat Heart Rate Changes on T-wave Amplitude*. Unpublished manuscript, Department of Psychology, University of Nevada, Reno.

Laird, J.D. (1984) 'The real role of facial response in the experience of emotion: A reply to Tourangeau and Ellsworth, and others', *Journal of Personality and Social Psychology*, 47 (4): 909–17.

Laird, J.D. and Bresler, C. (1992) 'The process of emotional experience: A self-perception theory', in M.S. Clark (ed.), *Emotion* (V. 13). London: Sage Publications.

LeDoux, J.E. (1993) 'Emotional networks in the brain', in M. Lewis and J.M. Haviland (eds), *Handbook of Emotions*. New York: Guilford Press.

LeDoux, J.E. (1995) 'Emotion: Clues from the brain', *Annual Review of Psychology*, 46: 209–35.

Levenson, R.W. (1992) 'Autonomic nervous system differences among emotions', *Psychological Science*, 3 (1): 23–7.

Levenson, R.W. (1994) 'The search for autonomic specificity', in P. Ekman and R.J. Davidson (eds), *The Nature of Emotion: Fundamental Questions*. New York: Oxford University Press.

Levenson, R.W., Ekman, P. and Friesen, W.V. (1990) 'Voluntary facial action generates emotion-specific autonomic nervous system activity', *Psychophysiology*, 27 (4): 363–84.

Lewis, M. (1993) 'The emergence of human emotions', in M. Lewis and J.M. Haviland (eds), *Handbook of Emotions*. New York: Guilford Press.

MacLean, P.D. (1949) 'Psychosomatic disease and the "visceral brain": Recent developments bearing on the Papez theory of emotion', *Psychosomatic Medicine*, 11: 338–53.

Messinger, D.S., Fogel, A. and Dickson, K.L. (in press). 'Some dynamic features of infant facial action', in J.A. Russell (ed.), *New Directions in the Study of Facial Expression*. New York: Cambridge University Press.

Olds, J. and Milner, P. (1954) 'Positive reinforcement produced by electrical stimulation of septal area and other regions of rat brain', *Physiological Psychology*, 47: 419–27.

Panksepp, J. (1989) 'The neurobiology of human emotions: Of animal brains and human feelings', in T. Manstead and H. Wagner (eds), *Handbook of Social Psychophysiology*. New York: Wiley.

Panksepp, J. (1993) 'Neurochemical control of moods and emotions: Amino acids to neuropeptides', in M. Lewis and J.M. Haviland (eds), *Handbook of Emotions*. New York: Guilford Press.

Panksepp. J. (1994) 'Subjectivity may have evolved in the brain as a simple value-coding process that promotes the learning of new behaviors', in P. Ekman and R.J. Davidson (eds), *The Nature of Emotion: Fundamental Questions*. New York: Oxford University Press.

Pittam, J. and Scherer, K.R. (1993) 'Vocal expression and communication of emotion', in M. Lewis and J.M. Haviland (eds), *Handbook of Emotions*. New York: Guilford Press.

Rolls, E.T. (1992) 'Neurophysiology and functions of the primate amygdala', in J.P. Aggleton (ed.), *The Amygdala: Neurobiological Aspects of Emotion, Memory, and Mental Dysfunction*. New York: Wiley-Liss.

Rolls, E.T. (1994) 'A theory of emotion and consciousness, and its application to understanding the neural basis of emotion', in M. Gazzinaga (ed.), *The Cognitive Neurosciences*. MIT Press.

Russell, J.A. (1991) 'Natural language concepts of emotion', *Perspectives in Personality*, V. 3A: 119-37.

Russell, J.A. (1994) 'Is there universal recognition of emotion from facial expression? A review of the cross-cultural studies', *Psychological Bulletin*, 115 (1): 102-41.

Santibanez-H., Guy and Bloch, S. (1986) 'A qualitative analysis of emotional effector patterns and their feedback', *Pavlovian Journal of Biological Science*, 21 (3): 108-16.

Stemmler, G. (1989) 'The autonomic differentiation of emotions revisited: Convergent and discriminant validation', *Psychophysiology*, 26 (6): 617-32.

Stotland, E. (1978) *Empathy, Fantasy and Helping*. Beverly Hills, CA: Sage.

Tomkins, S.S. (1962) *Affect, Imagery, Consciousness: Volume 1. The Positive Affects*. New York: Springer.

Tomkins, S.S. (1963) *Affect, Imagery, Consciousness: Volume 2. The Negative Affects*. New York: Springer.

Vallacher, R.R. and Nowak, A. (eds) (1994) *Dynamical Systems in Social Psychology*. San Diego: Academic Press.

Voglmaier, M.M. and Hakerem, G. (1989) *Facial Electromyography (EMG) in Response to Facial Expressions: Relation to Subjective Emotional Experience and Trait Affect*. Presented at the Annual Meeting of the Society for Psychophysiological Research.

Weiskrantz, L. (1956) 'Behavioral changes associated with ablation of the amygdaloid complex in monkeys', *Journal of Comparative and Physiological Psychology*, 49: 381-91.

Zajonc, R.B. and McIntosh, D.M. (1992) 'Emotions research: Some promising questions and some questionable promises', *Psychological Science*, 3 (1): 70-4.

Zajonc, R.B., Murphy, S.T. and McIntosh, D.M. (1993) 'Brain temperature and subjective emotional experience', in M. Lewis and J.M. Haviland (eds), *Handbook of Emotions*. New York: Guilford Press.

Zillman, D. (1983) 'Transfer of excitation in emotional behavior', in J.T. Cacioppo and R.E. Petty (eds), *Social Psychophysiology: A Sourcebook*. New York: Guilford Press.

Chapter 11

'Facial Expressions of Emotion' and the Delusion of the Hermetic Self

Alan J. Fridlund and Bradley Duchaine

In this chapter, we try to show how the standard thinking about facial expressions both discloses and perpetuates our implicit views about the nature of the self. Specifically, we contend that the mythic power of the romanticist Rousseauian view of human nature, which pits a natural and passionate 'authentic' self against a Janusian social self, explains our uncritical acceptance of the standard 'Emotions View' of the human face. Then we give examples of how contemporary evolutionary and biological thinking afford us a glimpse of a new way to understand what our faces do and how they serve us. This 'Behavioral Ecology View' implies a primordially social self – one that emerges from social interaction and transforms even ostensibly 'nonsocial' actions into social ones.

The 'emotions view' of faces as ideology

In the process of writing *Human Facial Expression: An Evolutionary View* (Fridlund, 1994), and in earlier papers (e.g., Fridlund, 1991a, 1992b), the first author reviewed much of the literature on human facial expressions, and summarized the 'emotions view' of faces that typified the research of the 1970s and 80s and is still popular today.

This emotions view was a corpus of contentions that bore upon the universality, emotionality, innateness, and 'authenticity' of facial displays. These are all classic issues, and the emotions view had – or so we thought – conveniently answered each, often with some supporting data. Here is how the recitation went:

1 Between 5 to 7 facial expressions occurred universally.
2 These canonical expressions were 'recognized' universally.
3 What was recognized universally in these facial expressions was 'emotion'.
4 By inference, there must be 5–7 universal, categorical emotions.
5 By virtue of their universality, the canonical facial expressions (and the emotions they express) must be innate.

6   Because the canonical facial expressions express emotion, they are 'authentic' expressions of ourselves.

7   Facial expressions of emotion (or the emotions they expressed) that departed from the 5–7 categorical ones were actually blends or mixtures of them.

8   Socialization, especially in childhood, could decouple facial expressions of emotion from the emotions they originally expressed.

9   The faces that resulted from socialization, because they became decoupled from the emotions they originally expressed, were no longer 'expressions' of the 'authentic self' but were dissimulations arising from the 'social self'.

10 Dissimulated 'social' faces are directed by internalized 'cultural display rules'.

11 Deception 'leaks' onto the face because of the incomplete suppression of the expressions of our 'authentic' selves by the dissimulated presentation of the 'social' self.

This emotions view of faces is schematized in Figure 11.1. It is a 'two-factor view' (Fridlund, 1994) which depicts human facial actions as authentic expressions of released emotion, which are suppressed, exaggerated, transmuted, or even 'faked' by the enculturated self.

The inclusiveness of this model was remarkable. All facial expressions were either identifiable as one or a combination of innate, canonical faces, and the exceptions were conventional dissimulations. Cynically, one might remark that the model survived by incorporating its own exceptions.

One view that could answer so many questions was compelling. Who wouldn't want closure? The problem is that we all got religion too soon, because many of the planks in this emotions view platform were considered either axiomatic or definitively answered are now suspect (for reviews see Fridlund, 1994; Russell, 1994). In hindsight, it appears that we fell prey to a sort of conjunction fallacy – the error of concluding that if *some* tenets are reasonable or true, then the whole edifice must be intact and allowed to stand (Tversky and Kahneman, 1988). The premature acceptance of the emotions view made it an ideology perpetuated more by arguments *ex cathedra* than a decisive body of data. Instead, we should have been more analytical and hewed instead to the truism that chains of evidence, like real ones, are only as strong as their weakest links.

Why the emotions view was so seductive

Why weren't we more astute? Why didn't we regard the emotions view skeptically as just another theory to evaluate? As discussed in *Human Facial Expression* and elsewhere (Fridlund, 1991a, 1992b, 1994), as an ideology the emotions view 'seemed true' because it conformed to a romanticist preconception of human nature that has become thoroughly embedded in Western cultures (Parrott and Sabini, 1989). When the

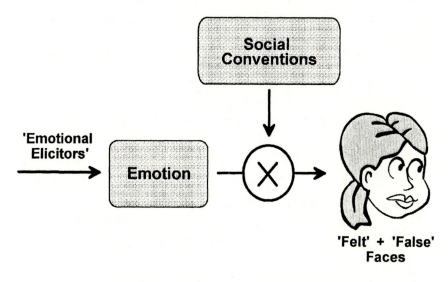

Figure 11.1 *Schematic of the two-factor model that underlies the common emotions view of facial expressions. In this model, everyday faces result from innate, prototypical facial expressions that read out emotional state, but which can be modified by socialization.*

emotions view posited a set of universal, natural 'authentic' expressions, this played into the romanticist sentiment that there is some 'natural' part of ourselves that is basic, insular and innate. And when dissimulative departures from the natural expressions were claimed to result from contamination by culture, this accorded entirely with the romanticist's assumption that our pristine natures are pitted against the forces of society that alienate us from our true selves and dictate that we conform via artifice. In this *Weltanshauung*, we are all 'two-faced' – we are Janus-like creatures who must reconcile the drives and passions of our 'true' natures with the marching orders of social life.

Sound familiar? It should. This is, of course, the romanticist doctrine of the philosopher Jean-Jacques Rousseau (e.g., his 1750 *Discourse on the Arts and Sciences*; Rousseau, 1950, and see Babbitt, 1919), who oxymoronically termed the human being a 'noble savage'. His pitting of a primitive, passionate natural self against a rational but corrupted social one neatly fits nearly all aspects of the emotions view of facial expressions of emotion. This is outlined in Table 11.1.

As Table 11.1 indicates, the emotions view posits that 'emotional' and 'social' faces, respectively: (1) belong to the 'animal' (primitive and impulsive) vs. 'human' (noble and rational) parts of our nature; (2) appear in natural (i.e., solitary) vs. civil (public) contexts; (3) owe to emotion vs. social convention; (4) are authentic (portraying 'real' feeling) vs. deceptive (representing Rousseau's 'corrupted', dissembling social self); (5) are released vs. deployed; with a quality (e.g., temporality) that is (6) reflexive

Table 11.1   *Romanticist* Leitmotif *underlying 'two-factor' theories of facial expression*

Aspect of expression	'Emotional' expressions	'Social' expressions
Creature domain	Animal (savage)	Human (noble)
Context of occurrence	Natural (private)	Civil (public)
Type of issuance	Released	Rule-governed
Quality of expression	Reflexive	Instrumental
Veridicality	Authentic	Deceptive
Governing mechanism	Endogenous 'facial affect programs'	Exogenous 'cultural display rules
Neurological bases	Subcortical ('passion')	Neocortical ('will', 'reason')

vs. instrumental; (7) are governed by endogenous 'facial affect programs' vs. exogenous 'display rules'; and (8) are instigated by 'primitive' subcortical 'emotional' parts of the brain vs. more recent neocortical 'willful' parts.

We believe that this romanticized view is so appealing and therefore so seductive simply because it is so flattering. While it admits to the taint of worldly duplicity, it sustains our belief that we have an 'authentic self', independent of the exigencies of social relations, that manifests itself in heartfelt emotion erupting on our faces. Put more theologically (Rousseau, after all, just re-expressed the Protestant doctrine of the Fall of Man), our 'self' is but a Soul caught in a struggle to preserve its Divinity amid the constant temptation to sin – and thus, no matter how corrupt we *act*, there is the young innocent somewhere 'inside' that is what we *are*.

Whether or not the transcendentalist and crypto-theological theme of Rousseau's view makes for good philosophy or workable theology, the 'two-factor' emotion view based upon it (depicted in Figure 11.1) makes for bad science. This is because, as detailed in *Human Facial Expression*, it depended upon several outmoded concepts. Among them, it:

• proposed a dichotomous, propositional view of displays as 'true' or 'false' (i.e., 'authentic' or 'inauthentic') based upon whether they – as presupposed – indicated the correct emotion.
• endorsed the recapitulationist notion that phylogenetically 'primitive' areas in our brain are held in check by other, more 'advanced' parts, and given this, that 'emotional' faces are based in more basic (primitive) biology. Conversely, the 'primitive' brain regions responsible for producing 'facial expressions of emotion' constitute evidence for the criticality of emotion in facial displays.

- was predicated upon an outdated concept of displays that conceives of them as issuing from the context-free, releaser-driven mechanisms of early ethology, which became recast as hermeutic emotion 'circuits' or 'facial affect programs'.
- assumed that we are innately innocent and egocentric, and must therefore *acquire* a social cognition.

In this chapter we consider just the first proposition, that there are 'authentic' displays of emotion which are interfered with by the dis-simulated faces of the 'social self'. We discuss two assumptions researchers commonly make which inadvertently perpetuate this divided-self, two-factor view of facial expression. These assumptions are: (1) that solitary faces are non-'social' and are thus the purest expressions of the emotional 'authentic' self; and (2) that studies of 'cultural display rules', particularly the oft-cited Japanese-American experiment, demonstrate how culture alters those authentic, solitary faces.

Assumption 1: Solitary faces represent the emergence of the 'emotional' self

Solitary faces do of course occur, and this fact is often touted as definitive evidence for some faces being by nature readouts or expressions of emotion rather than social communicative displays (see Buck, 1984, 1985; Cacioppo and Tassinary, 1987). As Buck put it,

> When a sender is alone . . . he or she should feel little pressure to present a proper image to others, and any emotion expression under such circumstances should be more likely to reflect an actual motivational/emotional state. (1984: 20)

Ekman took the same tack when he described a study of differences in facial displays among Japanese and Americans (explored in detail later). Ekman (1984) stated, 'In private, when no display rules to mask expression were operative, we saw the biologically based, evolved, universal facial expressions of emotion'. The most pointed declaration of the reliance of the emotions view upon the supposed emotional nature of solitary faces was provided by Ekman et al., who stated, 'Facial expressions do occur when people are alone . . . and contradict the theoretical proposals of those who view expressions solely as social signals' (1990: 351).

The belief that faces observed in solitude constitute the definitive evidence for 'facial expressions of emotion' is instantiated in the experiments typically conducted by proponents of the emotions view. Experimental subjects are usually isolated in a laboratory room and presented various kinds of 'emotional' elicitors. Many of these are depicted in the panels of Figure 11.2. These include panels: (*a*) face-to-face contact; (*b*) contact through a partition or laboratory wall; (*c*) watching television; (*d*) imagery tasks; and (*e*) viewing slides. Because subjects are physically alone in panels

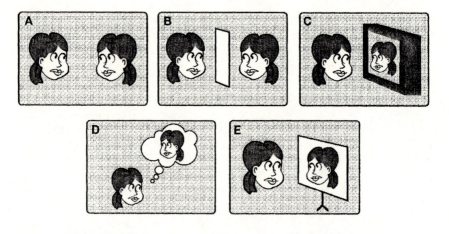

Figure 11.2 *Common methods of eliciting 'facial expressions of emotion' in the laboratory, arranged to show that they are disguised manipulations of sociality (see text for description). The implicit sociality in these manipulations mitigates the assumption that the facial displays issued by subjects who are physically alone are pure 'facial expressions of emotion' unaffected by social convention.*

(*b*) to (*e*), any facial displays elicited in subjects are considered 'expressions of emotion'. The exception is panel (*a*), face-to-face contact, which is considered 'social' and therefore produces a combination of both emotional and conventional faces.

Contrary to this categorization, we contend that a binary view of what is 'social' and what is 'non-social' is too absolutist. It is much more reasonable to suggest instead that the manipulations in Figure 11.2 vary in their sociality. Everyone considers face-to-face contact (*a*) quite social, but does speaking through a glass or partition (*b*) make it non-social? We think not, but then what if the glass is a CRT faceplate (*c*)? Asserting that watching a televised image is not social would be news to soap-opera lovers who consider the characters to be intimate acquaintances, and to sports fans who throw things at the screen. And what if the image is not on the CRT, but in our mind's eye (*d*)? Finally, what if we freeze a frame of an image and show a photo (*e*)? Would this make viewing a face non-social? Not necessarily, as sales of baby and family albums would attest; the photos in them are not mere spots of chromatic dye; they are cues to the reconstruction of interactions (i.e., panel *d*). In this sense, a still image of a face is a projective stimulus. When a patient examines a TAT card and begins to shake, blanch, and then burst into tears, it's not the ink on the card. Ditto for still images, but their use has nevertheless been canonized as the 'slide-viewing technique' (Buck, 1979), and pictorial depictions were used in nearly all studies of 'facial expressions of emotion' among different populations (see Russell, 1994).

Sociality does not conform to the All-or-None Law. Instead, the varying types of 'emotional elicitors' in Figure 11.2 represent simply different kinds of sociality. Even when an interactant has been physically removed from the room, he or she may still be present psychologically. This implicit sociality view is far from novel. Wundt (1896), Piderit (see Piderit, 1858, 1886), Gratiolet (1865), and Ribot (1897) all proposed 'imaginary object' accounts of solitary faces made toward absent others. Gratiolet, for example, provided the case of the indignant man who clenches his teeth (and, perhaps, his fists) toward an absent adversary. People may *blush* in private, a fact difficult to explain without imagining embarrassment in front of fantasized others. As Piderit (1858) stated, 'The muscular movements of expression are in part related to imaginary objects, and in part to imaginary sensory impressions. In this proposition lies the key to the comprehension of all expressive muscular movements.'

Darwin knew this argument. Unfortunately, he disposed of it peremptorily (Darwin, 1872: 6–8). We believe that this was due to his overriding interest in building a Lamarckian, reflexive model of faces as vestiges of once-serviceable habits (Fridlund, 1992b; Montgomery, 1985). In fact, Darwin had settled on the three principles of expression before he had completed many of his observations; they were contained in his *M* and *N* notebooks, which he began as early as 1838 (Gruber, 1974). With Darwin's success in explaining evolution in terms of natural selection, his 'latest hobby horse; (Browne, 1985), an emotional-reflexive view of expressions, became popular. This popularity led to the rise of the emotions view of faces as readouts, the 'decognitivizing' of solitary faces, and a longstanding neglect of imaginary objects accounts.

Darwin's disposal of implicit sociality in the *Expressions* volume was probably strategic. In that volume he aimed to show continuity by likening human faces to non-human movements. In *The Descent of Man*, he took the reverse tack, and tried to show that non-humans were strikingly similar to humans (i.e., they had dreams, memories, imagination, pride, shame, etc.). In this volume, he *endorsed* the concept of implicit sociality. It was an endorsement ignored by subsequent emotion theorists:

> Now with those animals which live permanently in a body, the social instincts are ever present and persistent . . . So it is with ourselves. Even when we are quite alone, how often do we think with pleasure or pain of what others think of us – of their imagined approbation or disapprobation; and all this follows from sympathy, a fundamental element of the social instincts. (Darwin, 1871: 114)

It seems obvious to us that the physical presence of others is one of the *least* important ways of assessing the sociality of facial displays. There are several ways in which people can be structurally alone, with their facial behavior implicitly social:

First, *when we are alone we often treat ourselves as interactants*. We talk to ourselves; reward or punish ourselves; hit, touch and stroke ourselves; and deploy facial displays in the course of these acts. Can it be said that talking to ourselves is not communicative, but a 'readout'? If so, what is being read out? In this sense, the faces made to oneself are as communicative as our 'self-talk'. That we are social interactants with ourselves at first seems absurdly solipsistic, but it is entirely consistent with views that emphasize the 'private, authentic self' as a social construction (Mead, 1934), and the dialogical nature of thought as internalized speech (Bakhtin, 1981; Vygotsky, 1962; Wertsch, 1985).

Second, *we often act as if others are present when they are not*. We curse them, or utter words of love to them, or rehearse what we will say to them when we see them. In many of these acts we deploy facial displays. Our acting as if others are there when they are not is usually done with prior knowledge of their absence (e.g., practicing for a play, talk, or interview). Occasionally it is done without prior knowledge of others' absence, as when we speak to, and make faces to, a person we believe is in the next room – when the other has in fact departed, and can no longer hear us. With or without prior knowledge, these faces, too, are communicative, although they are emitted when we are alone.

Third, *we often imagine that others are present when they are not*. In our imagination we engage in interactions with others who are not there, i.e., we 'simulate' interaction with them. We imagine talking to them, arguing with them, making love with them, and throughout these acts, we deploy facial displays. As in the previous example, we usually have prior knowledge that the others are absent. However, we sometimes become lost in reverie, and we momentarily forget that the imaginary others are actually absent. The facial displays made in reverie are also social and communicative, both when we are lost in reverie and *believe* they are there, and when we know that they are not. When we imagine a lover, and then smile and become sexually aroused, if we say that the smile was nonsocial, would we say that the arousal was non-sexual?

The importance of this kind of implicit audience as a mediator of solitary faces has been documented in several experiments. Fridlund et al. (1990) employed standard affective imagery procedures and established the role of imaginary audiences in mediating private faces. Subjects provided, and were then asked to imagine, situations that they enjoyed either alone (low-social) or with other people (high-social). We measured smiling during the imagery using facial electromyography (EMG) overlying the *zygomatic major* muscles, and asked subjects to rate how happy they felt during the imagery. These happiness ratings were then controlled statistically. Subjects showed more EMG activity in their *zygomatic major* sites in high-social than low-social imagery, even when their happiness ratings were equalized. For Fridlund et al., this increase implied that subjects were displaying to the 'people in their heads'. Fridlund et al. (1992) later extended these findings to dysphoric imagery using a standard imagery protocol.

Fridlund (1991b) attempted to circumvent the slipperiness of imagery manipulations by directly manipulating implicit audiences. Subjects watched an amusing videotape in one of four viewing conditions: (1) alone; (2) alone, but with the belief that a friend nearby was engaged in an irrelevant task;

(3) alone, but with the belief that a friend nearby was viewing the same videotape in another room; and (4) when a friend was physically present. Viewers' smiles were measured using facial electromyography (EMG) over the *zygomatic major* muscles responsible for smiling. Smiling (measured using EMG) among solitary viewers who believed a friend was viewing nearby equalled that shown in the actual presence of the friend, but was greater than that shown by subjects who simply viewed alone. Reported happiness did not differ among the viewing conditions, and within conditions it correlated negligibly with smiling.

Similar findings emerged from another study involving gradations in sociality. Chovil (1991) visually coded the types of gestures made in different social contexts. Her subjec (here, all females) heard stories about close calls in one of four conditions: (1) alone, from an audio tape recording; (2) alone, over the telephone; (3) from another subject across a partition; and (4) talking to another subject face-to-face. When these conditions were ordered according to their 'psychological presence', as determined by separate raters, Chovil's subjects exhibited facial displays – largely wincing and grimacing – that increased monotonically with sociality, a finding that mapped nearly identically onto that provided by Fridlund (1991a).

In these sociality studies, face-to-face interaction resulted in maximal facial behavior. This should not always be the case, however, because in many contexts we do *not* issue communications to others. Friends sharing a humorous experience face-to-face should exhibit greater facial behavior than if they are separated by a partition; friends asked to play poker should make less. One important determinant of our facial behavior is our social role with respect to our potential interactants. Commuters on a subway may be within inches of each other yet pretend not to notice; if they are friends, however, their talk and facial behavior may be incessant. (There are exceptions, as when we 'spill our guts' to a total stranger on a plane, and here, our faces pour out with our words). Just this kind of finding was reported by Wagner and Smith (1991), who videotaped pairs of subjects while they 'rated their emotions' to slides. The facial behavior of the subjects was more discernible if the two were friends than if they were strangers. In the behavioral ecology view, the subjects' faces were no more than a running commentary on the series of slides. Had they been permitted, the friends would have chatted while they made faces; and the strangers would have done neither. And it is hard to strip an experiment of the influence of such social roles. To the solitary subject, the experiment is a judge and the subject is in temporary solitary confinement awaiting parole for 'good behavior'. Two male or two female subjects in the same room may make a contest out of the experiment, whereas an experiment with a (heterosexual) male-female pair may become a 'blind date'.

Fourth, *we often forecast interaction and deploy displays appropriately*, consciously or not, even though no interactant is immediately present. These displays function in the service of seeking or shunning interaction. Most species have displays that function to deter potential interactants. In both gorillas and humans, a tongue-showing display deters others (Smith et al., 1974; Dolgin and Sabini, 1982). If we are in a bad mood, we scowl upon entering the office in the morning; the scowl discourages potential greeting. On the other hand, solicitation of interaction is omnipresent (cf., the 'readiness to interact' displays described by Smith, 1977). We deploy a smile seconds before greeting a neighbor at the front door. As T.S. Eliot stated, 'I must prepare a face to meet the faces that I meet.' Indeed, Kraut and Johnston (1979) found that bowlers were very unlikely to smile when they had just made a spare or strike, but were very likely to do so when they turned around to meet the gaze of those in their bowling party. And like the bird who calls continuously in case a suitable mate should fly past (Smith, 1977), the human infant solving a problem deploys a 'cognitive mastery' smile (Sroufe and Waters, 1976). The smile usually seduces any potential pedagogues who may encounter the infant.

This was confirmed by Sue Jones and colleagues, who developed an infant analog to Kraut and Johnston's (1979) bowling study. Infants were positioned such that they could either look at toys or at their mothers, and Jones et al. observed their facial behavior toward each. As early as 10 months of age, infant smiling was almost entirely dependent upon visual contact with the caregiver (Jones and Raag, 1989; Jones et al., 1991)

Fifth, *we often treat non-humans, and animate and inanimate objects, as interactants.* That we often treat non-human animals as humans is self-evident to any pet owner. We talk to them, confide in them, praise and curse them, and make faces and gesture to them. Most people have no difficulty according pets agency and treating them as autonomous inter-actants. What is more reluctantly acknowledged is the extent to which we accord agency to inanimate objects and regard *them* as interactants. Devotees of indoor gardening talk, gesture and make faces to their houseplants. Children do the same to their stuffed animals, dolls or toy soldiers. In outbursts of animism, most of us have pummeled intransigent soda machines that 'stole our money' or television sets that 'lost our station', or gesticulated wildly at willful, errant bowling balls, and in so doing we scolded them, called them names – and in the act, we made faces and gestures.

In new research on 'the animism of everyday life', Fridlund and Duchaine (1996) administered questionnaires to 700 undergraduates asking about the extent of their everyday animistic behavior. Students were polled regarding common ways in which we treat inanimate objects animistically: giving them names, speaking to them, acting non-verbally toward them, and holding them to conventions about social reciprocity (feeling cheated by them, or guilty about abandoning them). We also asked about the most common objects to receive such treatment. Table 11.2 shows subjects' responses.

As Table 11.2 shows, many students reported making faces to inanimate objects. Rates of animistic face-making, depending on the object, ranged from 2 percent to 28 percent of subjects. Over 20 percent reported making

Table 11.2 *Facial expressions made to inanimate objects (self-report)*

Inanimate object type	Percentage of *Ss* reporting facial expressions toward*
1 Alarm clocks	21.9
2 Answering/FAX/copy machines	18.1
3 Automobiles	8.7
4 Balls in games (softball, golf, etc.)	5.9
5 Bicycles	4.6
6 Computers	21.7
7 Elevators	7.6
8 Food	27.9
9 Household appliances	14.7
10 Houseplants	3.7
11 Musical instruments	5.1
12 Nonsexual body parts	12.4
13 Sexual body parts (genitals)	6.6
14 Soda machines	12.7
15 Television sets	26.1
16 Video games	19.4
17 Weather	18.3
18 Other object	2.1

*$N = 700$

faced toward such everyday items as alarm clocks, computers, food (probably reflecting judgments about taste), and television sets. We believe that these findings are conservative, given that subjects may not remember or be aware of their animistic face-making, and furthermore may not be willing to disclose its extent.

Is this implicit sociality account viable? In the implicit sociality view, implicit or imaginal interactants can never be excluded. Even recruiting subjects alone and leading them to believe that they are 'unobserved' (e.g., using a hidden camera) do not eliminate the implicit social context. At the limit, the *experimenters* still constitute an implicit audience; with the wall of the laboratory – with the experimenters behind it – constituting a de facto partition condition just as in Figure 11.2(b). The power of such an arrangement is commonly acknowledged as 'experimental demand', 'experimenter effects', or 'evaluation apprehension' (Latané, 1981).

Subjects' thoughts will *always* be populated, whether by thoughts or images either of the experimenter, or the others in their lives, or even themselves, and moreover, we convert inanimate objects into interactants. Fridlund (1994) called this process *restitutional interaction* (after Bleuler). Achieving pure 'aloneness' is thus a *reductio ad absurdum* that would require narcotization so complete that daydreaming stops, and this would terminate most overt subject behavior, not just facial movement. This fact carries a major implication for the laboratory study of facial behavior: it undercuts any presumption that isolating subjects or minimizing their physical contact with others actually 'purifies' their facial productions in any way. In other words, our solitary faces are just as conventional as our 'social' ones. When subjects are alone versus in the presence of others, what differs is not the 'amount' of sociality, but its directness, or the degree to which one's social engagement is entrained to *specifiable* others, that is, those planted in the room by the experimenter.

It might be objected that the implicit sociality view, then, is non-disconfirmable. In fact, it probably is unfalsifiable *in extremis*, but this is no impediment to its viability as a scientific concept. This feature is shared with many useful and established theories whose limiting cases are unattainable. There are several example. Superconductivity theory is alive and well. Despite the fact that the temperature of absolute zero is probably unattainable, potent and useful superconductivity effects can be observed as one approaches it. Similarly, special relativity theory holds that traveling at the speed of light is unattainable, but relativistic effects are well documented as the velocities of experimentally induced particle approach it. And scientists of all ilks – including psychologists themselves – exploit daily the utility of the natural logarithm, even though *in*(0) is entirely undefined. Like these well-established theories and entities, implicit sociality can be studied quite easily within experimentally manipulable ranges.

The strict falsifiability objection is also instructive, in that it reveals the extent to which we view most animals (especially humans) atomistically, instead of as components of, and agents within, an encompassing web of social relations – even when alone (see Mead, 1934). Indeed, 'solitude' – not implicit sociality – may be the odder concept.

Assumption 2: 'Display rules' represent the intrusion of the 'social self'

As mentioned earlier, the emotions view presupposes the universality of 'facial expressions of emotion', with any cultural differences in facial behavior necessarily due to cultural conventions about expression. The best-developed formulation of this concept is Ekman's 'cultural display rules' (Ekman and Friesen, 1969; Ekman, 1972), which comprise part of his 'neurocultural model' of facial expression. Display rules are 'overlearned habits about who can show what emotion to whom and when they can show it', and they ostensibly circumvent issuance of 'the biologically based, evolved, universal expressions of emotion' (Ekman, 1984: 320–1). In accordance with training or tradition, display rules are said to interfere with the patterned muscular output of the 'facial affect program' triggered by one's emotional state, in one of four ways: (1) attenuation; (2) histrionic intensification; (3) neutralization (i.e., making a 'poker face'); and (4) masking or camouflage with another type of face (Ekman, 1972: 225). Display rules could exert their effects at nearly any point ranging from the initial elicitation of an emotion, to the volley of neural activity to the facial muscles:

> Habits regarding the control of facial appearance . . . can interfere with the operation of the facial affect program, early or late in the sequence of internal events, in one of four ways: (a) they can prevent activation of the facial affect program with or without also preventing any other registration of emotion; or (b) if the facial affect program has been activated, they can prevent triggering of the facial muscles; or (c) if the facial muscles have been triggered, they can either interrupt the muscular contractions, making the appearance changes quite brief, or diminish the extent or scope of the muscular contractions, making the changes in appearance less pronounced; or (d) whether or not the facial muscles have been triggered by the facial affect program, these habits can override and thus mask with a different set of muscular contractions those directed by the affect program (Ekman, 1972: 217).

Ontological problems with the concept of 'cultural display rules'

Given any emotional state, people may make different faces in public than in private, with the public faces being distortions of the emotional faces that would naturally (i.e., in private) erupt by virtue of emotion. Obviously the display rules concept relies upon the premise that one's emotional state in public *could* be equivalent to one's state in private. Unfortunately, Ekman's neurocultural model does not specify criteria for discerning the occurrence of emotion independent of facial action. This point is crucial when we consider cultural display rules. Without independent criteria for emotion, how could one ever determine whether an individual's behavior indicated the operation of a cultural display rule? Within the emotions view, any differences in facial movements might simply reflect differences in emotion.

An example will clarify this point. An adult male who has suffered a loss should typically not cry in public, even if he cries copiously in private. This norm is often cited as a cultural display rule (see Ekman, 1972: 226). But the individual who is suffering in private may merely feel sad; in public, he may alternatively feel: (1) afraid of ridicule for crying; (2) guilty about foisting his suffering upon others; (3) relieved that he is not suffering alone; (4) angry that he cannot 'let out his tears', (5) humiliated if the loss engendered a fall in social status, etc. Any of these other emotional states would be more likely to co-occur with one's sadness when one is in public. According to the classical emotions view, any of these emotions would trigger its own facial expression; thus, the face made in public would represent not 'managed sadness', but sadness in combination with the ancillary emotions engendered by others' presence. Conceivably, the man who cries in private but refrains in public may merely be managing his facial muscles (and diaphragm) out of habit. However, invoking this display rules account requires that his emotional state must not differ in public vs. in private. This state of affairs would be most improbable.

Purported evidence for 'cultural display rules'

What constitutes the evidence for cultural display rules? Many studies claim to investigate display rules, but they either: (1) ask subjects to verbalize their beliefs about the appropriateness of certain faces in certain contexts, while assuming that these accounts have currency in explaining actual facial behavior; or (2) examine differences in facial behavior in various situations and then ascribe the difference *ad hoc* to display rules (see Cole, 1985, for review of studies).

Only one experiment was ever designed specifically to demonstrate cultural display rules. This is the study of Japanese vs. United States (hereafter, 'American') students reported by Ekman and Friesen (e.g., Ekman, 1972; Friesen, 1972). Like the 'cross-cultural studies' used to support the 'universality thesis' about facial expressions (Russell, 1994), the Japanese-American study and its conclusion about cultural display rules have gained canonical status, appearing not only in texts on emotion and facial expression, but also in many introductory psychology texts.

Unfortunately, the study and its findings were never described completely or accurately. Most sources depended on Ekman and Friesen's own description of the study and summary of the data. Here is the usual description of the Japanese-American study:

> Research conducted in our laboratory played a central role in settling the dispute over whether facial expressions are universal or specific to each culture. In one experiment, stress-inducing films were shown to college students in the United States and to college students in Japan. Part of the time, each person watched the film alone and part of the time the person watched while talking about the experience with a research assistant from the person's own culture. Measurements of the actual facial movements, captured on videotapes, showed that when they were alone, the Japanese and Americans had virtually identical facial expressions. When in the presence of another person, however, where cultural rules about the management of facial appearance (display rules) would be applied, there was little correspondence between Japanese and American facial expressions. The Japanese masked their facial expressions of unpleasant feelings more than did the Americans. This study was particularly important in demonstrating what about facial expression is universal and what differs for each culture. The universal feature is the distinctive appearance of the face for each of the primary emotions. But people in various cultures differ in what they have been taught about managing or controlling their facial expressions of emotion. (Ekman and Friesen, 1975: 24)

In this description, repeated often by Ekman and tertiary sources, Japanese and Americans viewed a film in each of two conditions, alone and with a same-culture experimenter. The facial expressions for the two groups were identical when subjects were alone, but dissimilar when 'in the presence of another person'. As will be apparent, the description and interpretation are inaccurate. Apart from the issue of reportage, the study itself illustrates the difficulties with the display rules concept. To obtain a fuller description of the Japanese-American display rules study, the first author obtained the unpublished dissertation by W.V. Friesen (1972) from the Microfilm Archives of the University of California.

According to Friesen (1972), the Japanese-American study actually involved *three* experimental conditions, not two as reported subsequently. Here were the conditions (actually phases or episodes, since the same subjects participated in all three):

Phase 1 Twenty-five Japanese and 25 American undergraduate males, each in his own country, individually viewed a total of four movies lasting 20 minutes. The first clip was designed to be mildly pleasant, and showed two men taking a canoe trip. The three remaining clips were intended to be stressful; these included ritual circumcision, a suction-aided delivery, and nasal sinus surgery.

Friesen did not include this solitary viewing phase in his dissertation. Instead, he referred to it as one previously conducted by Ekman, Friesen, and Malmstrom (unpublished), and reported in the chapter by Ekman (1972). Ekman's chapter contains the only published listing of any of the solitary viewing data, and this listing was only fragmentary.

Phase 2 Immediately following the solitary viewing, a graduate student of the subject's own culture entered the viewing room and engaged the subject in a one-minute face-to-face interview about his experience while viewing. The data for this second phase consisted of the subject's facial behavior in response to, and for approximately 10–20 seconds after, the graduate student began the interview with the question, 'How are you feeling right now?' (Friesen, 1972: 75).

Phase 3 Following this initial interview, the graduate student was positioned facing the subject with his back to the viewing screen. The most unpleasant portions of the final stressful clip (the nasal sinus surgery) were replayed. As the replay began, the graduate student resumed his interview with the question, 'Tell me how you feel right now as you look at the film' (Friesen, 1972: 75). The data for this third experimental consisted of about 20–30 seconds of the subject's facial behavior following this question.

For all phases, the subject's facial behavior was viewed and videotaped using a hidden camera. Facial behavior concurrent with speech was excluded. The facial behavior was then coded using the Facial Affect Scoring Technique (Ekman et al., 1971), a predecessor to Ekman and Friesen's Facial Action Coding System (Ekman and Friesen, 1978).

The first condition thus involved solitary viewing, and both the second and third conditions were conducted in the presence of an experimenter. This fact is crucial to the interpretation of the results for the three conditions; we have depicted the data for the stressful films in Figure 11.3. One interpretive problem is that the scoring method used for Phases 2 and 3 by Friesen (1972) differed from that reported for the solitary viewing by Ekman (1972). This prevents direct comparisons between solitary viewing and the two interview conditions (Friesen used part-face scoring; Ekman

274 *The Emotions*

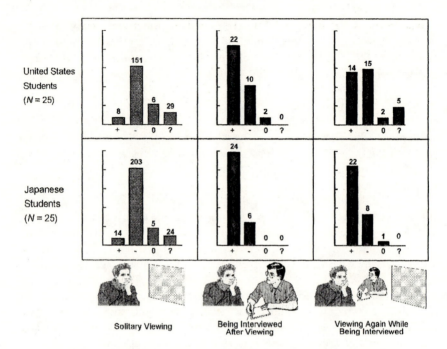

Figure 11.3 *Data from all three conditions of Ekman and Friesen's Japanese-American 'display rules' study. The study was never reported completely or accurately. These data were taken from Ekman's summary (Ekman, 1972), and from W.V. Friesen's unpublished dissertation (Friesen, 1972), as obtained from the Microfilm Archives of the University of California. Contrary to published interpretations of these data, the presence of an interviewer (second panel) produced* no *statistical differences between the facial behavior of the Japanese and American subjects; only when being interviewed* while *watching the films did differences appear. Across the three phases of the experiment, abcissas denote visually scored facial behavior which the experimenters believed indicated: (+) positive emotion and (−) negative emotion. The (0) symbol indicates no facial behavior during that experimental phase (this is a tally of subjects, not facial scores), and (?) signifies the number of facial movements unclassifiable within the coding system. Instances of facial behavior classifiable as concurrent positive and negative emotion were tallied in both categories. Faces classified 'surprise' were excluded. The absolute numbers listed for the Solitary Viewing condition (hatched bars in left panel) are not comparable to those for the two interview conditioned (solid bars in middle and right panels) due to procedural differences in scoring methods.*

reported mostly whole-face scoring data and only fragmentary part-face data).

A further problem is that these data do not depict facial behavior. Instead, subjects were categorized according to whether they showed (1) any 'positive-affect' faces (largely smiles), (2) any 'negative-affect' faces, (3) no facial behavior, or (4) unclassifiable facial behavior.

Inspection of the data in Figure 11.3 leads to three main conclusions:

1   Subjects in the first solitary viewing phase produced a preponderance of putative 'negative' affect' faces, equivalent for the two cultures. Eleven of the 50 subjects made no faces at all despite viewing such gory films.
2   In the second phase, about two-thirds of the faces made during this interview consisted of smiles, with the remainder interpreted as 'negative-affect' faces. Statistical analysis showed *no* differences between the two cultures (Friesen, 1972: 51–3).
3   In this third and final phase, the Japanese did not change either in smiling or negative-affect faces compared with the preceding interview. In contrast, the Americans smiled less and made more 'negative-affect' faces.

The standard interpretation of the findings is that the Americans' faces were more authentic, whereas the Japanese subjects masked their revulsion with a 'false smile' (Ekman, 1985).[1] This interpretation reinforces unfortunate jingoistic stereotypes ('orientals are inscrutable'; cf., Ekman, 1972: 241). It is also unsupportable on five counts. First, without direct comparisons between social and solitary viewing, no statement about 'masking' by the Japanese subjects is tenable. It may well have been that the Americans were histrionic.

Second, about 20 percent of the subjects in the solitary viewing condition (6 Americans and 5 Japanese) displayed no observable facial activity whatsoever. Is it conceivable that the stressful films left all of these subjects entirely unaffected? Moreover, if the Japanese 'masked' their revulsion with a false smile', then why did the 5 Japanese students who made *no* observable facial movements during solitary viewing make smiles during the interview?

Third, cultural differences were found only in the interview-while-viewing condition, and there was no prior basis for believing that any display rules would operate in one interview condition but not for another.

Fourth, subject's facial behavior in the solitary viewing was regarded as 'authentic' and unfettered by display rules; hence the faces were 'emotional'. To repeat Ekman's subsequent summary interpretation of the study:

> In private, when no display rules to mask expression were operative, we saw the biologically based, evolved, universal facial expressions of emotion. In a social situation, we had shown how rules for the management of expression led to culturally different facial expressions. (Ekman, 1984: 321)

As indicated in the previous discussion of implicit sociality, the absolutism about the solitary viewing condition is unwarranted. The Japanese-American study is of course a study of audience effects, and just because the viewer is alone *physically* does not mean that he is alone *psychologically*. Naturally, the experimenter is always an implicit audience, and his or her laboratory is always the stage for the directorial effort known as an 'experiment'. Thus the 'alone' phase of the study was implicitly social, and the two interview phases were simply more explicitly social. Contrasting the facial behavior in the 'alone' vs. interview phases as authentic vs. managed is overstatement at minimum.

It would also be presumptuous to regard subjects' facial activity as unrelated to speech. Even though facial behavior was selected so as to exclude concurrent speech, a facial movement that follows or precedes an utterance may be just as much a modifier of speech as one that occurs concurrently. In other words, much of the subjects' facial behavior was probably facial paralanguage (see Fridlund, 1994).

Finally, most critically, attributing the Japanese-American differences to display rules would, as the definition of display rules stipulates, have required verification that both cultures had equivalent emotions in the condition in which their faces differed. Ekman stipulated this qualification himself when he discussed facial behavior at funerals:

> All too often a common emotional state is inferred simply because the same event was compared. For example, at funerals Culture Y might show down-turned, partially open or trembling lips, inner corners of the brows drawn together and up, and tightened lower lids (the sad face), while Culture X might show up-turned, partially opened lips, deep nasolabial folds, wrinkling in the corners of the eyes, and bagging of the lower eyelid (the broad smiling face). Before declaring that the facial expression of sadness varies across these two cultures, it would be necessary to verify that the stimulus *funeral* normatively elicits the same emotion in the two cultures rather than being an occasion for sadness in one culture and happiness in another. (Ekman, 1972: 215)

By this reasoning, prerequisite to any comparisons of facial behavior in the Japanese-American study would be ensuring equivalence of emotion in the two groups of students. Above, we discussed the lack of independent criteria for emotion as a pitfall of the neurocultural model, and here the problem comes to roost. Ekman's discussion of the study admits this shortcoming (Ekman, 1972: 260), and suggests emotional self-report as possible validation. Curiously, these data were collected and available. After the conclusion of Phase 3, subjects completed questionnaires that inquired about their emotions during the viewing, as well as the entire California Psychological Inventory (Friesen, 1972: 25–6). Surprisingly, these data were not reported or considered either by Ekman (1972) or Friesen (1972).

There is a simpler explanation than masking via display rules to account for the results Friesen reports. Simply stated, the Japanese subjects smiled out of politeness to the graduate student interviewer. Indeed, Japanese custom is to smile when being addressed, especially by an authority. When the film was being replayed, the positioning of the interviewer left subjects the choice to look at him or the film. Although the object of the film replay was to obtain reactions to the film with the interviewer present, it would be rude for the Japanese student to ignore the interviewer who was addressing him, and thus the Japanese students' faces were unaffected by the replay. It would be far less rude for the American student to view the film while being addressed. Thus the cultural difference may not have been in managing facial behavior, but in attending to the film. In the behavioral ecology view, the faces issued by the Japanese and Americans were equally authentic displays of social motives. The Americans were authentically moved to comment facially on the film, whereas the Japanese were authentically moved to show *politesse*.

In cross-cultural studies, social roles and the context of interaction are potential confounds in assessing display rules. Thus in any 'display rules' study, not only must the emotion of the subject be controlled, but one's relation to those to whom one is displaying (i.e., in terms of power, status, obligation, etc.) must be controlled as well. These controls call for careful ethnographic or maturational comparison.[2]

These confounds also apply to studies claiming that at certain ages, children 'learn display rules' (see review by Cole, 1985). In explaining changes in facial behavior in child development, two alternatives must always be excluded: (1) changes in the behavior may be programmed as part of maturation; or (2) the child may learn not about faces but about social roles and contexts, and the appropriate facial role behavior is issued as a consequence. Furthermore, studies of 'display rules' that rely upon verbal accounts about facial manners (Saarni, 1978, 1982) must exclude the possibility that verbal accounts about facial manners may have little to do with actual facial behavior. When they do, they may result from observing one's own facial behavior, rather than as the cause of it.

To put it succinctly, demonstrating the operation of a display rule requires showing that what the individual is doing (and, as required by the neurocultural model, *learning* to do) is merely altering the predisposition to make a facial display by controlling the musculature – and nothing else. It is axiomatic that emotion and intention must be held constant in order to establish that the changes in facial expressions derive only from control of the *face*. Furthermore, attributing any facial behavior to 'display rules' requires that individuals not alter their facial behavior by other strategies (i.e., distracting themselves, inhibiting themselves emotionally, or reframing or reinterpreting the situation).

Thus, although individuals certainly do inhibit their own facial actions (i.e., holding back a belch), there is currently no acceptable evidence that display rules account for normal cultural or developmental differences in facial behavior.

Summary and implications

We have attempted to summarize two key assumptions of the common, 'two-factor' emotions views of facial expression: (1) that solitary faces are non-social and therefore expressions of the 'authentic', 'emotional' self; and (2) that faces observed in public are suppressed, inhibited, or 'masked' versions of the purportedly authentic ones. We hoped to show that, for both assumptions, the conceptual bases are problematic and the experimental support is weak.

The emotions view has outlived its usefulness not only because of its card-house of unsupported assumptions (many were itemized at the beginning of this chapter), and the insurmountable problems associated with some of its key tenets (two of which we detailed), but also because of its forced view of ourselves as split Janus-like between 'authentic' and 'social' selves.

For these reasons, the first author proposed an alternative view of facial expression. This 'behavioral ecology view' (Fridlund, 1991a, 1992b, 1994)[3] is based upon contemporary theory and findings about the evolution (both genetic and cultural) of signaling and social communication. Space allows only a summary.

In contrast to the emotions view, the behavioral ecology view of facial displays does not treat them as 'expressions' of discrete, internal emotional states, or the outputs of modular affect programs. For the contemporary ethologist or the behavioral ecologist, displays have their impact upon others' behavior because vigilance for and comprehension of signals co-evolved with the signals themselves. The balance of signaling and vigilance, countersignaling and countervigilance, produces a signaling 'ecology' that is analogous to the balance of resources and consumers, and predator and prey, that characterize all natural ecosystems.

Displays are specific to intent and context, rather than derivatives or blends of a small set of fundamental emotional displays. Indeed, simultaneously proposing a small set of fundamental affects, and then invoking 'blends' of them to explain why everyday displays are so varied, is considered procrustean, tautological and self-confirming (see Ortony and Turner, 1990, for a critique of theories of 'basic emotions'). Instead of there being six or seven displays of 'fundamental emotions' (for example, anger), there may be one dozen or one hundred 'about to aggress' displays appropriate to the identities and relationship of the interactants, and the context in which the interaction occurs. The topography of an 'about to aggress' display may depend on whether the interactant is dominant or non-dominant, conspecific or extraspecific, and whether one is defending territory or young, contesting for access to a female, or retrieving stolen food or property. Any genetic control might apply to one form but not another. Table 11.3 compares typical facial displays as interpreted by the emotions view and the behavioral ecology view.

Note that we have not depicted prototype faces for each category. This is because, *contra* the emotions view, there may be *no* prototypes faces for each category. Rather, displays exert their influence in the particular context of their issuance; a face interpreted as 'contemptuous' in one context may be interpreted as 'exasperated' or even 'constipated' in another (Russell, 1994, provided the evidence here). The table simply illustrates the kinds of descriptors that each view applies to facial displays. Thus, in

Table 11.3 *Emotions and behavioral ecology interpretations of common human facial displays*

Emotions view ('Facial expressions of emotion')	Behavioral ecology view (Signification of intent)
'Felt' ('Duchenne') smile (expression of happiness)	Readiness to play or affiliate ('Let's play [keep playing]', or 'Let's be friends')
'False' smile (feigned happiness)	Readiness to appease ('Whatever you say', or 'I give in')
'Sad' face	Recruitment of succor ('Take care of me', or 'Hold me')
'Anger' face	Readiness to attack ('Back off or I'll attack')
'Leaked' anger (inhibited anger)	Conflict about attacking ('I want to attack and I don't want to attack')
'Fear' face	Readiness to submit or escape ('Don't hurt me')
'Contentment' face	Readiness to continue current interaction ('Everything [you're doing] is just fine')
'Contempt' face	Declaration of superiority ('I can't even bother with you')
'Poker' face (suppressed emotion)	Declaration of neutrality ('I'm taking no position [on what you're doing or saying]')

contexts in which one would try to appease another, any smile one issued would tend to be labeled a 'false smile' in the emotions view, which would connote a masking smile over some other emotion. For the behavioral ecologist, the same smile would likely be labeled an 'about to appease' display and it would deliver the same message as the words 'I give in' or 'Whatever you say'.

Because facial displays are the results of a formalized coevolution with vigilance for them, they are not readouts but 'social tools' (Smith, 1977) that aid the negotiation of social encounters. Andrew captured the distinction when, in decrying the notion that instinct-like emotion underlies display, he stated, 'It is probably truer for a man to say 'I would like to hit you' than for him to say 'I am angry' (1963: 5). As Andrew's quote should not be construed to say that displays *express* intent; this would be yet another 'readout' view. Instead, displays are declarations that signify our trajectory in a given social interaction, i.e., what we will do in the current situation, or what we would like the other to do. And this 'context' depends considerably not only on the structural features of the situation, but on the succession of interactants' displays and their responses to them. This is similar to the notion (Clark and Brennan, 1991) that conversations are the progressive accumulation of common ground: actions at prior times in the course of an act constitute the context for current actions in that act. . . .

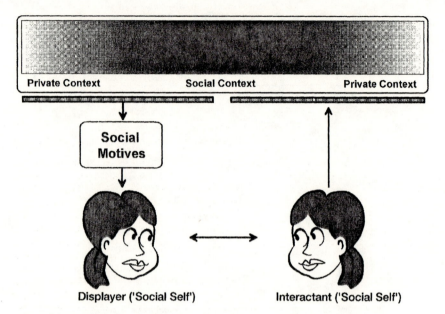

Figure 11.4 *The behavioral-ecology view of facial displays, showing that displays are issued in the service of social motives, and are interpretable in the context of interaction.*

And the current actions become incorporated as part of the context for subsequent actions.

Our conception of the behavioral ecology view is depicted in Figure 11.4. It is meant to contrast with the two-factor emotions view model in Figure 11.1. The figure makes obvious that the 'facial expressions of emotion' of the emotions view actually serve the social motives of the displayer. No distinction is made between 'felt' and 'false' displays issued by 'authentic' and 'social' selves; instead *all* displays are considered to arise out of social interaction, thus there is *only* a social self. Finally, displays are deployed and interpreted within the context of the interaction ('social context' in the figure). This context is formed from both its structural features (e.g., the setting as well as the relations of the interactants), and the accreted 'common ground' that arises from any previous interactions. Finally, the 'private context' of the participants consists of that set of expectations, needs, etc., that each brings to the interaction, and these in turn result in great part from one's prior interactions. For this reason, the figure depicts the interactants private contexts as melding with their shared social context.

Plainly, the behavioral ecology view is less romantic. There is no fundamental, innocent 'authentic' self to lose, because we are born into a social matrix, and evolved to maximal advantage within it. Facial displays have meanings in the social context of their issuance, and they reflect not any 'true' self or hermetic emotions but one's motives within a specific context of interaction. Adopting this view of faces and jettisoning two-factor emotion theories – and their hermetic, divided view of the 'self' – will obviously not be automatic or easy, because it will require our adopting new conceptions of ourselves.

Notes

Portions of this chapter are from Fridlund (1994), reprinted with permission.

1 Ekman and Friesen (1982) drew from Duchenne's observations (Duchenne, 1859/1990) in asserting that some facial expressions were 'felt' because they portrayed emotion (e.g., 'happy' smiles), and others were 'false' because they did not (e.g., the smiles in the Japanese-American study). They believed that these smiles differed in timing and topography, and data were collected to support this interpretation (Ekman et al., 1990). This felt/false view makes sense only if smiles are assumed *a priori* to portray happiness. In the behavioral ecology view, the smile of appeasement or politesse may have different timing and topography than the smile of play or amusement, but it is no less authentic. The felt/false dichotomy is erroneous because it: (1) so closely relates faces to emotion; (2) discounts as 'false' those faces that arise in the service of social motives like appeasement, placation, compliance, submission, and face-saving ('embarrassment'); and (3) ignores the probabilistic relation of display to behavior (Smith, 1985).

2 Importantly, this position is consistent with either genetic or epigenetic accounts of the faces made by the two cultures. Even if all facial displays were under substantial genetic control, a display could occur in one culture but not another because the social roles and contexts that release the displays are present in one culture but not the other. Indeed, the role specificity itself could be genetically determined. It is possible that humans are 'wired' to smile when addressed by certain kinds of authority, but only in Japanese culture did the graduate student interviewer possess the kind of authority requisite for the smiling.

3 'Behavioral ecology' is, technically, the branch of zoology in which behavior is examined for the ways that it contributes to reproductive success (see Krebs and Davies, 1987). Behavioral ecologists thus study how behavior emerges within an animal's 'ecology', that is, within its social organization and its environmental niche. Because it conceives of expressive movements and receptivity for them as highly interdependent, the terms 'interactional' or 'communicative' could easily be substituted.

References

Andrew, R.J. (1963) 'The origin and evolution of the calls and facial expressions of the primates', *Behaviour*, 20: 1–109.

Babbitt, I. (1919) *Rousseau and Romanticism*. New York: Houghton and Mifflin Co.

Baer, K.E. von (1828) *Entwicklungsgeschichte der Thiere: Beobachtung und Reflexion*. Königsberg, Germany: Bornträger.

Bakhtin, M.M. (1981) *The Dialogical Imagination* (M. Holquist, ed.). Austin, TX: University of Texas Press.

Browne, J. (1985) 'Darwin and the expression of the emotions', in D. Kohn (ed.), *The Darwinian Heritage*. Princeton: Princeton University Press. pp. 307–26.

Buck, R. (1979) 'Measuring individual differences in the nonverbal communication of affect: the slide-viewing paradigm', *Human Communication Research*, 6: 47–57.

Buck, R. (1984) *The Communication of Emotion*. New York: Guilford.

Buck, R. (1985) 'Prime theory: An integrated view of motivation and emotion', *Psychological Review*, 92: 389–413.

Cacioppo, J.T. and Tassinary, L.G. (1987) 'The relationship between EMG response and overt facial actions', *Face Value*, 1: 2–3.

Chovil, N. (1991) 'Social determinants of facial displays', *Journal of Nonverbal Behavior*, 15: 141–54.

Clark, H.H. and Brennan, S.E. (1991) 'Grounding in communication', in L.B. Resnick, J.M. Levine and S.D. Teasley (eds), *Perspectives in Socially Shared Cognition*. Washington, DC: American Psychological Association. pp. 127–49.

Cole, P.M. (1985) 'Display rules and socialization', in G. Zivin (ed.), *The Development of Expressive Behavior*. Orlando, FL: Academic Press. pp. 27–50.

Darwin, C.R. (1871) *The Descent of Man, and Selection in Relation to Sex*. London: Murray.

Darwin, C.R. (1872) *Expression of the Emotions in Man and Animals*. London: Albemarle.

Dolgin, K.M. and Sabini, J. (1982) 'Experimental manipulation of a human non-verbal display: The tongue show affects an observer's willingness to interact', *Animal Behaviour*, 30: 935–6.

Duchenne de Boulogne, G.B.A. (1990) *The mechanism of human facial expression*, in R.A. Cuthbertson (ed. and trans.). Cambridge: Cambridge University Press. (Original published 1859)

Ekman, P. (1972) 'Universals and cultural differences in facial expressions of emotion', in J. Cole (ed.), *Nebraska Symposium on Motivation, 1971* (Vol. 19). Lincoln, NE: University of Nebraska Press. pp. 207–83.

Ekman, P. (1984) 'Expression and the nature of emotion', in P. Ekman and K. Scherer (eds), *Approaches to Emotion*. Hillsdale, NJ: Erlbaum. pp. 319–43.

Ekman, P. (1985) *Telling Lies*. New York: Norton.

Ekman, P. and Friesen, W.V. (1969) 'The repertoire of nonverbal behavior: Categories, origins, usage, and coding', *Semiotica*, 1: 49–98.

Ekman, P. and Friesen, W.V. (1975) *Unmasking the Face*. Englewood Cliffs, NJ: Prentice-Hall.

Ekman, P. and Friesen, W.V. (1978) *The Facial Action Coding System*. Palo Alto, CA: Consulting Psychologists Press.

Ekman, P. and Friesen, W.V. (1982) 'Felt, false, and miserable smiles', *Journal of Nonverbal Behavior*, 6: 238–52.

Ekman, P., Davidson, R.J. and Friesen, W.V. (1990) 'The Duchenne smile: Emotional expression and brain physiology II', *Journal of Personality and Social Psychology*, 58: 342–53.

Ekman, P., Friesen, W.V. and Tomkins, S.S. (1971) 'Facial affect scoring technique (FAST): A first validity study', *Semiotica*, 3: 37–58.

Fridlund, A.J. (1991a) 'Evolution and facial action in reflex, social motive, and paralanguage', *Biological Psychology*, 32: 3–100.

Fridlund, A.J. (1991b) 'Sociality of solitary smiling: Potentiation by an implicit audience', *Journal of Personality and Social Psychology*, 69: 229–40.

Fridlund, A.J. (1992a) 'Darwin's Anti-Darwinism in *The Expression of the Emotions in Man and Animals*', in K. Strongman (ed.), *International Review of Emotion, Vol. 2*. Chichester: Wiley.

Fridlund, A.J. (1992b) 'The behavioral ecology and sociality of human faces', in M.S. Clark (ed.), *Review of Personality and Social Psychology, Vol. 13*. Newbury Park, CA: Sage. pp. 90–121.

Fridlund, A.J. (1994) *Human Facial Expression: An Evolutionary View*. San Diego, CA: Academic Press.

Fridlund, A.J. and Duchaine, B. (1996) Studies on the animism of everyday life. In preparation.

Fridlund, A.J., Kenworthy, K.G. and Jaffey, A.K. (1992) 'Audience effects in affective imagery: Replication and extension to affective imagery', *Journal of Nonverbal Behavior*, 16: 191–212.

Fridlund, A.J., Sabini, J.P., Hedlund, L.E., Schaut, J.A., Shenker, J.I. and Knauer, M.J. (1990) 'Social determinants of facial expressions during affective imagery: Displaying to the people in your head', *Journal of Nonverbal Behavior*, 14: 113–37.

Friesen, W.V. (1972) 'Cultural differences in facial expressions in a social situation: An experimental test of the concepts of display rules', Unpublished doctoral dissertation,

University of California, San Francisco. San Francisco: University of California Microfilm Archives.

Gratiolet, P. (1865) *De la physionomie et des mouvements d'expression*. Paris: J. Hetzel.

Gruber, H.E., with Barnett, H.P. (1974) *Darwin on Man: A Psychological Study of Scientific Creativity*. New York: Dutton.

Jones, S.S. and Raag, T. (1989) 'Smile production in older infants: The importance of a social recipient for the facial signal', *Child Development*, 69: 811–18.

Jones, S.S., Collins, K. and Hong, H.-W. (1991) 'An audience effect on smile production in 10-month-old infants', *Psychological Science*, 2: 45–9.

Kendon, A. (1981) 'Introduction: Current issues in the study of "nonverbal communication"', in A. Kendon (ed.), *Nonverbal Communication, Interaction, and Gesture*. Paris: Mouton. pp. 1–53.

Kraut, R.E. and Johnston, R.E. (1979) 'Social and emotional messages of smiling: An ethological approach', *Journal of Personality and Social Psychology*, 37: 1539–53.

Krebs, J.R. and Davies, N.B. (1987) *An Introduction to Behavioral Ecology* (2nd edn). Sunderland, MA: Sinauer.

Krebs, J.R. and Dawkins, R. (1984) 'Animal signals: Mind-reading and manipulation', in J.R. Krebs and N.B. Davies (eds), *Behavioural Ecology* (2nd edn). Oxford: Blackwell. pp. 380–402.

Latané, B. (1981) 'The psychology of social impact', *American Psychologist*, 36: 343–56.

Mead, G.H. (1934) *Mind, Self and Society from the Standpoint of a Social Behaviorist*. Chicago: University of Chicago Press.

Montgomery, W. (1985) 'Charles Darwin's thought on expressive mechanisms in evolution', in G. Zivin (ed.), *The Development of Expressive Behavior*. Orlando, FL: Academic Press. pp. 27–50.

Ortony, A. and Turner, T.J. (1990) 'What's so basic about basic emotions?', *Psychological Review*, 97: 315–31.

Parrott, W.G. and Sabini, J. (1989) 'On the "emotional" qualities of certain types of cognition: A reply to arguments for the independence of cognition and affect', *Cognitive Therapy and Research*, 13: 49–65.

Piderit, T. (1858) *Grundzüge der Mimik und physiognomik*. Brunswick, Germany: F. Vieweg und Sohn.

Piderit, T. (1886) *Mimik und physiognomik*. Detmold, Germany: Mayer.

Ribot, T. (1897) *The Psychology of the Emotions*. London: Walter Scott.

Ricklefs, R.E. (1979) *Ecology* (2nd edn). New York: Chiron Press.

Rousseau, J.-J. (1950) *Discourse on the Arts and Sciences*, in G.D.H. Cole (ed.), *The Social Contract and Discourses*. New York: E.P. Dutton and Co.

Russell, J.A. (1994) 'Is there universal recognition of emotion from facial expression?', *Psychological Bulletin*, 115: 102–41.

Saarni, C. (1978) 'Cognitive and communicative features of emotional experience, or do you show what you think you feel?', in M. Lewis and L. Rosenblum (eds), *The Development of Affect*. New York: Plenum.

Saarni, C. (1982) 'Social and affective functions of nonverbal behavior', in R.S. Feldman (ed.), *Development of Nonverbal Behavior in Children*. New York: Springer-Verlag.

Smith, W.J. (1977) *The Behavior of Communicating*. Cambridge, MA: Harvard University Press.

Smith, W.J. (1985) 'Consistency and change in communication', in G. Zivin (ed.), *The Development of Expressive Behavior*. Orlando, FL: Academic Press. pp. 51–75.

Smith, W.J. (1986) 'An "informational" perspective on manipulation', in R.W. Mitchell and N.S. Thompson (ed.), *Perspectives on Human and Nonhuman Deceit*. Albany, NY: State University of New York Press. pp. 71–87.

Smith, W.J., Chase, J. and Lieblich, A.K. (1974) 'Tongue showing: A facial display of humans and other primate species', *Semiotica*, 11: 201–46.

Sroufe, L.A. and Waters, E. (1976) 'The ontogenesis of smiling and laughter: A perspective on the organization of development in infancy', *Psychological Review*, 83: 173–89.

Tinbergen, N. (1953) *Social Behaviour in Animals*. London: Chapman and Hall.

Tversky, A. and Kahneman, D. (1988) 'Extensional versus intuitive reasoning: The conjunction fallacy in probability judgment', in A.M. Collins and E.E. Smith (eds), *Readings in Cognitive Science: A Perspective from Psychology and Cognitive Science*. San Mateo, CA: Kaufman. pp. 440–51.

Vygotsky, L.S. (1962) *Thought and Language*. Cambridge, MA: MIT Press.

Wagner, H.L. and Smith, J. (1991) 'Facial expression in the presence of friends and strangers', *Journal of Nonverbal Behavior*, 15: 201–14.

Wertsch, J.V. (1985) *Vygotsky and the Social Formation of Mind*. Cambridge, MA: Harvard University Press.

Wundt, W. (1896) *Outline of Psychology* (C.H. Judd, trans.). New York: Stechert.

Chapter 12

Emotional Self-control and Self-perception: Feelings are the Solution, not the Problem

James D. Laird and Nicholas H. Apostoleris

Whenever I feel afraid,
I hold my head erect
And whistle a happy tune
So no one will suspect I'm afraid.

The result of this deception
Is very strange to tell
For when I fool the people I fear
I fool myself as well

Make believe you're brave
And the trip will take you far
You may be as brave
As you make believe you are.

Rogers and Hammerstein (1956) 'I Whistle a Happy Tune'
from *The King and I*

A typically fluffy, silly idea. Just the sort of thing one would expect to find in a popular tune. How could it be that pretending could make something come true? And yet, a great deal of research suggests that Richard Rogers and Oscar Hammerstein had hit upon a particularly good way to control one's emotions. In this chapter we try to provide the scholarly, boring justification for the truth that the playwrights made real on the stage.

The very notion of self-control implies a person divided against him- or herself: one part of me needs to be controlled by some other part of me. The origin of this idea is obvious enough: we all do things that we regret, we struggle to avoid doing things we know are bad for us. But who are these warring parties? To understand self-control, we first must understand the nature and identity of the adversaries.

One popular view of self-control is that the conflict is between two parts of the mind or psyche. One side consists of immature, biological, animal-istic urges, while on the other are mature, distinctively human, rational judgments. The rational part of the mind is identified with thought, while the irrational is the domain of feelings and affect. Thus the conflict often is seen as between thoughts and feelings. I know that I should not strike out at my boss, but my feeling of rage impels me to attack. My hunger drives me to eat that extra slice of cake despite my rational judgment that I should not. In the common sense view, the problem of self-control is for the rational mind to anticipate and limit the irrational feelings which produce impulsive, primitive, uncontrolled behavior (Solomon, 1993). The stereotype of the self-controlled person is a lack of passion, a style like Mr Spock on *Star Trek*.

This view of self-control grows naturally from the broader notion, shared by common sense and many formal psychological theories, that feelings are the causes of actions. The problem of self-control becomes, therefore, a problem in the control of feelings. If we can foster 'good' feelings, and avoid bad feelings then we will act as we should.

Of course, such self-control is notoriously difficult for most of us, perhaps because the nature and origin of feelings are not very clearly identified in this common sense theory. Two other familiar ideas about feelings add to the difficulties. The first is the assumption that feelings are extremely difficult to resist. It is assumed that once one feels an emotion or desire intensely, the action is almost inevitable. A second, even more pernicious assumption is that even if possible, failing to act on one's feelings may be unhealthy. Feelings are seen as forces, like steam expanding in a boiling container, which, if not vented, may build up until they burst forth violently. As a result of this idea, sometimes people feel they should act on their feelings to relieve the pressure, whatever the consequences.

Self-perception theory suggests a quite different view of feelings, and consequently their role in self-control. In this chapter we describe that view of self-control and some of its practical and theoretical implications. First we begin with a summary of self-perception theory and its empirical support.

Self-perception theory

In contrast to the common sense view of feelings as the often powerful or even irresistible causes of behavior, the central tenet of self-perception theory, is that feelings are the consequences of behavior, not the causes. My feeling of anger doesn't make me strike out, but rather is a result of my having struck out. My feeling of sadness doesn't cause me to sit slumped in my chair, motionless for hours. Instead, my feeling of sadness is the consequence of my slumped posture and drooping face. My attraction to a political candidate is not the reason for the arguments I make, but the result of those arguments (Bem, 1972). Clearly, if self-perception theory is correct about the relationship between feelings and behaviors, then our usual ideas about self-control would need extensive re-thinking. Before we look at the self-perception view of control, we first need to look briefly at the evidence that would make us entertain such a counter-intuitive idea at all.

The evidence for self-perception

In psychology the clearest early statement of the self-perception view of feelings was William James' (1890) theory of emotion. In philosophy, Gilbert Ryle's (1949) *The Concept of Mind*, is a more general and elaborate version of the same point of view. In presenting his theory of emotion, James asserted

> Common sense says, we lose our fortune, are sorry and weep; we meet a bear, are frightened and run; we are insulted by a rival, are angry and strike. The hypothesis here to be defended says that this order of sequence is incorrect . . . and the more rational statement is that we feel sorry *because* we cry, angry *because* we strike, afraid *because* we tremble. (James, 1890: 449)

The basic test of James' (or the more general self-perception theory) view of emotion is contained in James' last sentence. If we feel angry because we strike, or afraid because we tremble, then a person induced to strike should report feeling anger; if induced to tremble, they should report feeling afraid, and so forth. So, dozens and dozens of experiments in the last 20 years have tested whether inducing emotional actions would produce emotional feelings (see reviews by Adelman and Zajonc, 1989; Capella, 1993; Izard, 1990; Laird, 1984; Laird and Bresler, 1990).

For many years James' theory was out of favor in psychology, and one of the few proponents was Sylvan Tomkins (1962). Tomkins focused his attention primarily on facial expressions, and, perhaps as a consequence, the largest body of research on self-perception approaches to feeling has concentrated on facial expressions. In these studies, people are induced to adopt facial expressions of emotion and then asked how they feel.

A great variety of techniques have been used to induce the facial expressions while disguising the purposes of the manipulations. For example, at Clark we have often (see Laird, 1984 for a summary) told participants that we were measuring electromyographic activity of muscles and asked them to contract and relax individual muscles while we made our measurements. The instructions to contract and relax muscles were the guise under which participants were induced to adopt facial expressions of happiness, anger, sadness, fear, and so on. Although participants do not ordinarily recognize the purpose, or even the nature of the expressions that they are led to adopt, they do report changes in feelings that correspond to the expressions.

A particularly well-disguised variation of this procedure was invented by Strack et al, (1988). They induced people to adopt facial expressions by asking them to hold a pen in their mouth either in a way that produced something like a smile or in a way that produced an expression more like disgust. This procedure also produced corresponding feelings. Another very well-disguised manipulation of expressions was invented by Zajonc and his associates (e.g., Zajonc et al., 1989). They induced facial expressions by asking people to pronounce different vowel sounds. For example, most of us know the photographer's trick of asking people to say 'cheese' to produce a kind of smile. Zajonc et al. asked participants to pronounce vowel sounds (including the 'ee' of 'cheese') which produced approxima- tions of facial expressions, and observed matching changes in the participants' reported feelings. Whatever the technique used to manipulate facial expressions, the results have been quite consistent. When participants are induced to adopt facial expressions of happiness, they feel happy, expressions of anger make people feel angry, and expressions of sadness produce feelings of sadness (Duclos et al., 1989).

James explicitly included a variety of other expressive behaviors in addition to facial expressions. A number of studies have examined these as well. For example, one very noticeable kind of emotional behavior are changes in posture. In a number of different studies, people have been induced to adopt postures of sadness, fear and anger, and in each case the participants reported feeling the appropriate emotion (Duclos et al., 1989; Stepper and Strack, 1993). Emotions also produce characteristic vocal patterns, and if participants are induced to produce these patterns, they also report feeling the appropriate emotion (Siegman and Boyle, 1993).

Another distinctive kind of emotional behavior is characteristic of romantic love. Only people in the throes of passionate love exchange long, unbroken mutual gazes. If self-perception theory is correct, then inducing strangers to gaze into each other's eyes should produce feelings of romantic attraction. Two different studies demonstrated that gazing does lead to loving (Kellerman et al., 1989). A recent study (Williams and Kleinke, 1993) replicated and extended these effects, by adding touching as another variable. Both touching and gazing led to increased attraction.

A third major component of emotional behavior is autonomic response. For centuries people have recognized that strong emotions are often accompanied by a pounding heart, sweaty palms and other symptoms of autonomic arousal. The famous Schachter experiments (Schachter and Singer, 1962) seemed to demonstrate that if these arousal symptoms were artificially produced by injections of adrenalin, people would then report more intense emotions. In recent years some uncertainty has arisen about those effects, but it seems to be the case that increasing arousal does increase some kinds of emotions. The emotions that are increased by arousal are also the ones that one might expect to be, since they are the emotions which involve high arousal, that is, anger, fear and romantic love (see Laird and Bresler, 1990 for a review).

In sum, dozens and dozens of studies confirm the predictions of James and self-perception theory, that if people act emotionally, they will feel the corresponding emotion. Furthermore, these effects are additive, so a person performing two emotional actions reports stronger feelings than when performing either alone (Flack et al., 1994; Flack et al., 1996).

The effects of behavior are not confined to emotional feelings. Numerous studies have shown that other feelings can be similarly evoked by inducing the behavior. For example, feelings of confidence and pride are affected by posture. Feelings of hunger and of liking and disliking, as in attitudes, and of other motives, all have been found to fit self-perception predictions (see Laird and Bresler, 1990 for a review).

All of this research indicates that self-perception theory at least deserves some serious attention. Literally hundreds of studies show that when people are induced to act as if they felt something, they do, indeed, feel it. Any of these studies could undoubtedly be 'explained away' by some method problem or another. However, it is hardly plausible that so large a number of investigators could have been deceived in so many different ways to produce such a coherent system of results. At some point the unifying theory that predicted these effects begins to seem more reasonable than a vast collection of ad hoc and post hoc methodological hypotheses.

If feelings are consequences of action, not the causes, new questions arise about both the feelings and the behaviors.

Self-perception and feelings

Common sense describes a clear role for feelings: they are the forces that push and pull our behavior. However, if feelings are not those forces, then what are they? The answer is that they seem to be information about that behavior. When we feel angry, that feeling is derived from the fact that our brows are drawn down, that our fists are clenched, that we are about to lash out, and so forth. And experiencing that feeling means that we 'know' all of this. That is, the feeling seems to consist of information about the behavior that we are in the middle of performing. In the self-perception view, then, feelings are a kind of information.

Obviously, since most of us are surprised by the results of self-perception experiments, these information-gathering processes must take place out of our awareness. Feelings of emotion or of attitudes or desire are complex integrations of a variety of 'cues' and information, but this information is acquired automatically (e.g. Shiffrin and Schneider, 1977), without the person knowing the basis of the feeling, or the way in which the behaviors lead to the feeling. Ordinarily, the only experience is of the final product (Bargh, 1984).

In this, 'affective' feelings are similar to the usual kinds of perceptual processes. The perception of depth, for example, involves the complex integration of cues from such diverse sources as linear perspective, gradients of texture and color, and binocular disparity, but the perceiver is unaware of the cues for depth and of the process that 'uses' them.

Many kinds of more cognitive feelings are also similar, in that the experiencer is unaware of the cues which lead to the feeling, and the processes which generate feelings. For example, the intuitions of experts (Chi et al., 1988) are often accurate integrations of very complex arrays of information, but are experienced simply as 'feelings' for which the expert can give little justification. The 'feeling of knowing' or having experienced an event before (Jacoby et al., 1989) also is based on cues the individual cannot identify, which result in a simple feeling of familiarity. Even the

perception of whether a remembered event was really experienced or not
(Johnson et al., 1988) is a direct feeling, based on cues and processes that
the experiencer cannot identify. In sum, there seems to be a multitude of
feelings, all of which consist of information about some aspect of the world
or one's own behavior. Indeed, all feelings, including affective feelings,
seem to be information, or knowledge. They are distinguished from what
we ordinarily think of as knowledge only by our inability to experience
directly the sources of that knowledge.

The objects of affective knowledge

All affective feelings are 'about' some kind of automatically performed,
more or less complex behavior. In the case of emotions, at least three kinds
of behaviors are easily distinguished: action, expressive behavior and autonomic response. Each of these seems to be 'innate' and to be systematically
coordinated with each other. For example, the basic patterns of action
associated with emotions are common to all people everywhere, and,
indeed, to all reasonably complex organisms: the prototypical action of
anger is attack or aggression, the prototypical action of fear is flight, and so
forth. Each of the more basic emotions have been associated with distinctive patterns of adaptive action (e.g. Buck, 1985; Ekman, 1992; Plutchik,
1980).

Each of these emotional action patterns is also associated with a
distinctive array of expressive behaviors; the smile of happiness, the scowl
of anger, the dejected posture of sadness, and so forth. A great deal of
evidence demonstrates that broadly similar patterns of expressive behavior
occur in all cultures and societies (Ekman, 1989; Izard, 1971). Equally
clearly, some, though not all of these emotional sequences include changes
in the activity of the autonomic nervous system. As long ago as Cannon's
work in the 1920s, it was clear that a pattern of mobilization for 'fight or
flight', as Cannon called it, was characteristic of anger and fear in most
mammals. Until recently it was generally accepted that Levenson et al.
(1992) had demonstrated the expectable cross-cultural similarities in
autonomic responses to different emotions, including the specific patterning
of responses for specific emotional feelings. There is now reason to think
that the tie between biology and emotion is much looser than was
previously thought (Fridlund, this volume). Whatever the nature of the tie
human beings do seem to be built with a complicated array of behaviors
which are highly coordinated and organized to achieve adaptive ends, and
many features of these organizations of behavior are shared with many
other animal species. These organized patterns of behavior begin to be 'run
off' automatically in response to general classes of stimuli (deRivera et al.,
1977; Mauro et al., 1992).

Of course, cultures may affect the shape of these patterns, when they are
incorporated in the complex cultural-cognitive phenomena we call

emotions. Different cultures define which kinds of situations call for particular emotions, and even which kinds of emotional patterns will be recognized and experienced (e.g. Lutz, 1988; Shaver et al., 1992). Cultures also provide 'display rules' (Ekman and Friesen, 1975) which govern the way in which emotional expressions appear and the context in which they are appropriate. However, these cultural variations seem to sit atop a broad base of biologically determined constancy, in much the same way that sexual behavior and sex differences begin with biology, but provide an exceptionally fertile ground for further cultural 'work' (Oatley, 1993).

So, when people are confronted with an appropriate environmental event, like a challenge, they begin to respond with a coordinated pattern of behavior, such as a frown, a increased heart rate, clenched fists, etc. When we feel an emotion like anger, we are detecting the beginnings of one of these automatic patterns of behavior. We are 'reading out' (Buck, 1985) the activities of our bodies, our arousal, our expressive behavior, and the action patterns that are at least incipient.

We have focused on the way in which emotional feelings provide information about emotional behavior in part because it is the most distinctive feature of self-perception theory, and in part because we do think that this is the most important content of feeling-knowledge. However, feelings certainly may provide information about other aspects of the emotional episode as well (Schwarz and Clore, 1988; Clore and Parrott, 1991). Since emotional episodes are tightly integrated sequences of activities, the occurrence of any one of them may be enough to induce a feeling. Consequently the feeling may consist of information that is 'about' some, but not necessarily all of the parts of an emotional episode: the instigating event, the expressive and autonomic responses, and actions. In this regard, again we see a parallel with perceptual processes like depth perception, in which the experience can be generated by some part of the usual array of cues, such as linear perspective or binocular disparity, without any of the others being available.

Self-perception theory of course extends to many other feelings beyond those of emotion. The patterns of action of many of these are unlikely to be as 'wired in' as emotional patterns are. When a person judges their own feelings of liking or disliking of a presidential candidate from how they have spoken about that candidate (Bem, 1972), both the form and meaning of the speech-making behavior and our comprehension of what it means to make a speech are products of a complicated social system and many years of learning and experience. Indeed, many of the emotional behaviors which lead to feelings are also probably the results of cultural shaping and individual experience. But the basic pattern remains the same for all feelings: a variety of complex behaviors are performed automatically in reaction to some appropriate context, and our perception of how we are behaving in relation to the context in which we behave is the source of our feeling.

Because self-perception theory asserts that action precedes feeling, people often erroneously assume that the theory assigns no functional role to feelings. After all, if feelings don't cause action, and even occur after the action is at least begun, what good are feelings? The potential for this misunderstanding is strengthened because the best known source of self-perception theory (and the source of the name) is Skinnerian behaviorism (Bem, 1967) which explicitly held that mental contents including feelings were only epiphenomenal.

Nonetheless, it is neither necessary nor reasonable to assume that feelings are epiphenomenal. Instead, the information of feelings clearly is used like any other information, to guide further action. In the case of emotions, for example, knowing that we are about to punch someone in the mouth is useful, because we can decide not to. Feelings guide behavior in just the same way that other information guides behavior. My feeling of anger may be the result of my scowl and clenched fists, but it has very useful consequences for the behavior that follows next. In the flow of human life, my scowl is upstream of my feeling of anger, but a great deal of behavior lies downstream, potentially subject to the impact of this information.

Self-control

The contestants involved in self-control can now be identified more clearly. The contest is not between thoughts and feelings. Instead, on one side are a variety of automatic patterns of action, and on the other are more or less conscious control processes which have the potential to modulate these patterns (Vallacher, 1993).

These patterns of action are not necessarily biological in origin. Some, such as those of emotions are, but others, such as automatic evaluative reactions to politicians, seem to depend on individual experience. Nor are these action patterns irrational. Many of these patterns seem to have been produced by our evolutionary history, and others by histories of reinforce-ment, and neither of these sources produces 'irrational' behavior. At most the behavior is inflexible, and potentially not well adapted to every situation in which it is called forth. So the conflict is between the automatic and the reflective, not between feeling and thought. And in this conflict, the feelings are tools of the rational, reflective processes, not representatives of the automatic processes. In the battle for self-control, feelings are like the scouts who bring information about the enemy, not the generals who command the enemy forces.

So, how will we go about self-control of emotions and other affective processes? There are two kinds of things which we might want to control. Sometimes we simply want to control our feelings – I'm afraid, but I will not flee, I will stay and speak to this group. More commonly, what we really want to control is our behavior: I don't particularly enjoy feeling angry at my boss, but it is essential that I don't tell the boss what I think of him. Ways of controlling feelings are the most straightforward, and are a good place to start.

Controlling feelings

There are times when we don't want or need to change our conduct, but would like to change our feelings. We may be sad at the loss of a loved one, annoyed at a trivial problem, or afraid of speaking in public. These are all situations in which we are able to do whatever we need without regard for our feelings, but we also wish we didn't feel the way we do.

Controlling expressive behavior   In these situations, self-perception theory suggests a direct means of control. The principle lesson of the self-perception research is that if you act as you wish you felt, you will feel that way. That is, we can, as the song from *The King and I* says:

Make believe you're brave
And the trip will take you far
You may be as brave
As you make believe you are.

This technique seems to lie at the heart of the behavior therapy technique of systematic desensitization (Wolpe, 1958). This therapy has been widely documented as effective in the treatment of phobias (see Deffenbacher and Suinn, 1988, for a review), which are the paradigms of unwanted feelings. Typically, clients first identify a hierarchy of increasingly anxiety-provoking activities. They then are taught to relax all of the muscles in their bodies. Once relaxation is mastered, they then proceed to imagine as vividly as possible each step in their hierarchy of threats. If they begin to feel anxious, they stop imagining, and return to relaxing their muscles, which prevents the anxiety. They repeat this procedure for each step in their hierarchy, until they can contemplate even the most terrifying level without tensing their muscles, or experiencing anxiety. The therapy works, according to the self-perception perspective, because clients who are relaxing their muscles cannot adopt the expressive behavior of fear, and instead are acting, and feeling, relaxed.

Sandy Duclos (1992) directly tested whether, in a less intense and non-therapeutic context, people could control their emotions simply by changing their emotional behavior. She asked her participants to deliberately adopt facial expressions in order to produce feelings, or to control their expressions to prevent emotional feelings. As a comparison, she also asked participants to create feelings through guided imagery, and inhibit them by a distraction task. The participants in her research were recruited from a church, were unacquainted with psychological research or theory, and were virtually unanimous in believing that changing their expressions would have no effect on their feelings. Nonetheless, in general their feelings were affected by their expressive behavior, and for some their intentional manipulations of their behavior were the most successful technique for producing or inhibiting their feelings.

Notice, incidentally, that this technique for changing feelings is different from simply trying to ignore a feeling, or trying to think only of happy things. In fact, the deliberate attempt to avoid feeling an emotion, has the paradoxical effect of increasing both one's awareness of the feeling and also increases at least some emotional behavior as well (Wegner, 1994). However, when one deliberately adopts expressive behaviors, ironic processes are less likely to occur to sabotage one's control efforts.

Individual differences Duclos' study makes salient an aspect of self-perception research that is important to the practices of controlling feeling, but has not been discussed thus far. In many self-perception experiments the effects of behavior on feelings are not observed in all people. Some people consistently feel whatever their behavior is expressing, whereas other people are unaffected. These individual differences have been observed in studies of manipulations of facial expressions (Laird and Crosby, 1974) and postures (Duclos et al., 1989), in the effects of counter-attitudinal behavior on attitudes (Laird and Berglas, 1975) and in the effects of overt behavior on attitudes (Wagener and Laird, 1980), and in many other self-perception tasks. These differences are stable over time, and related to other enduring attributes of the person, such as Field Dependence and body weight (Edelman, 1984).

These individual differences seem to reflect the extent to which people respond to cues from their own behavior ('self-produced cues') or from their circumstances ('situational cues') (Laird and Berglas, 1975). Response to one or the other kind of cues has been found to be consistent from behavior to behavior and from feeling to feeling. For example, someone whose emotional feelings are affected by their expressions will also be affected by their postures (Duclos et al., 1989) and gaze (Kellerman et al., 1989), and will change their attitudes to match their counter-attitudinal speeches (Duncan and Laird, 1977; Rhodewalt and Comer, 1979). In contrast, people who do not respond to any of these manipulations of self-produced cues are *more* responsive to conformity manipulations (Comer, 1975) and direct statements by an experimenter about how they should feel (Duncan and Laird, 1980; Kellerman and Laird, 1982). (See Laird and Bresler, 1992, for a more extensive discussion of these and other studies.) In sum, people differ in how much their emotional and other affective feelings are based on their behavior or on their understanding of what is appropriate for their circumstances.

In her study of deliberate expression control, Duclos (1992) used a separate and well-disguised procedure (which no subjects saw through) to assess response to self-produced cues. The most effective control procedure for those responsive to self-produced cues was to consciously control their facial expressions, whereas this technique was ineffective for people who were unresponsive to self-produced cues. The direct implication of these results is then, a qualification of Rogers and Hammerstein's (and our) recommendation that people act as they would like to feel. That technique will be more effective for some people than others.

Controlling action

Common sense holds that since we act because of feelings, the stronger the feeling the more inevitably we are compelled to act. Self-perception theory suggests the opposite: the more we are aware of feelings, the more likely we are to shape or inhibit our actions. Indeed, we have been arguing that feelings exist so that actions can be coordinated. Feelings are the tool by which automatic action patterns can be modified. In other words, knowing that we are angry allows us to control our anger. Conversely, an angry action is more likely to occur and continue if the person is unaware, if the feeling of anger is absent. It is only when we have the feeling, that we know that we are about to attack, and are thus able to exercise control over our actions.

Many everyday events confirm this insight. For example, people commonly lash out in anger and then almost immediately regret the action. The most unforgivable insults are usually emitted before the feeling of anger has been fully appreciated. The coward tends to flee immediately, and only feel the fear after he has begun to run.

Here we can see the wisdom of the usual advice for the management of anger, to 'count to 10'. Any delay in acting angrily provides the opportunity to become aware of the anger, and then to adjust one's behavior accordingly (Tavris, 1984). Similarly, it seems likely that becoming more alert and sensitive to one's emotional states – becoming more acutely aware of one's feelings – would lead to greater, not lesser self-control.

Self-perception theory predicts that people who are chronically unable to control their emotional behavior might experience less rather than more powerful emotional feelings. That appears to be precisely the case, at least for children who have been diagnosed as 'behavior disordered' (Buck et al., in press). Such children report feelings that are less intense than those that outside observers judge them to be enacting, and sometimes they act as if they were feeling one emotion when they report feeling another. The authors of this study recognized the problem of correctly experiencing, and observe, 'These children may need to learn to recognize when they are experiencing certain feelings, how to label them accurately, and how to express them appropriately' (Buck et al., in press). From the self-perception point of view, of course, there is no such thing as an 'unexperienced feeling', because feelings are identified exactly with the experienced. But we would agree with Buck et al. (in press) that the problem is in experiencing at all. Without the feelings, the children cannot control themselves.

Clinical experience with impulsivity is consistent with this view. Understood best as a symptom rather than a syndrome (Fink and McCown, 1993), impulsivity is a feature of a wide variety of childhood dysfunctions including Attention-Deficit Hyperactivity Disorder (ADHD) (see Koziol et al., 1993), affective, and anxiety-related difficulties (Fink and McCown, 1993). One successful technique for treating impulsivity associated with ADHD is cognitive-behavioral therapy (see Kendall and Braswell, 1993, for a review). Zentall (1989) proposed that hyperactive children maladaptively focus their attention on external stimuli. The suggested treatment approach is to redirect the attention of the child to their behaviors and what Zentall considers to be the underlying mentations of which the behaviors are a manifestation. While the self-perception approach differs from the cognitive-behavioral approach in the ascribed direction of causality, both theories predict that the treatment approach of increased emotional self-awareness would be beneficial.

In sum, self-perception theory views emotional feelings as information about relatively automatic patterns of behavior. These patterns of behavior are more or less hard wired and tend to run off rapidly and vigorously unless actively impeded. The essential function of feelings is then to provide the information that one of these patterns is occurring. One of the most important consequences of knowing about these patterns is being able to control them.

This is not to deny, of course, that people sometimes ruminate about their feelings of injustice or terror and then eventually act on these ruminations. But, these considered actions are what we would all understand to be premeditated. That is, in full recognition of the action pattern their feeling is reporting, they then proceed to act. The feeling provides the opportunity for self-control, but it doesn't guarantee that the particular choice of action will be inhibition. Indeed, their choice may well be a more targeted and effective attack on their enemy or avoidance of the object of their fear.

One of the ironic consequences of the common sense view of feelings and actions is that many of us are led to exercise much less self-control than we easily could. Believing that feelings are the causes of behavior, and that strong feelings are the strongest causes of behavior, we are often inclined to feel that we have little choice but to give in to our feelings, or in self-perception language, to let automatic patterns of behavior run their course. For example, many people feel that they have little choice but to act on fear. If they are afraid, then they must avoid the object of their fear, even if they know the fear is irrational. If they are angry, they must express that anger even if they know it will hurt. If they want a favorite, fatty food, they must eat it even if they know they neither need it nor should eat it. Believing that our behavior most commonly flows from our feelings, leads us to accept those feelings and, in a sense, passively emit their full expression. In contrast, both self-perception theory and the traditions of asceticism in the world's religions confirm that embracing one's feelings, becoming as acutely aware of them as possible, is the path to controlling the behaviors that accompany them.

Phobias might appear to represent a counter-argument to the view that more awareness of emotions is desirable. The problem in phobias is, after all, that the sufferer is too aware of his or her fear. The phobia sufferer comes to fear the fear, and to be vigilant in noticing the slightest signs (e.g. Mathews and MacLeod, 1986). But why does the phobic person fear the fear? Because they believe that if they experience fear, they will sweat and stammer, be compelled to run away, or in some other way publicly disgrace themselves. Thus, the outcomes they fear are precisely those contained in the erroneous folk belief that feelings are compelling forces. Phobic people are not victims of excessive fear, but of erroneous folk beliefs about fear. And the cure for them is, in part, to recognize that experiencing fear does not entail any social catastrophes, nor even any necessary action. No matter how strong the feeling of fear, one need not flee.

Earlier we noted one of the corollaries of common sense that has enjoyed a great deal of popularity in the last few decades, that feelings are in some way similar to mechanical or hydraulic forces. The very term 'expression' implies an internal pressure which must be released in action. This kind of idea gives rise to the assumption that catharsis, the bleeding off of emotional energy, is a route to self-control. The idea of catharsis has been used to explain and justify aspects of our culture such as violent movies and television, so naturally it has been the subject of considerable research. In studies attempting to show the effects of catharsis, subjects are characteristically encouraged to express angry feelings, usually verbally. If catharsis is at work, they should subsequently report feeling less anger, and act less angrily. Unfortunately for the catharsis hypothesis, however, the result is almost invariably the reverse. Subjects induced to say and do angry things then report feeling more, not less anger (e.g. Ebbesen et al., 1975; Kahn, 1966; Kaplan, 1975; Mallick and McCandless, 1966). After an exhaustive review of this literature, Tavris (1984) concluded, just as self-perception theory would have predicted, that acting angrily increased anger feelings, and future angry actions. Berkowitz (1993) points out that the best evidence is that aggressive stimuli incite aggressive behavior, and that angry acts and statements are aggressive stimuli. Thus it is no surprise that acting angrily increases, rather than decreases, anger.

Self-understanding

In other contexts, it is certainly not a new idea that awareness and knowledge are the prerequisites for change. Indeed, the whole rationale of psychotherapy, for example, is that knowledge permits control and, ultimately, change. The problem, of course, is that self-knowledge and self-understanding are extremely difficult. We all know the problems of trying to see ourselves as others see us. Even more difficult is to see ourselves as we truly are. The difficulty, according to common sense, is the difficulty of seeing the internal landscape where passions, desires, habits and motives exist and play out their dramas. Since the very core of self-perception theory is to deny that such an internal landscape exists, we would not be surprised to find that self-perception theory has a different view of self-understanding and its difficulties. In particular, self-perception theory argues that introspection, the quiet contemplation of one's interior, is precisely not the way to understand ourselves. All of the contents of our mind are, in fact, interpretations of our behavior. Consequently, the proper way to understand ourselves is to look outside, not in; to try to examine and understand our actions in the world, and, in particular, the repeating patterns of our actions.

Why is this so difficult? One reason is surely just that at the time that we are acting, we are not in a good position to see our actions as others would see them. We are too busy acting. We have to figure out what to do and how to do it, and we don't have the resources or leisure to reflect on our actions at the same time. A related and probably equally important problem is that as actors our perspective is not on our actions, but on those things that we are acting in response to. As Nisbett and others have shown repeatedly, the actor and the observer have very different perspectives on events, and while we are actors, it is extremely difficult for us to adopt the observer's perspective. But that is precisely what we need in order to understand ourselves in the way that we wish.

The route to self-understanding is to reflect at our leisure, but not to reflect introspectively, on our feelings, desires and thoughts, but rather to reflect on our actions, on the things that we have done and what those doings seem to imply about us. With greater understanding of the patterns of our lives, and the nature of our automatic, affective processes, self-control will follow naturally.

References

Adelman, P.K. and Zajonc, R.B. (1989) 'Facial efference and the experience of emotion', *Annual Review of Psychology*, 40: 249–80.

Bargh, J.A. (1984) 'Automatic and conscious processing of social information', in R.S. Wyer, Jr. and T.K. Srull (eds), *Handbook of Social Cognition* (Vol. 3). Hillsdale, NJ: Erlbaum.

Bem, D.J. (1967) 'Self-perception: An alternative interpretation of cognitive dissonance phenomena', *Psychological Review*, 74: 183–200.

Bem, D.J. (1972) 'Self-perception theory', in L. Berkowitz (ed.), *Advances in Experimental Social Psychology* (Vol. 6). New York: Academic Press.

Berkowitz, L. (1993) *Aggression: Its Causes, Consequences and Control*. New York: McGraw-Hill.

Buck, R. (1985) 'Prime theory: An integrated view of motivation and emotion', *Psychological Review*, 92: 389–413.

Buck R., Goldman, C.K., Easton, C.J. and Norelli-Smith, N. (in press) 'Social learning and emotional education: Emotional expression and communication in behaviorally-disordered children and schizophrenic patients', in W.F. Flack and J.D. Laird (eds), *Emotions and Psychopathology*. New York: Oxford University Press.

Capella, J.L. (1993) 'The facial feedback hypothesis in human interaction: Review and speculation', *Journal of Language and Social Psychology*, 12: 13–29.

Chi, M.T.H., Glaser, R. and Farr, M.J. (1988) *The Nature of Expertise*. Hillsdale, NJ: Erlbaum.

Clore, G.L. and Parrott, W.G. (1991) 'Moods and their vicissitudes: Thoughts and feelings as information', in J. Forgas (ed.), *Emotion and Social Judgment*. Oxford: Pergamon. pp. 107–23.

Comer, R. (1975) 'Individual differences in self-attribution behaviors: Dimensions and child-rearing correlates', Ph.D. Dissertation, Clark University.

Comer, R. and Rhodewalt, F. (1979) 'Cue utilization in the self-attribution of emotions and attitudes', *Personality and Social Psychology Bulletin*, 5: 320–4.

Deffenbacher, J.L. and Suinn, R.M. (1988) 'Systematic desensitization and the reduction of anxiety', *Counseling Psychologist*, 16: 9–30.

deRivera, J. (1977) 'A structural theory of the emotions', *Psychological Issues*, (4, Monograph 40): 40.

Duclos, S.E. (1992) 'The self-determination of emotional experience', Unpublished Ph.D. dissertation, Clark University, Worcester, MA.

Duclos, S., Laird, J.D., Schneider, E., Sexter, M., Stern, L. and Van Lighten, O. (1989) 'Categorical vs. dimensional effects of facial expressions and postures on emotional experience', *Journal of Personality and Social Psychology*, 57: 100–8.

Duncan, J.W. and Laird, J.D. (1977) 'Cross-modality consistencies individual differences in self-attribution', *Journal of Personality*, 45: 191–206.

Duncan, J.W. and Laird, J.D. (1980) 'Positive and reverse placebo effects as a function of differences in cues used in self-perception', *Journal of Personality and Social Psychology*, 39: 1024–36.

Ebbesen, E., Duncan, B. and Konecni, V. (1975) 'Effects of content of verbal aggression on future verbal aggression: A field experiment', *Journal of Experimental Social Psychology*, 11: 192–204.

Edelman, B. (1984) 'A multiple-factor of body weight control', *Journal of General Psychology*, 110: 99–114.

Ekman, P. (1989) 'The argument and evidence about universals in facial expressions of emotion', in H. Wagner and A.S.R. Manstead (eds), *Handbook of Social Psychophysiology*. Chichester: Wiley. pp. 143–64.

Ekman, P. (1992) 'An argument for basic emotions', *Cognition and Emotion*, 6: 169–200.

Ekman, P. and Friesen, W.V. (1975) *Unmasking the Face*. Englewood Cliffs, NJ: Prentice-Hall.

Fink, A.D. and McCown, W.G. (1993) 'Impulsivity in children and adolescents: Measurement, causes, and treatment', in W.G. McCown, J.L. Johnson and M.B. Shure (eds), *The Impulsive Client: Theory, Research and Treatment*. Washington, DC: APA. pp. 279–308.

Flack, W.F., Williams, C., Cavallaro, L.A. and Laird, J.D. (1994) 'Additive effects of postures and expressions on emotional experience'. Paper presented at the Eastern Psychological Association, Providence, RI, 22 April 1994.

Flack, W.F., Laird, J.D. and Cavallaro, L.A. (1996) 'Faces, postures and voices: Their separate and combined effects on emotional expression in psychoses and depression'. Paper presented at the XXVI International Congress of Psychology, Montreal, Canada, August 1996.

Izard, C.E. (1971) *The Face of Emotion*. New York: Appleton-Century-Crofts.

Izard, C.E. (1990) 'Facial expressions and the regulation of emotions', *Journal of Personality and Social Psychology*, 58: 487–98.

Jacoby, L.L., Kelley, C.M., Brown, J. and Jasechko, J. (1989) 'Becoming famous overnight: limits on the ability to avoid unconscious influences of the past', *Journal of Personality and Social Psychology*, 56: 326–38.

James, W. (1890) *Principles of Psychology*. New York: Holt.

Johnson, M.K., Foley, M.A., Suengas, A.G. and Raye, C.L. (1988) 'Phenomenal characteristics of memories for perceived and imagined events', *Journal of Experimental Psychology: General*, 117: 371–6.

Kahn, M. (1966) 'The physiology of catharsis', *Journal of Personality and Social Psychology*, 3: 278–86.

Kaplan, R. (1975) 'The cathartic value of self-expression: Testing catharsis, dissonance and interference explanations', *Journal of Social Psychology*, 97: 195–208.

Kellerman, J. and Laird, J.D. (1982) 'The effect of appearance on self-perception', *Journal of Personality*, 50: 296–315.

Kellerman, J., Lewis, J. and Laird, J.D. (1989) 'Looking and loving: The effects of mutual gaze on feelings of romantic love', *Journal of Research in Personality*, 23: 145–61.

Kendall, P. and Finch, A.J., Jr. (1979) 'Developing nonimpulsive behavior in children: Cognitive-behavioral strategies for self-control', in P.C. Kendall and S.D. Hollins (eds), *Cognitive-behavioral Interventions*. New York: Academic Press. pp. 37–80.

Kendall, P. and Braswell, L. (1993) *Cognitive-behavioral Therapy for Impulsive Children*. New York: Guilford.

Koziol, L.F., Stout, C.E. and Rubin, D.H. (eds) (1993) *Handbook of Childhood Impulse Disorders and ADHD: Theory and practice*. Springfield, IL: Charles C. Thomas.

Laird, J.D. (1974) 'Self-attribution of emotion: The effects of expressive behavior on the quality of emotional experience', *Journal of Personality and Social Psychology*, 33: 475–86.

Laird, J.D. (1984) 'The real role of facial response in experience of emotion: A reply to Tourangeau and Ellsworth, and others', *Journal of Personality and Social Psychology*, 47: 909–17.

Laird, J.D. and Berglas, S. (1975) 'Individual differences in the effects of engaging in counter-attitudinal behavior', *Journal of Personality*, 43: 286–304.

Laird, J.D. and Bresler, C. (1990) 'William James and the mechanisms of emotional experience', *Personality and Social Psychology Bulletin*, 16: 636–51.

Laird, J.D. and Bresler, C. (1992) 'The process of emotional experience: A self-perception theory', in M.S. Clark (ed.), *Emotion: Review of Personality and Social Psychology*, Vol. 13. Newbury Park: Sage. pp. 213–34.

Laird, J.D. and Crosby, M. (1974) 'Individual differences in the self-attribution of emotion', in H. London and R. Nisbett (eds), *Thinking and Feeling: The Cognitive Alteration of Feeling States*. Chicago: Aldine.

Levenson, R.W., Ekman, P., Heider, K. and Friesen, W.V. (1992) 'Emotion and autonomic nervous system activity in the Minangkabau of West Sumatra', *Journal of Personality and Social Psychology*, 62: 972–88.

Lutz, C. (1988) *Unnatural Emotions: Everyday Sentiments on a Micronesian Atoll and their Challenges to Western Theory*. Chicago: University of Chicago Press.

Mallick, S.K. and McCandless, B.R. (1966) 'A study of catharsis aggression', *Journal of Personality and Social Psychology*, 4: 591–6.

Mathews, A. and MacLeod, C. (1986) 'Discrimination of threat cues without awareness in anxious states', *Journal of Abnormal Psychology*, 95: 131–8.

Mauro, R., Sato, K. and Tucker, J. (1992) 'The role of appraisal in human emotions: A cross-cultural study', *Journal of Personality and Social Psychology*, 62: 301–17.

Oatley, K. (1993) 'Social construction in emotions', in M. Lewis and J.M. Haviland (eds), *Handbook of Emotions*. New York: Guilford. pp. 341–52.

Plutchik, R. (1980) *Emotion: A Psychoevolutionary Synthesis*. New York: Harper & Row.

Rhodewalt, F. and Comer, R. (1979) 'Induced-compliance attitude change: Once more with feeling', *Journal of Experimental Social Psychology*, 15: 35–47.

Ryle, G. (1949) *The Concept of Mind*. New York: Norton.

Schachter, S. and Singer, J.E. (1962) 'Cognitive, social and physiological determinants of emotional state', *Psychological Review*, 69: 379–99.

Schwarz, N. and Clore, G.L. (1988) 'How do I feel about it? The informative function of mood', in K. Fiedler and J. Forgas (eds), *Affect, Cognition, and Social Behavior*. Toronto: C.J. Hogrefe. pp. 44–62.

Shaver, P.R., Wu, S. and Schwartz, J.C. (1992) 'Cross-cultural similarities and differences in emotion and its representation: A prototype approach', in M.S. Clark (ed.), *Emotion: Review of Personality and Social Psychology* Vol. 13. Newbury Park: Sage. pp. 175–212.

Shiffrin, R.M. and Schneider, W. (1977) 'Controlled and automatic human information processing, II: Perceptual learning, automatic attending, and a general theory', *Psychological Review*, 84: 127–90.

Siegman, A.W. and Boyle, S. (1993) 'Voices of fear and anxiety and sadness and depression: The effects of speech rate and loudness on fear and anxiety and sadness and depression', *Journal of Abnormal Psychology*, 102: 430–37.

Solomon, R.C. (1993) 'The philosophy of emotions', in M. Lewis and J.M. Haviland (eds), *Handbook of Emotions.* New York: Guilford. pp. 3–15.

Stepper, S. and Strack, F. (1993) 'Proprioceptive determinants of emotional and nonemotional feelings', *Journal of Personality and Social Psychology*, 64: 211–20.

Strack, F., Martin, L.L. and Stepper, S. (1988) 'Inhibiting and facilitating conditions of facial expressions: A non-obtrusive test of the facial feedback hypothesis', *Journal of Personality and Social Psychology*, 54: 768–76.

Tavris, C. (1984) On the wisdom of counting to ten: Personal and social dangers of anger expression', in P. Shaver (ed.), *Review of Personality and Social Psychology*, Vol. 5. Beverly Hills, CA: Sage.

Tomkins, S.S. (1962) *Affect, Imagery and Consciousness.* New York: Springer.

Tomkins, S.S. (1982) 'Affect theory', in P. Ekman (ed.), *Emotion in the Human Face*, 2nd edn. Cambridge: Cambridge University Press.

Vallacher, R.R. (1993) 'Mental calibration: Forging a working relationship between mind and action', in D.M. Wegner and J.W. Pennebaker (eds), *Handbook of Mental Control.* Englewood Cliffs, NJ: Prentice Hall. pp. 443–72.

Vallacher, R.R. and Wegner, D.M. (1987) 'What do people think they are doing? Action identification and human behavior', *Psychological Review*, 94: 3–15.

Wagener, J.J. and Laird, J.D. (1980) 'The experimenters foot-in-the-door: Self-perception, body weight and volunteering', *Personality and Social Psychology Bulletin*, 6: 441–6.

Wegner, D.M. (1994) 'Ironic processes of mental control', *Psychological Review*, 101: 34–52.

Williams, G.P. and Kleinke, C.L. (1993) 'Effects of mutual gaze and touch on attraction, mood and cardiovascular reactivity', *Journal of Research in Personality*, 27: 170–83.

Wolpe, J. (1958) *Psychotherapy by Reciprocal Inhibitions.* Stanford, CA: Stanford University Press.

Wolpe, J. (1982) *The Practice of Behavior Therapy.* New York: Pergamon Press.

Zajonc, R.B., Murphy, S.T. and Inglehart, M. (1989) 'Feeling and facial efference: Implications of the vascular theory of emotion', *Psychological Review*, 96: 395–416.

Zentall, S.S. (1989) 'Self-control training with hyperactive and impulsive children', in J.N. Hughes and R.J. Hall (eds), *Cognitive Behavioral Psychology in the Schools: A Comprehensive Handbook.* New York: Guilford Press. pp. 305–46.

Chapter 13

Self-attention – Shame – Shyness – Modesty: Blushing

Charles Darwin

Blushing is the most peculiar and the most human of all expressions. Monkeys redden from passion, but it would require an overwhelming amount of evidence to make us believe that any animal could blush. The reddening of the face from a blush is due to the relaxation of the muscular coats of the small arteries, by which the capillaries become filled with blood; and this depends on the proper vaso-motor centre being affected. No doubt if there be at the same time much mental agitation, the general circulation will be affected; but it is not due to the action of the heart that the network of minute vessels covering the face becomes under a sense of shame gorged with blood. We can cause laughing by tickling the skin, weeping or frowning by a blow, trembling from the fear of pain, and so forth; but we cannot cause a blush, as Dr. Burgess remarks,[1] by any physical means – that is by any action on the body. It is the mind which must be affected. Blushing is not only involuntary; but the wish to restrain it, by leading to self-attention actually increases the tendency.

The young blush much more freely than the old, but not during infancy,[2] which is remarkable, as we know that infants at a very early age redden from passion. I have received authentic accounts of two little girls blushing at the ages of between two and three years; and of another sensitive child, a year older, blushing, when reproved for a fault. Many children, at a somewhat more advanced age blush in a strongly marked manner. It appears that the mental powers of infants are not as yet sufficiently developed to allow of their blushing. Hence, also, it is that idiots rarely blush. Dr. Crichton Browne observed for me those under his care, but never saw a genuine blush, though he has seen their faces flush, apparently from joy, when food was placed before them, and from anger. Nevertheless some, if not utterly degraded, are capable of blushing. A microcephalous idiot, for instance, thirteen years old, whose eyes brightened a little when he was pleased or amused, has been described by Dr. Behn,[3] as blushing and turning to one side, when undressed for medical examination.

Women blush much more than men. It is rare to see an old man, but not nearly so rare to see an old woman blushing. The blind do not escape. Laura Bridgman, born in this condition, as well as completely deaf, blushes.[4] The Rev. R.H. Blair, Principal of the Worcester College, informs me that three children born blind, out of seven or eight then in the Asylum, are great blushers. The blind are not at first conscious that they are observed, and it is a most important part of their education, as Mr. Blair informs me, to impress this knowledge on their minds; and the impression thus gained would greatly strengthen the tendency to blush, by increasing the habit of self-attention.

The tendency to blush is inherited. Dr. Burgess gives the case[5] of a family consisting of a father, mother, and ten children, all of whom, without exception, were prone to blush to a most painful degree. The children were grown up; 'and some of them were sent to travel in order to wear away this diseased sensibility, but nothing was of the slightest avail.' Even peculiarities in blushing seem to be inherited. Sir James Paget, whilst examining the spine of a girl, was struck at her singular manner of blushing; a big splash of red appeared first on one cheek, and then other splashes, variously scattered over the face and neck. He subsequently asked the mother whether her daughter always blushed in this peculiar manner; and was answered, 'Yes, she takes after me'. Sir J. Paget then perceived that by asking this question he had caused the mother to blush; and she exhibited the same peculiarity as her daughter.

In most cases the face, ears and neck are the sole parts which redden; but many persons, whilst blushing intensely, feel that their whole bodies grow hot and tingle; and this shows that the entire surface must be in some manner affected. Blushes are said sometimes to commence on the forehead, but more commonly on the cheeks, afterwards spreading to the ears and neck.[6] In two Albinos examined by Dr. Burgess, the blushes commenced by a small circumscribed spot on the cheeks, over the parotidean plexus of nerves, and then increased into a circle; between this blushing circle and the blush on the neck there was an evident line of demarcation; although both arose simultaneously. The retina, which is naturally red in the Albino, invariably increased at the same time in redness.[7] Every one must have noticed how easily after one blush fresh blushes chase each other over the face. Blushing is preceded by a peculiar sensation in the skin. According to Dr. Burgess the reddening of the skin is generally succeeded by a slight pallor, which shows that the capillary vessels contract after dilating. In some rare cases paleness instead of redness is caused under conditions which would naturally induce a blush. For instance, a young lady told me that in a large and crowded party she caught her hair so firmly on the button of a passing servant, that it took some time before she could be extricated; from her sensations she imagined that she had blushed crimson; but was assured by a friend that she had turned extremely pale.

I was desirous to learn how far down the body blushes extend; and Sir J. Paget, who necessarily has frequent opportunities for observation, has kindly attended to this point for me during two or three years. He finds that with women who blush intensely on the face, ears, and nape of neck, the blush does not commonly extend any lower down the body. It is rare to see it as low down as the collar-bones and shoulder-blades; and he has never himself seen a single instance in which it extended below the upper part of the chest. He has also noticed that blushes sometimes die away downwards, not gradually and insensibly, but by irregular ruddy blotches. Dr. Langstaff has likewise observed for me several women whose bodies did not in the least redden while their faces were crimsoned with blushes. With the insane, some of whom appear to be particularly liable to blushing, Dr. J. Crichton Browne has several times seen the blush extend as far down as the collarbones, and in two instances to the breasts. He gives me the case of a married woman, aged twenty-seven, who suffered from epilepsy. On the morning after her arrival in the Asylum, Dr. Browne, together with his assistants, visited her whilst she was in bed. The moment that he approached, she blushed deeply over her cheeks and temples; and the blush spread quickly to her ears. She was much agitated and tremulous. He unfastened the collar of her chemise in order to examine the state of her lungs; and then a brilliant blush rushed over her chest, in an arched line over the upper third of each breast, and extended downwards between the breasts nearly to the ensiform cartilage of the sternum. This case is interesting, as the blush did not thus extend downwards until it became intense by her attention being drawn to this part of her person. As the examination proceeded she became composed, and the blush disappeared; but on several subsequent occasions the same phenomena were observed.

The foregoing facts show that, as a general rule, with English women, blushing does not extend beneath the neck and upper part of the chest. Nevertheless Sir J. Paget informs me that he has lately heard of a case, on which he can fully rely, in which a little girl, shocked by what she imagined to be an act of indelicacy, blushed all over her abdomen and the upper parts of her legs. Moreau also[8] relates, on the authority of a celebrated painter, that the chest, shoulders, arms, and whole body of a girl, who unwillingly consented to serve as a model, reddened when she was first divested of her clothes.

It is a rather curious question why, in most cases the face, ears, and neck alone redden, inasmuch as the whole surface of the body often tingles and grows hot. This seems to depend, chiefly, on the face and adjoining parts of the skin having been habitually exposed to the air, light, and alternations of temperature, by which the small arteries not only have acquired the habit of readily dilating and contracting, but appear to have become unusually developed in comparison with other parts of the surface.[9] It is probably owing to this same cause, as M. Moreau and Dr. Burgess have remarked, that the face is so liable to redden under various circumstances, such as a fever-fit, ordinary heat, violent exertion, anger, a slight blow, &c.; and on the other hand that it is liable to grow pale from cold and fear, and to be discoloured during pregnancy. The face is also particularly liable to be affected by cutaneous complaints, by small-pox, erysipelas, &c. This view is likewise supported by the fact that the men of certain races, who habitually go nearly naked, often blush over their arms and chests and even down to their waists. A lady, who is a great blusher, informs Dr. Crichton Browne, that when she feels ashamed or is agitated, she blushes over her face, neck, wrists, and hands, – that is, all over the exposed portions of her skin. Nevertheless it may be doubted whether the habitual exposure of the skin of the face and neck, and its consequent power of reaction under stimulants of all kinds, is by itself sufficient to account for the much greater tendency in English women of these parts than of others to blush; for the hands are well supplied with nerves and small vessels, and have been as much exposed to the air as the face or neck, and yet the hands rarely blush. We shall presently see that the attention of the mind having been directed much more frequently and earnestly to the face than to any other part of the body, probably affords a sufficient explanation.

Blushing in the various races of man

The small vessels of the face become filled with blood, from the emotion of shame, in almost all the races of man, though in the very dark races no distinct change of colour can be perceived. Blushing is evident in all the Aryan nations of Europe, and to a certain extent with those of India. But Mr. Erskine has never noticed that the necks of the Hindoos are decidedly affected. With the Lepchas of Sikhim, Mr. Scott has often observed a faint blush on the cheeks, base of the ears, and sides of the neck, accompanied by sunken eyes and lowered head. This has occurred when he has detected them in a falsehood, or has accused them of ingratitude. The pale, sallow complexions of these men render a blush much more conspicuous than in most of the other natives of India. With the latter, shame, or it may be in part fear, is expressed, according to Mr. Scott, much more plainly by the head being averted or bent down, with the eyes wavering or turned askant, than by any change of colour in the skin.

The Semitic races blush freely, as might have been expected, from their general similitude to the Aryans. Thus with the Jews, it is said in the Book of Jeremiah (chap. vi. 15), 'Nay, they were not at all ashamed, neither could they blush'. Mrs. Asa Gray saw an Arab managing his boat clumsily on the Nile, and when laughed at by his companions, 'he blushed quite to the back of his neck'. Lady Duff Gordon remarks that a young Arab blushed on coming into her presence.[10]

Mr. Swinhoe has seen the Chinese blushing, but he thinks it is rare; yet they have the expression 'to redden with shame'. Mr. Geach informs me that the Chinese settled in Malacca and the native Malays of the interior both blush. Some of these people go nearly naked, and he particularly attended to the downward extension of the blush. Omitting the cases in which the face alone was seen to blush, Mr. Geach observed that the face, arms, and breast of a Chinaman, aged 24 years, reddened from shame; and with another Chinese, when asked why he had not done his work in better style, the whole body was similarly affected. In two Malays[11] he saw the face, neck, breast, and arms blushing; and in a third Malay (a Bugis) the blush extended down to the waist.

The Polynesians blush freely. The Rev. Mr Stack has seen hundreds of instances with the New Zealanders. The following case is worth giving, as it relates to an old man who was unusually dark-coloured and partly tattooed. After having let his land to an Englishman for a small yearly rental, a strong passion seized him to buy a gig, which had lately become the fashion with the Maoris. He consequently wished to draw all the rent for four years from his tenant, and consulted Mr. Stack whether he could do so. The man was old, clumsy, poor, and ragged, and the idea of his driving himself about in his carriage for display amused Mr. Stack so much that he could not help bursting out into a laugh; and then 'the old man blushed up to the roots of his hair'. Forster says that 'you may easily distinguish a spreading blush' on the cheeks of the fairest women in Tahiti.[12] The natives also of several of the other archipelagoes in the Pacific have been seen to blush.

Mr. Washington Matthews has often seen a blush on the faces of the young squaws belonging to various wild Indian tribes of North America. At the opposite extremity of the continent in Tierra del Fuego, the natives, according to Mr. Bridges, 'blush much, but chiefly in regard to women; but they certainly blush also at their own personal appearance'. This latter statement agrees with what I remember of the Fuegian, Jemmy Button, who blushed when he was quizzed about the care which he took in polishing his shoes, and in otherwise adorning himself. With respect to the Aymara Indians on the lofty plateaus of Bolivia, Mr. Forbes says,[13] that from the colour of their skins it is impossible that their blushes should be as clearly visible as in the white races; still under such circumstances as would raise a blush in us, 'there can always be seen the same expression of modesty or confusion; and even in the dark, a rise of temperature of the skin of the face can be felt, exactly as occurs in the European.' With the Indians who inhabit the hot, equable, and damp parts of South America, the skin apparently does not answer to mental excitement so readily as with the natives of the northern and southern parts of the continent, who have long been exposed to great vicissitudes of climate; for Humboldt quotes without a protest the sneer of the Spaniard, 'How can those be trusted, who know not how to blush?'[14] Von Spix and Martius, in speaking of the aborigines of Brazil, assert that they cannot properly be said to blush; 'it was only after long intercourse with the whites, and after receiving some education, that we perceived in the Indians a change of colour expressive of the emotions of their minds.'[15] It is, however, incredible that the power of blushing could have thus originated; but the habit of self-attention, consequent on their education and new course of life, would have much increased any innate tendency to blush.

Several trustworthy observers have assured me that they have seen on the faces of negroes an appearance resembling a blush, under circumstances which would have excited one in us, though their skins were of an ebony-black tint. Some describe it as blushing brown, but most say that the blackness becomes more intense. An increased supply of blood in the skin seems in some manner to increase its blackness; thus certain exanthematous diseases cause the affected places in the negro to appear blacker, instead of, as with us, redder.[16] The skin, perhaps, from being rendered more tense by the filling of the capillaries, would reflect a somewhat different tint to what it did before. That the capillaries of the face in the negro become filled with blood, under the emotion of shame, we may feel confident; because a perfectly characterized albino negress, described by Buffon,[17] showed a faint tinge of crimson on her cheeks when she exhibited herself naked. Cicatrices of the skin remain for a long time white in the negro, and Dr. Burgess, who had frequent opportunities of observing a scar of this kind on the face of a negress, distinctly saw that it 'invariably became red whenever she was abruptly spoken to, or charged with any trivial offence.'[18] The blush could be seen proceeding from the circumference of the scar towards the middle, but it did not reach the centre. Mulattoes are often great blushers, blush succeeding blush over their faces. From these facts there can be no doubt that negroes blush, although no redness is visible on the skin.

I am assured by Gaika and by Mrs. Barber that the Kafirs of South Africa never blush; but this may only mean that no change of colour is distinguishable. Gaika adds that under the circumstances which would make a European blush, his countrymen 'look ashamed to keep their heads up'. [. . .]

Movements and gestures which accompany blushing

Under a keen sense of shame there is a strong desire for concealment.[19] We turn away the whole body, more especially the face, which we endeavour in some manner to hide. An ashamed person can hardly endure to meet the gaze of those present, so that he almost invariably casts down his eyes or looks askant. As there generally exists at the same time a strong wish to avoid the appearance of shame, a vain attempt is made to look direct at the person who causes this feeling; and the antagonism between these opposite tendencies leads to various restless movements in the eyes. I have noticed two ladies who, whilst blushing, to which they are very liable, have thus acquired, as it appears, the oddest trick of incessantly blinking their eyelids with extraordinary rapidity. An intense blush is sometimes accompanied by a slight effusion of tears;[20] and this, I presume, is due to the lacrymal glands partaking of the increased supply of blood, which we know rushes into the capillaries of the adjoining parts, including the retina.

Many writers, ancient and modern, have noticed the foregoing movements; and it has already been shown that the aborigines in various parts of the world often exhibit their shame by looking downwards or askant, or by restless movements of their eyes. Ezra cries out (ch. ix. 6), 'O, my God! I am ashamed, and blush to lift up my head to thee, my God.' In Isaiah (ch.

1. 6) we meet with the words, 'I hid not my face from shame'. Seneca remarks (Epist. xi. 5) 'that the Roman players hang down their heads, fix their eyes on the ground and keep them lowered, but are unable to blush in acting shame.' According to Macrobius, who lived in the fifth century ('Saturnalia', B. vii. C. 11), 'Natural philosophers assert that nature being moved by shame spreads the blood before herself as a veil, as we see any one blushing often puts his hands before his face.' Shakespeare makes Marcus ('Titus Andronicus', act ii. sc. 5) say to his niece, 'Ah! now thou turn'st away thy face for shame'. A lady informs me that she found in the Lock Hospital a girl whom she had formerly known, and who had become a wretched castaway, and the poor creature, when approached, hid her face under the bed-clothes, and could not be persuaded to uncover it. We often see little children, when shy or ashamed, turn away, and still standing up, bury their faces in their mother's gown; or they throw themselves face downwards on her lap.

Confusion of mind

Most persons, whilst blushing intensely, have their mental powers confused. This is recognized in such common expressions as 'she was covered with confusion'. Persons in this condition lose their presence of mind, and utter singularly inappropriate remarks. They are often much distressed, stammer, and make awkward movements or strange grimaces. In certain cases involuntary twitchings of some of the facial muscles may be observed. I have been informed by a young lady, who blushes excessively, that at such times she does not even know what she is saying. When it was suggested to her that this might be due to her distress from the consciousness that her blushing was noticed, she answered that this could not be the case, 'as she had sometimes felt quite as stupid when blushing at a thought in her own room.'

I will give an instance of the extreme disturbance of mind to which some sensitive men are liable. A gentleman, on whom I can rely, assured me that he had been an eye-witness of the following scene: – A small dinner-party was given in honour of an extremely shy man, who, when he rose to return thanks, rehearsed the speech, which he had evidently learnt by heart, in absolute silence, and did not utter a single word; but he acted as if he were speaking with much emphasis. His friends, perceiving how the case stood, loudly applauded the imaginary bursts of eloquence, whenever his gestures indicated a pause, and the man never discovered that he had remained the whole time completely silent. On the contrary, he afterwards remarked to my friend, with much satisfaction, that he thought he had succeeded uncommonly well.

When a person is much ashamed or very shy, and blushes intensely, his heart beats rapidly and his breathing is disturbed. This can hardly fail to affect the circulation of the blood within the brain, and perhaps the mental powers. It seems however doubtful, judging from the still more powerful influence of anger and fear on the circulation, whether we can thus satisfactorily account for the confused state of mind in persons whilst blushing intensely.

The true explanation apparently lies in the intimate sympathy which exists between the capillary circulation of the surface of the head and face, and that of the brain. On applying to Dr. J. Crichton Browne for information, he has given me various facts bearing on this subject. When the sympathetic nerve is divided on one side of the head, the capillaries on this side are relaxed and become filled with blood, causing the skin to redden and to grow hot, and at the same time the temperature within the cranium on the same side rises. Inflammation of the membranes of the brain leads to the engorgement of the face, ears, and eyes with blood. The first stage of an epileptic fit appears to be the contraction of the vessels of the brain, and the first outward manifestation is an extreme pallor of countenance. Erysipelas of the head commonly induces delirium. Even the relief given to a severe headache by burning the skin with strong lotion, depends, I presume, on the same principle.

Dr. Browne has often administered to his patients the vapour of the nitrite of amyl[21] which has the singular property of causing vivid redness of the face in from thirty to sixty seconds. This flushing resembles blushing in almost every detail: it begins at several distinct points on the face, and spreads till it involves the whole surface of the head, neck, and front of the chest; but has been observed to extend only in one case to the abdomen. The arteries in the retina become enlarged; the eyes glisten, and in one instance there was a slight effusion of tears. The patients are at first pleasantly stimulated, but, as the flushing increases, they become confused and bewildered. One woman to whom the vapour had often been administered asserted that, as soon as she grew hot, she grew *muddled*. With persons just commencing to blush it appears, judging from their bright eyes and lively behaviour, that their mental powers are somewhat stimulated. It is only when the blushing is excessive that the mind grows confused. Therefore it would seem that the capillaries of the face are affected, both during the inhalation of the nitrite of amyl and during blushing, before that part of the brain is affected on which the mental powers depend.

Conversely when the brain is primarily affected, the circulation of the skin is so in a secondary manner. Dr. Browne has frequently observed, as he informs me, scattered red blotches and mottlings on the chests of epileptic patients. In these cases, when the skin on the thorax or abdomen is gently rubbed with a pencil or other object, or, in strongly-marked cases, is merely touched by the finger, the surface becomes suffused in less than half a minute with bright red marks, which spread to some distance on each side of the touched point, and persist for several minutes. These are the *cerebral maculæ* of Trousseau; and they indicate, as Dr. Browne remarks, a highly modified condition of the cutaneous vascular system. If, then, there exists, as cannot be doubted, an intimate sympathy between the capillary circulation in that part of the brain on which our mental powers depend, and in the skin of the face, it is not surprising that the moral causes which induce intense blushing should likewise induce, independently of their own disturbing influence, much confusion of mind.

The nature of the mental states which induce blushing

These consist of shyness, shame, and modesty; the essential element in all being self-attention. Many reasons can be assigned for believing that originally self-attention directed to personal appearance, in relation to the opinion of others, was the exciting cause; the same effect being subsequently produced, through the force of association, by self-attention in relation to moral conduct. It is not the simple art of reflecting on our own appearance, but the thinking what others think of us, which excites a blush. In absolute solitude the most sensitive person would be quite indifferent about his appearance. We feel blame or disapprobation more acutely than approbation; and consequently depreciatory remarks or ridicule, whether of our appearance or conduct, causes us to blush much more readily than does praise. But undoubtedly praise and admiration are highly efficient: a pretty girl blushes when a man gazes intently at her, though she may know perfectly well that he is not depreciating her. Many children, as well as old and sensitive persons blush, when they are much praised.

Notes

1 'The Physiology or Mechanism of Blushing', 1839, p. 156. I shall have occasion often to quote this work in the present chapter.

2 Dr. Burgess, ibid. p. 56. At p. 33 he also remarks on women blushing more freely than men, as stated below.

3 Quoted by Vogt, 'Mémoire sur les Microcéphales', 1867, p. 20. Dr. Burgess (ibid. p. 56) doubts whether idiots ever blush.

4 Lieber 'On the Vocal Sounds', &c.; Smithsonian Contributions 1851, vol. ii. p. 6.

5 Ibid. p. 182.

6 Moreau, in edit. of 1820 of Lavater, vol. iv. p. 303.

7 Burgess, ibid. p. 38, on paleness after blushing, p. 177.

8 See Lavater, edit. of 1820, vol. iv. p. 303.

9 Burgess, ibid. pp. 114, 122. Moreau in Lavater, ibid. vol. iv. p. 293.

10 'Letters from Egypt', 1865, p. 66. Lady Gordon is mistaken when she says Malays and Mulattoes never blush.

11 Capt. Osborn ('Quedah', p. 199), in speaking of a Malay, whom he reproached for cruelty, says he was glad to see that the man blushed.

12 J.R. Forster, 'Observations during a Voyage round the World', 4to, 1778, p. 229. Waitz gives ('Introduction to Anthropology', Eng. translat. 1863, vol. i. p. 135) references for other islands in the Pacific. See, also, Dampier 'On the Blushing of the Tunquinese' (vol. ii. p. 40); but I have not consulted this work. Waitz quotes Bergmann, that the Kalmucks do not blush, but this may be doubted after what we have seen with respect to the Chinese. He also quotes Roth, who denies that the Abyssinians are capable of blushing. Unfortunately, Capt. Speedy, who lived so long with the Abyssinians, has not answered my inquiry on this head. Lastly, I must add that the Rajah Brooke has never observed the least sign of a blush with the Dyaks of

Borneo; on the contrary under circumstances which would excite a blush in us, they assert 'that they feel the blood drawn from their faces'.

13 Transact. of the Ethnological Soc. 1870, vol. ii. p. 16.

14 Humboldt, 'Personal Narrative', Eng. translat. vol. iii. p. 229.

15 Quoted by Prichard, Phys. Hist. of Mankind, 4th edit. 1851, vol. i. p. 271.

16 See, on this head, Burgess, ibid. p. 32. Also Waitz, 'Introduction to Anthropology', Eng. edit. vol. i. p. 135. Moreau gives a detailed account ('Lavater', 1820, tom. iv. p. 302) of the blushing of a Madagascar negress-slave when forced by her brutal master to exhibit her naked bosom.

17 Quoted by Prichard, Phys. Hist. of Mankind, 4th edit. 1851, vol. i. p. 225.

18 Burgess, ibid. p. 31. On mulattoes blushing, see p. 33. I have received similar accounts with respect to mulattoes.

19 Mr. Wedgwood says (Dict. of English Etymology, vol. iii. 1865, p. 155) that the word shame 'may well originate in the idea of shade or concealment, and may be illustrated by the Low German *scheme*, shade or shadow'. Gratiolet (De la Phys. pp. 357–62) has a good discussion on the gestures accompanying shame; but some of his remarks seem to me rather fanciful. See, also, Burgess (ibid. pp. 69, 134) on the same subject.

20 Burgess, ibid. pp. 181, 182. Boerhaave also noticed (as quoted by Gratiolet, ibid. p. 361) the tendency to the secretion of tears during intense blushing. Mr. Bulmer, as we have seen, speaks of the 'watery eyes' of the children of the Australian aborigines when ashamed.

21 See also Dr. J. Crichton Browne's Memoir on this subject in the 'West Riding Lunatic Asylum Medical Report', 1871, pp. 95–8.

Emotions: Communications to the Self and Others

Keith Oatley

Emotions have functions. They communicate to ourselves, configuring mental resources and making ready for certain kinds of action. They can communicate also to others, causing changes in the modes of our inter-actions, from cooperation, to withdrawal, to conflict, to deference. The main role of emotions, according to this argument, is management of the flow of attention and readiness in beings who have many goals and plans but for whom, because of our embodiment and its limitations, these plans do not always go as foreseen. Not all emotions are connected with goals, but I believe that the relationship of emotions to goals and plans indicates their primary functions, and allows for productive theorizing and empirical investigation.

According to the communicative theory of emotions (Oatley and Johnson-Laird, 1987, 1995) emotions and moods are supported by the same mechanism, with the two phenomena distinguished in the same way as aspects of muscle control. Phasic muscle movements cause changes in position and tonic states maintain posture; similarly an emotion signal causes a phasic change from one goal or plan to another; a mood main-tains a tonic state of concentration.

To argue that emotions and moods have functions was not usual until recently in European and American theorizing. Darwin (1872) thought emotional expressions were those actions that once had functions in evolu-tionary or developmental history, but occur in human adulthood whether or not they are of any use. James (1884) thought that although emotions gave color to experience, they had no influence on mechanisms that produce behavior, because they resulted from that behavior.

In this vignette I briefly sketch a version of an alternative idea: emotions have personal and social functions (discussed at more length in Oatley, 1992). I consider first whether functions of a comparable kind have been found useful in technology, and then whether in the social world they are supported by distinct cultural practices.

In technology, time-limited emotions are like auditory warning signals. They depend on simple devices designed to monitor important types of event. When a signal sounds it does not tell you exactly what has happened, but it directs attention. If the signal is from a fire or burglar alarm you attend to the possibility that your house has been broken into or that a fire has started.

According to the communicative theory, emotion signals are like this. They are based on simple monitoring of events relevant to our goals and plans; they are typically triggered by something that makes a goal substantially more or less likely to be achieved. With events that make this achievement more likely the emotion is positive, and its effect is to prompt continuation, to reinforce engagement in the current activity, and to make for cooperation with others. With events that imply loss or damage to a goal or plan, emotions are negative, and they interrupt the current plan. There is more differentiation among negative emotions: sadness organizes the cognitive system to relinquish a goal, anger prompts new plans to surmount a frustration or remedy a wrong so that a goal may be reinstated, fear prompts escape, attention to safety, and deference.

According to the communicative theory an emotion signal has no propositional content; it does not require parsing into parts that will be interpreted and mapped onto corresponding elements of meaning. Instead, it has a simpler control function – just as there are fire alarms, ambulance sirens, and so forth, each prompting a different kind of response, so emotion signals are simple, and configure the cognitive system. There is just a small number of such signals – corresponding roughly to the English terms happiness, sadness, anger, fear, and some others. Each one constrains attention and calls into readiness a distinctive repertoire of actions. Just as the sound of an emergency vehicle's siren does not tell us what has happened but merely prompts us into a distinct mode of road-using, pulling over to let the emergency vehicle pass, so an emotion signal does not tell us exactly what has happened – it sets up a mode of the cognitive system. This helps to explain why some emotions can slide across different objects – anger for instance can be directed at inappropriate people (Berkowitz, 1993). It also helps explain how emotions often have an inchoate quality. Individuals may search across a range of meanings to make sense of what happened, and in different societies not only can eliciting situations for emotions differ, but so too can connotations. The structure of the typical emotion therefore allows for the social construction of emotions from universal (configurational) bases and culturally variable (semantic) elements.

According to Oatley and Johnson-Laird (1987, 1995), an emotion signal sets up a cognitive mode which has a distinctive phenomenological tone. Although setting up this mode is usually accompanied by signals carrying semantic information about the emotion's object, the semantic part is not necessary. In some 19 out of 20 incidents of emotion the two types of signal (configurational and semantic) are bound together, so that emotions are properly intentional. But these two types of signal can be dissociated. Thus some clinical anxiety states include free floating fear (apprehension with no object), certain drugs change mood without any perceptual influence from the outer world, and auras of temporal lobe epilepsy can occur as free-floating emotional states. In a study of people keeping structured diaries of incidents of emotion, Oatley and Duncan (1992) found that although in most incidents people knew what caused each emotion, psychiatric out-patients experienced more emotion incidents that they did not fully under-stand than a comparison sample of non-psychiatric patients. We found also that for emotion incidents reported by people who were not patients, in 6 per cent of emotion episodes subjects did not know what caused them. In all cases of objectless emotions or moods we believe no introspectable interpretation of events occurred; the states had no intentional content.

Further insights come from social practices that allow certain emotions to be enacted with elaborate cultural support. Thus vacations, games, sporting activities, maximize the opportunity for experiencing happiness. According to the communicative theory, happiness is the mood that occurs when sub-goals are being achieved. It signals encouragement to the self to continue the current action, and signals cooperativeness to others. So, in a vacation, game, or sport, the activity is set apart in a special time and place to minimize interruptions of the kind that might distract. As Goffman (1961) has pointed out, enjoyment arises from engagement in the activity, usually face to face with others. If someone says 'I had a great time, I thoroughly enjoyed it', we should not infer that nothing went wrong, but that this person was engaged in what he or she was doing, and that there were frequent occurrences of the emotion signal corresponding to happiness that prompted continuation and engagement.

We can make similar arguments for other kinds of social ritual: mourn-ing is the state of profound sadness and sometimes depression at the severe loss of an intimate. The problem is to disengage from this unique person, and hopelessness can occur. The effect of intense sadness is to prompt one to do little until new interests emerge. The social arrangements of mourning allow and acknowledge this.

For anger the clear social expression is the law suit. As Averill (1982) has shown the usual function of anger in Western individualistic societies is to readjust the terms of social relationships. We become angry when someone acts inappropriately to the kind of agreement we had with that person. An argument occurs, accusations are made. After the angry incident two people's relationship is on different terms than previously. A law suit enacts this scenario with formality and highly paid social functionaries. But the structure is the same: a conflict between people whose expectations of each other have been violated. The object is readjustment of the behavior of one or both.

Fear occurs for many reasons: one type is a response to physical danger, another is social (Öhman, 1986). Social fear has its societal expression. To someone higher in a hierarchy one shows deference. The class system in Britain with its codes of speech, the caste system in India, the rituals of bowing in Japan, formally define deference hierarchies, which are human enactments of hierarchies seen in other animals. Humans often negotiate hierarchies without fighting or overt threats, and a remarkable feature in both apes and humans is that once a hierarchy is negotiated people in lower positions remain comfortable – more or less – in the presence of those in higher positions.

According to the communicative theory, if an emotion is sufficiently intense it is always a signal to the self. It has, as it were, been expressly designed during evolution to call attention to itself, to induce preoccupation with the events that may have caused it. There is an analogy between how emotions spread internally among the processors of the cognitive system, and how they spread externally among members of a social group. This external spread is partly non-verbal. Oatley and Larocque (1995) have studied the extent to whic.. emotion signals are or are not transmitted to others. We asked people to keep a structured diary record of an incident in which an error occurred in a plan or arrangement they made with someone else. We also asked them to ask the other person involved to complete a written account of what happened. Thus we have understandings of the same incident by two people, X and Y. We asked both whether they experienced emotions, and if so what kind, and at what intensity. We also asked them if they thought the other person experienced an emotion. People had no difficulty recording and describing their own emotions: anger, fear, guilt, shame, and so on. We put no pressure on them to report emotions, and a small proportion did not.

As to communications to the other we found that on 73 per cent of occasions when person X said he or she felt angry following an error, person Y knew that X was angry. So an emotion experienced by X was also communicated quite efficiently to Y, as befits the explanation of anger as an occasion for readjustment in a continuing relationship.

By contrast five other emotions that we asked about specifically (happiness, anxiety, sadness, shame, guilt) were not well recognized by the other: averaging over incidents of all five of these emotions, when person X said he or she felt one of these, person Y only thought that X felt this on 29 per cent of occasions. Unlike anger which demanded engagement with the other person, and mutual working through, these other feelings were more often private: only one instance of shame experienced by X (out of 10) was correctly ascribed by Y, only six instances of fear (out of 26), and so forth.

Oatley and Johnson-Laird's theory is that the interpersonal effects of emotions occur with emotions generally, for example, that happiness tends to induce cooperation, that social fear is signalled by deference, and so forth. But the results of Oatley and Larocque indicate that on two-thirds of occasions when an interpersonal error occurred, emotions other than anger were communicated only to the self.

We received a hint of why transmission of emotions to the other person did not always occur by examining more closely our results for the emotion of guilt. We know that paradigmatically in our society guilt leads to confession, apologies, recompense – but what we found was that the occurrence of guilt bore no significant relationship to being at fault in an error. Instead, it was associated with having other goals that might have affected the performance of the plan, which were not mentioned or negotiated with the other person. When guilt of this kind remained after the error it existed purely as a communication to the self, perhaps to be worked through and understood privately. People were moderately successful in keeping it from the other (it was only correctly recognized by the other on 5 out of 12 occasions when it occurred).

Emotions, then, have communicative functions, some of which are sufficiently useful and sufficiently simple to be implemented in everyday pieces of technology, like acoustic warning signals. Some functions of emotions are also supported and elaborated in cultural institutions. The emphasis in research has shifted. Rather than seeing emotions as interfering with human action it has become difficult to understand important classes of human action without referring to them.

Note

This research is supported by a grant to Keith Oatley from the Social Science and Humanities Research Council of Canada.

References

Averill, J.R. (1982) *Anger and Aggression: An Essay on Emotion.* New York: Springer.
Berkowitz, L. (1993) 'Towards a general theory of anger and emotional aggression: Implications of a cognitive neo-associationistic perspective for the analysis of anger and other emotions', in R.S. Wyer and T. Srull (eds), *Advances in Social Cognition.* Hillsdale, NJ: Erlbaum.
Darwin, C. (1872) *The Expression of the Emotions in Man and Animals.* Reissued by Chicago: University of Chicago Press, 1965.
Goffman, E. (1961) *Encounters: Two Studies in the Sociology of Interaction.* Indianapolis, IN: Bobbs-Merrill.
James, W. (1884) 'What is an emotion?', *Mind*, 9: 188–205.
Oatley, K. (1992) *Best Laid Schemes: The Psychology of Emotions.* New York: Cambridge University Press.
Oatley, K. and Duncan, E. (1992) 'Incidents of emotion in daily life', in K.T. Strongman (ed.), *International Review of Studies on Emotion.* Chichester: Wiley. pp. 250–93.
Oatley, K. and Johnson-Laird, P.N. (1987) 'Towards a cognitive theory of emotions', *Cognition and Emotion*, 1: 29–50.
Oatley, K. and Johnson-Laird, P.N. (1995) 'The communicative theory of emotions: Empirical tests, mental models, and implications for social interaction', in L.L. Martin and A. Tesser (eds), *Goals and Affect.* Hillsdale, NJ: Erlbaum. pp. 363–93.
Oatley, K. and Larocque, L. (1995) 'Everyday concepts of emotions following every-other-day errors in joint plans', in J.A. Russell, J.-M. Fernandez-Dols, A.S.R. Manstead and J. Wellenkamp (eds), *Everyday Conceptions of Emotions: An Introduction to the Psychology, Anthropology, and Linguistics of Emotion. NATO ASI Series D 81.* Dordrecht: Kluwer. pp. 145–65.
Öhman, A. (1986) 'Face the beast and fear the face: Animal and social fears as prototypes for evolutionary analyses of emotion', *Psychophysiology*, 23: 123–45.

Vignette 7

A Private Eye into Disgust

K.T. Strongman

Imagine V.I. Warshawski, Sara Paretsky's feisty, quick-witted private eye. In *Tunnel Vision*, she is getting close to 40 and so is beginning to slow down a little. It is a Saturday morning and the case is nowhere near solved, in fact matters seem to be worsening. She goes up to her office in the old condemned Poulteney Building and discovers the body of a friend sprawled across her desk. The friend has been smashed over the head with a baseball bat, leaving a congealing 'pool of brain and blood'.

Behaving slightly out of character, and thereby proving that she has her limits, V.I. almost fainted. She fell to the floor and her hand went into the mess. This finished her. She vomited into a handily placed cardboard box. The fainting and vomiting were the first and the obvious manifestations of disgust. There follows a memorable description of how she managed to get herself to a washroom, keeping her hand well away from the rest of her as she went and held her hand under water until it was 'red and swollen with cold'.

Even this was not enough to rid herself of the disgust because she then became aware of the smell of sewer gas and urine in the washroom. She was so physically churned up by this that she had to hold her breath, get to another room and smash a window with her shoe until she could breathe the fine air of Chicago. In about 300 words, Sara Paretsky has given us a well-articulated description of disgust, all of which is based, not so much on V.I. finding a murdered person in her office, but because *her hand slid through the mixture of blood and brain*. This might be all in the day's work for her, but it leaves the psychologist with much to ponder on.

Why should touching something be more likely to produce disgust than merely seeing it?[1] Is it worse to slip and break one's fall by putting one's hand into a pile of dog faeces than it is merely to see the faeces? It is. What if the fall was more of a tumble and one's face went into the mess? Of course, this is worse still. Think of the old children's game, something to do with Nelson. The details don't matter, but it culminates in a child being persuaded to push his or her finger through a screen into a half tomato. This might be unusual but in the ordinary light of day is a perfectly innocuous activity. However, by then, the child has been persuaded, through a sort of systematic sensitization, that what he or she is experiencing is Nelson's eye. Apart from being a fine example of what adults find amusing in their power games with children, it is also a fine manipulation of a sort of safe disgust, again dependent on actually touching something.

It is clear that disgust has much to do with the expulsion from the body of unwanted (unwholesome, diseased, poisoned, etc.) material. And it also has to do with proximity to such material. It is as though the unpleasant stuff must be kept far enough away that there is no chance of it getting into the body. So, a horrible mess on the face is too close to the mouth for comfort. Similarly, a horrible mess on the fingers is conceptually too close to the mouth for comfort. During the course of the day, the fingers are often in or near the mouth. *Treading* in dog faeces is not quite so bad; even treading on them with bare feet would surely not be so bad as picking them up.

At this first and rather simple level of analysis then, one can begin to understand why touching something unpleasant leads so readily to disgust. At the very least it is also adding another dimension (touch) to those that are probably already there – sight and smell perhaps. However, what is less obvious in the case of the unfortunate V.I. Warshawski is why there should be such disgust about touching the mixture of blood and brain. Why should it be disgusting to put one's hand in a bowl of brains? Do brain surgeons feel disgust when they ply their trade? Probably not. What then is the difference?

It is perhaps the link with death. Death is inextricably entwined with decay, and it is decay that prompts us to disgust, for very good reason. Perhaps then, seeing, and more particularly feeling, parts of the body which are normally tucked away safely inside the skin prompt atavistic urges to expel all such material to a safe distance. The best V.I. could do was to vomit, wash her hand and get some cleaner air. All of which might also account for what seems to be a near universal aversion to cannibalism, but even this depends on the circumstances.

Note

1 A small study among Georgetown University undergraduates confirmed the role of touch, real or imagined, in the genesis of disgust (Eds).

Name Index

Only those names are recorded in this index which have been used by authors in the text proper. Citations, usually in brackets in the text, are identified in the bibliography to each chapter.

Adams, W. 80
Agamemnon 66, 67
Alcott, Louisa M. 135
Allport, G. 90, 111
Anaxagoras 207
Apostoleris, N. 17–18
Aquinas, St.T. 26, 211–213
Argyle, M. 245
Aristotle 2–3, 21–24, 52, 93, 207
Auden, W. 65
Augustine 213
Austin, J. 73n
Averill, J.R. 3, 14, 15, 316

Baudelaire, C. 117
Baxter, C. 89
Behn, Dr. 302
Benedict, R. 74, 178
Bernard, C. 216
Bichat, M.F.X. 215
Blair, R.H. 302
Blankenship, B. 141
Blascovich, J. 233, 239
Bowlby, J. 162, 162
Bradstreet, A. 79
Bridges, Mr. 306
Browne, C. 302, 304, 305, 309
Bull, N. 245, 249
Burgess, Dr. 303, 307
Burgess, T.H. 119
Bush, G. 94
Butler, S. 107
Byron, Lord 120–121

Camras, L.A. 240, 254n
Cannon, W. 216–217, 290
Chagnon, N.A. 186
Chovil, N. 267
Cooley, C. 5

Darwin, C. 18, 19, 50, 53, 217, 218, 265, 312

Davidson, R.J. 235
Davitz, J.R. 175
Dawes, R.M. 102
Demos, J. 6–7, 10
Descartes, R. 24–25, 29, 30, 209, 213, 214
Dickens, C. 64
Dimberg, U. 229, 230
Dostoevsky, F. 65, 73n
Duchenne, de B., G.B.A. 281
Duclos, S. 293, 294
Duff, A. 202
Duff-Gordon, Lady 305
Duchaine, B. 16–17

Ekman, P.E. 231, 243, 254n, 263, 270, 276, 281
Eliot, T.S. 117
Erskine, Mr. 305

Faulkner, W. 108
Finney, C.G. 86
Fogel, A. 242
Forbes, Mr. 306
Ford, H. 94
Foucault, M. 148
Freud, S. 65, 72n, 100, 110, 185
Fridland, A. 16–17, 244

Galen, 211, 214
Garrison, W.L. 84–85
Geach, Mr. 305
Geertz, C. 171, 177
Ginsburg, G.J. 15
Goethe, J.W. 117
Goffman, E. 39, 47, 51, 52, 53, 209
Gottman, J.M. 254n
Gratiolet, P. 262
Gray, Mrs.A. 305

Hallpike, C.R. 182, 183, 190
Haraway, D. 158

Subject Index

facial displays (*cont.*)
  'emotions' view 260–261
  social tools 279
fear, communicative function 315
feed forward mechanisms 247–248
feelings
  as context 248–250
  as products 17–18

grief
  children and 135, 141, 143–144
  cultural variations 132–133
  decline of Victorian 138–140, 146–147
  eighteenth century 133
  etiquette of 144–146
  First World War effects 141
  'good deaths' 133–134
  historical variations 10–11
  patterns of death and 133
  songs expressing 133–136
  therapeutic approach to 142–143, 147–148
  Victorian culture and 134
guilt 5–6, 57–73
  feeling and being guilty 59–60
  Protestant 7
  remorse and 65–72
  repayment and 62
  responsibility and 6
  salvation and 6
  shame and 5–6, 60, 62–64

Homeric Greek emotions 184–185
hope
  and fear 36–37
  as an emotion 26–28
  cultural variations 3–4, 25–26, 30–36
  metaphors of 28

inner states 179

Maori culture, access to 200–201
Maori emotions
  anger 202
  sincerity in 201
  vocabulary of 202
modesty 53–55

organs as emotion sites 180–181

penitentiaries 84
personalization of emotions 163–166
psychophysiological symbolism 14–15, 205
  biological facets of 217–218
  cognition and 223
  localization of 220–222

physiological correlates of 219–220
social construction of 223–225
psychophysiological symbolism in philosophy
  in Aquinas 211–213
  in Descartes 213
  in Plato 209–211
  in Plotinus 211
psychophysiological symbolism in physiology
  in Bernard 216
  in Bichat 215
  in Cannon 216–217
  in Galen 214
  in Lange 216
  in Willis 214–215, 218
Puritan character type 82

regret 6, 8–9, 89–112
  action and 105–108
  benefits of 99–101, 111–112
  contemporary 8
  defects of 92–93, 96–98
  dysfunctionality 91, 94–96
  instructive power 103–105
  integrity and 108–110
  pessimism and 98–99
  rationality of 102–103
remorse 6
rhetoric of control
  hierarchy and 155
  metaphors of 153
  ontological implications 154
  women and 154, 157–158, 167

self-control 285–286, 292
  of action 295–297
  of feelings 293–294
self-perception 17, 286–291
  evidence for 287–289
  feelings and 289–290
self-punishment 83–84
self-understanding 297–298
shame 6
  guilt and 76
  Puritan 6–7, 75
  religion and 79–82, 85–86
  reputation and 77–79
  'shaming' 76
slavery, shame and guilt 84–85

two factor theory 16, 262, 277, 280–281

vergüenza ajena 9–10, 122–130
  culture and 126–130
  honour and 128–130
  shame and 125

206 -
207 Latin Hebrew
words for
emotion signify
Some change that
a person is
undergoing

187
different cultures
view emotions
EFFECT ON THE
MORM ORDER
P. 197 DIFFERENTLY

P. 01 - Israelite
EMOTIONS
TAKING
place
in
Behavior
eye

P. 197
Ancient
Israelite
Emotions

209-210
Location of
emotions
in the
body

P. 180
EMOTIONS AND
The body ORGANS

35-36
Hope found
less in Eastern
Cauntries becau
7 Eastern Religions
Judeo Christian in
west

Printed in the United States
54644LVS00003B/151-159